Windows® PowerShell™ 2.0

Administrator's Pocket Consultant

William Stanek

PUBLISHED BY
Microsoft Press
A Division of Microsoft Corporation
One Microsoft Way
Redmond, Washington 98052-6399

Library of Congress Control Number: 2009927478

Printed and bound in the United States of America.

2 3 4 5 6 7 8 9 QWE 4 3 2 1 0 9

Distributed in Canada by H.B. Fenn and Company Ltd.

A CIP catalogue record for this book is available from the British Library.

Microsoft Press books are available through booksellers and distributors worldwide. For further information about international editions, contact your local Microsoft Corporation office or contact Microsoft Press International directly at fax (425) 936-7329. Visit our Web site at www.microsoft.com/mspress. Send comments to mspinput@microsoft.com.

Acquisitions Editor: Martin DelRe
Developmental Editor: Karen Szall
Project Editor: Denise Bankaitis
Editorial Production: Macmillan Publishing Solutions
Technical Reviewer: Technical Reviewer: LJ Zacker; Technical Review services provided by Content Master, a member of CM Group, Ltd.
Cover: Tom Draper Design

Body Part No. X15-58129

Contents at a Glance

Contents

Introduction

Windows PowerShell 2.0 Administrator's Pocket Consultant is designed to be a concise and compulsively usable resource for Windows administrators, developers, and programmers, and for anyone else who wants to use Windows PowerShell Version 2.0 to control and configure computers. This is the readable resource guide that you'll want on your desk or in your pocket at all times. The book discusses everything you need to perform the core administrative tasks using Windows PowerShell. Because the focus is directed to providing you with the maximum value in a pocket-sized guide, you don't have to wade through hundreds of pages of extraneous information to find what you're looking for. Instead, you'll find exactly what you need to get the job done.

In short, the book is designed to be the one resource you consult whenever you have questions regarding administration of computers using Windows PowerShell. To this end, the book concentrates on daily administration procedures, frequently used tasks, documented examples, and options that are representative but not necessarily inclusive. One of the goals is to keep the content so concise that the book remains compact and easy to navigate while ensuring that the book is packed with as much information as possible—making it a valuable resource. Thus, instead of a hefty 1,000-page tome or a lightweight 100-page quick reference, you get a valuable resource guide that can help you quickly and easily perform common tasks, solve problems, and implement such advanced administration areas as automated monitoring, performance tracking, network troubleshooting, security management, and remote configuration.

Who Is This Book For?

Windows PowerShell 2.0 Administrator's Pocket Consultant covers Windows PowerShell Version 2.0. The book is designed for:

- Current Windows administrators
- Support staff who maintain Windows systems
- Accomplished users who have some administrator responsibilities
- Administrators upgrading to Windows PowerShell 2.0 from previous versions

To pack in as much information as possible, I had to assume that you have basic networking skills and a basic understanding of Windows, and that Windows PowerShell is already installed on your systems. With this in mind, I don't devote entire chapters to understanding Windows architecture or installing Windows PowerShell. I do, however, cover using PowerShell to modify security descriptors, manage domain membership, create restore checkpoints, configure event logging, and much more.

I also assume that you are fairly familiar with Windows commands and procedures as well as the Windows command line. If you need help learning the Windows basics, you should read the Windows documentation.

How Is This Book Organized?

Windows PowerShell 2.0 Administrator's Pocket Consultant is designed to be used in the daily administration of Windows computers, and as such, the book is organized by job-related tasks rather than by Windows features. Speed and ease of reference is an essential part of this hands-on guide. The book has an expanded table of contents and an extensive index for finding answers to problems quickly. Many other quick-reference features have been added as well. These features include quick step-by-step instructions, lists, tables with fast facts, and extensive cross-references.

Chapter 1 provides an overview of PowerShell administration tools, techniques, and concepts. You'll learn about the graphical interface for PowerShell as well as the command-line interface. Chapter 2 is designed to help you get the most out of PowerShell. It details techniques for starting up the PowerShell console using parameters, how to run scripts, what formatting options are available, and how to use multiple commands in sequences.

Windows provides many PowerShell commands to help in the management of daily operations. Chapter 3 explores profiles and how the working environment is loaded. You'll also learn about techniques for extending PowerShell, including snap-ins that add providers to the working environment and module extensions that must be imported prior to use. Chapter 4 discusses remote execution of commands, remote sessions, and remote background jobs. When you work remotely, you type commands in Windows PowerShell on your computer but execute the commands on one or more remote computers. Chapter 5 examines the core structures you'll use to put PowerShell to work. You'll learn how to set variables, work with expressions, and manage strings, arrays, and collections. Chapter 6, focuses on aliases, functions, and objects. Whenever you work with PowerShell, you'll use aliases, functions, and objects to help you do more with less and to help you use PowerShell to perform any conceivable administrative task.

Chapter 7 tells you how to get more from your scripts, profiles, and commands. You'll learn how to create transcripts and transactions. You'll also learn about control loops and conditional statements. Chapter 8 discusses how to manage server roles, role services, and features of Windows using PowerShell. Chapter 9 examines techniques you can use to inventory your computers and evaluate hardware configurations. You'll also learn how to determine whether there are issues that need your attention. In Chapter 10, you learn techniques for managing file systems, security, and auditing. Because you are working with PowerShell, it's just as easy to manipulate multiple directories and files as it is to work with individual directories and files.

Chapter 11 explores how you can control and configure network shares, printers, and TCP/IP networking. Chapter 12 discusses managing and securing the registry. You'll learn how to read and write registry values, how to view and set the access control lists, and how to configure registry auditing. In Chapter 13, you'll learn about tools and techniques for monitoring computers and optimizing performance. Finally, Chapter 14 details how to fine-tune system performance. You'll also learn techniques that can help you identify and correct system problems.

Conventions Used in This Book

I've used a variety of elements to help keep the text clear and easy to follow. You'll find code terms and listings in monospace type, except when I tell you to actually type a command. In that case, the command appears in **bold** type. When I introduce and define a new term, I put it in *italics*.

Other conventions include:

- **Best Practices** To examine the best technique to use when working with advanced configuration and administration concepts
- **Cautions** To warn you when there are potential problems you should look out for
- **Notes** To provide details on a point that needs emphasis
- **More Info** To provide more information on the subject
- **Real World** To provide real-world advice when discussing advanced topics
- **Security Alerts** To point out important security issues
- **Tips** To offer helpful hints or additional information

I truly hope you find that *Windows PowerShell2.0 Administrator's Pocket Consultant* provides everything that you need to perform essential administrative tasks as quickly and efficiently as possible. You're welcome to send your thoughts to me at williamstanek@aol.com. Thank you.

Find Additional Content Online

As new or updated material becomes available that complements this book, it will be posted online on the Microsoft Press Online Windows Server and Client Web site. The type of material you might find includes updates to book content, articles, links to companion content, errata, sample chapters, and more. This Web site is available at *http://microsoftpresssrv.libredigital.com/serverclient/* and is updated periodically. You'll also find discussion about the book on my Web site, *www.williamstanek.com*, and you can follow me on Twitter at WilliamStanek.

Support

Every effort has been made to ensure the accuracy of this book. Microsoft Press provides corrections for books through the World Wide Web at the following address:

http://www.microsoft.com/mspress/support

If you have comments, questions, or ideas about this book, please send them to Microsoft Press using either of the following methods:

Postal Mail:

Microsoft Press
Attn: Editor, *Windows PowerShell 2.0 Administrator's Pocket Consultant*
One Microsoft Way
Redmond, WA 98052-6399

E-mail:

mspinput@microsoft.com

Please note that product support isn't offered through these mail addresses. For support information, visit Microsoft's Web site at *http://support.microsoft.com/*.

CHAPTER 1

Introducing Windows PowerShell

Chances are that if you're an IT professional you've heard of Windows PowerShell. You may even have read other books about PowerShell and put PowerShell to work. However, you probably still have many questions about PowerShell, or you may simply be curious about what Windows PowerShell version 2.0 (PowerShell V2) has to offer that its predecessor, Windows PowerShell Version 1.0 (PowerShell V1), didn't. After all, the title of this book is *Windows PowerShell 2.0 Administrator's Pocket Consultant.*

Every version of Windows has had a built-in command line that is used to run built-in commands, utilities, and scripts. Windows PowerShell extends the command line in new and exciting ways, opening the operating system in ways that were previously possible only with extensive programming. Whether you are an administrator, developer, programmer, or other IT professional, you can use PowerShell to control and configure computers running Windows-based operating systems, and that's what I'll teach you in this book.

This chapter focuses on Windows PowerShell essentials. You'll learn how to use PowerShell, how to run commands, and how to work with related features. For proficient Windows administrators, skilled support staff, and committed power users, Windows PowerShell will become increasingly indispensible. Knowing how to use PowerShell properly can save you time and effort and can mean the difference between smooth-running operations and frequent problems. Moreover, if you're responsible for multiple computers, learning the timesaving strategies that PowerShell offers is not just important, it's essential for sustaining day-to-day operations.

> ***REAL WORLD*** **In general, you can use techniques that you learn in this book on all versions of Windows on which you can install Windows PowerShell V2. However, some features, like remoting and background jobs, don't work on all platforms. For this reason, when you are working across operating systems, you should always test commands, options, and scripts in a development or test environment, where the computers with which you are working are isolated from the rest of the network, before using them in live production environments.**

Getting Started with Windows PowerShell

Anyone with a background in UNIX is probably familiar with the concept of a command shell. Most UNIX-based operating systems have several full-featured command shells available, including Korn Shell (KSH), C Shell (CSH), and Bourne Shell (SH). Although Windows operating systems have always had a command-line environment, they've lacked a full-featured command shell, and this is where Windows PowerShell comes into the picture.

Not unlike the less sophisticated Windows command prompt, the UNIX command shells operate by executing built-in commands, external commands, and command-line utilities and then returning the results in an output stream as text. The output stream can be manipulated in various ways, including redirecting it so that it can be used as input for another command. The process of redirecting one command's output to another command's input is called *piping*, and it is a widely used shell-scripting technique.

The C Shell is one of the more sophisticated UNIX shells. In many respects, C Shell is a marriage of some of the best features of the C programming language and a full-featured UNIX shell environment. Windows PowerShell takes the idea of a full-featured command shell built on a programming language a step further. It does this by implementing a scripting language based on C# and an object model based on the Microsoft .NET Framework.

Basing the scripting language for Windows PowerShell on C# ensures that the scripting language can be easily understood by current C# developers and also allows new developers to advance to C#. Using an object model based on the .NET Framework allows Windows PowerShell to pass complete objects and all their properties as output from one command to another. The ability to redirect objects is extremely powerful and allows for a much more dynamic manipulation of result sets. For example, you can get not only the name of a particular user but also the entire related user object. You can then manipulate the properties of this user object by referring to the properties you want to work with by name.

Running Windows PowerShell

Windows PowerShell V2 is an enhanced and extended edition of the original implementation of PowerShell. The changes are dramatic, and they improve both the performance capabilities of PowerShell and its versatility. You can do things with PowerShell V2 that you simply could not do with PowerShell V1, and you can perform standard tasks in much more efficient ways than before. The discussion that follows explores PowerShell options and configurations and also provides tips for using the command history.

Using the Windows PowerShell Console

Windows PowerShell Version 2.0 (PowerShell V2) is built into Windows 7, Windows Server 2008 Release 2, and later releases of the Windows operating system. Also, you can install PowerShell V2 on computers running Windows XP, Windows Server 2003, Windows Vista, and Windows Server 2008. Different builds are available for each version of Windows, in 32-bit and 64-bit editions, at the Microsoft Download Center (*http://download.microsoft.com*).

Windows PowerShell V2 has both a command-line environment and a graphical environment for running commands and scripts. The PowerShell console (powershell.exe) is a 32-bit or 64-bit environment for working with PowerShell at the command line. On 32-bit versions of Windows, you'll find the 32-bit executable in the %SystemRoot%\System32\WindowsPowerShell\v1.0 directory. On 64-bit versions of Windows, you'll find the 32-bit executable in the %SystemRoot%\SysWow64\WindowsPowerShell\v1.0 directory and the 64-bit executable in the %SystemRoot%\System32\WindowsPowerShell\v1.0 directory.

NOTE **%SystemRoot% refers to the SystemRoot environment variable. The Windows operating system has many environment variables, which are used to refer to user-specific and system-specific values. I'll often refer to environment variables using the standard Windows syntax %VariableName%.**

REAL WORLD **Windows PowerShell V2 depends on the .NET Framework. Your computers need to run at least .NET Framework 2.0 to use core PowerShell features. Only computers running Windows Vista and later support the advanced features in PowerShell V2, and they need to be running .NET Framework 3.5.1 or later to do so.**

You can start the PowerShell console by using the Search box on the Start menu. Click Start, type **powershell** in the Search box, and then press Enter. Or, you can click Start, point to All Programs, point to Accessories, Windows PowerShell, and then choose Windows PowerShell V2. On 64-bit systems, the 64-bit version of PowerShell is started by default. If you want to use the 32-bit PowerShell console on a 64-bit system, you must select the Windows PowerShell V2 (x86) option.

You can start Windows PowerShell from a Windows command shell (cmd.exe) by entering the following:

```
powershell
```

Figure 1-1 shows a PowerShell window. By default, the window is 120 characters wide and displays 50 lines of text. When additional text is to be displayed in the window or you enter commands and the PowerShell console's window is full, the current text is displayed in the window, and prior text is scrolled up. If you want to pause the display temporarily when a command is writing output, press Ctrl+S. Afterward, press Ctrl+S to resume or Ctrl+C to terminate execution.

FIGURE 1-1 When you work with PowerShell, you'll frequently use the command-line environment.

In this figure from Windows 7, the display text is:

```
Windows PowerShell V2
Copyright (c) 2008 Microsoft Corporation. All rights reserved.

PS C:\Users\wrstanek>
```

Here, the command prompt for the PowerShell shows the current working directory preceded by PS, which by default is %UserProfile%, meaning the user profile directory for the current user. A blinking cursor following the command prompt indicates that PowerShell is in interactive processing mode. In interactive mode, you can type commands directly after the prompt and press Enter to execute them. For example, type **get-childitem** and then press Enter to get a listing of the current directory.

Windows PowerShell also has a noninteractive processing mode, which is used when executing a series of commands. In noninteractive processing mode, PowerShell reads and executes commands one by one but doesn't present a prompt to the user. Typically, commands are read from a script file, but you can start the PowerShell console in noninteractive processing mode.

To exit PowerShell, type **exit**. If you started PowerShell from a command prompt, typing **exit** will return you to the command prompt. If you want to run a separate instance of PowerShell from within PowerShell, you also can type **powershell** at the

PowerShell prompt. Invoking PowerShell in this way allows you to use a separate session and initialize PowerShell with specific parameters.

Using the Windows PowerShell ISE

The official name of the graphical environment for Windows PowerShell is the Windows PowerShell Integrated Scripting Environment (ISE). Using the PowerShell application (powershell_ise.exe), you can run commands and write, run, and debug scripts in a single integrated interface. There are 32-bit and 64-bit graphical environments for working with PowerShell, and you'll find the related executables in the same location as the PowerShell console.

You can start the PowerShell application by using the Search box on the Start menu. Click Start, type **powershell** in the Search box, and then click the version of the PowerShell application you want to run. Or, you can click Start, point to All Programs, point to Accessories, Windows PowerShell, and then choose Windows PowerShell V2 ISE. On 64-bit systems, the 64-bit version of the PowerShell ISE is started by default. If you want to use the 32-bit application on a 64-bit system, you must select the Windows PowerShell V2 ISE (x86) option.

You can start the PowerShell application from a command prompt (cmd.exe) by entering:

```
powershell_ise
```

Figure 1-2 shows the main window for the PowerShell application. By default, the main window displays the Script pane, the Command pane, and the Output pane. In the Script pane, you can type the commands and text for PowerShell scripts. In the Command pane, you can enter commands at a prompt as you would using the PowerShell console. The Output pane shows you the results of running scripts or commands.

As you enter text into the Script or Command panes, the text is color coded depending on whether it is a cmdlet, function, variable, or other type of text. Options on the View menu allow you to control the view panes. Select Show Script Pane to display the Script pane if it is hidden. Select the option again to hide the Script pane if it is displayed. When the Script pane is displayed, you can select Script Pane Right to display the Script pane on the right rather than at the top of the main window. Select the option again to restore the original position. If you prefer that the Command pane be displayed above the Output pane, select Command Pane Up. The organization I prefer is with the Command pane up and the Script pane on the right (see Figure 1-3). This arrangement helps me keep the purpose of the windows clear as I work. You can resize the panes by clicking and dragging as well.

The PowerShell application supports multiple execution environments called sessions, where each session has its own working environment. By default, the PowerShell application starts with a single session, but you can add up to seven other sessions for a total of eight. You add a session by pressing Ctrl+T or by selecting New PowerShell Tab from the File menu.

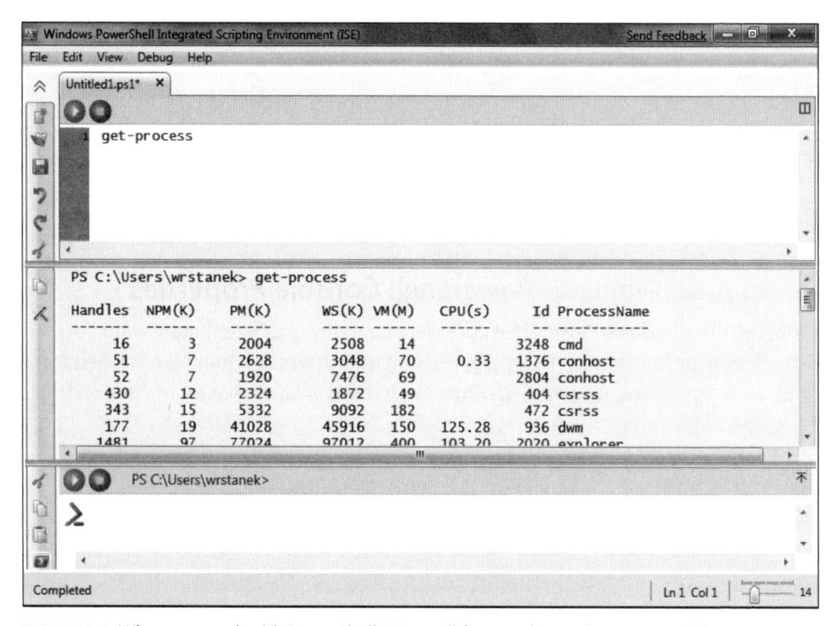

FIGURE 1-2 When you work with PowerShell ISE, you'll frequently use the command-line environment.

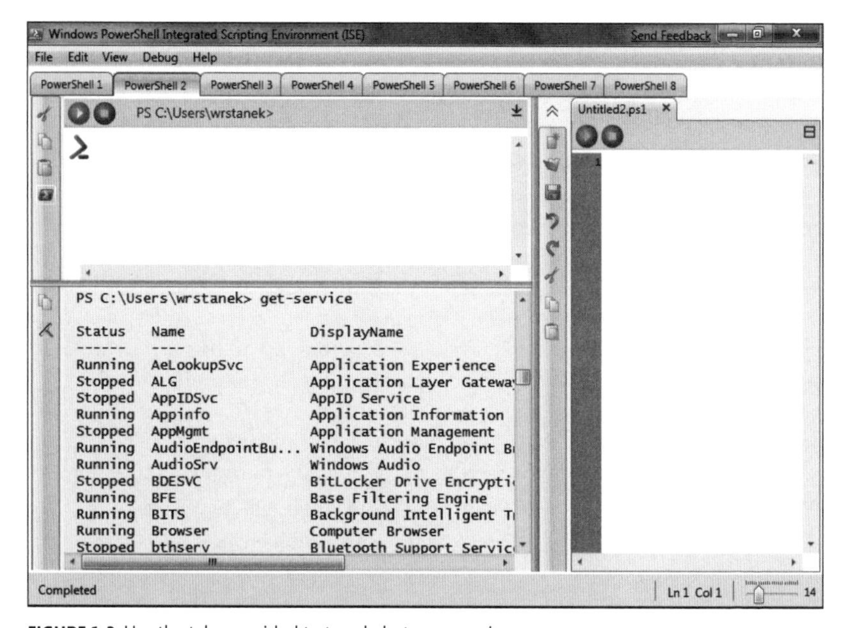

FIGURE 1-3 Use the tabs provided to toggle between sessions.

The default text size is fairly small. You can change the text size by using the Zoom slider in the lower-right corner of the main window. Alternatively, press Ctrl and+ to increase the text size, or press Ctrl and – to decrease the text size.

To close a session, press Ctrl+W or select the related Close option on the File menu. To exit the PowerShell application, press Alt+F4 or select the Exit option on the File menu. You can also exit by typing **exit** at the PowerShell prompt in the Command pane.

Configuring Windows PowerShell Console Properties

If you use the Windows PowerShell console frequently, you'll definitely want to customize its properties. For example, you can add buffers so that text scrolled out of the viewing area is accessible. You can resize the console, change its fonts, and more.

To get started, click the PowerShell prompt icon at the top of the console window or right-click the console's title bar and then select Properties. As Figure 1-4 shows, the Properties dialog box has four tabs:

- **Options** Allows you to configure cursor size, display options, edit options, and command history. Select QuickEdit Mode if you want to use a single mouse click to paste copied text into the PowerShell window. Clear QuickEdit Mode if you want to right-click and then select Paste to insert copied text. Clear Insert Mode to overwrite text as the default editing mode. Use the command history to configure how previously used commands are buffered in memory. (You'll find more information about the command history in the next section of this chapter, "Working with the Command History.")
- **Font** Allows you to set the font size and face used by the PowerShell prompt. Raster font sizes are set according to their pixel width and height. For example, the size 8 × 12 is 8 screen pixels wide and 12 screen pixels high. Other fonts are set by point size, such as 10-point Lucida Console. Interestingly, when you select a point size of n, the font will be n pixels high; therefore, a 10-point font is 10 screen pixels high. These fonts can be designated as a bold font type as well, which increases their screen pixel width.
- **Layout** Allows you to set the screen buffer size, window size, and window position. Size the buffer height so that you can easily scroll back through previous listings and script output. A good setting is in the range of 2,000 to 3,000. Size the window height so that you can view more of the PowerShell window at one time. A good setting is 60 lines on screens set to 1280 × 1024 resolution with a 12-point font. If you want the PowerShell window to be in a specific screen position, clear Let System Position Window and then specify a position, in pixels, for the upper-left corner of the PowerShell window by using Left and Top.
- **Colors** Allows you to set the text and background colors used by the PowerShell console. Screen Text and Screen Background control the respective color settings for the window. The Popup Text and Popup Background

options control the respective color settings for any pop-up dialog boxes generated when running commands at the PowerShell prompt.

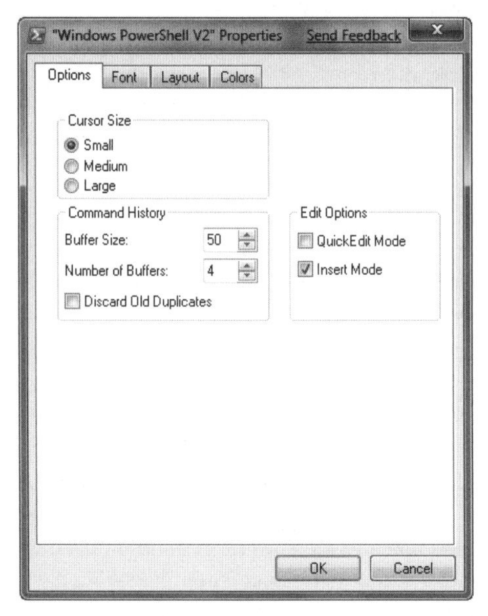

FIGURE 1-4 Configure PowerShell console properties for your environment.

When you are finished updating the window properties, click OK to save your settings to your user profile. Your settings modify only the shortcut that started the current window. Any time you start PowerShell using the applicable shortcut, PowerShell will use these settings. If, however, you start PowerShell using a different shortcut, you'll have the settings associated with that shortcut.

Working with the Command History

The command history buffer is a feature of Windows PowerShell that stores commands you've used in the current session and allows you to access them without having to retype the command text. The maximum number of commands to buffer is set through the PowerShell Properties dialog box discussed in the previous section. By default, up to 50 commands are stored.

You can change the history size by completing these steps:

1. Right-click the PowerShell console's title bar, select Properties, and then click the Options tab.
2. Use the Buffer Size field to set the maximum number of commands to store in the history, and then click OK to save your settings to your user profile.

Your settings modify only the shortcut that started the current window. Any time you start a PowerShell using the applicable shortcut, it will use these settings. If, however, you start a PowerShell using a different shortcut, you'll have the settings associated with that shortcut.

You can access commands stored in the history in the following ways:

- **Browsing with the arrow keys** Use the up arrow and down arrow keys to move up and down through the list of buffered commands. When you find the command you want to use, press Enter to execute it as entered previously, or you can modify the command text displayed by adding or changing parameters and then pressing Enter.
- **Browsing the command history pop-up window** Press F7 to display a pop-up window that contains a listing of buffered commands. Next, select a command using the arrow keys. (Alternatively, press F9, press the corresponding number on the keyboard, and then press Enter.) Execute the selected command by pressing Enter, or press Esc to close the pop-up window without executing a command.
- **Searching the command history** Enter the first few letters of the command you want to execute, and then press F8. PowerShell searches through the history for the first command that begins with the characters you entered. Press Enter to execute it, or press F8 again to search the history buffer for the next match in the command history.

As you work with the command history, keep in mind that each instance of Windows PowerShell has its own set of command buffers. Thus, buffers are valid only in the related PowerShell context.

Working with Cmdlets and Scripts

Windows PowerShell introduces the concept of a cmdlet (pronounced *commandlet*). A cmdlet is the smallest unit of functionality in Windows PowerShell. You can think of a cmdlet as a built-in command. Rather than being highly complex, most cmdlets are quite simple and have a small set of associated properties.

Using Cmdlets

You use cmdlets the same way you use any other commands and utilities. Cmdlet names are not case sensitive. This means you can use a combination of both uppercase and lowercase characters. After starting Windows PowerShell, you can enter the name of the cmdlet at the prompt, and it will run in much the same way as a command-line command.

For ease of reference, cmdlets are named using verb-noun pairs. As Table 1-1 shows, the verb tells you what the cmdlet does in general. The noun tells you what specifically the cmdlet works with. Verbs and nouns are always separated by a hyphen with no spaces. For example, the Get-Variable cmdlet gets a named Windows PowerShell variable and returns its value. If you don't specify which variable to get as a parameter, Get-Variable returns a list of all PowerShell variables and their values.

TABLE 1-1 Common Verbs Used with Cmdlets

CMDLET VERB	USAGE
Add	Adds an instance of an item, such as a history entry or snap-in.
Clear	Removes the contents of an item, such as an event log or variable value.
ConvertFrom	Converts an item from one format to another, such as converting from a list of comma-separated values to object properties.
ConvertTo	Converts an item to a particular format, such as converting object properties to a list of comma-separated values.
Disable	Disables an enabled setting, such as disabling remote connections.
Enable	Enables a disabled setting, such as enabling remote connections.
Export	Exports an item's properties in a particular format, such as exporting console properties in XML format.
Get	Queries a specific object or a subset of a type of object, such as getting a list of running processes.
Import	Imports an item's properties from a particular format, such as importing console properties from serialized XML.
Invoke	Executes an instance of an item, such as an expression.
New	Creates a new instance of an item, such as a new variable or event.
Remove	Removes an instance of an item, such as a variable or event.
Set	Modifies specific settings of an object.
Start	Starts an instance of an item, such as a service or process.
Stop	Stops an instance of an item, such as a service or process.
Test	Tests an instance of an item for a specific state or value, such as testing a connection to see if it is valid
Write	Performs a write operation on an instance of an item, such as writing an event to the system event log.

Table 1-2 provides a list of cmdlets you'll commonly use for administration. Although many other cmdlets are available, these are the ones you're likely to use the most.

TABLE 1-2 Cmdlets Commonly Used for Administration

CMDLET NAME	DESCRIPTION
Add-Computer, Remove-Computer	Adds or removes a computer's membership in a domain or workgroup.
Checkpoint-Computer, Restore-Computer	Creates a system restore checkpoint for a computer or restores a computer from a checkpoint.
Compare-Object, Group-Object, Sort-Object, Select-Object, New-Object	Cmdlets for comparing, grouping, sorting, selecting, and creating objects.
ConvertFrom-SecureString, ConvertTo-SecureString	Cmdlets for creating or exporting secure strings.
Debug-Process	Debugs a process running on a computer.
Get-Alias, New-Alias, Set-Alias, Export-Alias, Import-Alias	Cmdlets for getting, creating, setting, exporting, and importing aliases.
Get-AuthenticodeSignature, Set-AuthenticodeSignature	Cmdlets for getting or setting the signature object associated with a file.
Get-Command, Invoke-Command, Measure-Command, Trace-Command	Cmdlets for getting information about cmdlets, invoking commands, measuring the run time of commands, and tracing commands.
Get-Counter	Gets performance counter data.
Get-Credential	Gets a credential object based on a password.
Get-Date, Set-Date	Gets or sets the current date and time.
Get-EventLog, Write-EventLog, Clear-EventLog	Gets events, writes events, or clears events in an event log.
Get-ExecutionPolicy, Set-ExecutionPolicy	Gets or sets the effective execution policy for the current shell.
Get-Host	Gets information about the PowerShell host application.
Get-HotFix	Gets the hotfixes and other updates that have been applied to a computer.

TABLE 1-2 Cmdlets Commonly Used for Administration

CMDLET NAME	DESCRIPTION
Get-Location, Set-Location	Displays or sets the current working location.
Get-Process, Start-Process, Stop-Process	Gets, starts, or stops processes on a computer.
Get-PSDrive, New-PSDrive, Remove-PSDrive	Gets, creates, or removes a specified PowerShell drive.
Get-Service, New-Service, Set-Service	Gets, creates, or sets system services.
Get-Variable, New-Variable, Set-Variable, Remove-Variable, Clear-Variable	Cmdlets for getting, creating, setting, and removing variables as well as for clearing variable values.
Import-Counter, Export-Counter	Imports or exports performance counter log files.
Limit-EventLog	Sets the size and age limits for an event log.
New-EventLog, Remove-EventLog	Creates or removes a custom event log and event source
Ping-Computer	Sends Internet Control Message Protocol (ICMP) request packets to designated computers.
Pop-Location	Obtains a pushed location from the stack.
Push-Location	Pushes a location to the stack
Read-Host, Write-Host, Clear-Host	Reads input from, writes output to, or clears the host window.
Rename-Computer, Stop-Computer, Restart-Computer	Renames, stops, or restarts a computer.
Reset-ComputerMachinePassword	Changes and resets the machine account password that the computer uses to authenticate in a domain.
Show-EventLog	Displays a computer's event logs in Event Viewer.
Show-Service	Displays a computer's services in the Services utility.
Start-Sleep	Suspends shell or script activity for the specified period.

TABLE 1-2 Cmdlets Commonly Used for Administration

CMDLET NAME	DESCRIPTION
Stop-Service, Start-Service, Suspend-Service, Resume-Service, Restart-Service	Cmdlets for stopping, starting, suspending, resuming, and restarting system services.
Wait-Process	Waits for a process to be stopped before accepting input.
Write-Output	Writes an object to the pipeline.
Write-Warning	Displays a warning message.

You can work with cmdlets by executing them directly at the PowerShell prompt or by running commands from within scripts. At the Windows PowerShell prompt, you can get a complete list of cmdlets available by typing **get-command**. However, the output lists both cmdlets and functions by name and definition. With cmdlets, the definition provided is the syntax, but the full syntax rarely fits on the line. More often, you simply want to know if a cmdlet exists. You can display a formatted list of cmdlets by entering the following command:

```
get-command | format-wide -column 3
```

This command shows many of the features of PowerShell that you'll use regularly at the command line. The | symbol is called a pipe. Here, you pipe the output of Get-Command to Format-Wide. Format-Wide takes the output and formats it in multiple columns. The default number of columns is two, but here we used the –Column parameter to specify that we wanted to format the output into three columns, as shown in this example:

```
A:               Add-Computer     Add-Content
Add-History      Add-Member       Add-PSSnapin
Add-Type         B:               C:
cd..             cd\              Checkpoint-Computer
Clear-Content    Clear-EventLog   Clear-History
Clear-Host       Clear-Item       Clear-ItemProperty
Clear-Variable   Compare-Object   Complete-Transaction
Connect-WSMan    ConvertFrom-Csv  ConvertFrom-SecureString
```

A better way to get information about cmdlets is to use Get-Help. If you enter **get-help *-***, you get a list of all cmdlets, which includes a synopsis that summarizes the purpose of the cmdlet—much more useful than a list of commands.

Rather than list all commands, you can list specific commands by name or by using wildcards. For example, if you know the command you are looking for begins with Get, enter **get-help get*** to view all commands that start with Get. If you know the command includes the word *computer*, you could enter **get-help *computer*** to view all commands that included this keyword. Finally, if you are looking for related commands on a specific subject, such as aliases, enter **get-help *** and then the keyword, such as **get-command *alias**.

When you work with cmdlets, you'll encounter two standard types of errors:

- **Terminating errors** Errors that halt execution
- **Nonterminating errors** Errors that cause error output to be returned but do not halt execution

With both types of errors, you'll typically see error text that can help you resolve the problem that caused it. For example, an expected file might be missing or you may not have sufficient permissions to perform a specified task.

To help you examine cmdlet syntax and usage, Windows PowerShell provides three levels of Help documentation: standard, detailed, and full. To view the standard Help documentation for a specific cmdlet, type **get-help** followed by the cmdlet name, such as:

```
get-help new-variable
```

The standard Help documentation provides the complete syntax for using a cmdlet, which includes details on any parameters the cmdlet supports and examples. You can get detailed information about a cmdlet by adding the –Detailed parameter. Or you can get full technical information about a cmdlet by adding the –Full parameter. The detailed and the full documentation are both useful when you want to dig deeper, and usually either one will give you the information you are looking for.

Using Cmdlet Parameters

All cmdlet parameters are designated with an initial dash (–), as with –Detailed and –Full in the previous section. To reduce the amount of typing required, some parameters are position sensitive, so that you can sometimes pass parameters in a specific order without having to specify the parameter name. For example, in the syntax for the Get-Service cmdlet, you know the –Name parameter can be omitted because it is enclosed in brackets as shown here:

```
Get-Service [-ComputerName <string[]>] [-DependentServices]
[-Exclude <string[]>] [-Include <string[]>] [-ServicesDependedOn]
[[-Name] <string[]>] [<CommonParameters>]
```

Therefore, with Get-Service, you don't have to specify the –Name parameter; you can simply type the following:

```
get-service ServiceName
```

where *ServiceName* is the name of the service you want to examine, such as:

```
get-service winrm
```

This command line returns the status of the Windows Remote Management service. Because you can use wildcards, such as *, with name values, you can also type **get-service win*** to return the status of all services whose names begin with *win*. Typically, these will include the Windows Defender, Windows Management Instrumentation, and Windows Remote Management services, as shown in this example:

```
Status   Name               DisplayName
------   ----               -----------
Running  WinDefend          Windows Defender
Stopped  WinHttpAutoProx... WinHTTP Web Proxy Auto-Discovery
Running  Winmgmt            Windows Management Instrumentation
Stopped  WinRM              Windows Remote Management
```

All cmdlets support a common set of parameters. Most cmdlets that make changes support the risk mitigation parameters: –Confirm and –WhatIf. Table 1-3 lists the common and risk mitigation parameters. Although you can use the common parameters with any cmdlet, they don't necessarily have an effect with all cmdlets. For example, if a cmdlet doesn't generate verbose output, using the –Verbose parameter has no effect.

TABLE 1-3 Common and Risk Mitigation Parameters

PARAMETER NAME	DESCRIPTION
–Confirm	Pauses execution and requires the user to acknowledge the action before continuing.
–Debug	Provides programming-level debugging information about the operation.
–ErrorAction	Controls the command behavior when an error occurs. Valid values are SilentlyContinue (suppress the error and continue), Continue (display the error and continue), Inquire (display the error and prompt to confirm before continuing), and Stop (display the error and halt execution). The default value is Continue.
–ErrorVariable	Sets the name of the variable (in addition to the standard error) in which to store errors that have occurred.
–OutBuffer	Sets the output buffer for the cmdlet.
–OutVariable	Sets the name of the variable in which to place output objects.
–Verbose	Provides detailed information about the operation.

TABLE 1-3 Common and Risk Mitigation Parameters

PARAMETER NAME	DESCRIPTION
–WarningAction	Determines how a cmdlet responds to a warning message. Valid values are SilentlyContinue (suppress the warning and continue), Continue (display the warning and continue), Inquire (display the warning and prompt to confirm before continuing), and Stop (display the warning and halt execution). The default value is Continue.
–WarningVariable	Sets the name of the variable (in addition to the standard error) in which to store warnings that have occurred.
–WhatIf	Allows the user to view what would happen if a cmdlet were run with a specific set of parameters.

Using External Commands

Because Windows PowerShell runs within the context of the Windows command prompt, you can run all Windows command-line commands, utilities, and graphical applications from within the Windows PowerShell, either at the PowerShell prompt or in your scripts. However, it is important to remember that the Windows PowerShell interpreter parses all commands before passing off the command to the command-prompt environment. If the Windows PowerShell has a like-named command, keyword, alias, or function for a command, this command, and not the expected Windows command, is executed. (See the "Initializing the Environment" and "Understanding Command Input, Parsing, and Output" sections in Chapter 2, "Getting the Most from Windows PowerShell" for more information on aliases and functions.)

Non–Windows PowerShell commands and programs must reside in a directory that is part of the PATH environment variable. If the item is found in the path, it is run. The PATH variable also controls where the Windows PowerShell looks for applications, utilities, and scripts. In Windows PowerShell, you can work with Windows environment variables by using $env. If you want to view the current settings for the PATH environment variable, you type **$env:path**. If you want to add a directory to this variable, you can use the following syntax:

```
$env:path += ";DirectoryPathToAdd"
```

Here, *DirectoryPathToAdd* is the directory path you want to add to the path, such as:

```
$env:path += ";C:\Scripts"
```

To have this directory added to the path every time you start Windows PowerShell, you can add the command line as an entry in a PowerShell profile. A profile is a type of script used to set the working environment for PowerShell. Keep in mind that cmdlets are like built-in commands rather than stand-alone executables. Because of this, they are not affected by the PATH environment variable.

REAL WORLD **Computers running Windows Vista and later versions of Windows have the SETX utility. With the SETX utility, you can write environment variable changes directly to the Windows registry, which makes the changes permanent rather than temporary, as the $env:path command does. You can also use SETX to obtain current registry key values and write them to a text file.**

Using Scripts

Windows PowerShell scripts are text files with the .ps1 extension. You can enter any command or cmdlet that you can run at the PowerShell prompt into a script by copying the related command text to a file and saving the file with the .ps1 extension. You can then run the script in the same way you would any other command or cmdlet. However, when you are working with PowerShell scripts, the current directory might not be part of the environment path. For this reason, you might need to use "./" when you run a script in the current directory. For example, if you create a PowerShell script called run_all.ps1, and the script is in the current directory, you could run the script by entering the following command:

```
./run_all
```

NOTE **PowerShell is designed to accommodate users with backgrounds in UNIX or Windows operating systems. You can use a forward slash or backward slash as a directory separator. Following this, you can enter ./run_all or .\run_all to reference a script in the current working directory.**

Whenever you work with scripts, you need to keep in mind the current execution policy and whether signed scripts are required.

Understanding Execution Policy

The current execution policy for Windows PowerShell controls whether and how you can run configuration files and scripts. Execution policy is a built-in security feature of Windows PowerShell that is set on a per-user basis in the Windows registry. Although the default configuration depends on which operating system and edition is installed, you can quickly determine the execution policy by entering **get-executionpolicy** at the PowerShell prompt.

The available execution policies, from most secure to least secure, are:

- **Restricted** Does not load configuration files or scripts. This means all configuration files and scripts, regardless of whether they are signed or unsigned. Because a profile is a type of script, profiles are not loaded either.
- **AllSigned** Requires all configuration files and scripts from all sources—whether local or remote—to be signed by a trusted publisher. Because of this requirement, configuration files and scripts on the local computer must be signed as configuration files, and scripts from remote computers must be signed. PowerShell prompts you before running scripts from trusted publishers.
- **RemoteSigned** Requires all configuration files and scripts from remote sources to be signed by a trusted publisher. Configuration files and scripts on the local computer do not need to be signed. PowerShell does not prompt you before running scripts from trusted publishers.
- **Unrestricted** Allows all configuration files and scripts to run whether they are from local or remote sources and regardless of whether they are signed or unsigned. However, if you run a configuration file or script from a remote resource, you are prompted with a warning that the file comes from a remote resource before the configuration file is loaded or the script runs.

As you can see, execution policy determines whether you can load configuration files and run scripts as well as whether scripts must be digitally signed before they will run. When an execution policy prevents loading a file or running a script, a warning is displayed explaining applicable restrictions.

You can use Set-ExecutionPolicy to change the preference for the execution policy. Changes to the policy are written to the registry. However, if the Turn On Script Execution setting in Group Policy is enabled for the computer or user, the user preference is written to the registry, but it is not effective, and Windows PowerShell displays a message explaining the conflict. You cannot use Set-ExecutionPolicy to override a group policy, even if the user preference is more restrictive than the policy setting.

To set the execution policy to require that all scripts have a trusted signature to execute, enter the following command:

```
set-executionpolicy allsigned
```

To set the execution policy so that scripts downloaded from the Web execute only if they are signed by a trusted source, enter:

```
set-executionpolicy remotesigned
```

To set the execution policy to run scripts regardless of whether they have a digital signature and work in an unrestricted environment, you can enter the following command:

```
set-executionpolicy unrestricted
```

The change occurs immediately and is applied to the local console or application session. Because the change is written to the registry, the new execution policy will be used whenever you work with PowerShell.

> ***NOTE*** **Because only administrators are allowed to change the execution policy on Windows Vista or later, you must run Windows PowerShell with the Run As Administrator option.**

Understanding Script Signing

Signing scripts is much easier than you might think. To sign scripts, you can use the Set-AuthenticodeSignature cmdlet. This cmdlet creates digital signatures using a digital certificate. Digital certificates can be created by a certificate authority (CA), or you can create your own self-signed certificates. When you use certificates created by a CA, you can use the certificate on any computer that trusts the CA. When you use self-signed certificates, you can use the certificate on your local computer.

In Windows domains, you can use Active Directory Certificate Services to establish a certificate authority (CA) and create digital certificates. As most enterprises have CAs and use digital certificates to enhance security, you may already have been issued a digital certificate that you can use for code signing. To find out, enter the following command:

```
get-childitem cert:\CurrentUser\My -codesigningcert
```

Or you can examine the certificates store. The certificates store on a Windows computer stores trust information. In the certificates store, you can view information about the following:

- **Personal** Certificates stored on the local computer that are assigned to you for various uses.
- **Other People** Certificates stored on the local computer that are assigned to other people for various uses.
- **Trusted Root Certification Authorities** Root CAs your computer trusts. Your computer will trust any certificates from these root CAs.
- **Trusted Publishers** Publishers whose digitally signed scripts are trusted.
- **Untrusted Publisher** Publishers whose digitally signed scripts are not trusted.

You can access the certificates store through the Internet Properties dialog box. In Control Panel, select Network And Internet and then click Internet Options. In the Internet Properties dialog box, on the Content tab, click Certificates to display the Certificates dialog box. Use the Certificates store to examine the various types of trust information and related details.

PowerShell makes certificates available through the Cert provider. As you'll learn more about in the "Using Providers" section in Chapter 5, "Navigating Core PowerShell Structures," the data that a provider exposes appears as a drive that you can browse much like you browse a hard drive. If you enter **cd cert:** at the PowerShell prompt, you will access the certificates store on your computer. If you then enter **dir** (which is an alias for Get-ChildItem), you'll see a list of locations you can browse. Typically, this will include CurrentUser and LocalMachine, which are the certificate stores for the currently logged-on user and the local computer, respectively, as shown in the following example and sample output:

```
cd cert:
dir
```

```
Location   : CurrentUser
StoreNames : {SmartCardRoot, UserDS, AuthRoot, CA...}

Location   : LocalMachine
StoreNames : {SmartCardRoot, AuthRoot, CA, Trust...}
```

While you are working with the Cert provider, if you enter **cd currentuser** and then type **dir** again, you'll see all the substores for the current user. One of these stores is the My store, where personal certificates are stored, as shown in the following example and sample output:

```
cd currentuser
dir
```

```
Name : SmartCardRoot
Name : UserDS
Name : AuthRoot
Name : CA
Name : ADDRESSBOOK
Name : Trust
Name : Disallowed
Name : My
Name : Root
Name : TrustedPeople
Name : TrustedPublisher
```

You can see the personal certificates for code signing in the My store by entering **cd my** and then entering **dir –codesigningcert,** as shown in the following example and sample output:

```
cd my
dir -codesigningcert
```

```
Directory: Microsoft.PowerShell.Security\Certificate::currentuser\my
Thumbprint                                  Subject
----------                                  -------
D3828283483483882433482384238E2828282833    CN=WRSTANEK
AED382828383838484834838483483488AC39839    CN=WRSTANEK
```

Whether you enter Get-ChildItem –Codesigningcert or Dir –Codesigningcert, the results are the same. The command returns an array of certificates. In PowerShell, you can reference individual elements in an array by their index position. The first element in an array has the index position 0, the second 1, and so on.

If you have a personal certificate for code signing issued by a CA, you can sign unsigned scripts using the following command:

```
$cert = @(Get-ChildItem cert:\CurrentUser\My -codesigningcert)[0]
Set-AuthenticodeSignature ScriptName.ps1 $cert
```

Note that these are two separate commands and that ScriptName sets the name of the script to sign, such as:

```
$cert = @(Get-ChildItem cert:\CurrentUser\My -codesigningcert)[0]
Set-AuthenticodeSignature run_all.ps1 $cert
```

Here, you use Get-ChildItem to access the My certificates store and get the first personal certificate for code signing and then use the certificate to sign the run_all.ps1 script. As long as the certificate is signed by an enterprise CA, you can run the signed script on any computer in the enterprise that trusts the CA.

Creating and Using Self-Signed Certificates

You can create a self-signed certificate using makecert.exe. This utility is included in the Microsoft .NET Framework Software Development Kit (SDK) Versions 1.1 and later, and in the platform-specific Windows SDK. After you download and install the appropriate SDK, you must:

1. Open an elevated, administrator command prompt (cmd.exe).
2. Use the command prompt to create a local certificate authority for your computer.
3. Use the command prompt to generate a personal certificate via this certificate authority.

You create the local certificate authority by entering the following command:

```
makecert -n "CN=PowerShell Local Certificate Root" -a sha1
-eku 1.3.6.1.5.5.7.3.3 -r -sv root.pvk root.cer
-ss Root -sr localMachine
```

Here, you're running this from a command prompt with Administrator privileges in the directory where makecert is located. Note that this is a single command, and the parameters are used as follows:

- The –n parameter sets the certificate name. The name value is preceded by CN=.
- The –a parameter sets the signature algorithm as SHA1 as opposed to MD5 (the default value).
- The –eku parameter inserts the enhanced key usage object identifier: 1.3.6.1.5.5.7.3.3.
- The –r parameter specifies that you want to create a self-signed certificate.
- The –sv parameter sets the file names for the private key file and the certificate file that makecert will create.
- The –ss parameter sets the name of the store that stores the output certificate as Root for the Trusted Root Certificate Authorities store.
- The –sr parameter sets the certificate store location as the local machine, as opposed to the current user (the default value).

You generate a personal certificate via this certificate authority by entering the following command:

```
makecert -pe -n "CN=PowerShell User" -ss MY -a sha1
-eku 1.3.6.1.5.5.7.3.3 -iv root.pvk -ic root.cer
```

Note that this is a single command, and the parameters are used as follows:

- The –pe parameter marks the certificate's private key as exportable.
- The –n parameter sets the certificate name. Again, the name value is preceded by CN=.
- The –ss parameter sets the name of the store that stores the output certificate as MY, for the Personal store.
- The –a parameter sets the signature algorithm as SHA1.
- The –eku parameter inserts the enhanced key usage object identifier: 1.3.6.1.5.5.7.3.3.
- The –iv parameter specifies the name of the CA's private key file.
- The –ic parameter specifies the name of the CA's certificate file.

The first command generates two temporary files: root.pvk and root.cer. The second command uses these files to create a certificate that is stored in the Personal certificate store on the local computer.

MakeCert will prompt you for a private key password. The password ensures that no one can use or access the certificate without your consent. Create and enter a password that you can remember. You will use this password later to retrieve the certificate.

To verify that the certificate was generated correctly, use the following command to search for the certificate in the Personal certificate store on the computer:

```
get-childitem cert:\CurrentUser\My -codesigningcert
```

This command uses the Windows PowerShell Certificate provider to view information about certificates in the My personal certificate store. If the certificate was created, the output lists the certificate by its encrypted thumbprint and subject.

After you have a self-signed certificate, you can sign scripts as discussed previously. The signed script will run on the local computer. However, the signed script will not run on computers on which the execution policy requires a digital signature from a trusted authority. On these computers, Windows PowerShell reports that the script cannot be loaded and that the signature of the certificate cannot be verified.

CHAPTER 2

Getting the Most from Windows PowerShell

Windows PowerShell provides an effective environment for working with commands and scripts. As discussed in Chapter 1, "Introducing Windows PowerShell," you can run many types of commands at the command line, including built-in cmdlets, Windows utilities, and applications with command-line extensions. Regardless of its source, every command you'll use follows the same syntax rules. These rules state that a command consists of a command name followed by any required or optional arguments. Arguments, which include parameters, parameter values, and other command text, can also use piping to combine commands and redirection to specify the sources for inputs, outputs, and errors.

When you execute commands in PowerShell, you start a series of events that are similar to the following:

1. Multiple commands that are chained or grouped and passed on a single line are broken into individual units of execution. Values within a unit of execution are broken into a series of segments called *tokens*.
2. Each token is parsed, commands are separated from values, and values are evaluated as some kind of object type, such as String or Boolean. Variables in the command text are replaced with their actual values as appropriate during parsing.
3. The individual commands are then processed. If a command's name has a file path, PowerShell uses this path to find the command. If the command cannot be found in the specified location, PowerShell returns an error.
4. If a command's name doesn't specify a file path, PowerShell tries to resolve the command name internally. A match means that you've referenced a built-in command (including an alias to a command or a function) that can

be executed immediately. If no match is found, PowerShell searches the command path for a matching command executable. If the command cannot be found in any of those locations, PowerShell returns an error. Because PowerShell does not look in the current directory by default, you must explicitly specify the current directory.

5. If the command is located, the command is executed using any specified arguments, including those that specify the inputs to use. Command output and any errors are written to the PowerShell window or to the specified destinations for output and errors.

As you can see, many factors can affect command execution, including command path settings, redirection techniques, and whether commands are chained or grouped. In this chapter, I'll describe and show examples of this breakdown of command execution to help you get the most out of PowerShell. Before diving into those discussions, however, let's look at special considerations for starting PowerShell and examine the concepts of profiles and console files.

Initializing the Environment

Windows PowerShell provides a dynamic, extensible execution environment. You can initialize the environment for PowerShell in several ways, including passing startup parameters to Powershell.exe, using a customized profile, using a console file, or any combination of the three. You can extend the environment for PowerShell in several ways as well, including by installing providers and registering snap-ins as discussed in Chapter 3, "Managing Your PowerShell Environment."

Passing Startup Parameters

If you worked with PowerShell previously, you probably opened a console window by clicking Start, pointing to All Programs, pointing to Accessories, pointing to Windows PowerShell, and then choosing Windows PowerShell. This technique starts PowerShell with standard user privileges rather than administrator privileges, however, so you would not be able to perform many administrative tasks. To start PowerShell with administrator privileges, you need to click Start, point to All Programs, point to Accessories, point to Windows PowerShell, right-click Windows PowerShell, and then select Run As Administrator.

Other ways to start a PowerShell console are to use the Search box on the Start menu, use the Run dialog box, or type **powershell** in an open command-shell window. These techniques enable you to pass arguments to PowerShell, including switches that control how PowerShell works and parameters that execute additional commands. For example, you can start PowerShell in no-logo mode (meaning the logo banner is turned off) by using the startup command **powershell -nologo**. By default, when you start PowerShell via the command shell, PowerShell runs and then exits. If you want PowerShell to execute a command and not terminate, type **powershell /noexit** followed by the command text.

Listing 2-1 shows the basic syntax for invoking the PowerShell console. Table 2-1 lists the available startup parameters. By default, startup profiles are loaded when the PowerShell console starts. You can exit the console at any time by typing **exit**.

LISTING 2-1 PowerShell Syntax

```
powershell[.exe] [-PSConsoleFile FileName | -Version VersionNumber]
  [-NoLogo] [-NoExit] [-NoProfile] [-NonInteractive] [-Sta]
  [-InputFormat {Text | XML}] [-OutputFormat {Text | XML}]
  [-WindowsStyle Style] [-EncodedCommand Base64EncodedCommand]
  [-File ScriptFilePath] [-ExecutionPolicy PolicySetting]
  [-Command CommandText]
```

TABLE 2-1 PowerShell Startup Parameters

PARAMETER	DESCRIPTION
–Command	Specifies the command text to execute as though it were typed at the PowerShell command prompt.
–EncodedCommand	Specifies the base64-encoded command text to execute.
–ExecutionPolicy	Sets the default execution policy for the console session.
–File	Sets the name of a script file to execute.
–InputFormat	Sets the format for data sent to PowerShell as either text string or serialized XML. The default format is XML. Valid values are *text* and *XML*.
–NoExit	Does not exit after running startup commands. This parameter is useful when you run PowerShell commands or scripts via the command prompt (cmd.exe).
–NoLogo	Starts the PowerShell console without displaying the copyright banner.
–Noninteractive	Starts the PowerShell console in noninteractive mode. In this mode, PowerShell does not present an interactive prompt to the user.
–NoProfile	Tells the PowerShell console not to load the current user's profile.
–OutputFormat	Sets the format for output as either text string or serialized XML. The default format is text. Valid values are *text* and *XML*.

TABLE 2-1 PowerShell Startup Parameters

PARAMETER	DESCRIPTION
–PSConsoleFile	Loads the specified Windows PowerShell console file. Console files end with the .psc1 extension and can be used to ensure that specific snap-in extensions are loaded and available. You can create a console file using Export-Console in Windows PowerShell.
–Sta	Starts PowerShell in single-threaded mode.
–Version	Sets the version of Windows PowerShell to use for compatibility, such as 1.0.
–WindowStyle	Sets the window style as Normal, Minimized, Maximized, or Hidden. The default is Normal.

Invoking Windows PowerShell

Although you'll most often work with the PowerShell console or the PowerShell application, at times you might want to invoke PowerShell to run a cmdlet from the Windows command shell (cmd.exe) environment or a batch script. To do so, you use the –Command parameter. Generally, you will also want to suppress the Windows PowerShell logo with the –NoLogo parameter and stop execution of profiles with the –NoProfile parameter. For example, at a command prompt or in a batch script, you could get a list of running processes via PowerShell with the following command:

```
powershell -nologo -noprofile -command get-process
```

When you enter this command, the Windows command shell runs PowerShell as it would any other external program, passing in the parameters and parameter values you use and then exiting PowerShell when execution completes. If you want the command shell to run a PowerShell command and remain in PowerShell after execution, you can add the –NoExit parameter as shown in the following example:

```
powershell -noexit -command get-process
```

Using –Command to Run Commands

Because –Command is the most common parameter you'll use when invoking PowerShell from a command prompt or batch script, let's take a closer look at all the ways it can be used. If you enter – as the command, the command text is read from standard input. You also can use piping and redirection techniques to manipulate the output of a command. However, keep in mind that any characters typed after the command are interpreted as command arguments. Because of this, to write a command that includes piping or redirection, you must enclose the command text in double quotation marks. The following example gets information about currently running processes and sorts it by process identifier:

```
powershell -nologo -noprofile -command "get-process | sort-object Id"
```

> ***REAL WORLD*** **Most commands generate output that can be redirected to another command as input. To do this, you use a technique called *piping*, whereby the output of a command is sent as the input of the next command. Following this, you can see the general syntax for piping is**
>
> ```
> Command1 | Command2
> ```
>
> **where the pipe redirects the output of Command1 to the input of Command2. But you can also redirect output more than once by using this syntax:**
>
> ```
> Command1 | Command2 | Command3
> ```
>
> **Generally, if a cmdlet accepts input from another cmdlet, the cmdlet will have an –InputObject parameter and you can pipe output to the cmdlet.**

Windows PowerShell also supports script blocks. A script block is a series of commands executed in sequence. Script blocks are enclosed in braces ({}), and each command within a script block is separated by a semicolon. Although you can enter script blocks enclosed in braces, you can do so directly only when running Powershell.exe in Windows PowerShell. The results are then returned as deserialized XML objects rather than standard objects. For example, if you are already working at the PowerShell prompt and want to run a series of commands through a separate PowerShell instance, you can do so by enclosing the commands in braces and separating commands with semicolons, as shown in this example:

```
powershell -command {get-service; get-process}
```

Although this technique works if you are already working with the PowerShell prompt, it doesn't work when you want to run PowerShell from a command prompt. The workaround is to use the following format:

```
"& {CommandText}"
```

Here, the quotation marks indicate a string, and the ampersand (&) is an invoke operator that causes the command to be executed. After you write a string that runs a command, you will generally be able to run the command at either the command prompt or the PowerShell prompt. For example, even though you cannot enter **powershell -command {get-service; get-process}** at the command prompt, you can enter the following at a command prompt:

```
powershell -command "& {get-service; get-process}"
```

Here, you pass a code block to PowerShell as a string to parse and execute. PowerShell executes Get-Service and displays the results and then executes Get-Process and displays the results. If you want one syntax that will generally succeed whether you are working with strings, multiple commands, the command prompt, or the PowerShell prompt, this syntax is the one you should use.

Using –File to Run Scripts

When you are working with the Windows command shell and want to run a PowerShell script, you also can use piping and redirection techniques to manipulate the output of a command. However, instead of using the –Command parameter, you use the –File parameter to specify the script to run. As shown in the following example, you follow the –File parameter with the path to the script to run:

```
powershell -nologo -noprofile -file c:\scripts\run_all.ps1
```

If the script is in the current directory, simply enter the script name:

```
powershell -nologo -noprofile -file run_all.ps1
```

If the path name includes blank spaces, you must enclose the path in double quotation marks, as shown in this example:

```
powershell -nologo -noprofile -file "c:\data\current scripts\run_all.ps1"
```

REAL WORLD **You can specify parameters whether you start PowerShell from the menu or a command prompt. When starting PowerShell from the menu, edit the menu shortcut that starts the PowerShell console or the PowerShell application to specify parameters you want to use whenever you work with PowerShell. To do so, follow these steps:**

1. **On the menu, right-click the shortcut and then select Properties.**

   In the Properties dialog box, the Target entry on the Shortcut tab is selected by default.
2. **Without pressing any other key, press the Right arrow key. This places the insertion cursor at the end of the full path to PowerShell. Insert a space, and then type your parameters and parameter values.**
3. **Click OK to save the settings. If you make a mistake or no longer want to use parameters, repeat this procedure and remove any parameters and values you've added.**

Using Nested Consoles

Sometimes you might want to use different environment settings or parameters for a PowerShell console and then go back to your original settings without exiting the console window. To do this, you can use a technique called *nesting*. With nesting, you start a PowerShell console within another PowerShell console.

Unlike the command shell, the nested console opens with a new working environment and does not inherit its environment settings from the current console. You can work in this separate console environment and execute commands and scripts.

When you type **exit** to close the instance of the nested console, you return to the previous console, and the previous environment settings are restored.

Understanding Command Input, Parsing, and Output

As you've seen from examples in this chapter and in Chapter 1, typing commands at the PowerShell prompt is a fairly straightforward process. The most basic approach is simply to type your command text and then press Enter. When you press Enter, PowerShell processes and parses the command text.

Basic Line Editing

The PowerShell console includes some basic editing capabilities for the current line. Table 2-2 lists the editing keys. Alternatively, enter **get-history** to list all the commands in the command history, or enter **clear-history** to clear the command history. Get-History lists commands by command number, and you can pass this to Invoke-History to run a specific numbered command from your command history. In this example, you run command 35:

```
invoke-history 35
```

TABLE 2-2 Basic Editing Keys

KEY	USAGE
`	Press the backward apostrophe key to insert a line break or as an escape character to make a literal character. You can also break a line at the pipe (|) character.
Alt+Space+E	Displays an editing shortcut menu with Mark, Copy, Paste, Select All, Scroll, and Find options. You can then press K for Mark, Y for Copy, P for Paste, S for Select All, L to scroll through the screen buffer, or F to search for text in the screen buffer. To copy the screen buffer to the Clipboard, press Alt+Space+E+S and then press Alt+Space+E+Y.
Alt+F7	Clears the command history.
Ctrl+C	Press Ctrl+C to break out of the subprompt or terminate execution.
Ctrl+End	Press Ctrl+End to delete all the characters in the line after the cursor.
Ctrl+Left arrow / Ctrl+Right arrow	Press Ctrl+Left arrow or Ctrl+Right arrow to move left or right one word at a time.
Ctrl+S	Press Ctrl+S to pause or resume the display of output.

TABLE 2-2 Basic Editing Keys

KEY	USAGE
Delete / Backspace	Press Delete to delete the character under the cursor, or press the Backspace key to delete the character to the left of the cursor.
Esc	Press the Esc key to clear the current line.
F1	Moves the cursor one character to the right on the command line. At the end of the line, inserts one character from the text of your last command.
F2	Creates a new command line by copying your last command line up to the character you type.
F3	Completes the command line with the content from your last command line, starting from the current cursor position to the end of the line.
F4	Deletes characters from your current command line, starting from the current cursor position up to the character you type.
F5	Scans backward through your command history.
F7	Displays a pop-up window with your command history and allows you to select a command. Use the arrow keys to scroll through the list. Press Enter to select a command to run, or press the Right arrow key to place the text on the command line.
F8	Uses text you've entered to scan backward through your command history for commands that match the text you've typed so far on the command line.
F9	Runs a specific numbered command from your command history. Command numbers are listed when you press F7.
Home / End	Press Home or End to move to the beginning or end of the line.
Insert	Press Insert to switch between insert mode and overwrite mode.
Left / Right arrow keys	Press the Left or Right arrow key to move the cursor left or right on the current line.
Page Up / Page Down	Press the Page Up or Page Down key to access the first or last command in the command history.

TABLE 2-2 Basic Editing Keys

KEY	USAGE
Right-click	If QuickEdit is disabled, displays an editing shortcut menu with Mark, Copy, Paste, Select All, Scroll, and Find options. To copy the screen buffer to the Clipboard, right-click, choose Select, and then press Enter.
Tab / Shift+Tab	Press the Tab key or press Shift+Tab to access the tab expansion function as discussed in "Creating and Using Functions" in Chapter 6, "Mastering Aliases, Functions, and Objects."
Up / Down arrow keys	Press the Up or Down arrow key to scan forward or backward through your command history, as discussed in "Working with the Command History" in Chapter 1.
Windows key+R and then type **powershell**	Runs Windows PowerShell. However, if you've installed multiple versions of PowerShell or are using a 64-bit computer, the first version encountered runs (and this is not necessarily the one you want to use).

REAL WORLD **The way copying and pasting text works in the PowerShell console depends on whether QuickEdit mode is enabled or disabled. With QuickEdit enabled, you copy text by dragging the mouse and pressing Enter, and then paste text by clicking the mouse. When you drag the mouse to select text to copy, be careful not to pause momentarily when you start; otherwise, PowerShell will paste from the Clipboard. With QuickEdit disabled, you copy by right-clicking, selecting Mark, dragging the mouse to select the text, and then pressing Enter. You paste by right-clicking and selecting Paste. You can enable or disable QuickEdit using the Properties dialog box, as described in the "Configuring Windows PowerShell Console Properties" section of Chapter 1.**

How Parsing Works

In addition to the processing modes discussed previously in "Passing Startup Parameters," PowerShell also has parsing modes. Don't confuse processing modes with parsing modes. Processing modes control the way PowerShell processes commands. Generally speaking, processing occurs either interactively or noninteractively. Parsing modes control the way PowerShell parses each value within a command line.

PowerShell breaks down command lines into units of execution and tokens. A unit of execution includes everything from the first character on a line to either a semicolon or the end of a line. A token is a value within a unit of execution. Knowing this, you can:

- Enter multiple commands on a single command line by using semicolons to separate each command.
- Mark the end of a unit of execution by pressing Enter.

The way PowerShell parses values is determined by the first token encountered when parsing a unit of execution. PowerShell parses using one of these modes:

- **Expression mode** PowerShell uses expression mode when the first token encountered in a unit of execution *is not* the name of a cmdlet, keyword, alias, function, or external utility. PowerShell evaluates expressions as either numerical values or strings. Character string values must be contained in quotation marks, and numbers not in quotation marks are treated as numerical values (rather than as a series of characters).
- **Command mode** PowerShell uses command mode when the first token encountered in a unit of execution is the name of a cmdlet, keyword, alias, function, or external utility. PowerShell invokes command tokens. Values after the command token are handled as expandable strings except when they start with a special character that denotes the start of a variable, array, string, or subexpression. These special characters include $, @, ', " and (, and when these characters are encountered, the value is handled using expression mode.

With these rules in mind, you can see that the following are true:

- If you enter 5+5 at the PowerShell prompt, PowerShell interprets 5+5 as an expression to evaluate and displays the result as 10.
- If you enter Write-Host 5+5 at the PowerShell prompt, PowerShell interprets 5+5 as an argument to Write-Host and displays 5+5.
- If you enter Write-Host (5+5) at the PowerShell prompt, PowerShell interprets (5+5) as an expression to evaluate and then pass to Write-Host. As a result, PowerShell displays 10.

Parsing Assigned Values

In PowerShell, variable definitions begin with the dollar sign ($) and are followed by the name of the variable you are defining. To assign a value to a variable, you use the equals sign (=) and then specify the value you want. After you create a variable, you can reference or display the value of the variable by using the variable name.

Following this, if you enter $a = 5+5 at the PowerShell prompt, PowerShell interprets 5+5 as an expression to evaluate and assigns the result to the variable a. As a result, when you write the value of $a to the PowerShell prompt by entering

```
$a
```

or by entering

```
Write-Host $a
```

the output is

```
10
```

On the other hand, let's say you define a variable named $a and assign it a string value, such as:

```
$a = "This is a string."
```

Here, the value assigned to $a is handled as a literal string, and the string is processed in expression mode. You know this because when you write the value of $a to the PowerShell prompt by entering

```
$a
```

or by entering

```
Write-Host $a
```

the output is

```
This is a string.
```

Sometimes, however, you'll want to force PowerShell to interpret a string literal expression using command mode. To see why, consider the following example:

```
$a = "Get-Process"
```

If you write the value of $a to the PowerShell prompt by entering

```
$a
```

the output is

```
Get-Process
```

This occurs because the value assigned to $a is handled as a literal string, and the string is processed in expression mode. However, you might have wanted PowerShell to actually run the Get-Process cmdlet. To do this, you need PowerShell to parse the string and determine that it contains a token that should be processed in command mode. You can accomplish this by using the & operator when you reference the $a variable, as shown in this example:

```
&$a
```

Because PowerShell processes the string in command mode, Get-Process is seen as a command token, the Get-Process cmdlet is invoked, and the output displays the currently running processes. This technique can be used with any cmdlet, keyword, alias, function, or external utility name assigned to a variable in a string. However, if you want to add values in addition to the command name, for example parameters, or use multiple commands or piping, you must enclose your command or commands in curly braces rather than quotation marks. This denotes a script block. Here is an example:

```
$a = {get-eventlog -newest 25 -logname application}
```

The value assigned to $a is handled as a special string, and the string is processed in expression mode. You know this because when you write the value of $a to the PowerShell prompt, the output is:

```
get-eventlog -newest 25 -logname system
```

You can force PowerShell to parse the contents of the script block by using:

```
&$a
```

PowerShell will then parse each token in the script block. The result will be the same as when you enter the command text.

Parsing Exceptions

When you enter part of an expression on the command line but do not complete the expression, PowerShell displays the >> subprompt, indicating that it is waiting for you to complete the expression. For example, if you type **Write-Host (** and press Enter, PowerShell displays the >> subprompt and waits for you to complete the expression. You must then complete the command line by entering any additional required text, such as **5+5)**, and then press Enter. You must then press Enter again (without typing any additional text) to exit the subprompt and return. PowerShell then interprets this input as a completed unit of execution.

If you want to intentionally split command text across multiple lines of input, you can use the backward apostrophe character (`). This technique is handy when you are copying long command lines and pasting them into a PowerShell console so that you can run them. Here's how this works:

1. Enter part of the command text, and then type `. When you press Enter, PowerShell displays the >> subprompt.
2. Enter the next part of the command text. Then either enter ` to indicate that you want to continue the command text on the next line or press Enter to mark the end of the command text.
3. When you finally mark the end of the line by pressing Enter without using the backward apostrophe (and you've closed all expressions), PowerShell parses the command text as appropriate.

An example and partial output follows:

```
get-eventlog -newest 25 `
>> -logname system
>>
```

```
Index Time          EntryType   Source                 InstanceID Message
----- ----          ---------   ------                 ---------- -------
258248 Feb 28 16:12  Information Service Control M...   1073748860 The
description for Event ID '1073748860' in So...
258247 Feb 28 14:27  Information Service Control M...   1073748860 The
description for Event ID '1073748860' in So...
```

If your command text uses the pipe (|) character, you can also break a line and continue it on the next line at the pipe character, as shown in the following example and partial output:

```
get-process |
>> sort-object Id
>>
```

```
Handles  NPM(K)    PM(K)      WS(K) VM(M)   CPU(s)     Id ProcessName
-------  ------    -----      ----- -----   ------     -- -----------
      0       0        0         24     0               0 Idle
    710       0        0      12904    20               4 System
     28       1      360        816     4             516 smss
    666       6     1872       5212    94             592 csrss
```

Output from Parsing

After parsing commands and values, PowerShell returns output. Unlike with the command shell (Cmd.exe), built-in commands that you run in PowerShell return objects in the output. An object is a collection of data points that represent an item. Objects have a specific data type, such as String, Boolean, or Numeric, and have methods and properties. Object methods allow you to perform actions on the item the object represents. Object properties store information about the item the object represents. When you work with PowerShell, you can use an object's methods and properties to take specific actions and manipulate data.

When you combine commands in a pipeline, the commands pass information to each other as objects. When the first command runs, it sends one or more objects along the pipeline to the second command. The second command receives the objects from the first command, processes the objects, and then displays output or passes new or modified objects to the next command in the pipeline. This continues until all commands in the pipeline run and the final command's output is displayed. Because you and I can't read objects, PowerShell translates the objects for output on the screen as text. You can manipulate this output in many ways.

Writing and Formatting Output

Although PowerShell reads and writes objects, the various values associated with objects are converted to text as a final part of the cmdlet execution process. When output is written to the console, this output is said to be written to the *standard output stream*. PowerShell supports other output streams as well. Before I describe these output streams, however, I'll explain how output is formatted by default.

Using Formatting Cmdlets

When you are working with external utilities and programs, those utilities and programs determine how the output is formatted. With PowerShell cmdlets, PowerShell calls designated formatting cmdlets to format the output for you. The formatter determines which properties of the output are displayed and whether they are displayed in a list or table. The formatter makes this determination based on the type of data being displayed. Strings and objects are handled and processed in different ways.

> ***NOTE*** **The formatting cmdlets arrange the data to be displayed but do not actually display it. The output cmdlets, discussed next, are responsible for displaying output.**

You can explicitly specify the output format by using one of the following formatting cmdlets:

- **Format-List** Formats the output as a list of properties. All properties of the objects are formatted by default, with each property displayed on a separate line. Use –Properties to specify which properties to display by name. Enter property names in a comma-separated list. Use wildcard characters such as * to match any value as necessary.

```
Format-List [-DisplayError] [-ShowError] [-Expand String] [-Force]
[-GroupBy Object] [-InputObject Object] [-View String]
[[-Property] PropertyName]
```

- **Format-Table** Formats the output as a table with selected properties of the objects in each column. The object type determines the default layout and the properties that are displayed. Use –AutoSize to automatically adjust the column size and number of columns based on the width of the data. Use –HideTableHeaders to omit column headings. Use –Wrap to display text that exceeds the column width on the next line.

```
Format-Table [-DisplayError] [-ShowError] [-Expand String] [-Force]
[-GroupBy Object] [-InputObject Object] [-View String]
[-AutoSize] [-HideTableHeaders] [-Wrap] [[-Property] PropertyName]
```

- **Format-Wide** Formats the output as a multicolumned table, but only one property of each object is displayed. Use –AutoSize to automatically adjust the column size and number of columns based on the width of the data. Use –Columns to specify the number of columns to display.

```
Format-Wide [-DisplayError] [-ShowError] [-Expand String] [-Force]
[-GroupBy Object] [-InputObject Object] [-View String]
[-AutoSize] [-Column NumColumns] [[-Property] PropertyName]
```

- **Format-Custom** Formats the output using a predefined alternate view. You can determine the alternate view by reviewing the *format.PS1XML files in the Windows PowerShell directory. To create your own views in new .PS1XML files, use the Update-FormatData cmdlet to add them to Windows PowerShell. Use –Depth to specify the number of columns to display.

```
Format-Custom [-DisplayError] [-ShowError] [-Expand String]
[-Force] [-GroupBy Object] [-InputObject Object] [-View String]
[-Depth Num] [[-Property] PropertyName]
```

When working with the previous formatting cmdlets, you might also want to use these cmdlets:

- **Group-Object** Groups objects that contain the same value for specified properties. Objects are grouped in sequence, so if values aren't sorted you won't get the result you want. Use –CaseSensitive to use case-sensitive grouping rather than the default grouping, which is not case sensitive. Use –NoElement to omit the names of members of the group, such as file names if you are grouping files by extension.

```
Group-Object [-CaseSensitive] [-Culture String] [-NoElement]
[-InputObject Object] [[-Property] PropertyName]
```

- **Sort-Object** Sorts objects in ascending order based on the values of properties of the object. Use –Descending to reverse sort. Use –CaseSensitive to use case-sensitive sorting rather than the default sorting, which is not case sensitive. Use –Unique to eliminate duplicates and return only the unique members of a specified collection.

```
Sort-Object [-Culture String] [-CaseSensitive] [-Descending]
[-InputObject Object] [-Unique] [[-Property] PropertyName]
```

To change the format of the output from any cmdlet, use the pipeline operator (|) to send the output of the command to a formatter. For example, the default format for the Get-Service cmdlet is a table that displays the value of the Status, Name, and DisplayName properties, as shown in this command and sample output:

```
get-service
```

```
Status   Name               DisplayName
------   ----               -----------
Stopped  Adobe LM Service   Adobe LM Service
Running  Adobe Version C... Adobe Version Cue CS2
Stopped  Adobe Version C... Adobe Version Cue CS3
Running  AeLookupSvc        Application Experience
Running  AlertService       Intel(R) Alert Service
Stopped  ALG                Application Layer Gateway Service
```

Format-Wide formats the output as a multicolumned table, but only one property of each object is displayed. The following command sends the output of a Get-Service cmdlet to the Format-Wide cmdlet:

```
get-service | format-wide -column 3
```

```
Adobe LM Service          Adobe Version Cue CS2     Adobe Version Cue CS3
AeLookupSvc               AlertService              ALG
AOL ACS                   Appinfo                   Apple Mobile Device
AppMgmt                   AudioEndpointBuilder      Audiosrv
BFE                       BITS                      Bonjour Service
Browser                   CertPropSvc               clr_optimization_v2.0
COMSysApp                 CryptSvc                  CscService
DcomLaunch                DFSR                      Dhcp
```

As a result, the service data is formatted into multiple columns for each service. The output provides the name of each configured service.

Knowing the name of a service, you can then examine services by listing the value of each configured property. For example, the following command gets detailed information on the WinRM service:

```
get-service winrm | format-list
```

```
Name                : WinRM
DisplayName         : Windows Remote Management (WS-Management)
Status              : Stopped
DependentServices   : {}
ServicesDependedOn  : {RPCSS, HTTP}
CanPauseAndContinue : False
CanShutdown         : False
CanStop             : False
ServiceType         : Win32ShareProcess
```

In this format, the data appears in a list instead of a table, and there is additional information about the service that the previous output formatting omitted.

With any of the formatting cmdlets, you can use the –Properties parameter to specify properties to display by name. You can use wildcards such as * to match any value as necessary. For example, to display all the properties of the winlogon process, enter:

```
get-process winlogon | format-list -property *
```

```
__NounName                 : Process
Name                       : winlogon
Handles                    : 147
VM                         : 58609664
```

```
WS                          : 6696960
PM                          : 2437120
NPM                         : 3832
Id                          : 808
PriorityClass               :
HandleCount                 : 147
WorkingSet                  : 6696960
PagedMemorySize             : 2437120
PrivateMemorySize           : 2437120
VirtualMemorySize           : 58609664
```

To see all the properties of an object, send the output of a command to the Get-Member cmdlet. For example, to see all the properties of a service object, type:

```
get-service | get-member -membertype *property
```

```
   TypeName: System.ServiceProcess.ServiceController
Name                MemberType    Definition
----                ----------    ----------
Name                AliasProperty Name = ServiceName
CanPauseAndContinue Property      System.Boolean CanPauseAndContinue
{get;}
CanShutdown         Property      System.Boolean CanShutdown {get;}
CanStop             Property      System.Boolean CanStop {get;}
Container           Property      System.ComponentModel.IContainer
DependentServices   Property      System.ServiceProcess.ServiceController
DisplayName         Property      System.String DisplayName {get;set;}
MachineName         Property      System.String MachineName {get;set;}
ServiceHandle       Property      System.Runtime.InteropServices.SafeHand
ServiceName         Property      System.String ServiceName {get;set;}
ServicesDependedOn  Property      System.ServiceProcess.ServiceController
ServiceType         Property      System.ServiceProcess.ServiceType
Site                Property      System.ComponentModel.ISite Site
Status              Property      System.ServiceProcess.ServiceController
```

Because all these properties are in the object that Get-Service retrieves for each service, you can display any or all of them by using the –Property parameter. For example, the following command uses the Format-Table command to display only the Name, Status, ServiceType, and ServicesDependedOn properties of each service:

```
get-service | format-table Name, Status, ServiceType, ServicesDependedOn
```

```
Name                          Status      ServiceType ServicesDependedOn
                              ------      ----------- ------------------
Adobe LM Service              Stopped  Win32OwnProcess {}
Adobe Version C...            Running  Win32OwnProcess {}
Adobe Version C...            Stopped  Win32OwnProcess {}
```

```
AeLookupSvc                  Running Win32ShareProcess {}
AlertService                 Running ...ractiveProcess {}
ALG                          Stopped   Win32OwnProcess {}
AOL ACS                      Running ...ractiveProcess {}
Appinfo                      Stopped Win32ShareProcess {ProfSvc, RpcSs}
Apple Mobile De...           Running   Win32OwnProcess {Tcpip}
AppMgmt                      Stopped Win32ShareProcess {}
AudioEndpointBu...           Running Win32ShareProcess {PlugPlay}
Audiosrv                     Running Win32ShareProcess {AudioEndpoint...
BFE                          Running Win32ShareProcess {RpcSs}
BITS                         Running Win32ShareProcess {EventSystem, ...
Bonjour Service              Running   Win32OwnProcess {Tcpip}
Browser                      Running Win32ShareProcess {LanmanServer,...
CertPropSvc                  Running Win32ShareProcess {RpcSs}
clr_optimizatio...           Stopped   Win32OwnProcess {}
COMSysApp                    Stopped   Win32OwnProcess {SENS, EventSy...
```

In addition to formatting output for display, you might want to group and sort objects. All the formatting cmdlets include the –GroupBy parameter, which allows you to group output based on a specified property.

Using the –GroupBy parameter produces the same results as sending the output to the Group-Object cmdlet and then sending the output to a formatting cmdlet. However, these techniques probably won't generate the output you are looking for because these approaches generate a new header each time a new value is encountered for the specified property. For example, with the Get-Service cmdlet, you can group services by status, such as Running or Stopped, by using the following command:

```
get-service | format-list -groupby status
```

```
   Status: Stopped
Name                : WinRM
DisplayName         : Windows Remote Management (WS-Management)
Status              : Stopped
DependentServices   : {}
ServicesDependedOn  : {RPCSS, HTTP}
CanPauseAndContinue : False
CanShutdown         : False
CanStop             : False
ServiceType         : Win32ShareProcess

   Status: Running
Name                : Wlansvc
DisplayName         : WLAN AutoConfig
Status              : Running
DependentServices   : {}
ServicesDependedOn  : {Eaphost, RpcSs, Ndisuio, nativewifip}
```

```
CanPauseAndContinue : False
CanShutdown         : True
CanStop             : True
ServiceType         : Win32ShareProcess
```

When you use Group-Object and group by status, you get a different result entirely:

```
get-service | group-object status
```

```
Count Name                      Group
----- ----                      -----
   68 Stopped                   {System.ServiceProcess.ServiceControll
   89 Running                   {System.ServiceProcess.ServiceControll
```

Although both outputs can be useful, neither produces the result you need if you want to see all stopped services and all started services in sequence. The workaround is to sort the objects first and then group them. You sort objects by using the Sort-Object cmdlet. Sort-Object supports sorting on a single property and sorting on multiple properties. You specify the property or properties to sort on with the –Property parameter and separate multiple properties with commas. For example, if you want to sort services by status and name, you can use the following command:

```
get-service | sort-object status, name | format-table –groupby status
```

```
   Status: Stopped
Status   Name               DisplayName
------   ----               -----------
Stopped  Adobe LM Service   Adobe LM Service
Stopped  Adobe Version C... Adobe Version Cue CS3
Stopped  ALG                Application Layer Gateway Service
Stopped  Appinfo            Application Information
Stopped  AppMgmt            Application Management
Stopped  clr_optimizatio... Microsoft .NET Framework NGEN v2.0....
Stopped  COMSysApp          COM+ System Application
Stopped  DFSR               DFS Replication
Stopped  dot3svc            Wired AutoConfig

   Status: Running
Status   Name               DisplayName
------   ----               -----------
Running  Adobe Version C... Adobe Version Cue CS2
Running  AeLookupSvc        Application Experience
Running  AlertService       Intel(R) Alert Service
Running  AOL ACS            AOL Connectivity Service
Running  Apple Mobile De... Apple Mobile Device
```

```
Running  AudioEndpointBu... Windows Audio Endpoint Builder
Running  Audiosrv           Windows Audio
Running  BFE                Base Filtering Engine
Running  BITS               Background Intelligent Transfer Ser...
```

By default, properties are sorted in ascending order. You can sort in descending order with the –Descending parameter. For example, with the Get-Process cmdlet, sorting the working set in descending order can help you identify processes that are using the most resources on the computer. The command to do this is:

```
get-process | sort-object ws -descending
```

```
Handles  NPM(K)    PM(K)      WS(K) VM(M)   CPU(s)     Id ProcessName
-------  ------    -----      ----- -----   ------     -- -----------
    481      22    97236      79804   371     4.31   5276 powershell_ise
   1057      39    84208      78912   279    17.94   3664 iexplore
    743      16    69532      74688   188            1120 svchost
   1377      44    62880      73172   218            1132 svchost
    763      14    89156      66536   347             784 VersionCueCS2
    459      12    58148      64140   201     7.88   5520 powershell
    596      23    39208      63676   412   110.25   5400 WINWORD
    614      27    33284      56512   421     5.22   5776 OUTLOOK
    739       0        0      55780    68               4 System
   1113      12    45712      43988   154            2560 SearchIndexer
    588      19    26768      34592   193     5.33   1704 explorer
    378      13    54952      34056   132            1004 svchost
```

By default, properties are sorted using case-insensitive sorting. You can use case-sensitive sorting by adding the –CaseSensitive parameter. Finally, when you want to view only the unique values of a property, you can add the –Unique parameter. This eliminates multiple occurrences of members of a specified collection with the same value. When you are sorting based on object properties, this means only unique values for specified properties are returned, which may be what you want when you are sorting business names but probably isn't what you want when you are sorting process names. To see why, enter the following command to display a name-sorted list of running processes:

```
get-process | sort-object name
```

```
Handles  NPM(K)    PM(K)      WS(K) VM(M)   CPU(s)     Id ProcessName
-------  ------    -----      ----- -----   ------     -- -----------
     52       3     1292       3856    51     0.00   2204 acrotray
    139       4     2556       7356    75            1380 AlertService
    586       8    22100      19900   132             652 csrss
    658       6     1720       5160    95             592 csrss
```

```
     57       2       884       2860     23              2100 svchost
    306      24     17576      21816     86              1828 svchost
    680      20     20688      24184    119              1524 svchost
    135       5      2764       6036     52              2112 svchost
    105       4      1436       4076     46               640 wininit
    147       4      2380       6540     56               808 winlogon
    598      23     39240      63696    413   111.77     5400 WINWORD
```

In the output, you'll likely see multiple occurrences of some processes, such as powershell or svchost. If you enter the following command:

```
get-process | sort-object name -unique
```

```
Handles  NPM(K)    PM(K)      WS(K) VM(M)   CPU(s)     Id ProcessName
-------  ------    -----      ----- -----   ------     -- -----------
     52       3      1292       3856    51     0.00   2204 acrotray
    139       4      2556       7356    75            1380 AlertService
    586       8     22100      19900   132             652 csrss
     57       2       884       2860    23            2100 svchost
    105       4      1436       4076    46             640 wininit
    147       4      2380       6540    56             808 winlogon
    598      23     39240      63696   413   111.77   5400 WINWORD
```

In the output, you'll see only the first occurrence of each process, which doesn't give you a complete picture of how many processes are running and what resources are being used by those processes.

Writing to Output Streams

Windows PowerShell supports several Write cmdlets for writing to different output streams. The first thing to know about these cmdlets is that they don't actually render the output. They simply pipeline (send) the output to a specified output stream. Although some output streams modify formatting of the output, the job of actually rendering and finalizing output belongs to the Output cmdlets discussed in the next section.

The available output streams include the following:

- Standard output stream
- Verbose message stream
- Warning message stream
- Debugging message stream
- Error stream

Explicitly Writing Output

You can explicitly write output using one of the following output cmdlets:

- **Write-Host** Writes to the standard output stream and allows you to set the background color and foreground color for text. By default, any text you write is terminated with a newline character. Use –NoNewLine to write text without inserting a newline character. Use –Separator to specify a string to output between objects you are displaying. Use –Object to specify the object or string literal to display.

```
Write-Host [-BackgroundColor Color] [-ForegroundColor Color]
[-NoNewline] [-Separator Object] [[-Object] Object]
```

- **Write-Output** Sends a specified object down the pipeline to the next command or for display in the console. Because Write-Output accepts an input object, you can pipeline objects to it, and it in turn will pipeline objects to the next command or the console as appropriate.

```
Write-Output [[-InputObject] Object]
```

The main reason to use Write-Host is to take advantage of the formatting options it provides, which include alternative text and background colors. You use the –BackgroundColor parameter to set the background color for output text and the –ForegroundColor parameter to set the text color. The available colors are:

- Black, DarkBlue, DarkGreen, DarkCyan
- DarkRed, DarkMagenta, DarkYellow, Gray
- DarkGray, Blue, Green, Cyan
- Red, Magenta, Yellow, White

In the following example, you specify that you want black text on a yellow background:

```
write-host -backgroundcolor yellow -foregroundcolor black "This is text!"
```

```
This is text!
```

NOTE **The Write-Host cmdlet writes output to the application that is hosting PowerShell. Typically, this is the PowerShell console (powershell.exe) or the PowerShell application (powershell_ise.exe). Other applications can host the PowerShell engine, and those applications may handle Write-Host output in a different way. This means that you'll want to use Write-Host only when you know which host application will be used and how the host application will handle Write-Host output.**

The Write-Output cmdlet also writes to the standard output stream. Unlike Write-Host, which does not accept input objects, Write-Output accepts objects as input. However, the purpose of Write-Output is simply to send a specified object to the next command in the pipeline. If the command is the last in the pipeline, the object is displayed on the console.

One situation in which to use Write-Output is when you want to be explicit about what you are writing to output. For example:

```
get-process | write-output
```

```
Handles  NPM(K)    PM(K)      WS(K) VM(M)   CPU(s)     Id ProcessName
-------  ------    -----      ----- -----   ------     -- -----------
     52       3     1292       3856    51     0.00   2204 acrotray
    139       4     2556       7356    75            1380 AlertService
```

Here, you pipeline the output of Get-Process to Write-Output to show you are writing output.

When you are using variables, Write-Output is also helpful for being explicit about output you are writing. Consider the following example:

```
$p = get-process; $p
```

```
Handles  NPM(K)    PM(K)      WS(K) VM(M)   CPU(s)     Id ProcessName
-------  ------    -----      ----- -----   ------     -- -----------
     52       3     1292       3856    51     0.00   2204 acrotray
    139       4     2556       7356    75            1380 AlertService
```

Here you create the $p variable, store Process objects in it, and then write those objects to the output. To be explicit about the write operation, you can change the previous line of code to read as follows:

```
$p = get-process; write-output $p
```

```
Handles  NPM(K)    PM(K)      WS(K) VM(M)   CPU(s)     Id ProcessName
-------  ------    -----      ----- -----   ------     -- -----------
     52       3     1292       3856    51     0.00   2204 acrotray
    139       4     2556       7356    75            1380 AlertService
```

Using Other Output Streams

When you want to work with output streams other than the standard output stream, use the following Write cmdlets:

- **Write-Debug** Writes debug messages to the console from a script or command. By default, debug messages are not displayed in the console and do not cause execution to halt. You can display debug messages using the –Debug parameter (which is common to all cmdlets) or the $Debug-Preference variable. The –Debug parameter overrides the value of the $DebugPreference variable for the current command.

```
Write-Debug [-message] DebugMessage
```

- **Write-Error** Writes error messages to the console from a script or command. By default, error messages are displayed in the console but do not cause execution to halt. You can modify the behavior using the –ErrorAction parameter (which is common to all cmdlets) or the $ErrorActionPreference variable. The –ErrorAction parameter overrides the value of the $ErrorAction-Preference variable for the current command.

```
Write-Error -ErrorRecord ErrorRecord [AddtlParams]

Write-Error [-TargetObject Object] [-Message] String
[-ErrorId String] [AddtlParams]

Write-Error -Exception Exception [-Category String] [AddtlParams]

AddtlParams=
[-CategoryTargetName String] [-CategoryTargetType String]
[-CategoryReason String] [-CategoryActivity String]
[-RecommendedAction String]
```

- **Write-Warning** Writes warning messages to the console from a script or command. By default, warning messages are displayed in the console but do not cause execution to halt. You can modify the behavior using the –WarningAction parameter (which is common to all cmdlets) or the $WarningPreference variable. The –WarningAction parameter overrides the value of the $WarningPreference variable for the current command.

```
Write-Warning [-message] WarningMessage
```

- **Write-Verbose** Writes verbose messages to the console from a script or command. By default, verbose messages are not displayed in the console and do not cause execution to halt. You can display verbose messages using the –Verbose parameter (which is common to all cmdlets) or the

$VerbosePreference variable. The –Verbose parameter overrides the value of the $VerbosePreference variable for the current command.

```
Write-Verbose [-message] VerboseMessage
```

Write-Debug, Write-Error, Write-Warning, and Write-Verbose can each be managed using either a common parameter or a preference variable. In every case, the related parameter accepts a value of $true or $false, and the preference variable accepts one of the following values:

- Stop
- Inquire
- Continue
- SilentlyContinue

For example, the $DebugPreference variable determines how PowerShell handles debugging messages. You can specify:

- $DebugPreference=Stop to display debug messages and stop executing.
- $DebugPreference=Inquire to display debug messages that ask whether you want to continue.
- $DebugPreference=Continue to display debug messages and continue with execution.
- $DebugPreference=SilentlyContinue to not display debug messages and continue execution without interruption.

The –Debug parameter overrides the value of the $DebugPreference variable for the current command. You can specify –Debug:$true or –Debug to turn on debugging, or you can specify –Debug:$false to suppress the display of debugging messages when the value of $DebugPreference is not SilentlyContinue.

Rendering and Finalizing the Output

Whether you enter a single cmdlet, send output to other cmdlets using piping, or format output explicitly, the final part of parsing and displaying output is a hidden background call to an output cmdlet. By default, as the last part of the execution process, PowerShell calls the default output cmdlet, which is typically the Out-Host cmdlet.

You can explicitly specify the output cmdlet to use by sending the output to one of the following output cmdlets:

- **Out-File** Sends the output to a file. You must specify the path to the output file to use. If the output file exists, you can use the –Force parameter to overwrite it or the –Append parameter to add the output to the file. You can use Out-File instead of the standard redirection techniques discussed in the next section.

```
Out-File [-InputObject Object] [-NoClobber] [-Width NumChars]
[-Force] [-Append] [-FilePath] String [[-Encoding] String]
```

- **Out-GridView** Sends the output to a grid view window and displays the output in an interactive table. The grid view window supports sorting, grouping, copying, and filtering.

```
Out-GridView [-InputObject Object]
```

- **Out-Host** Sends the output to the command line. Add the –Paging parameter to display one page of output at a time (similar to using the More command in the command shell).

```
Out-Host [-InputObject Object] [-Paging]
```

- **Out-Null** Sends the output to the null port. This deletes the output without displaying it, which is useful for output that you don't need.

```
Out-Null [-InputObject Object]
```

- **Out-Printer** Sends the output to the default printer or to a named printer. Use the –Name parameter to specify the UNC path to the printer to use, such as –Name "\\PrintServer85\LaserP45".

```
Out-Printer [-InputObject Object] [[-Name] String]
```

- **Out-String** Converts the output of all objects to a single string and then sends the result to the console. Use the –Stream parameter to send the strings for each object separately. Use the –Width parameter to specify the number of characters to display in each line of output. Any additional characters are truncated. The default width is 80 characters.

```
Out-String [-InputObject Object] [-Width NumChars] [-Stream]
```

All these cmdlets accept input objects, which means you can pipeline objects to them. The following example writes events from the application log to the C:\logs\app\current.txt file:

```
get-eventlog -newest 10 -logname application | out-file -filepath
c:\logs\app\current.txt
```

All these cmdlets also allow you to use the –InputObject parameter to specify the input object. The following example displays the currently running processes in a grid view window:

```
$p = get-process; out-gridview -inputobject $p
```

Because these commands do not accept positional input, you must always explicitly declare the –InputObject parameter. Figure 2-1 shows the command output in grid view.

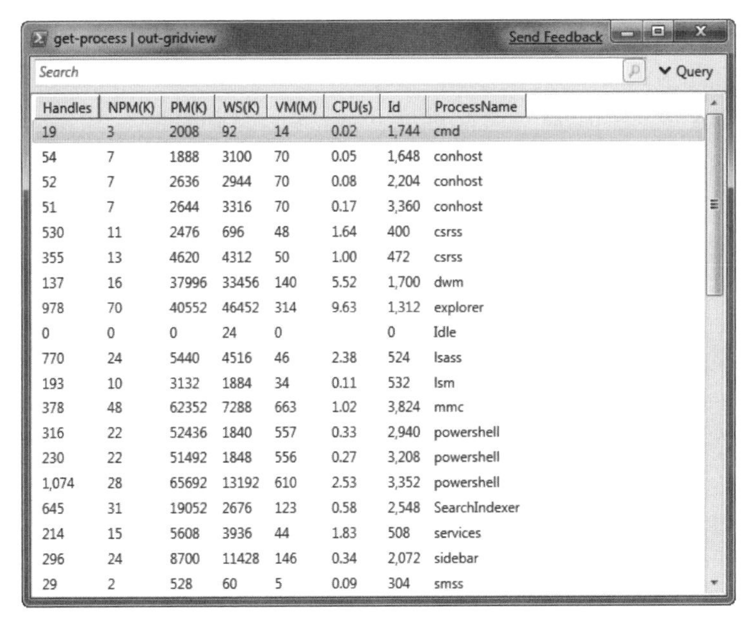

Handles	NPM(K)	PM(K)	WS(K)	VM(M)	CPU(s)	Id	ProcessName
19	3	2008	92	14	0.02	1,744	cmd
54	7	1888	3100	70	0.05	1,648	conhost
52	7	2636	2944	70	0.08	2,204	conhost
51	7	2644	3316	70	0.17	3,360	conhost
530	11	2476	696	48	1.64	400	csrss
355	13	4620	4312	50	1.00	472	csrss
137	16	37996	33456	140	5.52	1,700	dwm
978	70	40552	46452	314	9.63	1,312	explorer
0	0	0	24	0		0	Idle
770	24	5440	4516	46	2.38	524	lsass
193	10	3132	1884	34	0.11	532	lsm
378	48	62352	7288	663	1.02	3,824	mmc
316	22	52436	1840	557	0.33	2,940	powershell
230	22	51492	1848	556	0.27	3,208	powershell
1,074	28	65692	13192	610	2.53	3,352	powershell
645	31	19052	2676	123	0.58	2,548	SearchIndexer
214	15	5608	3936	44	1.83	508	services
296	24	8700	11428	146	0.34	2,072	sidebar
29	2	528	60	5	0.09	304	smss

FIGURE 2-1 Command output is displayed in the grid view.

More on Redirecting Input, Output, and Error

By default, commands take input from the parameters specified when they are called by PowerShell and then send their output, including errors, to the standard console window. Sometimes, however, you'll want to take input from another source or send output to a file or another output device, such as a printer. You might also want to redirect errors to a file rather than have them displayed in the console window. In addition to using the Output cmdlets discussed previously, you can perform these and other redirection tasks by using the techniques introduced in Table 2-3 and discussed in the examples that follow.

TABLE 2-3 Redirection Techniques for Input, Output, and Errors

REDIRECTION TECHNIQUE	DESCRIPTION
command1 | command2	Sends the output of the first command to be the input of the second command.
command > [path]filename	Sends output to the named file, creating the file if necessary or overwriting it if it already exists.
command >> [path]filename	Appends output to the named file if it exists or creates the file and then writes to it.

TABLE 2-3 Redirection Techniques for Input, Output, and Errors

REDIRECTION TECHNIQUE	DESCRIPTION
command 2> [path]filename	Creates the named file and sends any error output to it. If the file exists, it is overwritten.
command 2>> [path]filename	Appends errors to the named file if it exists or creates the file and then writes errors to it.
command 2>&1	Sends error output to the same destination as standard output.

Piping is the primary redirection technique, and you'll find examples of piping throughout this chapter. Another command redirection technique is to send output to a file. You can do this with the Out-File cmdlet. You also can use > to create or overwrite a named file, or >> to create or append data to a named file. For example, if you want to write the current status of running processes to a file, you can use the following command:

```
get-process > processes.txt
```

Unfortunately, if there is a file in the current directory with the same file name, this command overwrites the file and creates a new one. If you want to append this information to an existing file rather than overwrite an existing file, change the command text to read as follows:

```
get-process >> processes.txt
```

By default, errors from commands are written as output on the command line. As discussed previously, you can manage the error stream using Write-Error, the –ErrorAction parameter (which is common to all cmdlets), or the $ErrorActionPreference variable. Another way to redirect standard error is to tell PowerShell that errors should go to the same destination as standard output. To do this, type the 2>&1 redirection symbol as shown in this example:

```
chkdsk /r > diskerrors.txt 2>&1
```

Here, you send standard output and standard error to a file named Diskerrors.txt. If you want to track only errors, you can redirect only the standard error. In this example, standard output is displayed at the command line and standard error is sent to the file Diskerrors.txt:

```
chkdsk /r 2> diskerrors.txt
```

If the error file exists, it is overwritten automatically. To append to an existing file rather than overwrite it, you can use the append technique shown in the following example:

```
chkdsk /r 2>> diskerrors.txt
```

CHAPTER 3

Managing Your Windows PowerShell Environment

When you start Windows PowerShell, the working environment is loaded automatically. Many features of the working environment come from profiles, which are a type of script that run when you start PowerShell. However, the working environment is also determined by imported modules, snap-ins, providers, command paths, file extensions, and file associations. You'll learn about these features of PowerShell in this chapter.

Additionally, when you work remotely, your working environment is different from when you work locally. For this reason, you'll use different techniques when you work remotely than when you are working on your local computer. Not only does PowerShell V2 support remote execution of commands, but PowerShell V2 also supports remote sessions and remote background jobs. You'll learn about these features of PowerShell in Chapter 4, "Using Sessions, Jobs, and Remoting."

Using Profiles

Profiles end with the .ps1 file extension. Generally speaking, profiles are always loaded when you work with Windows PowerShell, but there are specific exceptions. For example, when testing a script, you might want to invoke PowerShell without loading a profile and then run the script. Doing so will help ensure that you've coded the script properly and haven't used any profile-specific settings.

You use profiles to store frequently used elements, including:

- **Aliases** An alias is an alternate name for a command, function, script, file, executable, or other command element. After you create an alias, you can use the alias as a keystroke shortcut or friendly name to invoke the related command element. For example, gsv is an alias for Get-Service. Instead of entering **get-service winrm** to get information about the WinRM service, you could enter **gsv winrm**. To list all available aliases, enter **get-alias** at the PowerShell prompt.

```
Get-Alias [-Exclude Strings] [[-Name Strings] |
[-Definition Strings]] [-Scope String]
```

- **Functions** A function is a named set of PowerShell commands. When you call a function by its name, the set of commands runs just as though you had typed each command at the command line. For example, you could create a function to examine critical processes and services on a computer and generate a report. By adding the function to a profile, you would then be able to run the function at any time by entering the function name at the PowerShell prompt. To list all available functions, enter **get-childitem function:** at the PowerShell prompt.

```
Get-ChildItem [[-Filter] Strings] [-LiteralPath] Strings [AddtlParams]

Get-ChildItem [[-Path] Strings] [[-Filter] Strings] [AddtlParams]

AddtlParams=
[-Exclude Strings] [-Force] [-Include Strings] [-Name] [-Recurse]
```

- **Variables** A variable is a placeholder for a value. In addition to environment variables from the operating system, PowerShell supports automatic, preference, and user-created variables. To reference a variable at the prompt or in scripts, you must precede the variable's name with a dollar sign ($). For example, to reference the home variable, you must enter **$home**. To list all available variables, enter **get-variable** at the PowerShell prompt.

```
Get-Variable [-Scope String] [-Exclude Strings] [-Include Strings]
[-ValueOnly] [[-Name] Strings]
```

NOTE Your scripts and command text can use any of the available variables. Automatic variables are fixed and are used to store state information. Preference variables are changeable and are used to store working values for PowerShell configuration settings. By default, variables you create exist only in the current session and are lost when you exit or close the session. To maintain user-created variables, you must store them in a profile. For detailed information on variables, see "Working with Variables and Values" in Chapter 5, "Navigating Core PowerShell Structures."

TIP You can view the value of an automatic or a preference variable simply by typing its name at the PowerShell prompt. For example, to see the current value of the $home variable, enter **$home** at the PowerShell prompt. Environment variables are accessed in a slightly different way. You must reference $env: and then the name of the variable. For example, to display the value of the %ComputerName% variable, you must enter **$env:computername**.

Creating Profiles

You can create a profile by using a standard text editor. Simply enter the commands that define the aliases, functions, variables, or other elements you want to use, and then save the file with the appropriate file name in the appropriate location on your computer. That's it. This means you can use the following technique to create a profile:

1. In Notepad or any other text editor, enter the command text for the aliases, functions, variables, and any other command elements you want to use.
2. Save the file with the appropriate file name and file extension for a profile, such as Profile.ps1.
3. Copy the profile file to the appropriate location, such as a folder named $pshome.

When you are working with the PowerShell console and the PowerShell application, there are six types of profiles you need to know about. Table 3-1 summarizes these profiles. $home and $pshome are automatic variables. The $home variable stores the current user's home directory. The $pshome variable stores the installation directory for PowerShell.

TABLE 3-1 Common PowerShell Profiles

PROFILE TYPE	DESCRIPTION	LOCATION
Current User, PowerShell Console	A profile specific to the user account for the current user context and applicable only to the PowerShell console.	Directory: $home\[My]Documents\WindowsPowerShell Name: profile.ps1
Current User, PowerShell ISE	A profile specific to the user account for the current user context and applicable only to the PowerShell application.	Directory: $home\[My]Documents\WindowsPowerShell Name: Microsoft.PowerShellISE_profile.ps1
Current User, All Hosts	A profile specific to the current user context and applicable to both the PowerShell console and the PowerShell application.	Directory: $home\[My]Documents Name: profile.ps1

TABLE 3-1 Common PowerShell Profiles

PROFILE TYPE	DESCRIPTION	LOCATION
All Users, PowerShell Console	A profile applicable to all users but specific to the PowerShell console.	Directory: $pshome Name: Microsoft.PowerShell_profile.ps1
All Users, PowerShell ISE	A profile applicable to all users but specific to the PowerShell application.	Directory: $pshome Name: Microsoft.PowerShellISE_profile.ps1
All Users, All Hosts	A profile applicable to all users for both the PowerShell console and the PowerShell application.	Directory: $pshome Name: profile.ps1

When PowerShell starts, PowerShell looks for profiles in the specified locations and runs the profiles in the following order:

1. The All Users, All Hosts profile
2. Either the All Users, PowerShell or All Users, PowerShell ISE profile as appropriate
3. The Current User, All Hosts profile
4. Either the Current User, PowerShell or Current User, PowerShell ISE profile as appropriate

The order of the profiles' execution determines the precedence order for any conflicts. Whenever there is a conflict, the last value written wins. Following this, an alias defined in the Current User, PowerShell profile or the Current User, PowerShell ISE profile has precedence over any conflicting entries in any other profile.

Understanding Execution Order

Whenever you work with Windows PowerShell and PowerShell profiles, don't overlook the importance of execution order and the PATH environment variable. It is important to keep in mind where the commands you are using come from. PowerShell searches for commands in the following order:

1. **Aliases** PowerShell looks for alternate built-in or profile-defined aliases for the associated command name. If an alias is found, the command to which the alias is mapped is run.
2. **Functions** PowerShell looks for built-in or profile-defined functions with the command name. If a function is found, the function is executed.

3. **Cmdlets or language keywords** PowerShell looks for built-in cmdlets or language keywords with the command name. If a cmdlet or language keyword is found, the appropriate action is taken.
4. **Scripts** PowerShell looks for scripts with the .ps1 extension. If a PowerShell script is found, the script is executed.
5. **External commands and files** PowerShell looks for external commands, non-PowerShell scripts, and utilities with the command name. If an external command or utility is found in a directory specified by the PATH environment variable, the appropriate action is taken. If you enter a file name, PowerShell uses file associations to determine whether a helper application is available to open the file.

Because of the execution order, contrary to what you might think, when you type **dir** and then press Enter to get a listing of the current directory, you are not running the dir command that is built into the Windows command shell (cmd.exe). Instead, when you type **dir** at the PowerShell prompt, you are actually running a PowerShell command. This command is called Get-ChildItem. Why does this occur? Although PowerShell does pass commands through to the Windows command shell, it does so only when a PowerShell command or an alias to a PowerShell command is not available. Because dir is a registered alias of Get-ChildItem, you are actually running Get-ChildItem when you enter **dir**.

Working with the Command Path

The Windows operating system uses the command path to locate executables. The types of files that Windows considers to be executables are determined by the file extensions for executables. You can also map file extensions to specific applications by using file associations.

Managing the Command Path

You can view the current command path for executables by displaying the value of the PATH environment variable. To do this, open a PowerShell console, type **$env:path** on a line by itself, and then press Enter. The results should look similar to the following:

```
C:\Windows\System32;C:\Windows;C:\Windows\System32\Wbem;
C:\Windows\System32\WindowsPowerShell\v1.0\
```

> ***NOTE*** **Observe the use of the semicolon (;) to separate individual paths. PowerShell uses the semicolon to determine where one file path ends and another begins.**

The command path is set during logon using system and user environment variables, namely the %PATH% variable. The order in which directories are listed in the path indicates the search order PowerShell uses when it searches for executables. In the previous example, PowerShell searches in this order:

1. C:\Windows\System32
2. C:\Windows
3. C:\Windows\System32\Wbem
4. C:\Windows\System32\PowerShell\v1.0

You can permanently change the command path in the system environment by using the SETX command. For example, if you use specific directories for scripts or applications, you may want to update the path information. You can do this by using the SETX command to add a specific path to the existing path, such as **setx PATH "%PATH%;C:\Scripts"**.

> ***NOTE*** **Observe the use of the quotation marks and the semicolon. The quotation marks are necessary to ensure that the value %PATH%;C:\Scripts is read as the second argument for the SETX command. As mentioned previously, the semicolon is used to specify where one file path ends and another begins. Because the command path is set when you open the PowerShell console, you must exit the console and open a new console to load the new path. If you'd rather not exit the console, you can update the PATH environment variable for the console as discussed in "Using External Commands" in Chapter 1, "Introducing Windows PowerShell."**

In this example, the directory C:\Scripts is appended to the existing command path, and the sample path listed previously would be modified to read as follows:

```
C:\Windows\System32;C:\Windows;C:\Windows\System32\Wbem;C:\Windows\
System32\PowerShell\v1.0;C:\Scripts
```

Don't forget about the search order that Windows uses. Because the paths are searched in order, the C:\Scripts directory will be the last one searched. This can sometimes slow execution of your scripts. To help Windows find your scripts faster, you may want C:\Scripts to be the first directory searched. In this case, you could set the command path by using the following command:

```
setx PATH "C:\Scripts;%PATH%"
```

Be careful when setting the command path. It is easy to overwrite all path information accidentally. For example, if you don't specify the %PATH% environment variable when setting the path, you will delete all other path information. One way to ensure that you can easily re-create the command path is to keep a copy of the command path in a file. To write the current command path to a file, type **$env:path > orig_path.txt**. Keep in mind that if you are using a standard console rather than an administrator console, you won't be able to write to secure system locations. In this case, you can write to a subdirectory to which you have access or your personal profile. To write the command path to the PowerShell console, type **$env:path**. Now you have a listing or a file that contains a listing of the original command path.

Managing File Extensions and File Associations

File extensions are what allow you to execute external commands by typing just their command name at the PowerShell prompt. Two types of file extensions are used:

- **File extensions for executables** Executable files are defined with the %PATHEXT% environment variable. You can view the current settings by typing **$env:pathext** at the command line. The default setting is .COM;.EXE;.BAT;.CMD;.VBS;.VBE;.JS;.JSE;.WSF;.WSH;.MSC;.PSC1. With this setting, the command line knows which files are executables and which files are not, so you don't have to specify the file extension at the command line.
- **File extensions for applications** File extensions for applications are referred to as *file associations*. File associations are what enable you to pass arguments to executables and to open documents, spreadsheets, or other application files by double-clicking file icons. Each known extension on a system has a file association that you can view by typing **cmd /c assoc** followed by the extension, such as **cmd /c assoc .exe**. Each file association in turn specifies the file type for the file extension. This information can be viewed using the FTYPE command followed by the file association, such as **cmd /c ftype exefile**.

NOTE **Observe that you call ASSOC and FTYPE via the command shell. The reason is that they are internal commands for the command shell.**

With executables, the order of file extensions sets the search order used by the command line on a per-directory basis. Thus, if a particular directory in the command path has multiple executables that match the command name provided, a .com file would be executed before a .exe file and so on.

Every known file extension on a system has a corresponding file association and file type—even extensions for executables. In most cases, the file type is the extension text without the period, followed by the keyword *file*, such as cmdfile, exefile, or batfile. The file association specifies that the first parameter passed is the command name and that other parameters should be passed on to the application.

You can look up the file type and file association for known extensions by using the ASSOC and FTYPE commands. To find the association, type **cmd /c assoc** followed by the file extension that includes the period. The output of the ASSOC command is the file type. So if you type **cmd /c ftype *association*** (where *association* is the output of the ASSOC command), you'll see the file type mapping. For example, if you type **cmd /c assoc .exe** to see the file associations for .exe executables, you then type **cmd /c ftype exefile** to see the file type mapping.

You'll see the file association is set to

```
exefile="%1" %*
```

Thus, when you run an .exe file, Windows knows the first value is the command that you want to run and anything else you've provided is a parameter to pass along.

> ***TIP*** File associations and types are maintained in the Windows registry and can be set using the ASSOC and FTYPE commands, respectively. To create the file association, type **cmd /c assoc** followed by the extension setting, such as **cmd /c assoc .pl=perlfile**. To create the file type, set the file type mapping, including how to use parameters supplied with the command name, such as cmd /c ftype **perlfile=C:\Perl\Bin\Perl.exe "%1" %***.

Navigating Windows PowerShell Extensions

Windows PowerShell can be extended in several different ways. Typically, extensions are in the form of PowerShell snap-ins that add PowerShell providers to the working environment. The data that a provider exposes appears in a drive that you can browse. PowerShell V2 introduces module extensions, which must be imported before you use them.

Working with Windows PowerShell Extensions

Cmdlets that you'll use to work with Windows PowerShell snap-ins, providers, and drives include:

- **Add-PSSnapin** Adds one or more registered snap-ins to the current session. After you add a snap-in, you can use the cmdlets and providers that the snap-in supports in the current session.

```
Add-PSSnapin [-PassThru] [-Name] Strings
```

- **Export-Console** Exports the names of PowerShell snap-ins in the current session to a PowerShell console file (.psc1). You can add the snap-ins in the console file to future sessions by using the –PSConsoleFile parameter of PowerShell.exe.

```
Export-Console [-NoClobber] [-Force] [[-Path] String]
```

- **Get-Module** Gets information modules. The first syntax shown in the following example gets information about imported modules that are on the computer and available in the current session. The second syntax shown gets information about available modules that you can use.

```
Get-Module [[-Name] Strings] [-All]
Get-Module [-ListAvailable [-Name] Strings] -Recurse
```

- **Get-PSProvider** Gets information about all or specified providers that are installed on the computer and available in the current session. Providers are listed by name, capability, and drive.

```
Get-PSProvider [[-PSProvider] Strings]
```

- **Get-PSSnapin** Gets objects representing snap-ins that were added to the current session or registered on the system. Snap-ins are listed in detection order. You can register snap-ins using the InstallUtil tool included with Microsoft .NET Framework 2.0.

```
Get-PSSnapin [-Registered] [[-Name] Strings]
```

- **Import-Module** Imports one or more available modules into the current session. After you add a module, you can use the cmdlets and functions that the module supports in the current session.

```
Import-Module [-Name] Strings [AddtlParams]
Import-Module [-Assembly] Assemblies [AddtlParams]
Import-Module [-ModuleInfo] ModGUIDs [AddtlParams]

AddtlParams=
[-Prefix String] [-Function Strings] [-Cmdlet Strings] [-Variable
Strings] [-Alias Strings] [-Force] [-PassThru] [-AsCustomObject]
[-Version Version] [-ArgumentList Objects]
```

- **New-Module** Creates a module based on script blocks, functions, and cmdlets that you specify. Also available are New-ModuleManifest and Test-ModuleManifest.

```
New-Module [-ScriptBlock] ScriptBlock [-Function Strings] [-Cmdlet
Strings] [-ReturnResult] [-AsCustomObject] [-ArgumentList Objects]

New-Module [-Name] String [-ScriptBlock] ScriptBlock [-Function
Strings] [-Cmdlet Strings] [-ReturnResult] [-AsCustomObject]
[-ArgumentList Objects]
```

- **Remove-Module** Removes a module that you added to the current session.

```
Remove-Module [-Name] Strings [-Force]
Remove-Module [-ModuleInfo] ModGUIDs [-Force]
```

- **Remove-PSSnapin** Removes a PowerShell snap-in that you added to the current session. You cannot remove snap-ins that are installed with Windows PowerShell.

```
Remove-PSSnapin [-PassThru] [-Name] Strings
```

Using Snap-ins

Windows PowerShell snap-ins are .NET programs that are compiled into DLL files. Snap-ins can include providers, cmdlets, and functions. PowerShell providers are .NET programs that provide access to specialized data stores so that you can access the data stores from the command line. Before using a provider, you must install the related snap-in and add it to your Windows PowerShell session.

PowerShell comes with a set of core snap-ins, but you can extend PowerShell by adding snap-ins that contain additional providers and cmdlets. For example, when you are working with servers and applications such as Microsoft Exchange Server 2007 SP1 or later or SQL Server 2008, those servers and applications include extended command environments for PowerShell. Exchange Server 2007 SP1 or later includes Exchange Management Shell, which is simply a PowerShell console loaded with the snap-ins and environment used by Exchange Server. SQL Server 2008 or later includes SQL Server PowerShell, which is a PowerShell console loaded with the snap-ins and environment used by SQL Server.

Similarly, when you add a snap-in, the providers and cmdlets that it contains are immediately available for use in the current session. To ensure that a snap-in is available in all future sessions, add the snap-in via your profile. You can also use the Export-Console cmdlet to save the names of snap-ins to a console file. If you start a console by using the console file, the named snap-ins are available.

To save the snap-ins from a session in a console file (.psc1), use the Export-Console cmdlet. For example, to save the snap-ins in the current session configuration to the MyConsole.psc1 file in the current directory, enter the following command:

```
export-console MyConsole
```

The following command starts PowerShell with the MyConsole.psc1 console file:

```
powershell.exe -psconsolefile MyConsole.psc1
```

You can list the available snap-ins by entering **get-pssnapin**. To find the snap-in for each Windows PowerShell provider, enter the following command:

```
get-psprovider | format-list name, pssnapin
```

To list the cmdlets in a snap-in, enter

```
get-command -module SnapinName
```

where *SnapinName* is the name of the snap-in you want to examine. The built-in snap-ins are summarized in Table 3-2.

TABLE 3-2 Built-In PowerShell Snap-Ins

NAME	DESCRIPTION
Microsoft.PowerShell.Core	Contains providers and cmdlets used to manage the basic features of Windows PowerShell. Includes the FileSystem, Registry, Alias, Environment, Function, and Variable providers and basic cmdlets like Get-Help, Get-Command, and Get-History.
Microsoft.PowerShell.Diagnostics	Contains the cmdlets used to read Windows event log and configuration data, for example, Get-WinEvent.
Microsoft.PowerShell.Host	Contains cmdlets used by the Windows PowerShell host, such as Start-Transcript and Stop-Transcript.
Microsoft.PowerShell.Management	Contains cmdlets used to manage Windows components, including Get-Service and Get-ChildItem.
Microsoft.PowerShell.Security	Contains cmdlets to manage Windows PowerShell security, such as Get-Acl, Get-AuthenticodeSignature, and ConvertTo-SecureString
Microsoft.PowerShell.Utility	Contains the cmdlets used to manipulate objects and data, such as Get-Member, Write-Host, and Format-List.
Microsoft.PowerShell.WSMan.Management	Contains the cmdlets used to manage WSMan operations, such as Get-WSManInstance and Set-WSManInstance.

The built-in snap-ins are registered in the operating system and added to the default session whenever you start Windows PowerShell. To use snap-ins that you create or obtain from other sources, you must register them and add them to your console session. To find registered snap-ins (other than the built-in snap-ins) on your system or to verify that an additional snap-in is registered, enter the following command:

```
get-pssnapin -registered
```

You can add a registered snap-in to the current session by using the Add-PSSnapin cmdlet. For example, to add the SQL Server snap-in to the session, type **add-pssnapin sqlserver**. Once you add the snap-in, its providers and cmdlets are available in the console session. If you add the necessary Add-PSSnapin commands to a relevant profile, you can be sure that modules you want to use are always loaded.

To remove a Windows PowerShell snap-in from the current session, use the Remove-PSSnapin cmdlet. For example, to remove the SQL Server snap-in from the current session, type **remove-pssnapin sqlserver**. This removes the snap-in from the session. The snap-in is still loaded, but the providers and cmdlets that it supports are no longer available.

When you are performing administrative tasks or creating scripts for later use, you'll often want to ensure that a particular PowerShell snap-in is available before you try to use its functions or cmdlets. The easiest way to do this is to attempt to perform the action or run a script only if the snap-in is available. Consider the following example:

```
if (get-pssnapin -name ADRMS.PS.Admin -erroraction silentlycontinue)
 {

   Code to execute if the snap-in is available.

} else {

   Code to execute if the snap-in is not available.

}
```

Here, when the ADRMS.PS.Admin snap-in is available, the statement in parentheses evaluates to True, and any code in the related script block is executed. When the ADRMS.PS.Admin snap-in is not available, the statement in parentheses evaluates to False, and any code in the Else statement is executed. Note also that I set the –ErrorAction parameter to SilentlyContinue so that error messages aren't written to the output if the snap-in is not found.

TIP **The same technique can be used with providers and modules.**

Using Providers

The data that a provider exposes appears in a drive that you can browse much like you browse a hard drive, allowing you to view, search though, and manage related data. To list all providers that are available, type **Get-PSProvider**. Table 3-3 lists the built-in providers. Note the drives associated with each provider.

TABLE 3-3 Built-In PowerShell Providers

PROVIDER	DATA ACCESSED	DRIVE
Alias	Windows PowerShell aliases	{Alias}
Certificate	X509 certificates for digital signatures	{Cert}
Environment	Windows environment variables	{Env}
FileSystem	File system drives, directories, and files	{C, D, E, ...}
Function	Windows PowerShell functions	{Function}
Registry	Windows registry	{HKLM, HKCU}
Variable	Windows PowerShell variables	{Variable}
WSMan	WS-Management	{WSMan}

PowerShell includes a set of cmdlets that are specifically designed to manage the items in the data stores that are exposed by providers. You use these cmdlets in the same ways to manage all the different types of data that the providers make available to you. Table 3-4 provides an overview of these cmdlets.

TABLE 3-4 Cmdlets for Working with Data Stores

CMDLET	DESCRIPTION

Get-PSDrive	Gets all or specified PowerShell drives in the current console. This includes logical drives on the computer, drives mapped to network shares, and drives exposed by Windows PowerShell providers. Get-PSDrive does not get Windows mapped drives that are added or created after you open PowerShell. However, you can map drives using New-PSDrive, and those drives will be available.
	`Get-PSDrive [-PSProvider Strings]`
	`[-Scope String]`
	`[[-LiteralName] | [-Name]] Strings`

TABLE 3-4 Cmdlets for Working with Data Stores

CMDLET	DESCRIPTION

New-PSDrive	Creates a PowerShell drive that is mapped to a location in a data store, which can include a shared network folder, a local directory, or a registry key. The drive is available only in the current PowerShell console.
	`New-PSDrive [-Credential Credential]`
	`[-Description String]`
	`[-Scope String] [-Name] String`
	`[-PSProvider] String [-Root] String`

Remove-PSDrive	Removes a PowerShell drive that you added to the current console session. You cannot delete Windows drives or mapped network drives created by using other methods.
	`Remove-PSDrive [-Force]`
	`[-PSProvider Strings] [-Scope String]`
	`[[-LiteralName] | [-Name]] Strings`

Get-ChildItem	Gets the items and child items in one or more specified locations.
	`Get-ChildItem [[-Path] Strings]`
	`[[-Filter] String] [AddtlParams]`
	
	`Get-ChildItem [[-Filter] String]`
	`[-LiteralPath] Strings [AddtlParams]`
	
	`AddtlParams=`
	`[-Exclude Strings] [-Force]`
	`[-Include Strings] [-Name]`
	`[-Recurse]`

Get-Item	Gets the item at the specified location.
	`Get-Item [[-LiteralPath] |`
	`[-Path]] Strings [AddtlParams]`
	
	`AddtlParams=`
	`[-Credential Credential]`
	`[-Exclude Strings] [-Filter String]`
	`[-Force] [-Include Strings]`

New-Item	Creates a new item.
	`New-Item [-Credential Credential]`
	`[-Force] [-ItemType String]`
	`[-Path Strings] [-Value Object]`
	`-Name String`

TABLE 3-4 Cmdlets for Working with Data Stores

CMDLET	DESCRIPTION

Set-Item	Changes the value of an item to the value specified in the command.
	`Set-Item [-Value] Object] [[-LiteralPath] | [-Path] Strings [AddtlParams]`
	
	`AddtlParams= [-Credential Credential] [-Exclude Strings] [-Filter String] [-Force] [-Include Strings] [-PassThru]`

Remove-Item	Deletes the specified item.
	`Remove-Item [[-LiteralPath] | [-Path]] Strings [AddtlParams]`
	
	`AddtlParams= [-Credential Credential] [-Exclude Strings] [-Filter String] [-Force] [-Include Strings] [-Recurse]`

Move-Item	Moves an item from one location to another.
	`Move-Item [[-Destination] String] [[-LiteralPath] | [-Path]] Strings [AddtlParams]`
	
	`AddtlParams= [-Credential Credential] [-Exclude Strings] [-Filter String] [-Force] [-Include Strings] [-PassThru]`

Rename-Item	Renames an item in a Windows PowerShell provider namespace. `Rename-Item [-Credential Credential] [-Force] [-PassThru] [-Path] String [-NewName] String`

TABLE 3-4 Cmdlets for Working with Data Stores

CMDLET	DESCRIPTION

Copy-Item	Copies an item from one location to another within a namespace.
	
	`Copy-Item [[-Destination] String] [[-LiteralPath] | [-Path]] Strings [AddtlParams]`
	
	`AddtlParams=`
	`[-Container] [-Credential Credential] [-Exclude Strings] [-Filter String] [-Force] [-Include Strings] [-PassThru] [-Recurse]`

Clear-Item	Deletes the contents of an item but does not delete the item.
	
	`Clear-Item [[-LiteralPath] | [-Path]] Strings [AddtlParams]`
	
	`AddtlParams=`
	`[-Credential Credential] [-Exclude Strings] [-Filter String] [-Force] [-Include Strings]`

Invoke-Item	Performs the default action on the specified item.
	
	`Invoke-Item [[-LiteralPath] | [-Path]] Strings [AddtlParams]`
	
	`AddtlParams=`
	`[-Credential Credential] [-Exclude Strings] [-Filter String] [-Include Strings]`

Clear-ItemProperty	Deletes the value of a property but does not delete the property.
	
	`Clear-ItemProperty [[-LiteralPath] | [-Path]] Strings [-Name] String [AddtlParams]`
	
	`AddtlParams=`
	`[-Credential Credential] [-Exclude Strings] [-Filter String] [-Force] [-Include Strings] [-PassThru]`

TABLE 3-4 Cmdlets for Working with Data Stores

CMDLET	DESCRIPTION

Copy-ItemProperty	Copies a property and value from a specified location to another location.
	`Copy-ItemProperty [[-LiteralPath] | [-Path]] Strings [-Destination] String [-Name] String [AddtlParams]`
	
	`AddtlParams= [-Credential Credential] [-Exclude Strings] [-Filter String] [-Force] [-Include Strings] [-PassThru]`

Get-ItemProperty	Gets the properties of a specified item.
	`Get-ItemProperty [-Name] String [[-LiteralPath] | [-Path]] Strings [AddtlParams]`
	
	`AddtlParams= [-Credential Credential] [-Exclude Strings] [-Filter String] [-Include Strings]`

Move-ItemProperty	Moves a property from one location to another.
	`Move-ItemProperty [[-LiteralPath] | [-Path]] Strings [-Destination] String [-Name] String [AddtlParams]`
	
	`AddtlParams= [-Credential Credential] [-Exclude Strings] [-Filter String] [-Force] [-Include Strings] [-PassThru]`

New-ItemProperty	Creates a property for an item and sets its value.
	`New-ItemProperty [-PropertyType String] [-Value Object] [[-LiteralPath] | [-Path]] Strings [-Name] String [AddtlParams]`
	
	`AddtlParams= [-Credential Credential] [-Exclude Strings] [-Filter String] [-Force] [-Include Strings]`

TABLE 3-4 Cmdlets for Working with Data Stores

CMDLET	DESCRIPTION

Remove-ItemProperty	Deletes the specified property and its value from an item.
	
	`Remove-ItemProperty [[-LiteralPath] | [-Path]] Strings [-Name] String [AddtlParams]`
	
	`AddtlParams= [-Credential Credential] [-Exclude Strings] [-Filter String] [-Force] [-Include Strings]`

Rename-Item-Property	Renames the specified property of an item.
	
	`Rename-ItemProperty [[-LiteralPath] | [-Path]] Strings [-Name] String [-NewName] String [AddtlParams]`
	
	`AddtlParams= [-Credential Credential] [-Exclude Strings] [-Filter String] [-Force] [-Include Strings] [-PassThru]`

Set-ItemProperty	Creates or changes the value of the specified property of an item.
	
	`Set-ItemProperty -InputObject Object [-LiteralPath] Strings [AddtlParams]`
	
	`Set-ItemProperty [-Name] String [-Value] Object [AddtlParams]`
	
	`Set-ItemProperty [-Path] Strings [AddtlParams]`
	
	`AddtlParams= [-Credential Credential] [-Exclude Strings] [-Filter String] [-Force] [-Include Strings] [-PassThru]`

In addition to the built-in cmdlets, providers can:

- Have custom cmdlets that are designed especially for related data.
- Add "dynamic parameters" to the built-in cmdlets that are available only when using the cmdlet with the provider data.

The drive associated with each provider is listed in the default display of Get-PSProvider, but you can get more information about a provider drive by using the Get-PSDrive cmdlet. For example, the Registry provider makes the HKEY_LOCAL_MACHINE root key available as the HKLM drive. To find all the properties of the HKLM drive, enter the following command:

```
get-psdrive hklm | format-list *
```

You can view and navigate through the data in a provider drive just as you would data in a file system drive. To view the contents of a provider drive, use the Get-Item or Get-ChildItem cmdlet. Type the drive name followed by a colon (:). For example, to view the contents of the Function drive, type:

```
get-childitem function:
```

You can view and manage the data in any drive from another drive by including the drive name in the path. For example, to view the HKLM\Software registry key in the HKLM drive from another drive, type:

```
get-childitem hklm:\software
```

To get into the drive, use the Set-Location cmdlet. Remember the colon when specifying the drive path. For example, to change your location to the root of the Function drive, type **set-location function:**. Then, to view the contents of the Function drive, type **get-childitem**.

You can navigate through a provider drive just as you would a hard drive. If the data is arranged in a hierarchy of items within items, use a backslash (\) to indicate a child item. The basic syntax is:

```
Set-location drive:\location\child-location\...
```

For example, to change your location to the HKLM\Software registry key, use a Set-Location command, such as:

```
set-location hklm:\software
```

You can also use relative references to locations. A dot (.) represents the current location. For example, if you are in the C:\Windows\System32 directory and you want to list its files and folders, you can use the following command:

```
get-childitem .\
```

When PowerShell loads providers, the providers can add dynamic parameters that are available only when the cmdlet is used with that provider. For example, the Certificate drive adds the –CodeSigningCert parameter to the Get-Item and Get-ChildItem cmdlets. You can use this parameter only when you use Get-Item or Get-ChildItem in the Cert drive.

Although you cannot uninstall a provider, you can remove the Windows PowerShell snap-in for the provider from the current session. To remove a provider, use the Remove-PSSnapin cmdlet. This cmdlet does not unload or uninstall providers. It removes all the contents of the snap-in, including providers and cmdlets. This makes the related providers and cmdlets unavailable in the current session.

Another way to remove features made available based on snap-ins is to use the Remove-PSDrive cmdlet to remove a particular drive from the current session. When you remove a drive, the data on the drive is not affected, but the drive is no longer available in the current session.

Often, you'll want to ensure that a particular PowerShell provider or PSDrive is available before you try to work with its features. The easiest way to do this is to attempt to perform the action or run a script only if the provider or PSDrive is available. Consider the following example:

```
iIf (get-psprovider -psprovider wsman -erroraction silentlycontinue)
 {

  Code to execute if the provider is available.

} else {

  Code to execute if the provider is not available.

}
```

Here, when the WSMan provider is available, the statement in parentheses evaluates to True, and any code in the related script block is executed. When the WSMan provider is not available, the statement in parentheses evaluates to False, and any code in the Else statement is executed. Note also that I set the –ErrorAction parameter to SilentlyContinue so that error messages aren't written to the output if the provider is not found.

Navigating and Using Provider Drives

When you are using provider drives, you might also want to manage content, configure locations, and work with paths. Table 3-5 provides an overview of cmdlets that you can use to perform related tasks.

TABLE 3-5 Cmdlets for Working with Provider Drives

CMDLET	DESCRIPTION
Add-Content	Adds content to the specified item, such as adding words to a file. Add-Content [[-LiteralPath] | [-Path]] *Strings* [-Value] *Objects* [AddtlParams] AddtlParams= [-Credential *Credential*] [-Encoding {<Unknown> | String | <Unicode> | <Byte> | <BigEndianUnicode> | <UTF8> | <UTF7> | <Ascii>}] [-Exclude *Strings*] [-Filter *String*] [-Force] [-Include *Strings*] [-PassThru]
Clear-Content	Deletes the contents of an item, such as deleting the text from a file, but does not delete the item. Clear-Content [[-LiteralPath] | [-Path]] *Strings* [AddtlParams] AddtlParams= [-Credential *Credential*] [-Exclude *Strings*] [-Filter *String*] [-Force] [-Include *Strings*]
Get-Content	Gets the content of the item at the specified location. Get-Content [[-LiteralPath] | [-Path]] *Strings* [AddtlParams] AddtlParams= [-Credential *Credential*] [-Delimiter *String*] [-Encoding {<Unknown> | *String* | <Unicode> | <Byte> | <BigEndianUnicode> | <UTF8> | <UTF7> | <Ascii>}] [-Exclude *Strings*] [-Filter *String*] [-Force] [-Include *Strings*] [-ReadCount <Int64>] [-TotalCount <Int64>] [-Wait]

TABLE 3-5 Cmdlets for Working with Provider Drives

CMDLET	DESCRIPTION

Set-Content	Writes content to an item or replaces the content in an item with new content.
	
	`Set-Content [[-LiteralPath] | [-Path]] Strings [-Value] Objects [AddtlParams]`
	
	`AddtlParams= [-Credential Credential] [-Encoding {<Unknown> | String | <Unicode> | <Byte> | <BigEndianUnicode> | <UTF8> | <UTF7> | <Ascii>}] [-Exclude Strings] [-Filter String] [-Force] [-Include Strings] [-PassThru]`

Get-Location	Gets information about the current working location.
	
	`Get-Location [-PSDrive Strings] [-PSProvider Strings]`
	
	`Get-Location [-Stack] [-StackName Strings]`

Set-Location	Sets the current working location to a specified location.
	
	`Set-Location [-PassThru] [[-Path] String]`
	
	`Set-Location [-PassThru] [-StackName String]`

Push-Location	Adds the current location to the top of a list of locations. ("stack"). `Push-Location [-PassThru] [-StackName String] [[-LiteralPath] | [-Path] String]`
Pop-Location	Changes the current location to the location most recently pushed onto the stack. `Pop-Location [-PassThru] [-StackName String]`
Join-Path	Combines a path and a child-path into a single path. The provider supplies the path delimiters. `Join-Path [-Credential Credential] [-Resolve] [-Path] Strings [-ChildPath] String`

TABLE 3-5 Cmdlets for Working with Provider Drives

CMDLET	DESCRIPTION
Convert-Path	Converts a path from a Windows PowerShell path to a Windows PowerShell provider path. Convert-Path [[-LiteralPath] | [-Path]] *Strings*
Split-Path	Returns the specified part of a path. Split-Path [-LiteralPath *Strings*] [-Path] *Strings* [AddtlParams] AddtlParams= [-Credential *Credential*] [-IsAbsolute | -Leaf | -Parent | -NoQualifier | -Qualifier] [-Resolve]
Test-Path	Determines whether all elements of a path exist. Test-Path [[-LiteralPath] | [-Path]] *Strings* [AddtlParams] AddtlParams= [-Credential *Credential*] [-Exclude *Strings*] [-Filter *String*] [-Include *Strings*] [-IsValid] [-PathType {<Any> | <Container> | <Leaf>}]
Resolve-Path	Resolves the wildcard characters in a path and displays the path's contents. Resolve-Path [-Credential *Credential*] [[-LiteralPath] | [-Path] *Strings*]

The currently selected provider drive determines what data store you are working with. The default data store is the file system, and the default path within the file system is the profile directory for the currently logged-on user (in most cases).

The current working location is the location that Windows PowerShell uses if you do not supply an explicit path to the item or location that is affected by the command. Typically, this is a directory on a hard drive accessed through the FileSystem provider. All commands are processed from this working location unless another path is explicitly provided.

PowerShell keeps track of the current working location for each drive even when the drive is not the current drive. This allows you to access items from the current working location by referring only to the drive of another location. For example, suppose that your current working location is C:\Scripts\PowerShell. Then you use the following command to change your current working location to the HKLM drive:

```
Set-Location HKLM:
```

Although your current location is now the HKLM drive, you can still access items in the C:\Scripts\PowerShell directory by using the C drive, as shown in the following example:

```
Get-ChildItem C:
```

PowerShell retains the information that your current working location for the C drive is the C:\Scripts\PowerShell directory, so it retrieves items from that directory. The results would be the same if you ran the following command:

```
Get-ChildItem C:\Scripts\PowerShell
```

You can use the Get-Location command to determine the current working location, and you can use the Set-Location command to set the current working location. For example, the following command sets the current working location to the Scripts directory of the C drive:

```
Set-Location c:\scripts
```

After you set the current working location, you can still access items from other drives simply by including the drive name (followed by a colon) in the command, as shown in the following example:

```
Get-ChildItem HKLM:\software
```

This example retrieves a list of items in the Software container of the HKEY Local Machine hive in the registry.

You use special characters to represent the current working location and its parent location. To represent the current working location, you use a single period. To represent the parent of the current working location, you use two periods. For example, the following command specifies the PowerShell subdirectory in the current working location:

```
Get-ChildItem .\PowerShell
```

If the current working location is C:\Scripts, this command returns a list of all the items in C:\Scripts\PowerShell. However, if you use two periods, the parent directory of the current working location is used, as shown in the following example:

```
Get-ChildItem ..\Data
```

In this case, PowerShell treats the two periods as the C drive, so the command retrieves all the items in the C:\Data directory.

A path beginning with a slash identifies a path from the root of the current drive. For example, if your current working location is C:\Scripts\PowerShell, the root of your drive is C. Therefore, the following command lists all items in the C:\Data directory:

```
Get-ChildItem \Data
```

If you do not specify a path beginning with a drive name, slash, or period when supplying the name of a container or item, the container or item is assumed to be located in the current working location. For example, if your current working location is C:\Scripts, the following command returns all the items in the C:\Scripts\PowerShell directory:

```
Get-ChildItem PowerShell
```

If you specify a file name rather than a directory name, PowerShell returns details about that file, as long as the file is available in the current working location. If the file is not available, PowerShell returns an error.

Using Modules

Windows PowerShell modules are self-contained, reusable units of execution that can include:

- Script functions that are made available through .PSM1 files.
- .NET assemblies that are compiled into .DLL files and made available through .PSD1 files.
- PowerShell snap-ins that are made available in .DLL files.
- Custom views and data types that are described in .PS1XML files.

Most modules have related snap-ins, .NET assemblies, custom views, and custom data types. In the .PSD1 files that define the included assemblies, you'll find an associative array that defines the properties of the module, as is shown in the example that follows and summarized in Table 3-6.

```
@{
GUID="{8FA5064B-8479-4c5c-86EA-0D311FE48875}"
Author="Microsoft Corporation"
CompanyName="Microsoft Corporation"
Copyright="© Microsoft Corporation. All rights reserved."
ModuleVersion="1.0.0.0"
Description="Powershell File Transfer Module"
PowerShellVersion="2.0"
CLRVersion="2.0"
NestedModules="Microsoft.BackgroundIntelligentTransfer.Management"
FormatsToProcess="FileTransfer.Format.ps1xml"
RequiredAssemblies=Join-Path $psScriptRoot "Microsoft.
BackgroundIntelligentTransfer.Management.Interop.dll"
}
```

TABLE 3-6 Common Properties of Modules

PROPERTY	DESCRIPTION
Author, CompanyName, Copyright	Provides information about the creator of the module and copyright.
CLRVersion	The common language runtime (CLR) version of the .NET Framework required by the module.
Description	The descriptive name of the module.
FormatsToProcess	A list of FORMAT.PS1XML files loaded by the module to create custom views for the module's cmdlets.
GUID	The globally unique identifier (GUID) of the module.
ModuleVersion	The version and revision number of the module.
NestedModules	A list of snap-ins, .NET assemblies, or both loaded by the module.
PowerShellVersion	The version of PowerShell required by the module. The version specified or a later version must be installed for the module to work.
RequiredAssemblies	A list of .NET assemblies that must be loaded for the module to work.
TypesToProcess	A list of TYPES.PS1XML files loaded by the module to create custom data types for the module's cmdlets.

Although PowerShell includes a New-Module cmdlet for creating modules, you'll more commonly use Get-Module, Import-Module, and Remove-Module to work with existing modules. You can list the available modules by entering **get-module -listavailable**. However, this will give you the full definition of each module in list format. A better way to find available modules is to look for them by name, path, and description:

```
get-module -listavailable | format-list name, path, description
```

You can also look for them only by name and description:

```
get-module -listavailable | format-table name, description
```

If you want to determine the availability of a specific module, enter the following command:

```
get-module -listavailable [-name] ModuleNames
```

where *ModuleNames* is a comma-separated list of modules to check. You can enter module names with or without the associated file extension and use wildcards such as. Note that when you use the –ListAvailable parameter, the –Name parameter is position sensitive, allowing you to specify modules using either

```
get-module -listavailable -name ModuleNames
```

or

```
get-module -listavailable ModuleNames
```

Here is an example:

```
get-module -listavailable -name networkloadbalancingclusters
```

The core set of modules available in PowerShell depends on the versions of Windows you are running as well as the components that are installed. Table 3-7 lists some of the most common modules as well as the operating systems they are commonly found on by default.

TABLE 3-7 Common PowerShell Modules

NAME	DESCRIPTION	OPERATING SYSTEM
ActiveDirectory	Provides a comprehensive set of cmdlets for working with Active Directory Domain Services (AD DS).	Windows Server 2008 Release 2 or later
ADRMS	Provides cmdlets for updating, installing, and uninstalling Active Directory Rights Management Services (AD RMS), including Update-ADRMS, Uninstall-ADRMS, Install-ADRMS.	Windows Server 2008 Release 2 or later
BestPractices	Provides cmdlets for testing best-practices scenarios, including Get-BPAModel, Invoke-BPAModel, Get-BPAResult, Set-BPAResult.	Windows Server 2008 Release 2 or later
FailoverClusters	Provides a comprehensive set of cmdlets for working with Microsoft Cluster Service.	Windows Server 2008 Release 2 or later

TABLE 3-7 Common PowerShell Modules

NAME	DESCRIPTION	OPERATING SYSTEM
FileTransfer	Provides cmdlets for working with Background Intelligent Transfer Service, including Add-FileTransfer, Clear-FileTransfer, Complete-FileTransfer, Get-FileTransfer, New-FileTransfer, Resume-FileTransfer Set-FileTransfer, Suspend-FileTransfer.	Windows Vista or later
GroupPolicy	Provides a comprehensive set of cmdlets for working with Group Policy objects (GPOs).	Windows Server 2008 Release 2 or later
NetworkLoadBalancing-Clusters	Provides a comprehensive set of cmdlets for working with Network Load Balancing (NLB) clusters.	Windows Server 2008 Release 2 or later
PSDiagnostics	Provides functions for performing event traces, including Disable-PSTrace, Disable-PSWSMan-CombinedTrace, Disable-WSManTrace, Enable-PSTrace, Enable-PSWSManCombinedTrace, Enable-WSManTrace, Get-LogProperties, Set-LogProperties, Start-Trace, Stop-Trace.	Windows Vista or later
RemoteDesktopServices	Provides cmdlets for working with Terminal Services running in Remote Desktop mode.	Windows Server 2008 Release 2 or later
ServerManager	Provides cmdlets for listing, adding, and removing Windows features, including Get-WindowsFeature, Add-WindowsFeature, Remove-WindowsFeature.	Windows Server 2008 Release 2 or later
TroubleshootingPack	Provides cmdlets for getting information about and running troubleshooting packs you've installed, including Get-TroubleshootingPack and Invoke-TroubleshootingPack.	Windows 7 or later
WebAdministration	Provides a comprehensive set of cmdlets for working with Internet Information Services (IIS).	Windows Server 2008 Release 2 or later

The components for available modules are registered in the operating system as necessary but are not added to your PowerShell sessions by default (in most instances). Therefore, to use functions, cmdlets, or other features of a module, you must first import the module. Modules such as PSDiagnostics that define functions and include .PSM1 files require an execution policy to be set so that signed scripts can run.

You can import an available module into the current session by using the Import-Module cmdlet. For example, to import the WebAdminstration module, type **import-module webadministration**. After you import a module, its providers, cmdlets, and other features are available in the console session.

If you add the necessary Import-Module commands to a relevant profile, you can be sure that modules you want to use are always loaded. To find imported modules or to verify that an additional module is imported, enter the following command:

```
get-module | format-table name, description
```

Any module listed in the output is imported and available.

To remove a module from the current session, use the Remove-Module cmdlet. For example, to remove the WebAdministration module from the current session, type **remove-module webadministration**. The module is still loaded, but the providers, cmdlets, and other features that it supports are no longer available.

You will often want to be sure that a particular module has been imported before you try to use its features. In the following example, when the WebAdministration module is available, the statement in parentheses evaluates to True, and any code in the related script block is executed:

```
if (get-module -name WebAdministration -erroraction silentlycontinue)
 {

  Code to execute if the provider is available.

} else {

  Code to execute if the provider is not available.

}
```

As shown previously, you could add an Else clause to define alternative actions. As before, I set the –ErrorAction parameter to SilentlyContinue so that error messages aren't written to the output if the module has not been imported.

REAL WORLD Although checking for modules is helpful, you'll want to consider the case of SQL Server separately. The SQL Server PowerShell console loads an extended environment designed specifically for working with SQL Server. You can re-create this environment using a lengthy script that loads all the right extensions. However, it usually is much easier to simply start the SQL Server PowerShell console when you want to manage SQL Server using PowerShell.

Generally, if the $sqlpsreg variable exists and has child items, the user is running the SQL Server PowerShell console. Knowing this, you can determine whether this console is available as shown in the following example:

```
if (Get-ChildItem $sqlpsreg -ErrorAction "SilentlyContinue")
{ throw "SQL Server PowerShell is not installed."
} else {
  $item = Get-ItemProperty $sqlpsreg
  $sqlpsPath = [System.IO.Path]::GetDirectoryName($item.Path)
}
```

Here, you determine whether the $sqlpsreg variable exists and has child items. If the variable doesn't exist, PowerShell throws an error. If the variable exists, you get the properties of the related object and then use the Path property to specify the path to use with SQL Server.

PowerShell Extensions for Exchange Server and SQL Server

PowerShell extensions are available for Exchange Server 2007 with Service Pack 1 or later and SQL Server 2008. The extensions for Exchange Server 2007 SP1 or later are implemented in a custom console called the Exchange Management Console. The extensions for SQL Server 2008 are implemented in a minishell called the SQL Server PowerShell console.

Custom consoles and minishells and modules are two different approaches for creating prepackaged PowerShell environments. A custom console automatically loads the snap-ins required to preconfigure the working environment, but it does not save the entire state. A minishell gives you a complete working environment with the entire state preserved, including any snap-ins, providers, and type extensions loaded previously. However, minishells are closed environments with their own security settings. Because of this, you cannot extend minishell environments and must manage security settings separately from the security settings in PowerShell.

TIP The PowerShell Software Developer's Kit allows developers to create minishells using make-shell. In PowerShell Version 1.0, custom consoles and minishells were the only way to create prepackaged PowerShell environments. As discussed previously, PowerShell V2 adds modules that extend the working environment using .NET assemblies and script functions. Because modules are more versatile and can be easily added to any console, Microsoft likely will use modules to implement PowerShell functionality for Exchange Server and SQL Server (and may have already done so by the time you read this).

When you are working on a server running Exchange Server 2007 SP1 or later, you can access Exchange cmdlets at the PowerShell prompt or in a script by loading the custom console for Exchange. To load the console for Exchange Server 2007, enter the following command:

```
powershell.exe -noexit -psconsolefile "C:\Program Files\Microsoft\Exchange
Server\Bin\exshell.psc1"
```

With scheduled tasks, don't forget that you must load the custom console for Exchange as shown in the following example:

```
at 05:30 /interactive powershell.exe -noexit -psconsolefile "C:\Program
Files\Microsoft\Exchange Server\Bin\exshell.psc1" -command "Move-Mailbox
-identity <wrstanek@cpandl.com> -TargetDatabase EngMailboxDB"
```

> ***NOTE*** **Both of the preceding examples are a single line. If you installed Exchange Server 2007 in a different location, modify the path so that it points to the Exchange Server bin directory on your server.**

When you are working on a server running SQL Server 2008, you can access SQL Server cmdlets at the PowerShell prompt or in a script by running the SQL Server PowerShell console or by loading the required startup environment from a script. The executable for the SQL Server PowerShell console is SQLPS.exe, and the required path to use the executable is configured automatically when you install SQL Server. To start the SQL Server PowerShell console, enter **sqlps** at a command prompt or PowerShell prompt. To load the SQL Server environment from a script, the script must add the SQL Server snap-ins, set certain global variables, and then load the SQL Server management objects. A sample initialization script follows.

```
#
# Add the SQL Server PowerShell Provider, if available
$ErrorActionPreference = "Stop"
$sqlpsreg="HKLM:\SOFTWARE\Microsoft\PowerShell\1\ShellIds\Microsoft.
SqlServer.Management.PowerShell.sqlps"

if (Get-ChildItem $sqlpsreg -ErrorAction "SilentlyContinue")
{ throw "SQL Server PowerShell Provider is not installed."
} else {
  $item = Get-ItemProperty $sqlpsreg
  $sqlpsPath = [System.IO.Path]::GetDirectoryName($item.Path)
}

#
# Set global variables
Set-Variable SqlServerMaximumChildItems 0 -scope Global
Set-Variable SqlServerConnectionTimeout 30 -scope Global
Set-Variable SqlServerIncludeSystemObjects $false -scope Global
Set-Variable SqlServerMaximumTabCompletion 1000 -scope Global
```

```
#
# Load the SQL Server Management Objects
$assemblylist = "Microsoft.SqlServer.Smo",
"Microsoft.SqlServer.Dmf ",
"Microsoft.SqlServer.SqlWmiManagement ",
"Microsoft.SqlServer.ConnectionInfo ",
"Microsoft.SqlServer.SmoExtended ",
"Microsoft.SqlServer.Management.RegisteredServers ",
"Microsoft.SqlServer.Management.Sdk.Sfc ",
"Microsoft.SqlServer.SqlEnum ",
"Microsoft.SqlServer.RegSvrEnum ",
"Microsoft.SqlServer.WmiEnum ",
"Microsoft.SqlServer.ServiceBrokerEnum ",
"Microsoft.SqlServer.ConnectionInfoExtended ",
"Microsoft.SqlServer.Management.Collector ",
"Microsoft.SqlServer.Management.CollectorEnum"

foreach ($asm in $assemblylist)
{ $asm = [Reflection.Assembly]::LoadWithPartialName($asm) }

#
# Load SQL Server snapins, type data and format data
Push-Location
cd $sqlpsPath
Add-PSSnapin SqlServerCmdletSnapin100
Add-PSSnapin SqlServerProviderSnapin100
Update-TypeData -PrependPath SQLProvider.Types.ps1xml
update-FormatData -prependpath SQLProvider.Format.ps1xml
Pop-Location
```

Before you use this type of initialization script, you should check current documentation for the version and service pack of SQL Server you are running to determine the required components. On the Microsoft Support site (at support.microsoft.com), you'll likely find examples of initialization scripts for your version and service pack.

CHAPTER 4

Using Sessions, Jobs, and Remoting

Windows PowerShell V2 supports remote execution of commands, remote sessions, and remote background jobs. When you work remotely, you type commands in Windows PowerShell on your computer but execute the commands on one or more remote computers. To work remotely, your computer and the remote computer must both have PowerShell V2, the Microsoft .NET Framework 2.0, and Windows Remote Management 2.0.

Enabling Remote Commands

The Windows PowerShell remoting features are supported by the WS-Management protocol and the Windows Remote Management (WinRM) service that implements WS-Management in Windows. Computers running Windows 7 and later include WinRM 2.0 or later. On computers running earlier versions of Windows, you need to install WinRM 2.0 or later as appropriate and if supported. Currently, remoting is supported only on Windows Vista with Service Pack 1 or later, Windows 7, Windows Server 2008, and Windows Server 2008 Release 2.

You can verify the availability of WinRM and configure a PowerShell for remoting by following these steps:

1. Start Windows PowerShell as an administrator by right-clicking the Windows PowerShell shortcut and selecting Run As Administrator.

2. The WinRM service is configured for manual startup by default. You must change the startup type to Automatic and start the service on each computer you want to work with. At the PowerShell prompt, you can verify that the WinRM service is running using the following command:

```
get-service winrm
```

As shown in the following example, the value of the Status property in the output should be Running:

```
Status   Name               DisplayName
------   ----               -----------
Running  WinRM              Windows Remote Management
```

3. To configure Windows PowerShell for remoting, type the following command:

```
Enable-PSRemoting -force
```

In many cases, you will be able to work with remote computers in other domains. However, if the remote computer is not in a trusted domain, the remote computer might not be able to authenticate your credentials. To enable authentication, you need to add the remote computer to the list of trusted hosts for the local computer in WinRM. To do so, type

```
winrm s winrm/config/client '@{TrustedHosts="RemoteComputer"}'
```

where *RemoteComputer* is the name of the remote computer, such as

```
winrm s winrm/config/client '@{TrustedHosts="CorpServer56"}'
```

When you are working with computers in workgroups or homegroups, you must either use HTTPS as the transport or add the remote machine to the TrustedHosts configuration settings. If you cannot connect to a remote host, verify that the service on the remote host is running and is accepting requests by running the following command on the remote host:

```
winrm quickconfig
```

This command analyzes and configures the WinRM service. If the WinRM service is set up correctly, you'll see output similar to the following:

```
WinRM already is set up to receive requests on this machine.
WinRM already is set up for remote management on this machine.
```

If the WinRM service is not set up correctly, you see output similar to the following and need to respond affirmatively to several prompts. When this process completes, WinRM should be set up correctly.

```
WinRM is not set up to receive requests on this machine.
The following changes must be made:

Set the WinRM service type to delayed auto start.
Start the WinRM service.
Configure LocalAccountTokenFilterPolicy to grant administrative rights
remotely to local users.

Make these changes [y/n]? y

WinRM has been updated to receive requests.
WinRM service type changed successfully.
WinRM service started.
Configured LocalAccountTokenFilterPolicy to grant administrative rights
remotely to local users.
WinRM is not set up to allow remote access to this machine for
management. The following changes must be made:

Create a WinRM listener on HTTP://* to accept WS-Man requests to any IP
on this machine.

Make these changes [y/n]? y

WinRM has been updated for remote management.
Created a WinRM listener on HTTP://* to accept WS-Man requests to any IP
on this machine.
```

To use PowerShell remoting features, you must start Windows PowerShell as an administrator by right-clicking the Windows PowerShell shortcut and selecting Run As Administrator. When starting PowerShell from another program, such as the command prompt (cmd.exe), you must start that program as an administrator.

Executing Remote Commands

You can use Windows PowerShell remoting to run cmdlets and external programs on remote computers. For example, you can run any built-in cmdlets and external programs accessible in the PATH environment variable ($env:path). However, because PowerShell runs as a network service or local service, you cannot use PowerShell to open the user interface for any program on a remote computer. If you try to start a program with a graphical interface, the program process starts but the command cannot complete, and the PowerShell prompt does not return until the program is finished or you press Ctrl+C.

Understanding Remote Execution

When you submit a remote command, the command is transmitted across the network to the Windows PowerShell client on the designated remote computers, and it runs in the Windows PowerShell client on the remote computer. The command results are sent back to the local computer and appear in the Windows PowerShell session on the local computer. Note that all of the local input to a remote command is collected before being sent to the remote computer, but the output is returned to the local computer as it is generated.

Whenever you use PowerShell remoting features, keep the following in mind:

- You must start Windows PowerShell as an administrator by right-clicking the Windows PowerShell shortcut and selecting Run As Administrator. When starting PowerShell from another program, such as the command prompt (cmd.exe), you must start that program as an administrator.
- The current user must be a member of the Administrators group on the remote computer or be able to provide the credentials of an administrator. When you connect to a remote computer, PowerShell uses your user name and password credentials to log on to the remote computer. The credentials are encrypted.
- When you work remotely, you use multiple instances of Windows PowerShell: a local instance and one or more remote instances. Generally, in the local instance, the policies and profiles on the local computer are in effect. On a remote instance, the policies and profiles on the remote computer are in effect. This means cmdlets, aliases, functions, preferences, and other elements in the local profile are not necessarily available to remote commands. To ensure you can use cmdlets, aliases, functions, preferences, and other elements in the local profile with remote commands, you must copy the local profiles to each remote computer.
- Although you can execute commands on remote computers, any files, directories, and additional resources that are needed to execute a command must exist on the remote computer. Additionally, your user account must have permission to connect to the remote computer, permission to run Windows PowerShell, and permission to access files, directories, and other resources on the remote computer.

Commands for Remoting

You can work with remote computers using the following remoting cmdlets:

- **Invoke-Command** Runs commands on a local computer or one or more remote computers, and returns all output from the commands, including errors. To run a single command on a remote computer, use the –ComputerName parameter. To run a series of related commands that share data, create a PowerShell session (PSSession) on a remote computer, and then use the –Session parameter of Invoke-Command to run the command in the PSSession.

```
Invoke-Command [-ArgumentList Args] [-InputObject Object]
[-ScriptBlock] ScriptBlock

Invoke-Command [[-ComputerName] Computers] [-ApplicationName
String] [-FilePath] String [-Port PortNum] [-UseSSL]
[BasicParams] [SecurityParams]

Invoke-Command [[-Session] Sessions] [-FilePath] String
[BasicParams]

Invoke-Command [[-ConnectionURI] URIs] [-AllowRedirection]
[-FilePath] String [BasicParams] [SecurityParams]

Invoke-Command [[-Session] Sessions] [-ScriptBlock] ScriptBlock
[BasicParams]

Invoke-Command [[-ConnectionURI] URIs] [-AllowRedirection]
[-ScriptBlock] ScriptBlock [BasicParams] [SecurityParams]

BasicParams=
[-ArgumentList Args] [-AsJob] [-HideComputerName] [-InputObject
Object] [-JobName String] [-ThrottleLimit Limit]

SecurityParams=
[-Authentication {<Default> | <Basic> | <Negotiate> |
<NegotiateWithImplicitCredential> | <Credssp>}]
[-CertificateThumbprint String] [-ConfigurationName String]
[-Credential Credential] [-NoCompression]
[-SessionOption SessionOption]
```

- **New-PSSession** Creates a PowerShell session (PSSession) on a local or remote computer. When you create a PSSession, Windows PowerShell establishes a persistent connection to the remote computer, and you can use the PSSession to interact directly with the computer.

```
New-PSSession [[-Session] Sessions] [BasicParams]

New-PSSession [[-ComputerName] Computers] [-ApplicationName
Application] [-UseSSL] [BasicParams] [SecurityParams]

New-PSSession [-ConnectionURI] URIs [-AllowRedirection]
[BasicParams] [SecurityParams]

BasicParams=
[-Noprofile] [-ThrottleLimit Limit] [-TimeOut Num]

SecurityParams=
[-Authentication {<Default> | <Basic> | <Negotiate> |
```

```
<NegotiateWithImplicitCredential> | <Credssp>}]
[-CertificateThumbprint String] [-ConfigurationName String]
[-Credential Credential] [-Name Names] [-NoCompression]
[-Port PortNum] [-SessionOption SessionOption]
```

- **Get-PSSession** Gets the PowerShell sessions (PSSessions) that were created in the current session. Without parameters, this cmdlet returns all of the PSSessions created in the current session. You can use the parameters of Get-PSSession to get the sessions that are connected to particular computers or identify sessions by their names, IDs, or instance IDs. For computers, type the NetBIOS name, IP address, or fully qualified domain name. To specify the local computer, type the computer name, **localhost**, or a dot (**.**). For IDs, type an integer value that uniquely identifies the PSSession in the current session. PSSessions can be assigned friendly names with the –Name parameter. You can specify the friendly names using wildcards. To find the names and IDs of PSSessions, use Get-PSSession without parameters. An instance ID is a GUID that uniquely identifies a PSSession, even when you have multiple sessions running in PowerShell. The instance ID is stored in the RemoteRunspaceID property of the RemoteRunspaceInfo object that represents a PSSession. To find the InstanceID of the PSSessions in the current session, type **get-pssession | Format-Table Name, ComputerName, RemoteRunspaceId**.

```
Get-PSSession [[-ComputerName] Computers] | [-InstanceID GUIDs] |
[-Name Names] | [-ID IDs]
```

- **Enter-PSSession** Starts an interactive session with a single remote computer. During the session, you can run commands just as if you were typing directly on the remote computer. You can have only one interactive session at a time. Typically, you use the –ComputerName parameter to specify the name of the remote computer. However, you can also use a session that you created previously by using New-PSSession for the interactive session.

```
Enter-PSSession [[-Session] Session] | [-InstanceID GUID] |
[-Name Name] | [-ID ID]

Enter-PSSession [-ComputerName] Computer [-ApplicationName String]
[-UseSSL] [SecurityParams]

Enter-PSSession [[-ConnectionURI] URI][-AllowRedirection]
[SecurityParams]

SecurityParams=
[-Authentication {<Default> | <Basic> | <Negotiate> |
<NegotiateWithImplicitCredential> | <Credssp>}]
[-CertificateThumbprint String] [-ConfigurationName String]
[-Credential Credential] [-NoCompression]
[-SessionOption SessionOption]
```

- **Exit-PSSession** Ends an interactive session and disconnects from the remote computer. You can also type **exit** to end an interactive session. The effect is the same as using Exit-PSSession.

```
Exit-PSSession
```

- **Import-PSSession** Imports cmdlets, aliases, functions, and other command types from an open session on a local or remote computer into the current session. You can import any command that Get-Command can find in the other session. To import commands, first use New-PSSession to connect to the session from which you will import. Then use Import-PSSession to import commands. By default, Import-PSSession imports all commands except for commands that exist in the current session. To overwrite a command, specify the command in the –CommandName parameter. PowerShell adds the imported commands to a temporary module that exists only in your session, and it returns an object that represents the module. Although you can use imported commands just as you would use any command in the session, the imported part of the command actually runs in the session from which it was imported. Because imported commands might take longer to run than local commands, Import-PSSession adds an –AsJob parameter to every imported command. This parameter allows you to run the command as a PowerShell background job.

```
Import-PSSession [-CommandType {Alias | Function | Filter | Cmdlet
| ExternalScript | Application | Script | All}]
[-FormatTypeName Types] [-PSSnapin Snapins] [[-CommandName]
Commands] [[-ArgumentList] Args] [-Session] Session
```

- **Export-PSSession** Gets cmdlets, functions, aliases, and other command types from an open session on a local or remote computer, and saves them in a Windows PowerShell script module file (.psm1). When you want to use the commands from the script module, use the Add-Module cmdlet to add the commands to the local session so that they can be used. To export commands, first use New-PSSession to connect to the session that has the commands that you want to export. Then use Export-PSSession to export the commands. By default, Export-PSSession exports all commands except for commands that already exist in the session. However, you can use the –PSSnapin, –CommandName, and –CommandType parameters to specify the commands to export.

```
Export-PSSession [-CommandType {Alias | Function | Filter | Cmdlet
| ExternalScript | Application | Script | All}]
[-Encoding String] [-Force] [-NoClobber] [-PSSnapin Snapins]
[[-CommandName] Commands] [[-ArgumentList] Args] [-Session] Session
```

Invoking Remote Commands

One way to run commands on remote computers is to use the Invoke-Command cmdlet. With this cmdlet, you can do the following:

- Use the –ComputerName parameter to specify the remote computers to work with by DNS name, NetBIOS name, or IP address.
- When working with multiple remote computers, separate each computer name or IP address with a comma.
- Enclose your command or commands to execute in curly braces, which denotes a script block, and use the –ScriptBlock parameter to specify the command or commands to run.

After completing any of the preceding actions, you can type the following command as a single line to run a Get-Process command remotely:

```
invoke-command -computername Server43, Server27, Server82
-scriptblock {get-process}
```

> ***TIP*** **By default, Invoke-Command runs under your user name and credentials. Use the –Credential parameter to specify alternate credentials, such as UserName or Domain\UserName. You will be prompted for a password.**

> ***REAL WORLD*** **When you connect to a remote computer that is running Windows Vista, Windows Server 2003, or later versions of either one, the default starting location is the home directory of the current user, which is stored in the %HomePath% environment variable ($env:homepath) and the Windows PowerShell $home variable. When you connect to a remote computer that is running Windows XP, the default starting location is the home directory of the default user, which is stored in the %HomePath% environment variable ($env:homepath) for the default user.**

When you use Invoke-Command, the cmdlet returns an object that includes the name of the computer that generated the data. The remote computer name is stored in the PSComputerName property. Typically, the PSComputerName property is displayed by default. You can use the –HideComputerName parameter to hide the PSComputerName property.

If the PSComputerName property isn't displayed and you want to see the source computer name, use the Format-Table cmdlet to add the PSComputerName property to the output as shown in the following example:

```
$procs = invoke-command -script {get-process |
sort-object -property Name} -computername Server56, Server42, Server27

&$procs | format-table Name, Handles, WS, CPU, PSComputerName -auto
```

```
Name                 Handles       WS        CPU PSComputerName
----                 -------       --        --- --------------
acrotray                  52  3948544          0 Server56
AlertService             139  7532544            Server56
csrss                    594 20463616            Server56
csrss                    655  5283840            Server56
CtHelper                  96  6705152   0.078125 Server56
  . . .
acrotray                  43  3948234          0 Server42
AlertService             136  7532244            Server42
csrss                    528 20463755            Server42
csrss                    644  5283567            Server42
CtHelper                  95  6705576   0.067885 Server42

acrotray                  55  3967544          0 Server27
AlertService             141  7566662            Server27
csrss                    590 20434342            Server27
csrss                    654  5242340            Server27
CtHelper                  92  6705231   0.055522 Server27
```

PowerShell includes a per-command throttling feature that lets you limit the number of concurrent remote connections that are established for a command. The default is 32 or 50 concurrent connections, depending on the cmdlet. You can use the –ThrottleLimit parameter to set a custom throttle limit for a command. Keep in mind the throttling feature is applied to each command, not to the entire session or to the computer. If you are running a command concurrently in several sessions, the number of concurrent connections is the sum of the concurrent connections in all sessions.

Keep in mind that although PowerShell can manage hundreds of concurrent remote connections, the number of remote commands that you can send might be limited by the resources of your computer and its ability to establish and maintain multiple network connections. To add more protection for remoting, you can use the –UseSSL parameter of Invoke-Command. This option uses an HTTPS channel over Port 443 instead of HTTP over Port 80. As with commands that are run locally, you can pause or terminate a remote command by pressing Ctrl+S or Ctrl+C.

REAL WORLD **PowerShell remoting is available even when the local computer is not in a domain. For testing and development, you can use the remoting features to connect to and create sessions on the same computer. PowerShell remoting works the same as when you are connecting to a remote computer.**

To run remote commands on a computer in a workgroup, you might need to change Windows settings on the computer. In Windows XP with Service Pack 2 (SP2), use Local Security Settings (secpol.msc) to change the setting of the Network Access: Sharing And Security Model For Local Accounts policy in Security Settings\Local Policies\Security Options to Classic. In Windows Vista, create the LocalAccountTokenFilterPolicy registry entry in HKLM\SOFTWARE\Microsoft\Windows\CurrentVersion\Policies\System and set its value to 1.

In Windows 2003, no changes are needed in most cases because the default setting of the Network Access: Sharing And Security Model For Local Accounts policy is Classic. However, you should check the setting to be sure it wasn't changed.

Establishing Remote Sessions

Windows PowerShell 2.0 supports both local and remote sessions. A *session* is a runspace that establishes a common working environment for commands. Commands in a session can share data. Although you'll learn more about sessions in upcoming chapters, let's look now at how remote sessions are used.

Invoking Sessions

You can establish a local or remote session to create a persistent connection using the New-PSSession cmdlet. Unless you use the –ComputerName parameter and use it to specify the name of one or more remote computers, PowerShell assumes you are creating a session for the local computer. With New-PSSession, you must use the –Session parameter with Invoke-Command to run the command in the named session. For example, you can establish a session by typing the following command:

```
$s = new-PSSession -computername Server24
```

Here, *$s* is a variable that sets the name of the session. Because you've used the –ComputerName parameter, PowerShell knows you are creating a remote session rather than a local session. PowerShell creates a persistent connection with the specified computer. You can then use Invoke-Command with the –Session parameter to run the command in the named session as shown in this example:

```
invoke-command -session $s -scriptblock {get-process}
```

Here, you use Invoke-Command to run Get-Process in the $s session. Because this session is connected to a remote computer, the command runs on the remote computer.

You can just as easily establish a session with multiple computers. Simply establish the session and name all the computers. Generally, you might also need to specify your credentials using the –Credential parameter.

The –Credential parameter specifies a user account that has permission to perform an action. The default user account is the current user. You can provide alternative credentials in one of two ways. You can:

- Pass in a Credential object to provide the information required for authentication. A Credential object has UserName and Password properties. Although the user name is stored as a regular string, the password is stored as a secure, encrypted string. You can learn more about Credential objects in "Specifying Authentication Credentials" in Chapter 9, "Inventorying and Evaluating Windows Systems."

- Specify the user account that has permission to perform the action. Enter the user name as Domain\UserName or simply as UserName. If you specify a user name, PowerShell displays a prompt for the user's password. When prompted, enter the password and then click OK.

To see how the –Credential parameter can be used, consider the following example:

```
$t = new-PSSession -computername Server24, Server45, Server36
-Credential Cpandl\WilliamS
```

Here, you establish a session with Server24, Server45, and Server36 and specify your domain and user name. As a result, when you use Invoke-Command to run commands in the $t session, the commands run on each remote computer with those credentials. Note that although this is a single session, each runspace on each computer is separate.

Extending this idea, you can also just as easily get the list of remote computers from a text file. In this example, servers.txt contains a comma-separated list of computers:

```
$ses = get-content c:\test\servers.txt | new-PSSession
-Credential Cpandl\WilliamS
```

Here, the contents of this file are piped to New-PSSession. As a result, the $ses session is established with all computers listed in the file.

Sometimes, you'll want to execute an application or external utility on a remote computer as shown in the following example:

```
$comp = get-content c:\computers.txt
$s = new-pssession -computername $comp
invoke-command -session $s { powercfg.exe -energy }
```

Here, C:\Computers.txt is the path to the file containing the list of remote computers to check. On each computer, you run PowerCfg with the –Energy parameter. This generates an Energy-Report.html file in the default directory for the user account used to access the computer. The energy report provides details on power configuration settings and issues that are causing power management not to work correctly. If you'd rather not have to retrieve the report from each computer, you can write the report to a share and base the report name on the computer name, as shown in the following example:

```
$comp = get-content c:\computers.txt
$s = new-pssession -computername $comp
invoke-command -session $s { powercfg.exe -energy -output
"\\fileserver72\reports\$env:computername.html"}
```

Here, you write the report to the \\fileserver72\reports share and name the file using the value of the ComputerName environment variable. Note that when you work with PowerShell and are referencing applications and external utilities, you must specify the .exe file extension with the program name.

When you are running commands on many remote computers, you might not want to wait for the commands to return before performing other tasks. To avoid having to wait, use Invoke-Command with the –AsJob parameter to create a background job in each of the runspaces:

```
invoke-command -session $s -scriptblock {get-process moddr |
stop-process -force } -AsJob
```

Here, you use Invoke-Command to get and stop a named process via the $s session. Because the command is run as a background job, the prompt returns immediately without waiting for the command to run on each computer.

Although being able to establish a session on many computers is handy, sometimes you might want to work interactively with a single remote computer. To do this, you can use the Enter-PSSession cmdlet to start an interactive session with a remote computer. At the Windows Powershell prompt, type **Enter-PSSession *ComputerName***, where *ComputerName* is the name of the remote computer. The command prompt changes to show that you are connected to the remote computer, as shown in the following example:

```
[Server49]: PS C:\Users\wrstanek.cpandl\Documents>
```

Now the commands that you type run on the remote computer just as if you had typed them directly on the remote computer. For enhanced security through encryption of transmissions, the Enter-PSSession cmdlet also supports the –Credential and –UseSSL parameters. You can end the interactive session using the command Exit-PSSession or by typing **exit**.

Understanding Remote Execution and Object Serialization

When you are working with remote computers, you need to keep in mind the following:

- How commands are executed
- How objects are serialized

Whether you use Invoke-Command or Enter-PSSession with remote computers, Windows PowerShell establishes a temporary connection, uses the connection to run the current command, and then closes the connection each time you run a command. This is an efficient method for running a single command or several unrelated commands, even on a large number of remote computers.

The New-PSSession cmdlet provides an alternative by establishing a session with a persistent connection. With New-PSSession, Windows PowerShell establishes a persistent connection and uses the connection to run any commands you enter. Because you can run multiple commands in a single, persistent runspace, the commands can share data, including the values of variables, the definitions of aliases, and the contents of functions. New-PSSession also supports the –UseSSL parameter.

When you use Windows PowerShell locally, you work with live .NET Framework objects, and these objects are associated with actual programs or components. When you invoke the methods or change the properties of live objects, the changes affect the actual program or component. And, when the properties of a program or component change, the properties of the object that represent them change too.

Because live objects cannot be transmitted over the network, Windows PowerShell serializes the objects sent in remote commands. This means it converts each object into a series of Constraint Language in XML (CLiXML) data elements for transmission. When Windows PowerShell receives a serialized file, it converts the XML into a deserialized object type. Although the deserialized object is an accurate record of the properties of the program or component at execution time, it is no longer directly associated with the originating component, and the methods are removed because they are no longer effective. Also, the serialized objects returned by the Invoke-Command cmdlet have additional properties that help you determine the origin of the command.

> ***NOTE*** **You can use Export-Clixml to create XML-based representations of objects and store them in a file. The objects stored in the file are serialized. To import a CLiXML file and create deserialized objects, you can use Import-CLixml.**

Establishing Remote Background Jobs

Windows PowerShell 2.0 supports both local and remote background jobs. A background job is a command that you run asynchronously without interacting with it. When you start a background job, the command prompt returns immediately, and you can continue to work in the session while the job runs, even if it runs for an extended period of time.

Using Background Jobs

PowerShell runs background jobs on the local computer by default. You can run background jobs on remote computers by

- Starting an interactive session with a remote computer and starting a job in the interactive session. This approach allows you to work with the background job the same way as you would on the local computer.
- Running a background job on a remote computer that returns results to the local computer. This approach allows you to collect the results of background jobs and maintain them from your computer.

- Running a background job on a remote computer and maintaining the results on the remote computer. This approach helps ensure the job data is secure.

PowerShell has several commands for working with background jobs. These commands include

- **Get-Job** Gets objects that represent the background jobs started in the current session. Without parameters, Get-Job returns a list of all jobs in the current session. The job object returned does not contain the job results. To get the results, use the Receive-Job cmdlet. You can use the parameters of Get-Job to get background jobs by their command text, names, IDs, or instance IDs. For command text, type the command or the part of the command with wildcards. For IDs, type an integer value that uniquely identifies the job in the current session. For names, type the friendly names previously assigned to the job. An instance ID is a GUID that uniquely identifies a job, even when you have multiple jobs running in PowerShell. To find the names, IDs, or instance IDs of jobs, use Get-Jobs without parameters. You can use the –State parameter to get only jobs in the specified state. Valid values are NotStarted, Running, Completed, Stopped, Failed, and Blocked.

```
Get-Job [-Command Commands] | [[-InstanceId] GUIDs] | [[-Name]
Names] | [[-Id] IDs] | [-State JobState]
```

- **Receive-Job** Gets the output and errors of the PowerShell background jobs started in the current session. You can get the results of all jobs or identify jobs by their name, ID, instance ID, computer name, location, or session, or by inputting a job object. By default, job results are deleted after you receive them, but you can use the –Keep parameter to save the results so that you can receive them again. To delete the job results, receive them again without the –Keep parameter, close the session, or use the Remove-Job cmdlet to delete the job from the session.

```
Receive-Job [[-ComputerName Computers] | [-Location Locations] |
[-Session Session]] [-Job] Jobs [BasicParams]

Receive-Job [[-Id] IDs] | [[-InstanceId] GUIDS] | [[-Name] Names] |
[-State States] [BasicParams]

BasicParams=
[-Error] [-Keep] [-NoRecurse]
```

- **Remove-Job** Deletes PowerShell background jobs that were started by using Start-Job or the –AsJob parameter of a cmdlet. Without parameters or parameter values, Remove-Job has no effect. You can delete all jobs or selected jobs based on their command, name, ID, instance ID, or state, or by passing a job object to Remove-Job. Before deleting a running job, you should use Stop-Job to stop the job. If you try to delete a running job, Remove-Job fails. You can use the –Force parameter to delete a running job. If you do not delete a background job, the job remains in the global job cache until you close the session in which the job was created.

```
Remove-Job [-Force] [-Command Commands] | [[-Job] Jobs] |
[[-Id] IDs] | [[-InstanceId] GUIDS] | [[-Name] Names] |
[-State States]
```

- **Start-Job** Starts a Windows PowerShell background job on the local computer. To run a background job on a remote computer, use the –AsJob parameter of a cmdlet that supports background jobs, or use the Invoke-Command cmdlet to run a Start-Job command on the remote computer. When you start a Windows PowerShell background job, the job starts, but the results do not appear immediately. Instead, the command returns an object that represents the background job. The job object contains useful information about the job, but it does not contain the results. This approach allows you to continue working while the job runs.

```
Start-Job [-FilePath Path] [AddtlParams]
Start-Job [-ScriptBlock] ScriptBlock [AddtlParams]

AddtlParams=
[-ArgumentList Args] [-Authentication {<Default> | <Basic> |
<Negotiate> | <NegotiateWithImplicitCredential> | <Credssp>}]
[-ConfigurationName String] [-Credential Credential]
[-InputObject Object] [-Name String] [-NoCompression]
```

- **Stop-Job** Stops PowerShell background jobs that are in progress. You can stop all jobs or stop selected jobs based on their name, ID, instance ID, or state, or by passing a job object to Stop-Job. When you stop a background job, PowerShell completes all tasks that are pending in that job queue and then ends the job. No new tasks are added to the queue after you stop the job. Stop-Job does not delete background jobs. To delete a job, use Remove-Job.

```
Stop-Job [-PassThru] [[-Job] Jobs] | [[-Id] IDs] |
[[-InstanceId] GUIDS] | [[-Name] Names] | [-State States]
```

- **Wait-Job** Waits for PowerShell background jobs to complete before it displays the command prompt. You can wait until any specific background jobs are complete or until all background jobs are complete. Use the –Timeout parameter to set a maximum wait time for the job. When the commands in the job are complete, Wait-Job displays the command prompt and returns a job object so that you can pipe it to another command. Use the –Any parameter to display the command prompt when any job completes. By default,

Wait-Job waits until all of the specified jobs are complete before displaying the prompt.

```
Stop-Job [-Any] [-TimeOut WaitTime] [[-Job] Jobs] | [[-Id] IDs] |
[[-InstanceId] GUIDS] | [[-Name] Names] | [-State States]
```

Some cmdlets can be run as background jobs automatically using an –AsJob parameter. You can get a complete list of all cmdlets with an –AsJob parameter by typing the following command: **get-help * -parameter AsJob**. These cmdlets include:

- **Invoke-Command** Runs commands on local and remote computers.
- **Invoke-WmiMethod** Calls Windows Management Instrumentation (WMI) methods.
- **Test-Connection** Sends Internet Control Message Protocol (ICMP) echo request packets (*pings*) to one or more computers.
- **Restart-Computer** Restarts (*reboots*) the operating system on local and remote computers.
- **Stop-Computer** Stops (shuts down) local and remote computers.

The basic way background jobs work is as follows:

1. You start a background job using Start-Job or the –AsJob parameter of a cmdlet.
2. The job starts, but the results do not appear immediately. Instead, the command returns an object that represents the background job.
3. As necessary, you work with the job object. The job object contains useful information about the job, but it does not contain the results. This approach allows you to continue working while the job runs.
4. To view the results of a job started in the current session, you use Receive-Job. You can identify jobs by their name, ID, instance ID, computer name, location, or session, or by inputting a job object to Receive-Job. After you receive a job, the job results are deleted (unless you use the –Keep parameter).

Starting Jobs in Interactive Sessions

You can start any interactive session. The procedure for starting a background job is almost the same whether you are working with your local computer or a remote computer. When you work with the local computer, all operations occur on the local computer. When you work with a remote computer, all operations occur on the remote computer.

You can use the Enter-PSSession cmdlet to start an interactive session with a remote computer. Use the –ComputerName parameter to specify the name of the remote computer, such as in the following:

```
enter-pssession -computername filesvr32
```

NOTE To end the interactive session later, type **exit-pssession**.

You start a background job in a local or remote session using the Start-Job cmdlet. You can reference a script block with the –ScriptBlock parameter or a local script using the –FilePath parameter.

The following command runs a background job that gets the events in the System, Application, and Security logs. Because Start-Job returns an object that represents the job, this command saves the job object in the $job variable. Type the command as a single line:

```
$job = start-job -scriptblock {$share = "\\FileServer85\logs";
$logs = "system","application","security";
foreach ($log in $logs) {
$filename = "$env:computername".ToUpper() + "$log" + "log" +
(get-date -format yyyyMMdd) + ".log";
Get-EventLog $log | set-content $share\$filename; }
}
```

Or use the back apostrophe to continue the line as shown here:

```
$job = start-job -scriptblock {$share = "\\FileServer85\logs"; `
$logs = "system","application","security"; `
foreach ($log in $logs) { `
$filename = "$env:computername".ToUpper() + "$log" + "log" + `
(get-date -format yyyyMMdd) + ".log"; `
Get-EventLog $log | set-content $share\$filename; } `
}
```

Alternatively, you can store the commands as a script on the local computer and then reference the local script using the –FilePath parameter as shown in the examples that follow.

Command line

```
$job = start-job -filepath c:\scripts\eventlogs.ps1
```

Source for Eventlogs.ps1

```
$share = "\\FileServer85\logs"
$logs = "system","application","security"

foreach ($log in $logs) {
  $filename = "$env:computername".ToUpper() + "$log" + "log" + `
(get-date -format yyyyMMdd) + ".log"
  Get-EventLog $log | set-content $share\$filename
}
```

The script must reside on the local computer or in a directory that the local computer can access. When you use FilePath, Windows PowerShell converts the contents of the specified script file to a script block and runs the script block as a background job.

While the job runs, you can continue working and run other commands, including other background jobs. However, you must keep the interactive session open until the job completes. Otherwise, the jobs will be interrupted, and the results will be lost.

> ***NOTE*** **You don't have to store Job objects in variables. However, doing so makes it easier to work with Job objects. But if you do use variables and you run multiple jobs, be sure that you store the returned Job objects in different variables, such as $job1, $job2, and $job3.**

You use the Get-Job cmdlet to do the following:

- Find out if a job is complete.
- Display the command passed to the job.
- Get information about jobs so that you can work with them.

You can get all jobs or identify jobs by their name, ID, instance ID, computer name, location, or session, or by inputting a job object. PowerShell gives jobs sequential IDs and names automatically. The first job you run has an ID of 1 and a name of Job1, the second job you run has an ID of 2 and a name of Job2, and so on. You can also name jobs when you start them using the –Name parameter. In the following example, you create a job named Logs:

```
start-job -filepath c:\scripts\eventlogs.ps1 -name Logs
```

You can then get information about this job using Get-Job and the –Name parameter as shown in the following example and sample output:

```
get-job -name Logs
```

```
Id  Name  State   HasMoreData  Location   Command
--  ----  -----   -----------  --------   -------
1   Logs  Failed  False        filesvr32  $share = "\\FileServer...
```

Because this job failed to run, you won't necessarily be able to receive its output or error results. You can, however, take a closer look at the job information. For more detailed information, you need to format the output in a list as shown in this example and sample output:

```
get-job -name logs | format-list
```

```
HasMoreData   : False
StatusMessage :
Location      : filesvr32
Command       : $share = "\\FileServer85\logs"; $logs = "system",
"application","security"; foreach ($log in $logs) { $f
ilename = "$env:computername".ToUpper() + "$log" + "log" + (get-date
-format yyyyMMdd) + ".log"; Get-Ev
entLog $log | set-content $share\$filename; }
JobStateInfo  : Failed
Finished      : System.Threading.ManualResetEvent
InstanceId    : 679ed475-4edd-4ba5-ae79-e1e9b3aa590e
Id            : 3
Name          : Logs
ChildJobs     : {Job4}
Output        : {}
Error         : {}
Progress      : {}
Verbose       : {}
Debug         : {}
Warning       : {}
```

If you are running several jobs, type **get-job** to check the status of all jobs as shown in the following example and sample output:

```
get-job
```

```
Id Name  State     HasMoreData  Location   Command
-- ----  -----     -----------  --------   -------
1  Job1  Completed False        localhost  $share = "\\FileServer...
3  Job3  Running   True         localhost  $logs = "system","appl...
```

When a job completes, you can use the Receive-Job cmdlet to get the results of the job. However, keep in mind that if a job doesn't produce output or errors to the PowerShell prompt, there won't be any results to receive.

You can receive the results of all jobs by typing **receive-job**, or you can identify jobs by their name, ID, instance ID, computer name, location, or session, or by inputting a job object. The following example receives results by name:

```
receive-job -name Job1, Job3
```

The following example receives results by ID:

```
receive-job -id 1, 3
```

Job results are deleted automatically after you receive them. Use the –Keep parameter to save the results so that you can receive them again. To delete the job results, receive the job results again without the –Keep parameter, close the session, or use the Remove-Job cmdlet to delete the job from the session.

Alternatively, you can write the job results to a file. The following example writes the job results to C:\logs\mylog.txt:

```
receive-job -name Job1 > c:\logs\mylog.txt
```

When working with a remote computer, keep in mind that this command runs on the remote computer. As a result, the file is created on the remote computer. If you are using one log for multiple jobs, be sure to use the append operator as shown in this example:

```
receive-job -name Job1 >> c:\logs\mylog.txt
receive-job -name Job2 >> c:\logs\mylog.txt
receive-job -name Job3 >> c:\logs\mylog.txt
```

While in the current session with the remote computer, you can view the contents of the results file by typing the following command:

```
get-content c:\logs\mylog.txt
```

If you close the session with the remote computer, you can use Invoke-Command to view the file on the remote computer as shown here:

```
$ms = new-pssession -computername fileserver84
invoke-command -session $ms -scriptblock {get-content c:\logs\mylog.txt}
```

Running Jobs Noninteractively

Rather than working in an interactive session, you can use the Invoke-Command cmdlet with the –AsJob parameter to start background jobs and return results to the local computer. When you use the –AsJob parameter, the job object is created on the local computer, even though the job runs on the remote computer. When the job completes, the results are returned to the local computer.

In the following example, we create a noninteractive PowerShell session with three remote computers and then use Invoke-Command to run a background job that gets the events in the System, Application, and Security logs. This is the same job created earlier, only now the job runs on all the computers listed in the –ComputerName parameter. Type the command as a single line:

```
$s = new-pssession -computername fileserver34, dataserver18, dcserver65
Invoke-command -session $s
-asjob -scriptblock {$share = "\\FileServer85\logs";
$logs = "system","application","security";
foreach ($log in $logs) {
$filename = "$env:computername".ToUpper() + "$log" + "log" +
(get-date -format yyyyMMdd) + ".log";
Get-EventLog $log | set-content $share\$filename; }
}
```

Or use the back apostrophe to continue the line as shown here:

```
$s = new-pssession -computername fileserver34, dataserver18, dcserver65 `
Invoke-command -session $s `
-asjob -scriptblock {$share = "\\FileServer85\logs"; `
$logs = "system","application","security"; `
foreach ($log in $logs) { `
$filename = "$env:computername".ToUpper() + "$log" + "log" + `
(get-date -format yyyyMMdd) + ".log"; `
Get-EventLog $log | set-content $share\$filename; } `
}
```

Alternatively, you can store the commands as a script on the local computer and then reference the local script using the –FilePath parameter as shown in the examples that follow.

Command line

```
$s = new-pssession -computername fileserver34, dataserver18, dcserver65
Invoke-command -session $s -asjob -filepath c:\scripts\eventlogs.ps1
```

Source for Eventlogs.ps1

```
$share = "\\FileServer85\logs"
$logs = "system","application","security"

foreach ($log in $logs) {
  $filename = "$env:computername".ToUpper() + "$log" + "log" + `
(get-date -format yyyyMMdd) + ".log"
  Get-EventLog $log | set-content $share\$filename
}
```

The script must reside on the local computer or in a directory that the local computer can access. As before, when you use FilePath, Windows PowerShell converts the contents of the specified script file to a script block and runs the script block as a background job.

Now, you don't necessarily have to run Invoke-Command via a noninteractive session. However, the advantage of doing so is that you can now work with the job objects running in the session. For example, to get information about the jobs on all three computers, you type the following command:

```
get-job
```

To receive job results you type this command:

```
receive-job -keep
```

Or you can type the following if you want to save the results to a file on the local computer:

```
receive-job > c:\logs\mylog.txt
```

A variation on this technique is to use the Invoke-Command cmdlet to run the Start-Job cmdlet. This technique allows you to run background jobs on multiple computers and keep the results on the remote computers. Here's how this works:

1. You use Invoke-Command without the –AsJob parameter to run the Start-Job cmdlet.
2. A job object is created on each remote computer.
3. Commands in the job are run separately on each remote computer.
4. Job results are maintained separately on each remote computer.
5. You work with the job objects and results on each remote computer separately.

Here, you use Invoke-Command to start jobs on three computers and store the Job objects in the $j variable:

```
$s = new-pssession -computername fileserver34, dataserver18, dcserver65
$j = invoke-command -session $s {start-job -filepath c:\scripts\elogs.ps1}
```

Again, you don't necessarily have to run Invoke-Command via a noninteractive session. However, the advantage of doing so is that you can now work with the job objects running on all three computers via the session. For example, to get information about the jobs on all three computers, you type the following command:

```
invoke-command -session $s -scriptblock {get-job}
```

Or, because you stored the Job objects in the $j variable, you also could enter:

```
$j
```

To receive job results, you type this command:

```
invoke-command -session $s -scriptblock { param($j) receive-job -job $j
-keep} -argumentlist $j
```

Or you can do the following if you want to save the results to a file on each remote computer:

```
invoke-command -session $s -command {param($j) receive-job -job $j > c:\
logs\mylog.txt} -argumentlist $j
```

In both examples, you use Invoke-Command to run a Receive-Job command in each session in $s. Because $j is a local variable, the script block uses the "param" keyword to declare the variable in the command and the ArgumentList parameter to supply the value of $j.

Working Remotely Without WinRM

Some cmdlets have a –ComputerName parameter that lets you work with a remote computer without using Windows PowerShell remoting. This means you can use the cmdlet on any computer that is running Windows PowerShell, even if the computer is not configured for Windows PowerShell remoting. These cmdlets include the following:

Get-WinEvent	Get-Counter	Get-EventLog
Clear-EventLog	Write-EventLog	Limit-EventLog
Show-EventLog	New-EventLog	Remove-EventLog
Get-WmiObject	Get-Process	Get-Service
Set-Service	Get-HotFix	Restart-Computer
Stop-Computer	Add-Computer	Remove-Computer
Rename-Computer	Reset-ComputerMachinePassword	

Because these cmdlets don't use remoting, you can run any of these cmdlets on a remote computer in a domain simply by specifying the name of one or more remote computers in the –ComputerName parameter. However, Windows policies and configuration settings must allow remote connections, and you must still have the appropriate credentials.

The following command runs Get-WinEvent on PrintServer35 and FileServer17:

```
get-winevent -computername printserver35, fileserver17
```

When you use ComputerName, these cmdlets return objects that include the name of the computer that generated the data. The remote computer name is stored in the MachineName property. Typically, the MachineName property is not displayed by default. The following example shows how you can use the Format-Table cmdlet to add the MachineName property to the output:

```
$procs = {get-process -computername Server56, Server42, Server27 |
sort-object -property Name}

&$procs | format-table Name, Handles, WS, CPU, MachineName -auto
```

```
Name                    Handles       WS        CPU MachineName
----                    -------       --        --- -----------
acrotray                     52  3948544          0 Server56
AlertService                139  7532544            Server56
csrss                       594 20463616            Server56
csrss                       655  5283840            Server56
CtHelper                     96  6705152   0.078125 Server56
 . . .
acrotray                     43  3948234          0 Server42
AlertService                136  7532244            Server42
```

```
csrss                              528 20463755              Server42
csrss                              644  5283567              Server42
CtHelper                            95  6705576     0.067885 Server42

acrotray                            55  3967544            0 Server27
AlertService                       141  7566662              Server27
csrss                              590 20434342              Server27
csrss                              654  5242340              Server27
CtHelper                            92  6705231     0.055522 Server27
```

You can get a complete list of all cmdlets with a –ComputerName parameter by typing the following command: **get-help * -parameter ComputerName**. To determine whether the –ComputerName parameter of a particular cmdlet requires Windows PowerShell remoting, display the parameter description by typing **get-help *CmdletName* -parameter ComputerName**, where *CmdletName* is the actual name of the cmdlet, such as

```
get-help Reset-ComputerMachinePassword -parameter ComputerName
```

If the parameter doesn't require remoting, this is stated explicitly, as shown in this example:

```
-ComputerName <string[]>

Resets the password for the specified computers. Specify one or more remote
computers. The default is the local computer.
```

Type the NetBIOS name, an IP address, or a fully qualified domain name of a remote computer. To specify the local computer, type the computer name, a dot (**.**), or **localhost**.

This parameter does not rely on Windows PowerShell remoting. You can use the –ComputerName parameter even if your computer is not configured to run remote commands.

CHAPTER 5

Navigating Core Windows PowerShell Structures

The core structures of any programming language determine what you can do with the available options and how you can use the programming language. The programming language at the heart of Windows PowerShell is C#, and the core structures of PowerShell include

- Expressions and operators
- Variables, values, and data types
- Strings, arrays, and collections

Whenever you work with Windows PowerShell, you use these core structures. You'll want to read this chapter closely to learn the core mechanics and determine exactly how you can put PowerShell to work. Because we discuss these core mechanics extensively in this chapter, we won't rehash these discussions when we put the core mechanics to work in upcoming chapters.

Working with Expressions and Operators

In Windows PowerShell, an expression is a calculation that evaluates an equation and returns a result. PowerShell supports many types of expressions, including arithmetic expressions (which return numerical values), assignment expressions (which assign or set a value), and comparison expressions (which compare values).

An *operator* is the element of an expression that tells PowerShell how to perform the calculation. You use operators as part of expressions to perform mathematical operations, make assignments, and compare values. The three common operator types are arithmetic operators, assignment operators, and comparison operators. Windows PowerShell also supports an extended type of operator used with regular expressions, logical operators, and type operators.

Arithmetic, Grouping, and Assignment Operators

Windows PowerShell supports a standard set of arithmetic operators. These operators are summarized in Table 5-1.

TABLE 5-1 Arithmetic Operators in Windows PowerShell

OPERATOR	OPERATION	FOR NUMBERS	FOR STRINGS	FOR ARRAYS	EXAMPLE
+	Addition	Returns their sum	Returns a joined string	Returns a joined array	3 + 4
/	Division	Returns their quotient	N/A	N/A	5 / 2
%	Modulus	Returns the remainder of their division	N/A	N/A	5 % 2
*	Multiplication	Returns their product	Appends the string to itself the number of times you specify	Appends the array to itself the number of times you specify	6 * 3
–	Subtraction, negation	Returns their difference	N/A	N/A	3 – 2

Table 5-2 lists the assignment operators available in PowerShell. Assignment operators assign one or more values to a variable and can perform numeric operations on the values before the assignment. PowerShell supports two special assignment operators that you might not be familiar with: the increment operator (++) and the decrement operator (--). These operators provide a quick way to add or subtract 1 from the value of a variable, property, or array element.

TABLE 5-2 Windows PowerShell Assignment Operators

OPERATOR	OPERATION	EXAMPLE	MEANING
=	Assign value	$a = 7	$a = 7
+=	Add or append to current value	$g += $h	$g = $g + $h
–=	Subtract from current value	$g –= $h	$g = $g – $h

TABLE 5-2 Windows PowerShell Assignment Operators

OPERATOR	OPERATION	EXAMPLE	MEANING
*=	Multiply current value	$g *= $h	$g = $g * $h
/=	Divide current value	$g /= $h	$g = $g / $h
%=	Modulus current value	$g %= $h	$g = $g % $h
++	Increment by 1	$g++ or ++$g	$g = $g + 1
--	Decrement by 1	$g-- or --$g	$g = $g – 1

As you can see in Tables 5-1 and 5-2, there are few surprises when it comes to PowerShell's arithmetic and assignment operators. Still, there are a few things worth mentioning. In PowerShell, you determine remanders using the Modulus function. In this example, $Remainder is set to 0 (zero):

```
$Remainder = 12 % 4
```

However, $Remainder is set to 1 with the following expression:

```
$Remainder = 10 % 3
```

You can negate a value using the – operator. In the following example, $Answer is set to –15:

```
$Answer = -5 * 3
```

Command expansion and execution operators bring together sets of elements. The grouping operators are described in the following list and examples:

- **&** Used to invoke a script block or the name of a command or function.

```
$a = {Get-Process -id 0}
&$a
```

```
Handles  NPM(K)    PM(K)     WS(K) VM(M)   CPU(s)     Id ProcessName
-------  ------    -----     ----- -----   ------     -- -----------
      0       0        0        24     0              0 Idle
```

- **( )** Used to group expression operators. It returns the result of the expression.

```
$a = (5 + 4) * 2; $a
```

```
18
```

- **$( )** Used to group collections of statements. The grouped commands are executed, and then results are returned.

```
$($p= "win*"; get-process $p)
```

```
Handles  NPM(K)  PM(K)    WS(K) VM(M)   CPU(s)     Id ProcessName
-------  ------  -----    ----- -----   ------     -- -----------
    106       4   1448     4092    46             636 wininit
    145       4   2360     6536    56             780 winlogon
```

- **@( )** Used to group collections of statements, execute them, and insert the results into an array.

```
@(get-date;$env:computername;$env:logonserver)
```

```
Friday, February 12, 2010 9:01:49 AM
CORSERVER34
\\CORDC92
```

> ***NOTE*** **An array is simply a data structure for storing a series of values. You'll learn more about arrays in the "Working with Arrays and Collections" section.**

If you mix operators, PowerShell performs calculations using the same precedence order you learned in school. For example, multiplication and division in equations are carried out before subtraction and addition, which means

```
5 + 4 * 2 = 13
```

and

```
10 / 10 + 6 = 7
```

Table 5-3 shows the precedence order for arithmetic operators. As the table shows, the grouping is always evaluated first, and then PowerShell determines whether any values have been incremented or decremented. Next, PowerShell sets positive and negative values as such. Then PowerShell performs multiplication and division before performing any modulus operations. Finally, PowerShell performs addition and subtraction and then assigns the results as appropriate.

TABLE 5-3 Operator Precedence in Windows PowerShell

ORDER	OPERATION
1	Grouping ( ) { }
2	Increment ++, Decrement --
3	Unary + -

TABLE 5-3 Operator Precedence in Windows PowerShell

ORDER	OPERATION
4	Multiplication *, Division /
5	Remainders %
6	Addition +, Subtraction –
7	Assignment =

One of the interesting things about Windows PowerShell is that it supports the data storage concepts of

- Kilobytes (KB)
- Megabytes (MB)
- Gigabytes (GB)
- Terabytes (TB)
- Petabytes (PB)

Knowing this, you can perform some simple calculations at the prompt. For example, if you are backing up a drive that uses 1 TB of storage to Blu-Ray DVD, you might want to find out the maximum number of dual-layer Blu-Ray DVDs you'll need, and you can do this simply by entering

```
1TB / 50GB
```

The answer is

```
20.48
```

In the following example, you list all files in the C:\Data directory that are larger than 100 KB:

```
get-item c:\data\* | where-object {$_.length -gt 100kb}
```

Comparison Operators

When you perform comparisons, you check for certain conditions, such as whether A is greater than B or whether A is equal to C. You primarily use comparison operators with conditional statements, such as If and If Else.

Table 5-4 lists the comparison operators available in PowerShell. Most of these operators are straightforward. By default, PowerShell uses non–case-sensitive comparisons. However, you can perform case-sensitive and non–case-sensitive comparisons, respectively, by adding the letter C or I to the operator, such as –ceq or –ieq.

TABLE 5-4 Windows PowerShell Comparison Operators

OPERATOR	OPERATION	EXAMPLE	MEANING	OUTPUT
–eq	Equal	$g –eq $h	Is g equal to h?	Boolean
	Include string	$g –eq $h	Does g include h?	Boolean
–ne	Not equal	$g –ne $h	Is g not equal to h?	Boolean
	Different string	$g –ne $h	Does g include a different value than h?	Boolean
–lt	Less than	$g –lt $h	Is g less than h?	Boolean
–gt	Greater than	$g –gt $h	Is g greater than h?	Boolean
–le	Less than or equal	$g –le $h	Is g less than or equal to h?	Boolean
–ge	Greater than or equal	$g –ge $h	Is g greater than or equal to h?	Boolean
–contains	Contains	$g –contains $h	Does g include h?	Boolean
–notcontains	Does not contain	$g –notcontains $h	Does g not include h?	Boolean
–like	Like	$g –like $h	Does g include a value like h?	Boolean
–notlike	Not like	$g –notlike $h	Does g not include a value like h?	Boolean
–match	Match	$g –match $h	Does g include any matches for the expression defined in h?	Boolean
–notmatch	Not match	$g –notmatch $h	Does g not include matches for the expression defined in h?	Boolean
–replace	Replace	$g –replace $h, $i	If g has occurrences of h, replace them with i.	String

Note that you can use these operators to compare numbers as well as strings and that there is no set precedence order for comparisons. Comparisons are always performed from left to right.

Most of the comparison operators return a Boolean value that indicates whether a match was found in the compared values. In this example and sample output, we evaluate whether $a equals $b, and the output is False because the values are different:

```
$a = 5; $b = 6
$a -eq $b
```

```
False
```

In this example and sample output, we evaluate whether $a does not equal $b, and the output is True because the values are different:

```
$a = 5; $b = 6
$a -ne $b
```

```
True
```

In this example and sample output, we evaluate whether $a is less than $b, and the output is True:

```
$a = 5; $b = 6
$a -lt $b
```

```
True
```

When you are working with arrays and collections, the –eq, –ne, –lt, –gt, –le, and –ge operators return all values that match the given expression. For example, the –eq operator checks to see if an array of values contains any identical values. If it does, the output shows all the identical values as shown in this example:

```
$a = "iexplorer", "iexplorer", "powershell"; $b = "iexplorer"
$a -eq $b
```

```
iexplorer
iexplorer
```

Similarly, when you are working with arrays and collections, the –ne operator checks to see if an array of values contains values other than a particular value. If it does, the output shows the different values as shown in this example:

```
$a = "svchost", "iexplorer", "powershell"; $b = "iexplorer"
$a -ne $b
```

```
svchost
powershell
```

You use the –contains and –notcontains operators with strings, arrays, and collections. These operators are used to determine whether there is or is not an identical match for a value. In the following example, you check to see whether $a has a resulting match for winlogon:

```
$a = "svchost", "iexplorer", "powershell"
$a -contains "winlogon"
```

```
False
```

The –like, –notlike, –match, and –notmatch operators are used for pattern matching. With –like and –notlike, you can use wildcard characters to determine whether a value is like or not like another value. In the following example, you check to see whether $a has a resulting match for *host:

```
$a = "svchost"
$a -like "*host"
```

```
True
```

In examples in other chapters, I've used the *match all* wildcard (*) to match part of a string. PowerShell supports several other wildcards as well, including ? and [ ]. Table 5-5 summarizes these wildcards and their uses.

TABLE 5-5 Wildcard Characters in Windows PowerShell

WILDCARD CHARACTER	DESCRIPTION	EXAMPLE	MATCH
*	Matches zero or more characters	help *-alias	export-alias, import-alias, get-alias, new-alias, set-alias
?	Matches exactly one character in the specified position	help ??port-alias	export-alias, import-alias
[ ]	Matches one character in a specified range of characters	help [a-z]e[t-w]-alias	get-alias, new-alias, set-alias
[ ]	Matches one character in a specified subset of characters	help [efg]et-alias	get-alias

When you are working with arrays and collections, the –like and –notlike operators return all values that match the given expression. The following example returns two values that are like 4:

```
1,1,2,3,4,5,5,6,3,4 -like 4
```

```
4
4
```

The following example returns five values that are not like 4:

```
2,3,4,5,5,6,4 -notlike 4
```

```
2
3
5
5
6
```

With –match and –notmatch, you use regular expressions to determine whether a value does or does not contain a match for an expression. You can think of regular expressions as an extended set of wildcard characters. In the following example, you check to see whether $a contains the letter s, t, or u:

```
$a = "svchost"
$a -match "[stu]"
```

```
True
```

Table 5-6 shows the characters you can use with regular expressions. When you use .NET Framework regular expressions, you also can add .NET Framework quantifiers to more strictly control what is considered a match.

TABLE 5-6 Characters Used with Regular Expressions

CHARACTER	DESCRIPTION	RETURNS TRUE…
[chars]	Matches exact characters anywhere in the original value.	"powershell" –match "er"
.	Matches any single character.	"svchost" –match "s.....t"
[value]	Matches at least one of the characters in the brackets.	"get" –match "g[aeiou]t"

TABLE 5-6 Characters Used with Regular Expressions

CHARACTER	DESCRIPTION	RETURNS TRUE...
[range]	Matches at least one of the characters within the range. Use a hyphen (-) to specify a block of contiguous characters.	"out" –match "[o-r]ut"
[^]	Matches any character except those in brackets.	"bell" –match "[^tuv]ell"
^	Matches the beginning characters.	"powershell" –match "^po"
$	Matches the end characters.	"powershell" –match "ell$"
*	Matches any pattern in a string.	"powershell" –match "p*"
?	Matches a single character in a string.	"powershell" –match "powershel?"
+	Matches repeated instances of the preceding characters.	"zbzbzb" –match "zb+"
\	Matches the character that follows as a literal character. For example, when \ precedes a double quotation mark, PowerShell interprets the double quotation mark as a character, not as a string delimiter.	"Shell$" –match "Shell\$"
.NET REGEX		
\p{name}	Matches any character in the named character class specified by {name}. Supported names are Unicode groups and block ranges—for example, Ll, Nd, Z, IsGreek, and IsBoxDrawing.	"abcd" –match "\p{Ll}+"
\P{name}	Matches text not included in groups and block ranges specified in {name}.	1234 –match "\P{Ll}+"
\w	Matches any word character. Equivalent to the Unicode character categories [\p{Ll} \p{Lu}\p{Lt}\p{Lo}\p{Nd}\p{Pc}]. If ECMAScript-compliant behavior is specified with the ECMAScript option, \w is equivalent to [a-zA-Z_0-9].	"abcd defg" –match "\w+"

TABLE 5-6 Characters Used with Regular Expressions

CHARACTER	DESCRIPTION	RETURNS TRUE...
\W	Matches any nonword character. Equivalent to the Unicode categories [^\p{Ll}\p{Lu}\p{Lt} \p{Lo}\p{Nd}\p{Pc}].	"abcd defg" –match "\W+"
\s	Matches any white-space character. Equivalent to the Unicode character categories [\f\n\r\t\v\x85\p{Z}].	"abcd defg" –match "\s+"
\S	Matches any non–white-space character. Equivalent to the Unicode character categories [^\f\n\r\t\v\x85\p{Z}].	"abcd defg" –match "\S+"
\d	Matches any decimal digit. Equivalent to \p{Nd} for Unicode and [0–9] for non-Unicode behavior.	12345 –match "\d+"
\D	Matches any nondigit. Equivalent to \P{Nd} for Unicode and [^0-9] for non-Unicode behavior.	"abcd" –match "\D+"
.NET FRAMEWORK QUANTIFER		
*	Matches zero or more occurrences of a pattern specified in a .NET Framework regex.	"abc" –match "\w*"
?	Matches zero or one occurrences of a pattern specified in a .NET Framework regex.	"abc" –match "\w?"
{n}	Matches exactly *n* occurrences of a pattern specified in a .NET Framework regex.	"abc" –match "\w{2}"
{n,}	Matches at least *n* occurrences of a pattern specified in a .NET Framework regex.	"abc" –match "\w{2,}"
{n,m}	Matches at least *n* occurrences of a pattern specified in a .NET Framework regex, but no more than *m*.	"abc" –match "\w{2,3}"

In addition to using the –match and –notmatch operators with regular expressions, you can explicitly declare regular expressions and then check values against the regular expression. The following example declares a regular expression that matches strings with the letters a to z or A to Z:

```
[regex]$regex="^([a-zA-Z]*)$"
```

When you work with regular expressions, you use the ^ to represent the beginning of a string and $ to represent the end of a string. You then use parentheses to define a group of characters to match. The value [a-zA-Z]* specifies that we want to match zero or more occurrences of the letters a to z or A to Z.

Now that we've defined a regular expression, we can use the IsMatch() method of the expression to verify that a value matches or does not match the expression as shown in the following example:

```
$a ="Tuesday"
[regex]$regex="^([a-zA-Z]*)$"
$regex.ismatch($a)
```

```
True
```

However, if we use a string with numbers, spaces, punctuation, or other special characters, the IsMatch test fails as shown in the following example:

```
$days ="Monday Tuesday"
[regex]$regex="^([a-zA-Z]*)$"
$regex.ismatch($days)
```

```
False
```

> ***TIP*** **PowerShell also provides operators for splitting, joining, and formatting strings. These operators are discussed in the "Working with Strings" section later in this chapter.**

Another comparison operator you can use is –replace. You use this operator to replace all occurrences of a value in a specified element. In the following example, you replace all occurrences of "host" in $a with "console":

```
$a = "svchost", "iexplorer", "loghost"
$a -replace "host", "console"
```

```
svcconsole
iexplorer
logconsole
```

Other Operators

Windows PowerShell includes several other types of operators, including logical and type operators. Table 5-7 provides an overview of these additional operators.

TABLE 5-7 Logical and Type Operators in Windows PowerShell

OP	OPERATION	DESCRIPTION	EXAMPLE
–and	Logical AND	True only when both statements are True.	(5 –eq 5) –and (3 –eq 6) False
–or	Logical OR	True only when either statement or both statements are True.	(5 –eq 5) –or (3 –eq 6) True
–xor	Logical XOR	True only when one of the statements is True and one is False.	(5 –eq 5) –xor (3 –eq 6) True
–not, !	Logical NOT	Negates the statement that follows it. True only when the statement is False. False only when the statement is True.	–not (5 –eq 5) False ! (5 –eq 5) False
–is	Object equality	Returns True only when the input is an instance of a specified .NET Framework type.	(get-date) –is [datetime] True
–isnot	Object inequality	Returns True only when the input is not an instance of a specified .NET Framework type.	(get-date) –isnot [datetime] False
–as	Object conversion	Converts the input to the specified .NET Framework type.	"3/31/10" –as [datetime] Wednesday, March 31, 2010 12:00:00 AM
,	Array constructor	Creates an array from the comma-separated values.	$a = 1,2,4,6,4,2
..	Range operator	Establishes a range of values.	$a = 2..24
–band	Binary AND	Performs a binary AND.	–
–bor	Binary OR	Performs a binary OR.	–
–bnot	Binary NOT	Performs a binary complement.	–
–bxor	Binary XOR	Performs a binary exclusive OR.	–

One operator you should learn about is the special operator Is. You use Is to compare objects according to their .NET Framework type. If the objects are of the same type, the result of the comparison is True. If the objects are not of the same type, the result of the comparison is False.

Table 5-8 shows the expanded precedence order for all available operators. This precedence order takes into account all the possible combinations of operators and defines an order of evaluation.

TABLE 5-8 Extended Operator Precedence in Windows PowerShell

ORDER	OPERATION
1	Grouping ( ) { }
2	Command expansion @ $
3	Not !
4	Wildcard expansion [ ]
5	Dot sourcing .
6	Invoke &
7	Increment ++, Decrement --
8	Unary + –
9	Multiplication *, Division /
10	Remainders %
11	Addition +, Subtraction –
12	Comparison operators
13	–and, –or
14	Pipelining |
15	Redirection > >>
16	Assignment =

Working with Variables and Values

Variables are placeholders for values. A value can be a string, a number, or an object. You can access this information later simply by referencing the variable name. With variables that store objects (from the output of commands), you can pass the stored information down the pipeline to other commands as if it were the output of the original command.

Your scripts and command text can use any of the available variables. By default, variables you create exist only in the current session and are lost when you exit or close the session. To maintain your variables, you must store them in a profile. For detailed information on profiles, see Chapter 3, "Managing Your PowerShell Environment."

In scripts, if configuration information doesn't need to be hard-coded, you should consider using variables to represent the information because this makes scripts easier to update and maintain. Additionally, you should try to define your variables in one place at the beginning of a script to make it easier to find and maintain variables.

PowerShell supports four classes of variables: automatic, preference, environment, and user-created variables. Unlike the command line, where variable values are stored as text strings, PowerShell stores values as either text strings or objects. Technically, a string is a type of object as well, and you'll learn more about strings in "Working with Strings" later in this chapter.

Variable Essentials

The following cmdlets are available for working with variables:

- **Get-Variable** Lists all or specified variables set in the current session by name and value.

```
Get-Variable [[-Name] VarNames] [AddtlParams]

AddtlParams=
[-Scope String] [-Exclude Strings] [-Include Strings] [-ValueOnly]
```

- **New-Variable** Creates a new variable.

```
New-Variable [[-Value] Object] [-Name] VarName [AddtlParams]

AddtlParams=
[-Description String] [-Force] [-Option None | ReadOnly | Constant
| Private | AllScope] [-PassThru] [-Scope String] [-Visibility
Public | Private]
```

- **Set-Variable** Creates a new variable or changes the definition of an existing variable.

```
Set-Variable [[-Value] Object] [-Name] VarNames [AddtlParams]

AddtlParams=
[-Description String] [-Exclude Strings] [-Force] [-Include
Strings] [-Option None | ReadOnly | Constant | Private | AllScope]
[-PassThru] [-Scope String] [-Visibility Public | Private]
```

- **Remove-Variable** Removes a variable and its value. Use the –Force parameter to remove a read-only variable.

```
Remove-Variable [-Name] VarNames[AddtlParams]

AddtlParams=
[-Scope String] [-Force] [-Exclude Strings] [-Include Strings]
```

- **Clear-Variable** Deletes the value of a variable. The value of the variable is then set to NULL.

```
Clear-Variable [-Force] [-PassThru] [-Scope String] [-Exclude
Strings] [-Include Strings] [-Name] VarNames
```

Regardless of the class of variable you are working with, you reference variables by preceding the variable name with a dollar sign ($). This is true whether you are defining a new variable or trying to work with a value stored in an existing variable. The dollar sign helps distinguish variables from aliases, functions, cmdlets, and other elements you use with PowerShell. Table 5-9 provides an overview of the options for defining variables.

TABLE 5-9 Windows PowerShell Variable Syntaxes

SYNTAX	DESCRIPTION
$myVar = "*Value*"	Defines a variable with a standard name, which is prefixed by $ and can contain the alphanumeric characters (a to z, A to Z, and 0–9) and the underscore (_). Variable names are not case sensitive.
${my.var!!!!} = "*Value*"	Defines a variable with a nonstandard name, which is prefixed by $, is enclosed in curly braces, and can contain any character. If curly braces are part of the name, you must prevent substitution using the back apostrophe (`).
[*type*] $myVar = "*Value*"	Defines a strongly typed variable that ensures the variable can contain only data of the specified type. PowerShell throws an error if it cannot coerce the data into the declared type.
$*SCOPE*:$myVar = "*Value*"	Declares a variable with a specific scope. Scopes set the logical boundaries for variables. For more information, see "Managing Variable Scopes" later in the chapter.
New-Item Variable:\myVar –Value *Value*	Creates a new variable using the variable provider. For more on providers, see the "Using Providers" section in Chapter 3.

TABLE 5-9 Windows PowerShell Variable Syntaxes

SYNTAX	DESCRIPTION
Get-Item Variable:\myVar Get-Variable myVar	Gets a variable using the variable provider or the Get-Variable cmdlet.
${*path\filename.ext*}	Defines a variable using the Get-Content and Set-Content syntax. If the *path\filename.ext* value points to a valid path, you can get and set the content of the item by reading and writing to the variable.

To define a variable, you must assign the variable a name and a value using the equals operator (=). Standard variable names are not case sensitive and can contain any combination of alphanumeric characters (a to z, A to Z, and 0–9) and the underscore (_) character. Following these rules, these are all valid and separate variables:

```
$myString = "String 1"
$myVar = "String 2"
$myObjects = "String 3"
$s = "String 4"
```

To access the value stored in a variable, you simply reference the variable name. For example, to display the contents of the $myString variable defined earlier, you type **$myString** at the PowerShell prompt, and you get the following output:

```
String 1
```

You can list available variables by typing **get-variable** at the PowerShell prompt. The output includes variables you've defined as well as current automatic and preference variables. Because environment variables are accessed through the environment provider, you must reference $env: and then the name of the variable you want to work with. For example, to display the value of the %UserName% variable, you must enter **$env:username**.

Variables can have nonstandard names that include special characters, such as dashes, periods, colons, and parentheses, but you must enclose nonstandard variable names in curly braces. Enclosing the variable name in curly braces forces PowerShell to interpret the variable name literally. Following these rules, these are all valid and separate variables:

```
${my.var} = "String 1"
${my-var} = "String 2"
${my:var} = "String 3"
${my(var)} = "String 4"
```

To refer to a variable name that includes braces, you must enclose the variable name in braces and use the back apostrophe character (`) to force PowerShell to interpret the brace characters literally when used as part of the variable name. For example, you can create a variable named "my{var}string" with a value of "String 5" by typing

```
${my`{var`}string} = "String 5"
```

In previous examples, we assigned string values to variables, but you can just as easily assign numeric, array, and object values. Numeric values are values entered as numbers rather than strings. Arrays are data structures for storing collections of like-typed data items. The values stored in an array can be delimited with a comma or initialized using the range operator (..). A collection of objects can be obtained by assigning the output of a cmdlet to a variable. Consider the following examples:

```
$myFirstNumber = 10
$mySecondNumber = 500
$myFirstArray = 0,1,2,3,4,8,13,21
$mySecondArray = 1..9
$myString = "Hello!"
$myObjectCollection1 = get-service
$myObjectCollection2 = get-process -name svchost
```

Here, you create variables to store integer values, arrays of values, strings, and collections of objects. You can then work with the values stored in the variable just as you would the original values. For example, you can count the number of service objects stored in $myObjectCollection1 by typing the following:

```
$myObjectCollection1.Count
```

You even can sort the service objects by status and display the sorted output by typing the following command:

```
$myObjectCollection1 | sort-object -property status
```

You aren't limited to values of these data types. You can assign any .NET Framework data type as a value, including the common data types listed in Table 5-10.

TABLE 5-10 Data Type Aliases

DATA TYPE ALIAS	DATA TYPE
[adsi]	An Active Directory Services Interface (ADSI) object
[array]	An array of values
[bool]	A Boolean value (True/False)

TABLE 5-10 Data Type Aliases

DATA TYPE ALIAS	DATA TYPE
[byte]	An 8-bit unsigned integer in the range 0 to 255
[char]	A Unicode 16-bit character
[datetime]	A datetime value
[decimal]	A 128-bit decimal value
[double]	A double-precision, 64-bit floating-point number
[float]	A single-precision, 32-bit floating-point number
[hashtable]	An associative array defined in a hashtable object
[int]	A 32-bit signed integer
[long]	A 64-bit signed integer
[psobject]	A common object type that can encapsulate any base object
[regex]	A regular expression
[scriptblock]	A series of commands
[single]	A single-precision, 32-bit floating-point number
[string]	A fixed-length string value with Unicode characters
[wmi]	A Windows Management Instrumentation (WMI) object
[xml]	An XML object

Variables also can be used to store the results of evaluated expressions. Consider the following example and result:

```
$theFirstResult = 10 + 10 + 10
$theSecondResult = $(if($theFirstResult -gt 25) {$true} else {$false})
write-host "$theFirstResult is greater than 25? `t $theSecondResult"
```

```
30 is greater than 25?        True
```

Here, Windows PowerShell evaluates the first expression and stores the result in the first variable. Next PowerShell evaluates the second expression and stores the result in the second variable. The expression determines whether the first variable is greater than 25. If it is, PowerShell sets the second variable to True. Otherwise, PowerShell sets the second variable to False. Finally, PowerShell displays output to the console containing the results.

In these examples, the first variable is defined as the Integer data type, and the second is defined as the Boolean data type. Generally, if you use whole numbers (such as 3 or 5) with a variable, PowerShell creates the variable as an Integer.

Variables with values that use decimal points, such as 6.87 or 3.2, are generally assigned as Doubles—that is, double-precision, floating-point values. Variables with values entered with a mixture of alphabetical and numeric characters, such as Hello or S35, are created as Strings.

In PowerShell, you use Boolean values quite frequently. Whenever PowerShell evaluates variables as part of a Boolean expression, such as in an If statement, PowerShell maps the result to a Boolean representation. A Boolean value is always either Tue or False, and it can be represented literally using the values $true for True or $false for False.

Table 5-11 shows examples of items and results and how they are represented as Booleans by PowerShell. Note that a reference to any object is represented as True whereas a reference to $null is represented as False.

TABLE 5-11 Results Represented as Boolean Values

ITEM OR RESULT	BOOLEAN REPRESENTATION
$true	True
$false	False
$null	False
Object reference	True
Nonzero number	True
Zero	False
Nonempty string	True
Empty string	False
Nonempty array	True
Empty array	False
Empty associative array	True
Nonempty associative array	True

Assigning and Converting Data Types

You can directly assign values without declaring the data type because PowerShell has the built-in capability to automatically determine the data type. If you ever have a question about a variable's data type, you can display the data type using the following syntax:

```
VariableName.GetType()
```

where *VariableName* is the actual name of the variable as shown in the following example and sample output:

```
$myFirstNumber.GetType()
```

```
IsPublic IsSerial Name                                     BaseType
-------- -------- ----                                     --------
True     True     Int32                                    System.ValueType
```

Note that the base type is listed as System.ValueType, and the name is listed as Int32. Based on this output, you know the base type for the variable is a valid type in the System namespace and that the specific value type is Int32, meaning a 32-bit integer value.

Although the easiest way to declare a variable type is to use an alias, you also can declare variable types using the following:

- Fully qualified class names, such as [System.Array], [System.String], or [System.Diagnostics.Service]
- Class names under the System namespace, such as [Array], [String], or [Diagnostics.Service]

Be careful though: PowerShell throws an error if it cannot coerce the data into the specified data type. This is why you'll typically want to allow PowerShell to determine the data type for you. That way, you don't have to worry about PowerShell throwing errors if data cannot be coerced into a specified data type. However, after the data type is set, PowerShell tries to coerce any subsequent values you add to a variable to be of this type and throws an error if data types are mismatched. Consider the following example:

```
$myNumber = 52
$myNumber += "William"
```

Here, you create a variable and assign an integer value of 52. Next, you try to add a string value to the existing value using the increment operator (+=). This causes PowerShell to throw the following type mismatch error:

```
Cannot convert value "William" to type "System.Int32". Error: "Input
string was not in a correct format."
At line:1 char:13
+ $myNumber += <<<<  "William"
    + CategoryInfo          : NotSpecified: (:) [], RuntimeException
    + FullyQualifiedErrorId : RuntimeException
```

This error occurs because PowerShell cannot automatically convert the string value to a numeric value. However, in other cases, PowerShell silently converts value types for you. Consider the following example:

```
$myNumber = "William"
$myNumber += 52
```

Here, you create a variable and assign a string value. Next, you try to add the numeric value 52 to the existing string value using the increment operator (+=). This causes PowerShell to silently convert a numeric value to a string, and the result is that the value of $myNumber is then set to "William52".

When you create variables, you can specify the value type using any of the data type aliases listed previously in Table 5-1. These data type aliases are used in the same way whenever you declare a data type in PowerShell.

In the following example, you declare the data type as a 32-bit integer, specify the variable name as $myNumber, and assign a value of 10:

```
[int]$myNumber = 10
```

This creates a strongly typed variable and ensures that the variable can contain only the data of the type you declare. PowerShell throws an error if it cannot coerce the data to this type when you assign it. For more information about data types, see the "Object Types" section in Chapter 6, "Mastering Aliases, Functions, and Objects."

To explicitly assign a number as a long integer or decimal, you can use the suffixes L and D, respectively. Here are examples:

```
$myLongInt = 52432424L
$myDecimal = 2.2425D
```

Windows PowerShell also supports scientific notation. For example,

```
$mathPi = 3141592653e-9
```

sets the value for $mathPi as 3.141592653.

> ***TIP*** **In Windows PowerShell, you can reference the mathematical constants Pi and E via the static properties of the [System.Math] class. [System.Math]::Pi equals 3.14159265358979. [System.Math]::E equals 2.71828182845905.**

You can enter hexadecimal numbers using the 0x prefix, and PowerShell stores the hexadecimal number as an integer. If you enter the following statement

```
$ErrorCode = 0xAEB4
```

PowerShell converts the hexadecimal value AEB4 and then stores that value as 44724.

PowerShell does not natively support other number bases. However, you can use the [Convert] class in the .NET Framework to perform many types of data conversions. The [Convert] class supports the static conversion methods shown in Table 5-12.

TABLE 5-12 Commonly Used Static Methods of the [Convert] Class

STATIC METHOD	DESCRIPTION
ToBase64CharArray()	Converts the value to a base64 character array
ToBase64String()	Converts the value to a base64 string
ToBoolean()	Converts the value to a Boolean
ToByte()	Converts the value to an 8-bit unsigned integer
ToChar()	Converts the value to a Unicode 16-bit char
ToDateTime()	Converts the value to a datetime value
ToDecimal()	Converts the value to a decimal value
ToDouble()	Converts the value to a double-precision, 64-bit floating-point number
ToInt16()	Converts the value to a 16-bit integer
ToInt32()	Converts the value to a 32-bit integer
ToInt64()	Converts the value to a 64-bit integer
ToSByte()	Converts the value to an 8-bit signed integer
ToSingle()	Converts the value to a single-precision, 32-bit floating-point number
ToString()	Converts the value to a string
ToUInt16()	Converts the value to an unsigned 16-bit integer
ToUInt32()	Converts the value to an unsigned 32-bit integer
ToUInt64()	Converts the value to an unsigned 64-bit integer

You can use the [Convert] class methods to convert to and from binary, octal, decimal, and hexadecimal values. The following example converts the binary value to a 32-bit integer:

```
$myBinary = [Convert]::ToInt32("1011111011110001", 2)
```

The result is 48881. The following example converts an octal value to a 32-bit integer:

```
$myOctal = [Convert]::ToInt32("7452", 8)
```

The result is 3882. The following example converts a hexadecimal value to a 32-bit integer:

```
$myHex = [Convert]::ToInt32("FEA07E", 16)
```

The result is 16687230. You can just as easily convert an integer value to binary, octal, or hexadecimal. The following example takes the value 16687230 and converts it to a string containing a hexadecimal value:

```
$myString = [Convert]::ToString(16687230, 16)
```

The result is "FEA07E".

Although PowerShell can convert between some variable types, you might sometimes want to force PowerShell to use a variable value as a string rather than another data type. To do this, you can use the ToString() method to convert a variable value to a string. This works with Boolean, Byte, Char, and Datetime objects, as well as any of the numeric data types. It does not work with most other data types.

To convert a value to a string, just pass the value to the ToString() method as shown in this example and sample output:

```
$myNumber = 505
$myString = $myNumber.ToString()
$myString.GetType()
```

```
IsPublic IsSerial Name                                     BaseType
-------- -------- ----                                     --------
True     True     String                                   System.Object
```

In the [System.Datetime] and [System.Math] classes, you find other useful static methods and properties. Table 5-13 lists the class members you'll use most often.

TABLE 5-13 Commonly Used Static Members of the [DateTime] and [Math] Classes

CLASS/MEMBERS	DESCRIPTION	SYNTAX
[Datetime]		
Compare()	Compares two date objects. Returns 0 if they are equal and –1 otherwise.	[Datetime]::Compare(d1,d2)
DaysInMonth()	Returns the number of days in a given year and month.	[Datetime]::DaysInMonth(year, month)
Equals	Determines if two date objects are equal. Returns True if they are equal.	[Datetime]::Equals(d1,d2)
IsLeapYear	Returns True if the specified year is a leap year.	[Datetime]::IsLeapYear(year)
Now	Returns the current date and time.	[Datetime]::Now

TABLE 5-13 Commonly Used Static Members of the [DateTime] and [Math] Classes

CLASS/MEMBERS	DESCRIPTION	SYNTAX
Today	Returns the current date as of 12:00 A.M.	[Datetime]::Today
[MATH]		
Abs()	Returns the absolute value.	[Math]::Abs(value1)
Acos()	Returns the arccosine of the value.	[Math]::Acos(value1)
Asin()	Returns the arcsine of the value.	[Math]::Asin(value1)
Atan()	Returns the arctangent of the value.	[Math]::Atan(value1)
Atan2()	Returns the inverse arccosine of the value.	[Math]::Atan2(value1)
BigMul()	Returns the multiple as a 64-bit integer.	[Math]::BigMul(val1,val2)
Ceiling()	Returns the mathematical ceiling of the value.	[Math]::Ceiling(val1)
Cos()	Returns the cosine of the value.	[Math]::Cos(val1)
Cosh()	Returns the inverse cosine of the value.	[Math]::Cosh(val1)
DivRem()	Returns the dividend remainder for value1 / value2.	[Math]::DivRem(val1,val2)
Equals()	Evaluates whether object1 equals object2.	[Math]::Equals(obj1,obj2)
Exp()	Returns the exponent.	[Math]::Exp(value1)
Floor()	Returns the mathematical floor of the value.	[Math]::Floor(val1)
Log()	Returns the Log of the value.	[Math]::Log(value1)
Log10()	Returns the Log10 of the value.	[Math]::Log10(value1)
Max()	Returns the larger of two values.	[Math]::Max(val1,val2)

TABLE 5-13 Commonly Used Static Members of the [DateTime] and [Math] Classes

CLASS/MEMBERS	DESCRIPTION	SYNTAX
Min()	Returns the smaller of two values.	[Math]::Min(val1,val2)
Pow()	Returns the value to the power of the exponent.	[Math]::Pow(val1,val2)
Round()	Returns the rounded value.	[Math]::Round(val1)
Sign()	Returns a signed 16-bit integer value.	[Math]::Sign(val1)
Sin()	Returns the sine of the value.	[Math]::Sin(value1)
Sinh()	Returns the inverse sine of the value.	[Math]::Sinh(value1)
Sqrt()	Returns the square root of the value.	[Math]::Sqrt(value1)
Tan()	Returns the tangent of the value.	[Math]::Tan(value1)
Tanh()	Returns the inverse tangent of the value.	[Math]::Tanh(value1)
Truncate()	Truncates the decimal value.	[Math]::Truncate(value1)
E	Returns the mathematical constant E.	[Math]::E
Pi	Returns the mathematical constant Pi.	[Math]::Pi

Table 5-14 provides an overview of the instance methods and properties of the String object. You'll use the String object often when working with values in PowerShell.

TABLE 5-14 Commonly Used Instance Methods and Properties of String Objects

INSTANCE MEMBER	DESCRIPTION	EXAMPLE
Length	Returns the character length of the string.	$s.Length
Contains()	Returns True if string2 is contained within string1.	$s.Contains("string2")
EndsWith()	Returns True if string1 ends with string2.	$s.EndsWith("string2")

TABLE 5-14 Commonly Used Instance Methods and Properties of String Objects

INSTANCE MEMBER	DESCRIPTION	EXAMPLE
Insert()	Inserts string2 into string1 at the specified character position.	$s.Insert(0,"string2") $s.Insert($s.Length,"string2")
Remove()	Removes characters from string1 based on a starting position and length. If no length is provided, all characters after the starting position are removed.	$s.Remove(5,3) $s.Remove(5)
Replace()	Replaces occurrences of substr1 in the string with the substr2 value.	$s.Replace("this","that")
StartsWith()	Returns True if string1 starts with string2.	$s.StartsWith("string2")
SubString()	Gets a substring from string1 based on a starting position and length. If no length is provided, all characters after the starting position are returned.	$s.Substring(3,5) $s.Substring(3)
ToLower()	Converts the string to lowercase letters.	$s.ToLower()
ToString()	Converts an object to a string.	$s.ToString()
ToUpper()	Converts the string to uppercase letters.	$s.ToUpper()

Managing Variable Scopes

The scope of a variable determines its logical boundaries. You can set variable scope as global, local, script, or private. The scopes exist in a logical hierarchy in which scope information is accessible downward in this order:

global > script/local > private

Following this, you can see that the local and script scopes can read information from the global scope, but the global scope cannot read a local or script scope. Further, private scopes can read information from higher-level scopes, but other scopes cannot read the contents of a private scope.

REAL WORLD Scope applies to aliases, functions, and PowerShell drives as well as to variables. You can think of the global scope as the parent or root scope and script/local scripts as child scopes of the global scope. Child scopes can always read information from parent scopes. Technically speaking, variables, aliases, and functions in a parent scope are not part of the child scope. A child scope does not inherit the variables, aliases, or functions from the parent scope. However, a child scope can view the variables, aliases, or functions from the parent scope, and it can change these items in the parent scope by explicitly specifying the parent scope.

The default scope for a script is a script scope that exists only for that script. The default scope for a function is a local scope that exists only for that function, even if the function is defined in a script.

Regardless of whether you are working with variables, aliases, functions, or PowerShell drives, scopes work the same. An item you include in a scope is visible in the scope in which it was created and any child scopes, unless you explicitly make it private. An item in a particular scope can be changed only in that scope, unless you explicitly specify a different scope. If you create an item in a child scope and that item already exists in another scope, the original item is not accessible in the child scope, but it is not overridden or changed in the original (parent) scope.

You can create a new scope by running a script or function, by defining a script block, by creating a local or remote session, or by starting a new instance of PowerShell. When you create a new scope through a script, function, script block, or nesting of instances, the scope is a child scope of the original (parent) scope. However, when you create a new session, the session is not a child scope of the original scope. The session starts with its own global scope, and that global scope is independent from the original scope.

You can explicitly or implicitly set the scope of a variable. You explicitly set scope by adding the Global, Local, Script, or Private keyword prefix to the variable name. The following example creates a global variable:

```
$Global:myVar = 55
```

You implicitly set scope whenever you define a variable at the prompt, in a script, or in a function. A variable with an implicit scope resides in the scope in which it is defined.

The default scope is the current scope and is determined as follows:

- Global when defined interactively at the PowerShell prompt
- Script when defined outside functions or script blocks in a script
- Local within functions, script blocks, or anywhere else

The global scope applies to an entire PowerShell instance. Because data defined in the global scope is inherited by all child scopes, this means any commands, functions, or scripts that you run can make use of variables defined in the global scope.

Global scopes are not shared across instances of PowerShell. With regard to the PowerShell console, this means the variables you define in one console are not available in another console (unless you define them in that console session). With regard to the PowerShell application, this means variables you define in one tab are not available in another tab (unless you define them in that tab session).

Local scopes are created automatically each time a function, script, or filter runs. A local scope can read information from the global scope, but it can make changes to global information only by explicitly declaring the scope. After a function, script, or filter has finished running, the information in the related local scope is discarded.

To learn more about scopes, consider the following example and sample output:

```
function numservices {$serv = get-service}
numservices
write-host "The number of services is: `t" $serv.count
```

```
The number of services is:
```

Here, $serv is created as a variable inside the numservices function. As a result, when you run the function, a local variable instance is created. When you then try to access the $s variable in the global scope, the variable has no value. In contrast, if you explicitly declare the variable as global, you can access the variable in the global scope as shown in the following example and sample output:

```
function numservices {$Global:serv = get-service}
numservices
write-host "The number of services is: `t" $serv.count
```

```
The number of services is:        157
```

Script scopes are created whenever a script runs. Only commands in a script run in the script scope; to these commands, the script scope is the local scope. As functions in a script run in their own local scope, any variables set in a script function are not accessible to the script itself. To remedy this, you can set the scope of variables defined in a script function explicitly as shown in this example:

```
function numservices {$Script:serv1 = get-service}
numservices
write-host "The number of services is: `t" $serv1.count
```

Normally, when a function or script finishes running, the related scope and all related information is discarded. However, you can use dot sourcing to tell PowerShell to load a function's or script's scope into the calling parent's scope rather than creating a new local scope for the function or script. To do this, simply prefix the function or script name with a period (.) when running the function or script, as shown in this example:

```
. c:\scripts\runtasks.ps1
```

The final scope type you can use is the private scope. You must create privately scoped items explicitly. Because any information in a private scope is not available to any other scopes, including child scopes, a privately scoped variable is available only in the scope in which it is created. The following example and sample output shows this:

```
function numservices {$Private:serv = get-service

write-host "The number of services is: `t" $serv.count

 &{write-host "Again, the number of services is: `t" $serv.count}

}
numservices
```

```
The number of services is:        157
Again, the number of services is:
```

Here, you create a function with a private variable and then define a script block within the function. Within the function, you have access to the private variable, and this is why you can write the number of services when you call the function. Because the script block automatically runs in its own local scope, you cannot access the private variable in the script block. This is why you cannot write the number of services from within the script block when you call the function.

Automatic, Preference, and Environment Variables

In addition to user-created variables, PowerShell supports automatic, preference, and environment variables. Automatic variables are fixed and used to store state information. Preference variables are changeable and used to store working values for PowerShell configuration settings. Environment variables store the working environment for the current user and the operating system.

Table 5-15 lists the common automatic variables in PowerShell. You'll use many of these variables when you are working with PowerShell, especially $_, $Args, $Error, $Input, and $MyInvocation.

TABLE 5-15 Common Automatic Variables in Windows PowerShell

AUTOMATIC VARIABLE	DESCRIPTION
$$	Stores the last token in the last line received by the PowerShell session.
$?	Stores the execution status of the last operation as TRUE if the last operation succeeded or as FALSE if it failed.
$^	Stores the first token in the last line received by the session.

TABLE 5-15 Common Automatic Variables in Windows PowerShell

AUTOMATIC VARIABLE	DESCRIPTION
$_	Stores the current object in the pipeline object set. Use this variable in commands that perform an action on every object or on selected objects in a pipeline.
$Args	Stores an array of the undeclared parameters, parameter values, or both that are passed to a function, script, or script block.
$ConsoleFileName	Stores the path of the console file (.psc1) that was most recently used in the session.
$Error	Stores an array of error objects that represent the most recent errors. $Error[0] references the most recent error in the array.
$ExecutionContext	Stores an EngineIntrinsics object that represents the execution context of the Windows PowerShell host.
$False	Stores FALSE. It can be used instead of the string "false".
$ForEach	Stores the enumerator of a ForEach-Object loop.
$Home	Stores the full path of the user's home directory.
$Host	Stores an object that represents the current host application.
$Input	Stores the input that is passed to a function or script block. The $Input variable is case sensitive. When the Process block is completed, the value of $Input is NULL. If the function does not have a Process block, the value of $Input is available to the End block, and it stores all the input to the function.
$LastExitCode	Stores the exit code of the last Windows-based program that was run.
$Matches	Stores a hash table of any string values that were matched when you use the –Match operator.
$MyInvocation	Stores an object with information about the current command, including the run path and file name for scripts.
$NestedPromptLevel	Stores the current prompt level. A value of 0 (zero) indicates the original prompt level. The value is incremented when you enter a nested level and decremented when you exit nested levels.

TABLE 5-15 Common Automatic Variables in Windows PowerShell

AUTOMATIC VARIABLE	DESCRIPTION
$NULL	Stores a NULL or empty value. It can be used instead of the string "NULL".
$PID	Stores the process identifier (PID) of the process that is hosting the current Windows PowerShell session.
$Profile	Stores the full path of the Windows PowerShell profile for the current user and the current host application.
$PSBoundParameters	Stores a hash table of the active parameters and their current values.
$PsCulture	Stores the name of the culture setting currently in use in the operating system.
$PSDebugContext	Stores information about the debugging environment (if applicable). Otherwise, it stores a NULL value.
$PsHome	Stores the full path of the installation directory for Windows PowerShell.
$PsUICulture	Stores the name of the user interface (UI) culture that is currently in use in the operating system.
$PsVersionTable	Stores a read-only hash table with the following items: PSVersion (the Windows PowerShell version number), BuildVersion (the build number of the current version), CLRVersion (the version of the common language runtime), and PSCompatibleVersions (versions of Windows PowerShell that are compatible with the current version).
$Pwd	Stores a path object representing the full path of the current working directory.
$ShellID	Stores the identifier of the current shell.
$This	Defines a script property or script method within a script block. Refers to the object that is being extended.
$True	Stores TRUE. It can be used instead of the string "true".

You use $_ with the Where-Object cmdlet to perform an action on every object or on selected objects in a pipeline. The basic syntax is

```
where-object {$_.PropertyName -ComparisonOp "Value"}
```

where *PropertyName* is the name of the object property to examine, *–ComparisonOp* specifies the type of comparison to perform, and *Value* sets the value to compare—for example:

```
get-process | where-object {$_.Name -match "svchost"}
```

Here, you use $_ to examine the Name property of each object passed in the pipeline. If the Name property is set to "svchost", you pass the related object along the pipeline.

You can extend this example using a regular expression, such as:

```
get-process | where-object {$_.Name -match "^s.*"}
```

Here, you examine the Name property of each object passed in the pipeline. If the Name property begins with the letter S, you pass the related object along the pipeline. You can just as easily use any other comparison operator listed previously in Table 5-4, such as –eq, –ne, –gt, –lt, –le, –ge, –contains, –notcontains, –like, or –notlike.

Another useful automatic variable is $Error. You use $Error to list all error objects for the current session and $Error[0] to access the most recent error object. Simply type **$Error** or **$Error[0]**. Because errors are represented in objects, you can format the properties of error objects as you would any other output, such as

```
$error[0] | format-list -property * -force
```

Error objects have the following properties:

- **CategoryInfo** Indicates the category under which an error is classified, such as InvalidArgument or PSArgumentException
- **Exception** Provides detailed information about the error that occurred
- **FullyQualifiedErrorId** Identifies the exact error that occurred, such as Argument
- **InvocationInfo** Provides detailed information about the command that caused an error
- **PipelineIterationInfo** Provides detailed information about the pipeline iteration
- **PSMessageDetails** Provides PowerShell message details, if applicable
- **TargetObject** Indicates the object being operated on

You can access any of these properties via a specified error object. To list detailed information about the command that caused the last error, you can use the InvocationInfo property as shown in the following example and sample output:

```
$currError = $error[0]
$currError.InvocationInfo
```

```
MyCommand           : Sort-Object
BoundParameters     : {}
UnboundArguments    : {}
ScriptLineNumber    : 1
OffsetInLine        : 25
ScriptName          :
Line                : $p | sort-object -status
PositionMessage     :
                      At line:1 char:25
                      + $p | sort-object -status <<<<
InvocationName      : sort-object
PipelineLength      : 0
PipelinePosition    : 0
ExpectingInput      : False
CommandOrigin       : Internal
```

You can clear all the errors in the current sessions by entering the following command:

```
$error.clear()
```

Another handy automatic variable is $Args. You can access command-line arguments using the array stored in this variable—for example:

```
$argCount = $args.Count
$firstArg = $args[0]
$secondArg = $args[1]
$lastArg = $args[$args.Count -1]
```

Here, you determine the number of arguments passed in the command line using $args.Count. You get the first argument using $args[0], the second argument using $args[1], and the last argument using $args[$args.Count -1].

Data being passed to a function or script block via the pipeline is stored in the $Input variable. This variable is a .NET Framework enumerator. With enumerators, you can access the input stream but not an arbitrary element as you can with an array. After you process the input stream, you must call the Reset() method on the $Input enumerator before you can process the elements again. One way to access the input stream is in a For Each loop, such as

```
foreach($element in $input) { "The input was: `t $element" }
```

Or you can store the input element in an array, such as

```
$iArray = @($input)
```

You can access information about the context under which you are running a script using $MyInvocation. In a script, you can access detailed information about the current command through $MyInvocation.MyCommand. To access the path and file name of the script, use $MyInvocation.MyCommand.Path. Use $MyInvocation.MyCommand.Name to identify the name of a function. Use $MyInvocation.ScriptName to display the name of the script.

Table 5-16 provides a summary of the common preference variables. As you use these variables to customize how PowerShell works, you should familiarize yourself with them. Some of these variables were discussed previously in the "Writing to Output Streams" section in Chapter 2, "Getting the Most from Windows PowerShell."

TABLE 5-16 Common Preference Variables in Windows PowerShell

PREFERENCE VARIABLE	DESCRIPTION	DEFAULT
$ConfirmPreference	Controls whether cmdlet actions request confirmation from the user before they are performed. Acceptable values are **High** (actions with a high risk are confirmed), **Medium** (actions with a medium or high risk are confirmed), **Low** (actions with a low, medium, or high risk are confirmed), or **None** (no actions are confirmed; use the –Confirm parameter to request confirmation).	High
$DebugPreference	Controls how PowerShell responds to debugging messages.	Silently Continue
$ErrorAction Preference	Controls how PowerShell responds to an error that does not stop the cmdlet processing.	Continue
$ErrorView	Controls the display format of error messages in PowerShell. Acceptable values are **NormalView** (the detailed normal view) or **CategoryView** (a streamlined view).	Normal View
$FormatEnumeration-Limit	Controls how many enumerated items are included in a grouped display. Acceptable values are **Integers**.	4
$LogCommand HealthEvent	Controls whether errors and exceptions in command initialization and processing are written to the PowerShell event log. Acceptable values are **$true** (logged) or **$false** (not logged).	$false

TABLE 5-16 Common Preference Variables in Windows PowerShell

PREFERENCE VARIABLE	DESCRIPTION	DEFAULT
$LogCommand LifecycleEvent	Controls whether PowerShell logs the starting and stopping of commands and command pipelines and security exceptions in command discovery. Acceptable values are **$true** (logged) or **$false** (not logged).	$false
$LogEngine HealthEvent	Controls whether PowerShell logs errors and failures of sessions. Acceptable values are **$true** (logged) or **$false** (not logged).	$true
$LogEngine LifecycleEvent	Controls whether PowerShell logs the opening and closing of sessions. Acceptable values are **$true** (logged) or **$false** (not logged).	$true
$LogProvider HealthEvent	Controls whether PowerShell logs provider errors, such as read and write errors, lookup errors, and invocation errors. Acceptable values are **$true** (logged) or **$false** (not logged).	$true
$LogProvider LifecycleEvent	Controls whether PowerShell logs adding and removing of PowerShell providers. Acceptable values are **$true** (logged) or **$false** (not logged).	$true
$MaximumAlias Count	Specifies how many aliases are permitted in a PowerShell session. Valid values are **1024–32768**. Count aliases using (get-alias).count.	4096
$MaximumDrive Count	Specifies how many PowerShell drives are permitted in a session. This includes file system drives and data stores that are exposed by providers and appear as drives. Valid values are **1024–32768**. Count drives using (get-psdrive).count.	4096
$MaximumError Count	Specifies how many errors are saved in the error history for the session. Valid values are **256–32768**. Objects that represent each retained error are stored in the $Error automatic variable. Count errors using $Error.count.	256

TABLE 5-16 Common Preference Variables in Windows PowerShell

PREFERENCE VARIABLE	DESCRIPTION	DEFAULT
$MaximumFunction Count	Specifies how many functions are permitted in a given session. Valid values are **1024–32768**. Count functions using (get-childitem function:).count.	4096
$MaximumHistory Count	Specifies how many commands are saved in the command history for the current session. Valid values are **1–32768**. Count commands saved using (get-history).count.	64
$MaximumVariable Count	Specifies how many variables are permitted in a given session, including automatic variables, preference variables, and user-created variables. Valid values are **1024–32768**. Count variables using (get-variable).count.	4096
$OFS	Sets the Output Field Separator. This determines the character that separates the elements of an array when the array is converted to a string. Valid values are **Any string**, such as "+" instead of " ".	" "
$OutputEncoding	Sets the character encoding method used by PowerShell when it sends text to other applications. Valid values are **ASCII-Encoding**, **SBCSCodePageEncoding**, **UTF7Encoding**, **UTF8Encoding**, **UTF32Encoding**, and **UnicodeEncoding**.	ASCII Encoding
$ProgressPreference	Specifies how PowerShell responds to progress updates generated by Write-Progress. Valid values are **Stop** (displays an error and stops executing), **Inquire** (prompts for permission to continue), **Continue** (displays the progress bar and continues), and **SilentlyContinue** (executes the command but does not display the progress bar).	Continue
$PSMaximumReceived ObjectSizeMB	Limits the size of any single object that a command returns. Apply only to commands that use PowerShell remoting.	10 MB for remote, no limit local

TABLE 5-16 Common Preference Variables in Windows PowerShell

PREFERENCE VARIABLE	DESCRIPTION	DEFAULT
$PSMaximumReceivedDataSizePer-CommandMB	Limits the size of the data set that any single command returns. Apply only to commands that use PowerShell remoting.	50 MB for remote, no limit local
$PSSessionApplicationName	Specifies the default application that is used when you identify a remote computer by an HTTP endpoint. Internet Information Services (IIS) forwards requests to WSMAN by default.	WSMAN
$PSSessionConfigurationName	Specifies the default session configuration for remote sessions. The value must be a name that appears in the WinRM custom remote session table and that is associated with the executable file that runs the session and a URI for the session resource.	Microsoft.PowerShell
$VerbosePreference	Controls how PowerShell responds to verbose messages.	SilentlyContinue
$WarningPreference	Controls how PowerShell responds to warning messages.	Continue
$WhatIfPreference	Specifies whether the –WhatIf parameter is automatically enabled for every command that supports it. When –WhatIf is enabled, the cmdlet reports the expected effect of the command, but it does not execute the command. Valid values are **0** (disabled) and **1** (enabled).	0
$WsmanMaxRedirectionCount	Controls how many times PowerShell redirects a connection to an alternate URI before the connection fails. A value of 0 prevents redirection.	5

You can view the value of automatic and preference variables simply by typing their name at the PowerShell prompt. For example, to see the current value of the $pshome variable, type **$pshome** at the PowerShell prompt. Although you cannot change the value of automatic variables, you can change the value of preference variables. To do so, you use the basic assignment syntax as with user-created variables. For example, if you want to set $WarningPreference to SilentlyContinue, you can do this by typing the following command:

```
$warningpreference = "silentlycontinue"
```

With environment variables, you must work within the context of the environment provider. One way to do this is to reference the $env: provider drive and then reference the name of the variable, such as

```
$env:logonserver
```

You also can get or set the location with respect to the env: provider drive. For example, if you set the location to the env: provider drive as shown in this example

```
set-location env:
```

the PowerShell prompt changes to

```
PS Env:\>
```

You can then work with any or all environment variables. To list all environment variables you type the following command:

```
get-childitem
```

To list a particular environment variable, you use Get-ChildItem and type the variable name or part of the variable name with wildcards, such as

```
get-childitem userdomain
get-childitem user*
```

When you are finished working with the environment provider, you can return to the file system drive you were using by typing **set-location** and the drive designator, such as

```
set-location c:
```

Another way to work with the environment provider is to use the Get-Item cmdlet to examine its path values. If you do this, you don't need to switch to the environment provider drive. For example, regardless of which provider drive you are working with, you can type the following command to list all environment variables:

```
get-item -path env:*
```

You also can get an environment variable by name:

```
get-item -path env:username
```

Or you can get it by using a wildcard:

```
get-item -path env:user*
```

You can change environment variables using the Set-Item cmdlet. The basic syntax is

```
set-item -path env:VariableName -value NewValue
```

where *VariableName* is the name of the environment variable you want to change, and *NewValue* sets the desired value, such as

```
set-item -path env:homedrive -value D:
```

You also can change the value of an environment variable using simple assignment, such as

```
$env:homedrive = D:
```

When you change environment variables using either technique, the change is made only for the current session. To permanently change environment variables, you can use the Setx command-line utility.

Working with Strings

Although we've used strings in some previous examples, we haven't really talked about what exactly a string is and isn't. A string is a series of alphanumeric or non-alphanumeric characters. PowerShell has several parsing rules for strings, and these rules modify the way values are handled. You need a good understanding of how strings are parsed to be successful with PowerShell, whether you enter commands at the PowerShell prompt or use PowerShell scripts.

Single-Quoted and Double-Quoted Strings

You use quotation marks to denote the beginning and ending of literal string expressions. You can enclose strings in single quotation marks (' ') or double quotation marks (" "). However, PowerShell parses values within single-quoted strings and double-quoted strings differently.

When you enclose a string in single-quotation marks, the string is passed to the command exactly as you type it. No substitution is performed. Consider the following example and output:

```
$varA = 200
Write-Host 'The value of $varA is $varA.'
```

The output of this command is

```
The value $varA is $varA.
```

Similarly, expressions in single-quoted strings are not evaluated. They are interpreted as literals—for example:

```
'The value of $(2+3) is 5.'
```

The output of this command is

```
The value of $(2+3) is 5.
```

When you enclose a string in double quotation marks, variable names that are preceded by a dollar sign ($) are replaced with the variable's value before the string is passed to the command for processing. Consider the following example:

```
$varA = 200
Write-Host "The value of $varA is $varA."
```

The output of this command is

```
The value 200 is 200.
```

To prevent the substitution of a variable value in a double-quoted string, use the back apostrophe character (`), which serves as the escape character as well as the line-continuation character. Consider following example:

```
$varA = 200
Write-Host "The value of `$varA is $varA."
```

Here, the back apostrophe character that precedes the first variable reference prevents Windows PowerShell from replacing the variable name with its value. This means the output is

```
The value $varA is 200.
```

Additionally, in a double-quoted string, expressions are evaluated, and the result is inserted in the string. Consider the following example:

```
"The value of $(100+100) is 200."
```

The output of this command is

```
The value of 200 is 200.
```

You can make double quotation marks appear in a string by enclosing the entire string in single quotation marks or by using double quotation marks, such as

```
'He said, "Hello, Bob"'
```

or

```
"He said, ""Hello, Bob"""
```

You can include a single quotation mark in a single-quoted string as well. Simply use a second single quote, such as

```
'He won''t go to the store.'
```

Finally, you can use the back apostrophe (`) character to force PowerShell to interpret a single quotation mark or a double quotation mark literally, such as

```
"You use a double quotation mark (`") with expandable strings."
```

Escape Codes and Wildcards

In several previous examples, we used the back apostrophe (`) as an escape character to force PowerShell to interpret a single quotation mark, a double quotation mark, or a variable literally. When an escape character precedes a single or double quotation mark, Windows PowerShell interprets the single or double quotation mark as a literal character, not as a string delimiter. When an escape character precedes a variable, it prevents a value from being substituted for the variable.

Within a string, the escape character also can indicate a special character. PowerShell recognizes the special characters listed in Table 5-17. To see how you can use a tab character in a string, review the following example and sample output:

```
$s = "Please specify the computer name `t []"
$c = read-host $s
write-host "You entered: `t $c"
```

```
Please specify the computer name        []: corpserver45
You entered:         corpserver45
```

Here, you create a string with a tab character. You then use the Read-Host cmdlet to display the string while waiting for input from the user. You store the input from the user in a variable for later user, and then you use the Write-Host cmdlet to display a string with a tab character and the value the user entered.

TABLE 5-17 Escape Codes in Windows PowerShell

ESCAPE CODE	MEANING
`'	Single quotation mark
`"	Double quotation mark

TABLE 5-17 Escape Codes in Windows PowerShell

ESCAPE CODE	MEANING
`0	Null character
`a	Alert (sends a bell or beep signal to the computer speaker)
`b	Backspace
`f	Form feed (used with printer output)
`n	New line
`r	Carriage return
`t	Horizontal tab (eight spaces)
`v	Vertical tab (used with printer output)

Often when you are working with strings, you might need to match part of a string to get a desired result. To do this, you use the wildcards listed previously in Table 5-5. When you work with character ranges and subsets, keep in mind the characters can be in these ranges:

- [a to z] or [A to Z] for alphabetic characters
- [0-9] for numeric characters

Generally, PowerShell matches characters whether they are uppercase or lowercase. Because of this, in most instances, these ranges are interpreted the same whether you use uppercase or lowercase letters—for example:

- [a-c] and [A-C] are the same.
- [abc] and [ABC] are the same.

However, when you get into regular expressions, there are times when PowerShell performs case-sensitive matches. As you've seen in past examples, wildcards are useful when you want to perform pattern matching within strings, especially when you are passing string values to cmdlet parameters. Although some cmdlet parameters support wildcards being passed in values, not all do, and you'll want to confirm whether a parameter supports wildcards using the –Full help details. For example, if you type **get-help get-alias –full**, you see the full help details for the Get-Alias cmdlet as shown partially in this example:

```
NAME
    Get-Alias

SYNOPSIS
    Gets the aliases for the current session.

SYNTAX
    Get-Alias [-Exclude <string[]>] [-Name <string[]>] [-Scope <string>]
[<CommonParameters>]
```

```
DETAILED DESCRIPTION
    The Get-Alias cmdlet gets the aliases (alternate names for commands
and executable files) in the current session.

PARAMETERS
    -Definition <string[]>
        Gets the aliases for the specified item. Enter the name of a
cmdlet, function, script, file, or executable file.

        Required?                    false
        Position?                    named
        Default value
        Accept pipeline input?       false
        Accept wildcard characters?  true
```

Here, you know the –Definition parameter accepts wildcards being passed in values because Accept WildCard Characters is set to True. If the parameter does not accept wildcards, Accept WildCard Characters is set to False.

Multiline Strings

When you want a string to have multiple lines, precede and follow the string value with @. This type of string is referred to as a *here-string*, and the same rules for single quotes and double quotes apply. Consider the following example and sample output:

```
$myString = @"
=========================
$env:computername
=========================
"@
write-host $myString
```

```
=========================
EngPC85
=========================
```

Data strings are another type of multiline string. PowerShell supports data strings primarily for script internationalization because data strings make it easier to separate data and code by isolating strings that might be translated into other languages. There's no reason, however, that you can't use data strings for other purposes, and they are much more versatile than other types of strings. Primarily, this is because data strings are referenced with a variable name and can include programming logic.

The basic syntax for a data string is

```
DATA StringName {
   StringText
}
```

where *StringName* sets the name for the data string as a variable, and *StringText* can include the following: one or more single-quoted strings, double-quoted strings, here-strings, or any combination thereof. Note that the DATA keyword is not case sensitive, meaning you can use DATA, data, or even Data to denote the beginning of the data string.

The following example declares a data string named MyValues:

```
DATA MyValues {
  "This is a data string."
  "You can use data strings in many different ways."
}
```

You use or reference the MyValues string by its name. To display the data string's contents at the prompt, type the following command:

```
Write-Host $MyValues
```

You can also type

```
$MyValues
```

The extended syntax for data strings is

```
DATA StringName [-supportedCommand CmdletNames] {
PermittedContent
}
```

Here, *CmdletName* provides a comma-separated list of cmdlets that you use in the data string, and *PermittedContent* includes any of the following elements:

- Strings and string literals
- Any PowerShell operators, except –match
- If, Else, and ElseIf statements
- Certain automatic variables, including $PsCulture, $PsUICulture, $True, $False, and $Null
- Statements separated by semicolons, comments, and pipelines

Adding cmdlets and programming elements to data strings makes them work much like functions, and in many cases you'll find it easier to simply use a function than to treat a data string like a function. For more information on functions, see the "Creating and Using Functions" section in Chapter 6, "Mastering Aliases, Functions, and Objects."

Strings that contain prohibited elements, such as variables or subexpressions, must be enclosed in single-quoted strings or here-strings so that the variables are not expanded and subexpressions are not executable. The only cmdlet you don't have to declare as supported is ConvertFrom-StringData. The ConvertFrom-StringData cmdlet converts strings that contain one or more "name=value" pairs into associative arrays. Because each "name=value" pair must be on a separate line, you typically use here-strings as the input format. However, PowerShell allows you to use single-quoted or double-quoted strings or here-strings.

The following example shows how the ConvertFrom-StringData cmdlet can be used with data strings:

```
DATA DisplayNotes {
   ConvertFrom-StringData -stringdata @'
   Note1 = This appears to be the wrong syntax.
   Note2 = There is a value missing.
   Note3 = Cannot connect at this time.
   '@
}
```

In this example, you create a data string called DisplayNotes and use ConvertFrom-StringData to create a related associative array with three separate strings: Note1, Note2, and Note3. You are then able to reference the strings using dot notation. To display the first string, you use $DisplayNotes.Note1; for the second string, you use $DisplayNotes.Note2; and for the third string, you use $DisplayNotes.Note3. To display all the notes, you simply type **$DisplayNotes**.

With a here-string, you can use a similar technique to create an array of strings—for example:

```
$string = @'
   Note1 = This appears to be the wrong syntax.
   Note2 = There is a value missing.
   Note3 = Cannot connect at this time.
   '@

$strArray = $string | convertfrom-stringdata
```

The here-string defined in this example contains the same strings as the previous example. You then use a pipeline operator (|) to send the value of the here-string to ConvertFrom-StringData. The command saves the result in the $strArray variable, and you can use the same techniques discussed previously to access the strings.

String Operators

As you learned in "Comparison Operators" earlier in the chapter, you can use many operators with strings and arrays. These include –eq, –ne, –lt, –gt, –le, –ge, –like, –notlike, –match, –notmatch, –contains, –notcontains, and –replace.

You also can use the following special operators with strings:

- = Assigns a string value to a variable
- + Concatenates strings by adding them together
- * Repeats a string some number of times

- **–Join** Joins strings by adding them together with or without delimiters
- **–Split** Splits a string on spaces or a specified delimiter
- **–f** Formats a string using the extended formatting syntax

The most common string operations you'll want to perform are assignment and concatenation. As you've seen in previous examples, you assign values to strings using the equal sign, such as

```
$myString = "This is a String."
```

Concatenation is the technical term for adding strings together. The normal operator for string concatenation is the + operator. Using the + operator, you can add strings together as follows:

```
$streetAdd = "123 Main St."
$cityState = "Anywhere, NY"
$zipCode = "12345"
$custAddress = $streetAdd + " " + $cityState + " " + $zipCode
$custAddress
```

```
123 Main St. Anywhere, NY 12345
```

Sometimes you might also want to add a string stored in a variable to output you are displaying. You can do this simply by referencing the variable containing the string as part of the double-quoted output string as shown here:

```
$company = "XYZ Company"
Write-Host "The company is: $company"
```

```
The company is: XYZ Company
```

Concatenation of arrays works much like concatenation of strings. Using the + operator, you can add arrays together as shown in this example:

```
$array1 = "PC85", "PC25", "PC92"
$array2 = "SERVER41", "SERVER32", "SERVER87"
$joinedArray = $array1 + $array2
$joinedArray
```

```
PC85
PC25
PC92
SERVER41
SERVER32
SERVER87
```

Multiplication of strings and arrays can be handy when you want to repeat the character in a string or the values in an array a specified number of times. For example, if you have a string with the + character stored in it, you might want to make an 80-character string of + characters act as a dividing line in output. You can do this as shown in the following example and sample output:

```
$separator = "+"
$sepLine = $separator * 60
$sepLine
```

```
++++++++++++++++++++++++++++++++++++++++++++++++++++++++++++
```

You use the –Join and –Split operators to join and split strings, respectively. The basic syntaxes for joining strings are

```
-Join (String1, String2, String3 …)

String1, String2, String3 … -Join "Delimiter"
```

The first syntax simply joins a collection of strings together. The second syntax joins a collection of strings while specifying a delimiter to use between them. To see how you can join strings without delimiters, consider the following example and sample output:

```
$a =  -join ("abc", "def", "ghi")
$a
```

```
abcdefghi
```

To see how you can join strings with delimiters, consider the following example and sample output:

```
$a = "abc", "def", "ghi" -join ":"
$a
```

```
abc:def:ghi
```

The basic syntaxes for splitting strings are

```
-Split String

String -Split "Delimiter" [,MaxSubStrings]
```

With the first syntax, you can split a string using the spaces between words as delimiters. To see how, consider the following example and sample output:

```
$a = "abc def ghi"
-Split $a
```

```
abc
def
ghi
```

You also can split strings based on a delimiter as shown in this example:

```
$a = "jkl:mno:pqr"
$a -Split ":"
```

```
jkl
mno
pqr
```

You use the –f operator to format a string using the extended formatting syntax. With this syntax, you specify exactly how you want to format a series of numeric, alphabetic, or alphanumeric values.

The basic structure is to specify the desired formatting on the left of the –f operator and the values to format in a comma-separated list on the right, as shown in this example:

```
'FormatingInstructions' -f "Value1", "Value2", "Value3", …
```

In the formatting instructions, {0} represents the first value, {1} the second value, and so on. Knowing this, you can use the formatting instructions to modify the order of values, convert values to different formats, or both. In the following example and sample output, you reverse the order of the values in the output:

```
'{2} {1} {0}' -f "Monday", "Tuesday", "Wednesday"
```

```
Wednesday Tuesday Monday
```

You are not limited to forward or reverse order. You control the output order and can specify any desired order, such as

```
'{2} {0} {1}' -f "Cloudy", "Sunny", "Rainy"
```

```
Rainy Cloudy Sunny
```

The number of formatting instructions must exactly match the number of values to format. Otherwise, values will be omitted, which is fine if this is your intention. In the following example, you omit the second value:

```
'{0} {2}' -f "Server15", "Server16", "Server17"
```

```
Server15 Server17
```

To each individual formatting instruction, you can add one of the conversion indicators listed in Table 5-18.

TABLE 5-18 Conversion Indicators for Formatting

FORMAT SPECIFIER	DESCRIPTION	EXAMPLE	OUTPUT
:c or :C	Converts a numeric format to currency format (based on the computer's locale).	'{0:c}' –f 145.50	$145.50
:e or :E	Converts to scientific (exponential) notation. Add a numeric value to specify precision (the number of digits past the decimal point).	'{0:e4}' –f [Math]::Pi	3.1416e+000
:f or :F	Converts to fixed-point notation. Add a numeric value to specify precision (the number of digits past the decimal point).	'{0:f4}' –f [Math]::Pi	3.1426
:g or :G	Converts to the most compact notation, either fixed-point or scientific notation. Add a numeric value to specify the number of significant digits.	'{0:g3}' –f [Math]::Pi	3.14
:n or :N	Converts to a number with culture-specific separators between number groups. Add a numeric value to specify precision (the number of digits past the decimal point).	'{0:n2}' –f 1GB	1,073,741,824.00
:p or :P	Converts a numeric value to a percentage. Add a numeric value to specify precision (the number of digits past the decimal point).	'{0:p2}' –f .112	11.20 %

TABLE 5-18 Conversion Indicators for Formatting

FORMAT SPECIFIER	DESCRIPTION	EXAMPLE	OUTPUT
:r or :R	Converts a number with precision to guarantee the original value is returned if parsing is reversed.	'{0:r}' –f (1GB/2.0)	536870912 Note: (536870912 * 2) = 1,073,741,824
:x or :X	Converts the numeric value to hexadecimal format.	'{0:x}' –f 12345678	bc614e
{*N*:hh} : {*N*:mm} : {*N*:ss}	Converts a datetime object to a two-digit hour, minute, and second format. You can omit any portion to get a subset.	'{0:hh:0:mm}' –f (get-date)	12:35
{*N*:ddd}	Converts a datetime object to a day of the week. It can be combined with the previous format listed.	'{0:ddd} {0:hh:0:mm}' –f (get-date)	Mon 12:57

Working with Arrays and Collections

In Windows PowerShell, the terms *array* and *collection* are interchangeable. Arrays are data structures for storing a series of values. Using arrays, you can group related sets of data together, and PowerShell doesn't care whether the data you group is like-typed or not. For example, although you can group sets of numbers, strings, or objects in separate arrays, you also can combine values of different types in the same array.

The most common type of array you'll use is a one-dimensional array. A one-dimensional array is like a column of tabular data, a two-dimensional array is like a spreadsheet with rows and columns, and a three-dimensional (3-D) array is like a 3-D grid.

Elements in an array are indexed and can be accessed by referencing their index position. With a one-dimensional array, you access elements in the array by specifying a single index value. You also can create arrays with multiple dimensions if you want to. With multidimensional arrays, you access elements in the array by specifying multiple index values.

NOTE Windows PowerShell also supports associative arrays, which are name-value pairs stored in arrays. For more information, see the "Multiline Strings" section earlier in this chapter.

Creating and Using One-Dimensional Arrays

Windows PowerShell has several operators for working with arrays. The one you'll use most is the comma. You use the comma to separate elements in a one-dimensional array. The basic syntax for this type of array is

```
$VarName = Element1, Element2, Element3, …
```

where *VarName* is the variable in which the array will be stored, *Element1* is the first item in the array, *Element2* is the second, and so on.

The following example creates an array of numbers:

```
$myArray = 2, 4, 6, 8, 10, 12, 14
```

You can just as easily create an array of strings, such as

```
$myStringArray = "This", "That", "Why", "When", "How", "Where"
```

You access the elements in the array by passing the index position to the [ ] operator. PowerShell numbers the array elements starting from zero. This means the first element has an index position of 0, the second has an index position of 1, and so on. The basic syntax is

```
$VarName[Index]
```

where *VarName* is the variable in which the array is stored, and *Index* is the index position you want to work with. Knowing this, you can return the first element in the $myStringArray as shown here:

```
$myStringArray[0]
```

```
This
```

You can work with the index in several ways. You can use an index value of –1 to reference the last element of the array, –2 to reference the second to last, and so on. This example returns the last element in the array:

```
$myStringArray[-1]
```

```
Where
```

You also can access ranges of elements in an array using the range operator (..). The following example returns elements 1, 2, and 3:

```
$myStringArray[0..2]
```

```
This
That
Why
```

By mixing these techniques, you can work with arrays in different ways. For example, the following statement returns the last, first, and second elements in the array:

```
$myStringArray[-1..1]
```

```
Where
This
That
```

This example goes through the array backward from the last to the second-to-last to the third-to-last:

```
$myStringArray[-1..-3]
```

```
Where
How
When
```

However, to return both a series of elements and a range of elements, you must separate the series and the range using the + operator. The following example returns element 1, element 2, and elements 4 to 6:

```
$myStringArray[0,1+3..5]
```

```
This
That
When
How
Where
```

Using the Length property, you can determine the number of elements in an array. For example, typing **$myArray.Length** returns a value of 7. You can use the Length property when accessing elements in the array as well. The following example returns elements 5 to 6:

```
$myStringArray[4..($myArray.Length-1)]
```

```
How
Where
```

Using the Cast Array Structure

Another way to create an array is to use the array cast structure. The basic syntax is

```
$VarName = @(Element1, Element2, Element3, …)
```

where *VarName* is the variable in which the array will be stored, *Element1* is the first item in the array, *Element2* is the second, and so on.

The following example creates an array of numbers:

```
$myArray = @(3, 6, 9, 12, 15, 18, 21)
```

The advantage of the cast array syntax is that if you use semicolons instead of commas to separate values, PowerShell treats each value as command text. This means PowerShell executes the value as if you typed it at the prompt and then stores the result. Consider the following example:

```
$myArray = @(14; "This"; get-process)
```

As shown in the following example and sample output, the first element is created as an integer:

```
$myArray[0].gettype()
```

```
IsPublic IsSerial Name                                     BaseType
-------- -------- ----                                     --------
True     True     Int32                                    System.ValueType
```

The second element is created as a string:

```
$myArray[1].gettype()
```

```
IsPublic IsSerial Name                                     BaseType
-------- -------- ----                                     --------
True     True     String                                   System.Object
```

And the third element is created as a collection of Process objects:

```
$myArray[2].gettype()
```

```
IsPublic IsSerial Name                                     BaseType
-------- -------- ----                                     --------
True     False    Process                                  System.ComponentModel.Component
```

Assigning and Removing Values

After you create an array, you can change the array's values through a simple assignment. For example, if you define the following array,

```
$myArray = @(3, 6, 9, 12, 15, 18, 21)
```

you can change the value of the second element in $myArray using the following assignment:

```
$myArray[1] = 27
```

You also can use the SetValue() method to change a value in an array. The syntax is

```
$VarName.SetValue(NewValue,IndexPos)
```

where *VarName* is the variable in which the array was stored, *NewValue* is the new value you want to assign, and *IndexPos* is the index position of the value to change. Following this, you can change the value of the first element in $myArray using the following assignment:

```
$myArray.SetValue(52,0)
```

To add elements to an existing array, you can use the += operator to assign a new value. For example, to append an element to $myArray with a value of 75, you type the following command:

```
$myArray += 75
```

PowerShell won't let you easily delete elements in an array, but you can create a new array that contains only a subset of elements from an existing array. For example, to create the $myNewArray array with all elements in $myArray, except for the value at index position 3, you type

```
$myNewArray = $myArray[0..2+4..($myArray.length - 1)]
```

You can combine multiple arrays into a single array using the plus operator (+). The following example creates three arrays and then combines them into one array:

```
$array1 = 1,2,3,4
$array2 = 5,6,7,8
$array3 = 9,10,11,12
$cArray = $array1 + $array2 + $array3
```

Because large arrays can use up memory, you might want to delete an array when you are finished working with it. To delete an array, use the Remove-Item cmdlet to delete the variable that contains the array. The following command deletes $myArray:

```
remove-item variable:myArray
```

Using Strict Types in Arrays

Sometimes when you are working with arrays, you might want to ensure an array can store only strings, numbers, or objects of a particular type. The way to do this is to declare the array's type when you create the array.

You can declare an array of any type, but the declared type uses the [] operator as shown here:

- **[int32[]]$myArray** Creates an array of integers
- **[bool[]]$myArray** Creates an array of Booleans
- **[object[]]$myArray** Creates an array of objects
- **[string[]]$myArray** Creates an array of strings

For example, if you want to create an array of integers and assign integer values, you can use the following declaration:

```
[int32[]]$myArray = 5,10,15,20,25,30,35
```

Because the array is strictly typed, you can use only the declared value type with it. For example, if you try to change a value to a string, you get an error as shown in the following example and sample output:

```
$myArray[0]= "Kansas"
```

```
Array assignment to [0] failed: Cannot convert value "Kansas" to type
"System.Int32". Error: "Input string was not in a correct format.".
At line:1 char:10
+ $myArray[ <<<< 0]= "Kansas"
   + CategoryInfo : InvalidOperation: (Kansas:String) [], RuntimeException
   + FullyQualifiedErrorId : ArrayAssignmentFailed
```

Using Multidimensional Arrays

Multidimensional arrays are arrays that support multiple index positions. With a two-dimensional array, you create a table with rows and columns. Because you access any row using the first index and any column using the second index, these can be thought of as x-coordinates and y-coordinates as well.

Consider the following example.

INDEX	COLUMN 0	COLUMN 1	COLUMN 2
ROW 0	Red	Green	Blue
ROW 1	Washington	Ohio	Florida
ROW 2	Ocean	Lake	Stream
ROW 3	Sky	Clouds	Rain

Here, you have a table with rows and columns that you want to store in an array. The convention is to reference the row index and then the column index. The value in row 0, column 0 is Red. The value in row 0, column 1 is Green, and so on.

Although you can create one-dimensional arrays with simple constructors, PowerShell handles arrays of two or more dimensions as objects. Because of this, you must first create the array and then populate the array. The syntax for creating a two-dimensional array is

```
$VarName = new-object 'object[,]' numRows,numColumns
```

where *VarName* is the variable in which the array will be stored, *object[,]* specifies you are creating a two-dimensional array, *numRows* sets the number of rows, and *numColumns* sets the number of columns.

The following example creates an array with 4 rows and 3 columns:

```
$myArray = new-object 'object[,]' 4,3
```

After you create the array, you can populate each value according to its row and column index position as shown in this example:

```
$myArray[0,0] = "Red"
$myArray[0,1] = "Green"
$myArray[0,2] = "Blue"
$myArray[1,0] = "Washington"
$myArray[1,1] = "Ohio"
$myArray[1,2] = "Florida"
$myArray[2,0] = "Ocean"
$myArray[2,1] = "Lake"
$myArray[2,2] = "Stream"
$myArray[3,0] = "Sky"
$myArray[3,1] = "Clouds"
$myArray[3,2] = "Rain"
```

After you populate the array, you can return a value at a row/column position, such as

```
$myArray[0,1]
```

```
Green
```

Creating an array of three or more dimensions works in much the same way. The difference is that you must accommodate dimension. The syntax for creating a three-dimensional array is

```
$VarName = new-object 'object[,,]' numX,numY,numZ
```

where *VarName* is the variable in which the array will be stored, *object[,,]* specifies you are creating a three-dimensional array, and *numX*, *numY*, and *numZ* set the X, Y, and Z grid coordinates.

The following example creates an array with 5 rows, 5 columns, and 3 levels:

```
$a = new-object 'object[,,]' 5,5,3
```

This array is like 3 tables, each of 5 rows and 5 columns, stacked on top of each other. Knowing this, you can set the value for the 0, 0, 0 coordinate as

```
$a[0,0,0] = "Texas"
```

At the time of this writing, PowerShell supports up to 17 dimensions, and you can create an array of 17 dimensions, using 16 commas for the object[] constructor and then entering 17 coordinate values, as in the following example:

```
$myHugeArray = new-object 'object[,,,,,,,,,,,,,,,,]'
5,5,5,5,3,3,3,3,3,3,3,3,3,3,3,3,4
```

If you create such a large array, be sure to remove it when you are finished, to free up memory.

CHAPTER 6

Mastering Aliases, Functions, and Objects

Beyond the core structures discussed in the previous chapter, you'll find a number of other essential elements you'll use whenever you work with Windows PowerShell. These include

- Aliases
- Functions
- Objects

Whenever you work with Windows PowerShell, you'll use these essential elements to help you do more with less and to help you use PowerShell to perform any conceivable administrative task. Because the discussion in this chapter ties in closely with the discussion in previous chapters, you should read those chapters before continuing with this chapter. Also, as with the core structures, once we examine these essential elements, we won't rehash these discussions when we put these essential elements to work in upcoming chapters. For example, if we use Get-WmiObject to access Windows Management Instrumentation (WMI) objects on a computer and retrieve the Win32_Processor object, we won't go into detail on how this works (because this is already discussed here); instead, we'll focus on the new concept we are introducing, such as how to evaluate the clock speed of a computer's processor or how to take an inventory of all computers running a specified version of Windows.

Creating and Using Aliases

PowerShell aliases provide alternate names for commands, functions, scripts, files, executables, and other command elements. PowerShell has many default aliases that map to commands, and you can create your own aliases as well. Aliases are designed to save you keystrokes, and each command can have multiple aliases. For example, ls is also an alias of Get-ChildItem. In UNIX environments, ls is used to list the contents of a directory and, in fact, the output of Get-ChildItem is more similar to UNIX ls than to Windows dir.

Using the Built-In Aliases

Table 6-1 shows some of the default aliases. Although there are many other default aliases, you'll use these aliases most frequently.

TABLE 6-1 Commonly Used Aliases

ALIAS	ASSOCIATED CMDLET
clear, cls	Clear-Host
diff	Compare-Object
cp, copy	Copy-Item
epal	Export-Alias
epcsv	Export-Csv
foreach	ForEach-Object
fl	Format-List
ft	Format-Table
fw	Format-Wide
gal	Get-Alias
ls, dir	Get-ChildItem
gcm	Get-Command
cat, type	Get-Content
h, history	Get-History
gl, pwd	Get-Location
gps, ps	Get-Process
gsv	Get-Service
gv	Get-Variable

TABLE 6-1 Commonly Used Aliases

ALIAS	ASSOCIATED CMDLET
group	Group-Object
ipal	Import-Alias
ipcsv	Import-Csv
r	Invoke-History
ni	New-Item
mount	New-MshDrive
nv	New-Variable
rd, rm, rmdir, del, erase	Remove-Item
rv	Remove-Variable
sal	Set-Alias
sl, cd, chdir	Set-Location
sv, set	Set-Variable
sort	Sort-Object
sasv	Start-Service
sleep	Start-Sleep
spps, kill	Stop-Process
spsv	Stop-Service
write, echo	Write-Output

Table 6-2 lists commands that exist internally within the Windows command shell (cmd.exe) and do not have separate executable files. Each internal command is followed by a brief description. Because cmdlets behave differently from these commands, you must know exactly what you are executing. For this reason, I also provide a notation when a default alias precludes use of the command. You can run commands internal to the Windows command shell at the PowerShell prompt or in a PowerShell script. To do so, invoke the command shell with appropriate parameters followed by the name of the internal command to execute. Typically, you'll want to use the /c parameter, which tells the command shell to carry out the specified command and then terminate. For example, if you want to use the internal dir command, you can type the following at the PowerShell prompt:

```
cmd /c dir
```

TABLE 6-2 Internal Commands for the Windows Command Shell

NAME	DESCRIPTION	OVERRIDDEN BY
assoc	Displays or modifies the current file extension associations.	
break	Sets breaks for debugging.	
call	Calls a procedure or another script from within a script.	
cd (chdir)	Displays the current directory name, or changes the location of the current directory.	Set-Location
cls	Clears the command window and erases the screen buffer.	Clear-Host
color	Sets the text and background colors of the command-shell window.	
copy	Copies files from one location to another, or concatenates files.	Copy-Item
date	Displays or sets the system date.	
del (erase)	Deletes the specified file, files, or directory.	Remove-Item
dir	Displays a list of subdirectories and files in the current or specified directory.	Get-ChildItem
dpath	Allows programs to open data files in specified directories as if they were in the current directory.	
echo	Displays text strings to PowerShell; sets command echoing state (on | off).	Write-Output
endlocal	Ends localization of variables.	
exit	Exits the command shell.	
for	Runs a specified command for each file in a set of files.	
ftype	Displays current file types, or modifies file types used in file extension associations.	
goto	Directs the command interpreter to a labeled line in a batch script.	
if	Performs conditional execution of commands.	

TABLE 6-2 Internal Commands for the Windows Command Shell

NAME	DESCRIPTION	OVERRIDDEN BY
md (mkdir)	Creates a subdirectory in the current or specified directory.	*md invokes mkdir (via cmd.exe)
mklink	Creates either a symbolic link or a hard link, for either a file or a directory.	
move	Moves a file or files from the current or designated source directory to a designated target directory. It can also be used to rename a directory.	Move-Item
path	Displays or sets the command path the operating system uses when searching for executables and scripts.	
pause	Suspends processing of a batch file, and waits for keyboard input.	
popd	Makes the directory saved by PUSHD the current directory.	Pop-Location
prompt	Sets the text for the command prompt.	
pushd	Saves the current directory location and then optionally changes to the specified directory.	Push-Location
rd (rmdir)	Removes a directory or a directory and its subdirectories.	Remove-Item
rem	Sets a remark in batch scripts or Config.sys.	
ren (rename)	Renames a file or files.	Rename-Item (for ren only)
set	Displays current environment variables, or sets temporary variables for the current command shell.	Set-Variable
setlocal	Marks the start of variable localization in batch scripts.	
shift	Shifts the position of replaceable parameters in batch scripts.	
start	Starts a separate window to run a specified program or command.	Start-Process
time	Displays or sets the system time.	

TABLE 6-2 Internal Commands for the Windows Command Shell

NAME	DESCRIPTION	OVERRIDDEN BY
title	Sets the title for the command-shell window.	
type	Displays the contents of a text file.	Get-Content
verify	Causes the operating system to verify files after writing files to disk.	
vol	Displays the disk's volume label and serial number.	

Creating Aliases

The following cmdlets are available for working with aliases:

- **Get-Alias** Lists all or specified aliases set in the current session by name and definition.

```
Get-Alias [[-Name | -Definition] Strings] [AddtlParams]

AddtlParams=
[-Exclude Strings] [-Scope String]
```

- **New-Alias** Creates a new alias.

```
New-Alias [-Description String] [-Name] String [-Value] String
[AddtlParams]

AddtlParams=
[-Force] [-PassThru] [-Scope String] [-Option None | ReadOnly |
Constant | Private | AllScope]
```

- **Set-Alias** Creates a new alias, or changes the definition of an existing alias.

```
Set-Alias [-Description String] [-Name] String [-Value] String
[AddtlParams]

AddtlParams=
[-Force] [-PassThru] [-Scope String] [-Option None | ReadOnly |
Constant | Private | AllScope]
```

- **Export-Alias** Exports all the aliases that are currently in use in the Power-Shell console to an alias file. This includes the built-in aliases as well as aliases you've created.

```
Export-Alias [-Append] [-As Csv | Script] [-Path] String
[AddtlParams]

AddtlParams=
[-Description String] [-Force] [-NoClobber] [-PassThru]
[-Scope String] [[-Name] Strings]
```

- **Import-Alias** Imports an alias file into a PowerShell console. The aliases can then be used in that PowerShell session. You must reload the aliases each time you open a PowerShell console.

```
Import-Alias [-Path] String [AddtlParams]

AddtlParams=
[-PassThru] [-Force] [-Scope String]
```

As mentioned previously, you can use the Get-Alias cmdlet to list all of the available aliases. To get particular aliases, use the –Name parameter of the Get-Alias cmdlet. For example, to get aliases that begin with "a", use the following command:

```
get-alias -name a*
```

To get aliases according to their values, use the –Definition parameter. For example, to get aliases for the Remove-Item cmdlet, type the following command:

```
get-alias -definition Remove-Item
```

You can create aliases using either the New-Alias cmdlet or the Set-Alias cmdlet. The primary difference between them is that New-Alias creates an alias only if a like-named alias does not yet exist, while Set-Alias overwrites an existing alias with the new association you provide. The basic syntax is

```
set-alias -name AliasName -value CommandName
```

where *AliasName* is the alias you want to use or modify, and *CommandName* is the cmdlet you want to associate with the alias. The following example creates a "cm" alias for Computer Management:

```
set-alias -name cm -value c:\windows\system32\compmgmt.msc
```

Because the –Name and –Value parameters are position sensitive, you pass the related values in order without having to specify the parameter name, as shown in this example:

```
set-alias cm c:\windows\system32\compmgmt.msc
```

MORE INFO Sometimes, you might want to use the –Option parameter to set optional properties of an alias. Valid values are None, ReadOnly, Constant, Private, and AllScope. The default, None, sets no options. ReadOnly specifies that the alias cannot be changed unless you use the –Force parameter. Constant specifies that the alias cannot be changed, even by using the –Force parameter. Private specifies that the alias is available only within the scope specified by the –Scope parameter. AllScope specifies that the alias is available in all scopes.

You can use the alias with any applicable parameters just as you would the full command name. If you always want to use certain startup parameters, external utilities, or applications, you can define those as well as part of the alias. To do this, enclose the value in double quotation marks as shown in this example:

```
set-alias cm "c:\windows\system32\compmgmt.msc /computer=engpc57"
```

However, you cannot define startup parameters for cmdlets in this way. For example, you can create an alias of *gs* for Get-Service, but you cannot create an alias with the following definition: get-service –name winrm. The workaround is to create a function that includes the command as discussed in the "Creating and Using Functions" section later in this chapter.

Importing and Exporting Aliases

Normally, you save the aliases you want to use by typing the related commands into a profile file. If you create a number of aliases in a PowerShell session and want to save those aliases, you also can use the Export-Alias cmdlet to do so. This cmdlet exports all the aliases that are currently in use in the PowerShell console to an alias file. You can export aliases as a list of comma-separated values or a list of Set-Alias commands in a PowerShell script.

The basic syntax for Export-Alias is

```
export-alias -path AliasFileName
```

where *AliasFileName* is the full file path to the alias file you want to create, such as

```
export-alias -path myaliases.csv
```

The default output format is a list of comma-separated values. You can use the –As parameter to set the output format as a script containing Set-Alias commands as shown in this example:

```
export-alias -as script -path myaliases.ps1
```

Other parameters you can use include

- –Append, to write the output to the end of an existing file rather than overwrite the file as per the default setting

- –Force, to force overwriting an existing alias file if the read-only attribute is set
- –Noclobber, to prevent automatic overwriting of an existing alias file

The Import-Alias cmdlet imports an alias file into the PowerShell console. The basic syntax for Import-Alias is

```
import-alias -path AliasFileName
```

where *AliasFileName* is the full file path to the alias file you want to import, such as

```
import-alias -path c:\powershell\myaliases.csv
```

Use the –Force parameter to import aliases that are already defined and set as read-only.

Creating and Using Functions

Windows PowerShell functions are named sets of commands that can accept input from the pipeline. When you call a function by its name, the related commands run just as if you had typed them at the command line. Normally, you save functions that you want to use frequently by typing the related commands into a profile file. You also can add functions to scripts.

Creating Functions

To create a function, type the word **function** followed by a name for the function. Type your command text, and enclose it in braces ({ }). For example, the following command creates the getwinrm function. This function represents the "get-service -name winrm" command:

```
function getwinrm {get-service -name winrm}
```

The braces ({ }) create a code block that the function uses. You can now type **getwinrm** instead of the command. And you can even create aliases for the getwinrm function. For example, you can create a *gr* alias for the getwinrm function using the following command:

```
new-alias gr getwinrm
```

Because functions use code blocks, you can create functions with multiple commands. Functions also can use piping, redirection, and other coding techniques. For example, you can use piping to format the output of Get-Service as shown in this example:

```
function getwinrm {get-service -name winrm | format-list}
```

Functions are very powerful because you can define parameters for them and use the parameter names to pass in values. The basic syntax for using parameters with functions is

```
function FunctionName {
  param ($Parameter1Name, $Parameter2Name, ...)
  Commands }
```

where *FunctionName* sets the name of the function, *$Parameter1Name* sets the name of the first parameter, *$Parameter2Name* sets the name of the second parameter, and so on. Consider the following example:

```
function ss {param ($status) get-service | where { $_.status -eq $status} }
```

This line of code defines an *ss* function with a parameter called *status*. The *ss* function examines all the configured services on the computer and uses the Where-Object cmdlet to return a formatted list of services with the status you specify. To return a list of all services with a status of Stopped, you type

```
ss -status stopped
```

To return a list of all services with a status of Running, you type

```
ss -status running
```

Because the name of the parameter is optional, you also can simply specify the value to check, such as

```
ss stopped
```

or

```
ss running
```

Keep in mind that functions run within the context of their own local scope. The items created in a function, such as variables, exist only in the function scope. Additionally, if a function is part of a script, the function is available only to statements within that script. This means a function in a script is not available at the command prompt by default. When you define a function in the global scope, you can use the function in scripts, in functions, and at the command line.

To set the scope for a function, simply prefix the name of the function with the desired scope. This example sets the scope of the function to *global*:

```
function global:getwinrm {get-service -name winrm}
```

Using Extended Functions

Now that you know the basics, let's look at the extended syntax for functions:

```
function $FunctionName {
  param ($Parameter1Name, $Parameter2Name, ...)
  Begin {
    <one-time, pre-processing commands>
  }
  Process{
    <commands to execute on each object>
  }
  End{
    <one-time, post-processing commands>
  }
}
```

In the extended syntax, you can add Begin, Process, and End code blocks to make a function behave exactly like a cmdlet. The Begin block is optional and used to specify one-time preprocessing commands. Statements in the Begin block are executed before any objects in the pipeline are evaluated by the function. This means no pipeline objects are available.

The Process block is required if you want to process input. In the basic syntax, the Process block is implied. However, when you use the other optional blocks and want to process input, you must explicitly declare the Process block. Statements in the Process block are executed once for each object in the pipeline.

The End block is optional and used to specify one-time postprocessing commands. Statements in the End block are executed after all objects in the pipeline are evaluated by the function. As with the Begin block, this means no pipeline objects are available.

The following example uses Begin, Process, and End code blocks:

```
function scheck {
param ($status)
 Begin {
  Write-Warning "############## Services on $env:computername"
 }
 Process {
  get-service | where { $_.status -eq $status}
 }
 End {
  Write-Warning "##############################################"
 }
}
```

If you define this function at the prompt or use it in a script, you can return a list of all services with a status of Stopped by typing

```
scheck stopped
```

To return a list of all services with a status of Running, you type

```
ss -status running
```

Using Filter Functions

Filters are a type of function that run on each object in the pipeline. You can think of a filter as a function with all its statements in a Process block.

The basic syntax for a filter is

```
filter FilterName {
  param ($Parameter1Name, $Parameter2Name, ...)
  Commands }
```

where *FilterName* sets the name of the filter, *$Parameter1Name* sets the name of the first parameter, *$Parameter2Name* sets the name of the second parameter, and so on.

The power of a filter is that it processes a single pipeline object at a time. This makes a filter ideal for working with large amounts of data and returning an appropriate subset of the pipeline data. As with functions, you can specify a scope for a filter. Simply prefix the name of the function with the desired scope.

When you work with filters, you'll often use the $_ automatic variable to operate on the current object in the pipeline as shown in this example:

```
filter Name { $_.Name }
```

Here, you define a filter that outputs the name property of any object sent to the filter. For example, if you pipeline the output of Get-PSDrive to the function as shown here:

```
get-psdrive | name
```

the filter returns the name of each PSDrive that is available. Because a filter is essentially a function with only a Process block, the following function works the same as the previously defined filter:

```
function Name {
   Process { $_.Name }
}
```

Digging Deeper into Functions

You can extend the function concepts we've discussed previously in many ways. For example, you can set a default value for a parameter by assigning an initial value as shown in this example:

```
function ss {param ($status = "stopped") get-service |
where { $_.status -eq $status} }
```

Now the –Status parameter is set to Stopped by default. You can override the default by specifying a different value.

When you create functions, you can specify the parameter value type using any of the data type aliases listed previously in Table 6-1. These data type aliases are used in the same way whenever you declare a data type in PowerShell.

In the following example, you create a function to dynamically set the PowerShell window size:

```
function set-windowsize {

param([int]$width=$host.ui.rawui.windowsize.width,
[int]$height=$host.ui.rawui.windowsize.height)

$size=New-Object System.Management.Automation.Host.Size($width,$height);

$host.ui.rawui.WindowSize=$size

}
```

The function defines two parameters: $width and $height. Both parameters are defined as having 32-bit integer values. Because of this, PowerShell expects the parameters to be in this format when you call the function. If you pass values in another format, PowerShell attempts to convert the values you provide to the correct format. If PowerShell cannot do this, an error is returned stating that the value cannot be converted to the specified type and that the input string was not in the correct format.

The Get-Command cmdlet lists all currently defined cmdlets and functions. If you want to see only the available functions, you can filter the output using the Where-Object cmdlet as shown in the following example:

```
get-command | where {$_.commandtype -eq "function"}
```

Here, you look for command objects where CommandType is set as Function. This lists all the functions that currently are defined. Add **| format-list** to see the extended definition of each function, such as

```
get-command | where {$_.commandtype -eq "function"} | format-list
```

The technique of calling a function and passing parameter values directly works great when you want to do either of the following:

- Define a function at the prompt and then run the function from the prompt.
- Define a function in a script and then run the function in the script.

However, this technique won't work if you want to pass parameter values to a function in a script from the prompt. The reason for this is that values passed to a script are read as arguments. For example, if you save a library of functions in a script and then want to run the functions from the prompt, you have to design the function to understand script-passed arguments or modify the script to work with arguments. One solution is shown in this example script:

Contents of CheckIt.ps1

```
function scheck {param ($status)
 Begin {
  Write-Warning "############### Services on $env:computername"
 }
 Process {
  get-service | where { $_.status -eq $status}
 }
 End {
  Write-Warning "###############################################"
 }
}
if ($args[0] = "scheck") {scheck $args[1]}
```

Note that the last line of the script determines whether the Scheck function is called. If you call the script with the first argument as *scheck* and the second argument as the status to check, the Scheck function is called and you get a list of services with that status. An alternative solution is to simply set the Status parameter to the value of the first argument passed to the script, as shown in the example that follows. You can then call the script with the first argument as the status to check. Note that the last line of the script invokes the function.

Contents of CheckIt2.ps1

```
function scheck {param ($status = $args[0])
 Begin {
  Write-Warning "############### Services on $env:computername"
 }
 Process {
  get-service | where { $_.status -eq $status}
 }
 End {
  Write-Warning "###############################################"
 }
}
scheck
```

Examining Function Definitions

If desired, you can work with functions via the *function:* provider drive. For example, if you set the location to the function: provider drive as shown in this example

```
set-location function:
```

the PowerShell prompt changes to

```
PS Function:\>
```

You can then work with any function or all functions. To list all functions by name and definition, you type

```
get-childitem
```

To list a particular function by name and definition, you use Get-ChildItem and type the function name or part of the function name with wildcards, such as

```
get-childitem enable-psremoting
get-childitem *psremoting
```

When you are finished working with the function: provider drive, you can return to the file system drive you were using by typing **set-location** and the drive designator, such as

```
set-location c:
```

Another way to work with the function: provider drive is to use the Get-Item cmdlet to examine its definitions. If you do this, you don't need to switch to the function: provider drive. For example, regardless of which provider drive you are working with, you can type the following command to list all functions:

```
get-item -path function:*
```

You also can get a function by name:

```
get-item -path function:prompt
```

Or you can get it by wildcard:

```
get-item -path function:pr*
```

Using the Built-In Functions

Table 6-3 shows the default functions. As you can see, most of the default functions are created to allow you to access drives and file paths, and the definition for these matches the definition set in the actual function. For other functions, the definition shows the essential command text at the heart of the function when possible.

TABLE 6-3 Default Functions

FUNCTION NAME	DEFINITION	PURPOSE
A:, B:, C:, D:, E:, F:, G:, H:, I:, J:, K:, L:, M:, N:, O:, P:, Q:, R:, S:, T:, U:, V:, W:, X:, Y:, Z:	Set-Location *DriveLetter*, where *DriveLetter* is the letter of the drive you want to access.	Allows you to change to a particular drive letter. Thus, rather than having to type **Set-Location C:**, you can simply type **C:**.
CD..	Set-Location ..	Allows you to go back one directory level. Thus, rather than having to type **Set-Location ..**, you can simply type **CD..**.
CD\	Set-Location \	Allows you to go to the root directory of the current drive. Thus, rather than having to type **Set-Location **, you can simply type **CD**.
Clear-Host	$space = New-Object System. Management. Automation. Host. BufferCell $space.Character = ' '	Clears the history buffer in the PowerShell console. Thus, rather than having to invoke the host run space and clear the buffer, you can simply type **Clear-Host**.
Disable-PSRemoting	Disable-PSSessionConfiguration * –force:$force	Disables the PowerShell remoting capabilities. Thus, rather than having to try several approaches to disabling remoting, you can simply type **Disable-PSRemoting**.
Enable-PSRemoting	Enable-PSSessionConfiguration * –force:$force	Enables the PowerShell remoting capabilities. Thus, rather than having to try several approaches to enabling remoting, you can simply type **Enable-PSRemoting**.

TABLE 6-3 Default Functions

FUNCTION NAME	DEFINITION	PURPOSE
Help	Get-help | More	Gets the help text for a cmdlet and pages it one screen at a time. Thus, rather than having to type **get-help *CmdletName* | More**, you can simply type **Help *CmdletName***.
Mkdir	New-Item –path *Path* –name *Name* –type directory	Creates a directory with a specified name along a specified path. Thus, rather than having to use New-Item to create a directory in a named path, you can simply type **mkdir *DirName***.
More	| More	Pages file contents or output one screen at a time. Thus, rather than having to type ***CommandText* | More**, you can simply type **More *CommandText***.
Prompt	$(if (test-path variable:/ PSDebugContext) { '[DBG]: ' } else { '' }) + 'PS ' + $(Get-Location) + $(if ($nestedpromptlevel –ge 1) { '>>' }) + '> '	Displays the PowerShell prompt. By default, the prompt displays PS, a space, and then the current directory. The prompt changes to >> when you do not terminate a line properly and PowerShell is looking for more input to complete the command entry.
TabExpansion	*	Enables tab expansion of command and parameter names. When you are typing part of a name value, press Tab to expand.

Practice using these functions because they provide handy shortcuts for many common tasks, especially the Prompt and TabExpansion functions. By default, the prompt displays PS, a space, and then the current directory. Also, the prompt changes to >> when you do not terminate a line properly and PowerShell is looking for more input to complete the command entry. When you are in debugging mode, the prompt changes to [DBG]:.

You can create your own Prompt function. If you do, your Prompt function simply overwrites and takes the place of the default prompt function. For example, if you want to the prompt to display the date instead of the current location, you can define the Prompt function as

```
function prompt {"$(get-date)> "}
```

Or to display the computer name, define the prompt as

```
function prompt {"PS [$env:computername]> "}
```

To maintain the original behavior of the prompt, copy the original definition and then modify it to meet your needs. The original prompt is created using the following function entered as a single line of code:

```
function prompt {
$(if (test-path variable:/PSDebugContext) { '[DBG]: ' }
else { '' }) + 'PS ' + $(Get-Location)
+ $(if ($nestedpromptlevel -ge 1) { '>>' }) + '> '
}
```

Typically, you'll want to replace the bold text with the desired value. For example, to display the date, you enter the following definition as a single line:

```
function prompt {
$(if (test-path variable:/PSDebugContext) { '[DBG]: ' }
else { '' }) + "$(get-date)> "
+ $(if ($nestedpromptlevel -ge 1) { '>>' }) + '> '
}
```

To display the computer name, you enter the following definition as a single line:

```
function prompt {
$(if (test-path variable:/PSDebugContext) { '[DBG]: ' }
else { '' }) + "PS [$env:computername]> "
+ $(if ($nestedpromptlevel -ge 1) { '>>' }) + '> '
}
```

While the Prompt function is a nice extra, the TabExpansion function is one you won't be able to live without once you start using it. The TabExpansion function allows you to complete cmdlet names, parameter names, and even parameter values using the Tab key. Here's how it works:

- When you are typing a cmdlet name, type the first few letters of the name and then press the Tab key to cycle through matching cmdlet names in alphabetical order. For example, if you know the cmdlet you want to use begins with Get-, you can type **Get-** and then press Tab to cycle through the matching cmdlets. Here, Get-Acl is listed first, followed by Get-Alias, Get-AuthenticateSignature, and so on. Similarly, if you know the cmdlet verb is Get and the cmdlet noun begins with C, you can type **Get-C** and then press Tab to cycle through possible values. A little-known secret is that you can press Shift+Tab to go through the values backwards, such as when you know the value you are looking for is later in the alphabet.
- After you type a cmdlet name, you can use tab expansion to select parameter names as well. If you don't know what parameter to use, type a hyphen (-) and then press Tab to cycle through all available parameter names. If you know a parameter begins with a certain letter, type a hyphen (-) followed by the letters you know and then press Tab. Again, you can press Shift+Tab to go through the values backward.

NOTE **Pressing Tab on a blank line inserts the tab character. If you press Tab when a parameter value is expected, PowerShell cycles through file and folder names in the current directory.**

Working with Objects

Every action you take in Windows PowerShell occurs within the context of objects. Objects are the fundamental unit in object-oriented programming. Programming languages that follow object-oriented concepts describe the interaction among objects, and PowerShell uses objects in exactly the same way.

Object Essentials

In Windows PowerShell, objects do the real work. As data moves from one command to the next, it moves as it does within objects. Essentially, this means that objects are simply collections of data that represent items in defined namespaces.

All objects have a type, state, and behavior. The type provides details about what the object represents. For example, an object that represents a system process is a Process object. The state of an object pertains to data elements and their associated values. Everything the object knows about these elements and values describes the state of the object. Data elements associated with objects are stored in properties.

The behavior of an object depends on the actions the object can perform on the item that the object represents. In object-oriented terminology, this construct is called a *method*. A method belongs to the object class it is a member of, and you use a method when you need to perform a specific action on an object. For example, the Process object includes a method for stopping the process. You can use this method to halt execution of the process that the object represents.

Putting this together, you can see that the state of an object depends on the things the object knows, and the behavior of the object depends on the actions the object can perform. Objects encapsulate properties and related methods into a single identifiable unit. Therefore, objects are easy to reuse, update, and maintain.

Object classes encapsulate objects. A single class can be used to instantiate multiple objects. This means that you can have many active objects or instances of a class. By encapsulating objects within a class structure, you can group sets of objects by type. For example, when you type **get-process** at the PowerShell prompt, PowerShell returns a collection of objects representing all processing that are running on the computer. Although all the objects are returned together in a single collection, each object is separate, retaining its own states and behaviors.

PowerShell supports several dozen object types. When you combine commands in a pipeline, the commands pass information to each other as objects. When the first command runs, it sends one or more objects of a particular class along the pipeline to the second command. The second command receives the collection of objects from the first command, processes the objects, and then either displays output or passes new or modified objects to the next command in the pipeline. This continues until all commands in the pipeline run and the final command's output is displayed.

You can examine the properties and methods of any object by sending the output through the Get-Member cmdlet. For example, system processes and services are represented by the Process and Service objects, respectively. To determine the properties and methods of a Process object, you type **get-process | get-member**. To determine the properties and methods of a Service object, you type **get-service | get-member**. In both instances, the pipe character (|) sends the output of the first cmdlet to the Get-Member cmdlet, and Get-Member shows you the formal type of the object class and a complete listing of its members, as shown in the following example and sample output:

```
get-service | get-member
```

```
   TypeName: System.ServiceProcess.ServiceController

Name                    MemberType    Definition
----                    ----------    ----------
Name                    AliasProperty Name = ServiceName
Disposed                Event         System.EventHandler Disposed
Close                   Method        System.Void Close()
. . .
CanPauseAndContinue     Property      System.Boolean CanPauseAndCo
. . .
Status                  Property      System.ServiceProcess.Service
```

TIP By default, the Get-Member cmdlet does not show you the static methods and static properties of object classes. To get the static members of an object class, type **get-member –static**. For example, to get the static members of the ServiceProcess object, you'd enter **get-service | get-member –static**.

In the output, note that each facet of the Service object is listed by member type. You can make better sense of the list of available information when you filter for elements you want to see by adding the –MemberType parameter. The allowed values of –MemberType include

- AliasProperty, CodeProperty, NoteProperty, ParameterizedProperty, Property, PropertySet, ScriptProperty, CodeMethod, MemberSet, Method, and ScriptMethod, for examining elements of a particular type
- Properties, for examining all property-related elements
- Methods, for examining all method-related elements
- All, for examining all properties and methods (the default)

When you examine an object using Get-Member, note the alias properties. Aliases to properties work the same as other aliases. They're friendly names that you can use as shortcuts when you are working with an object. Whereas Service objects have only one alias property (Name), most well-known objects have several alias properties. For example, Process objects have the alias properties shown in the following example and sample output:

```
get-process | get-member
```

```
   TypeName: System.Diagnostics.Process

Name                           MemberType     Definition
----                           ----------     ----------
Handles                        AliasProperty  Handles = Handlecount
Name                           AliasProperty  Name = ProcessName
NPM                            AliasProperty  NPM = NonpagedSystemMemory
PM                             AliasProperty  PM = PagedMemorySize
VM                             AliasProperty  VM = VirtualMemorySize
WS                             AliasProperty  WS = WorkingSet
```

And these aliases are displayed when you list running processes, as shown in the following example and sample output:

```
get-process
```

```
Handles  NPM(K)    PM(K)      WS(K) VM(M)   CPU(s)     Id ProcessName
-------  ------    -----      ----- -----   ------     -- -----------
     52       3     1296       3844    51     0.00   3004 acrotray
    139       4     2560       7344    75            1292 AlertService
    573      14    14680      11028   120     7.41   2764 aolsoftware
     97       4     2872       4476    53            1512 AppleMobil...
```

When you type **get-process | get-member** and see that Process objects have dozens of other properties not listed, you might wonder what happened to these other properties and why they aren't listed. This occurs because PowerShell shows only streamlined views of well-known objects as part of the standard output. Typically, this output includes only the most important properties of an object.

PowerShell determines how to display an object of a particular type by using information stored in XML files that have names ending in .format.ps1xml. The formatting definitions for many well-known objects are in the types.ps1xml file. This file is stored in the $pshome directory.

The properties you don't see are still part of the object, and you have full access to them. For example, if you type **get-process winlogon | format-list –property ***, you get complete details on every property of the Winlogon process by name and value.

Object Methods and Properties

Some methods and properties relate only to actual instances of an object, and this is why they are called *instance methods* and *instance properties*. The term *instance* is simply another word for *object*.

Often you will want to reference the methods and properties of objects through a variable in which the object is stored. To see how this works, consider the following example:

```
$myString = "THIS IS A TEST!"
```

Here, you store a character string in a variable named $myString. In PowerShell, the string is represented as a String object. String objects have a Length property that stores the length of the string. Therefore, you can determine the length of the string created previously by typing the following command:

```
$myString.Length
```

In this example, the length of the string is 15 characters, so the output is 15.

Although String objects have only one property, they have a number of methods, including ToUpper() and ToLower(). You use the ToUpper() method to display all the characters in the string in uppercase letters. You use the ToLower() method to display all the characters in the string in lowercase letters. For example, to change the previously created string to "this is a test!", you type the following command:

```
$myString.ToLower()
```

From these examples, you can see that you access a property of an object by placing a dot between the variable name that represents the object and the property name as shown here:

```
$ObjectName.PropertyName
$ObjectName.PropertyName = Value
```

And you can see that you access a method of an object by placing a dot between the variable name that represents the object and the method name, such as

```
$ObjectName.MethodName()
```

Because methods perform actions on objects, you often need to pass parameter values in the method call. The syntax for passing parameters in a method call is

```
$ObjectName.MethodName(parameter1, parameter2, …)
```

So far the techniques we've discussed for working with methods and properties are for actual instances of an object. However, you won't always be working with a tangible instance of an object. Sometimes, you'll want to work directly with the static methods and static properties that apply to a particular .NET Framework class type as a whole.

The .NET Framework includes a wide range of class types. Generally, .NET Framework class names are always enclosed in brackets. Examples of class type names include [System.Datetime], for working with dates and times, and [System.Diagnostics.Process], for working with system processes. However, PowerShell automatically prepends *System.* to type names, so you can also use [Datetime] for working with dates and times and [Diagnostics.Process] for working with system processes.

Static methods and static properties of a .NET Framework class are always available when you are working with an object class. However, if you try to display them with the Get-Member cmdlet, you won't see them unless you use the –Static parameter as well, such as

```
[System.Datetime] | get-member -Static
```

You access a static property of a .NET Framework class by placing two colon characters (::) between the bracketed class name and the property name as shown here:

```
[ClassName]::PropertyName
[ClassName]::PropertyName = Value
```

In this example, you use a static property of the [System.Datetime] class to display the current date and time:

```
[System.Datetime]::Now
```

```
Monday, February 15, 2010 11:05:22 PM
```

You access a static method of a .NET Framework class by placing two colon characters (::) between the bracketed class name and the method name, such as

```
[ClassName]::MethodName()
```

The syntax for passing parameters in a call to a static method is

```
[ClassName]::MethodName(parameter1, parameter2, …)
```

In this example, you use a static method of the [System.Diagnostics.Process] class to display information about a process:

```
[System.Diagnostics.Process]::GetProcessById(0)
```

```
Handles  NPM(K)    PM(K)      WS(K) VM(M)   CPU(s)     Id ProcessName
-------  ------    -----      ----- -----   ------     -- -----------
      0       0        0         24     0               0 Idle
```

Object Types

By default, all object types that are used by PowerShell are defined in .ps1xml files in the $pshome directory. The default formatting and type files include the following:

- **Certificate.Format.ps1xml** Provides formatting guidelines for certificate objects and X.509 certificates
- **Diagnostics.Format.ps1xml** Provides formatting guidelines for objects created when you are working with performance counters and diagnostics in PowerShell
- **DotNetTypes.Format.ps1xml** Provides formatting guidelines for .NET Framework objects not covered in other formatting files, including CultureInfo, FileVersionInfo, and EventLogEntry objects
- **FileSystem.Format.ps1xml** Provides formatting guidelines for file system objects
- **GetEvent.Types.ps1xml** Provides formatting guidelines for event log configuration, event log records, and performance counters
- **Help.Format.ps1xml** Provides formatting guidelines for the views PowerShell uses to display help file content
- **PowerShellCore.Format.ps1xml** Provides formatting guidelines for objects that are created by the PowerShell core cmdlets
- **PowerShellTrace.Format.ps1xml** Provides formatting guidelines for PSTraceSource objects generated when you are performing traces in PowerShell
- **Registry.Format.ps1xml** Provides formatting guidelines for Registry objects
- **Types.ps1xml** Provides formatting guidelines for System objects
- **WSMan.Format.ps1xml** Provides formatting guidelines for objects created when you are working with WS Management configurations in PowerShell

PowerShell accomplishes automatic typing by using a common object that has the capability to state its type dynamically, add members dynamically, and interact with other objects through a consistent abstraction layer. This object is the PSObject. The PSObject can encapsulate any base object, whether it is a system object, a WMI object, a Component Object Model (COM) object, or an Active Directory Service Interfaces (ADSI) object.

By acting as a wrapper for an existing base object, the PSObject can be used to access adapted views of a base object or to extend a base object. Although an adapted view of a base object exposes only members that are directly accessible, you can access alternate views of a base object, and those alternate views can provide access to the extended members of a base object. Available views for base objects include the following:

- **PSBase** Used to access the original properties of the object without extension or adaptation
- **PSAdapted** Used to access an adapted view of the object
- **PSExtended** Used to access the extended properties and methods of the object that were added in the Types.ps1xml files or by using the Add-Member cmdlet
- **PSObject** Used to access the adapter that converts the base object to a PSObject
- **PSTypeNames** Used to access a list of types that describe the object

By default, PowerShell returns information only from the PSObject, PSExtended, and PSTypeNames views. However, you can use dot notation to access alternate views. In the following example, you obtain a Win32_Process object representing the winlogon.exe process:

```
$pr = Get-WmiObject Win32_Process | where-object { $_.ProcessName -eq
"winlogon.exe" }
```

If you then type **$pr** at the PowerShell prompt, you see all the information for this process from the PSObject, PSExtended, and PSTypeNames views. You can then access the PSBase view to expose the members of the base object as shown in this example:

```
$pr.PSBase.Properties
```

Because there might be times when you want to extend an object yourself, you can do this using a custom Types.ps1xml file or by using the Add-Member cmdlet. The three most common extensions you'll want to use are

- **ScriptProperty** Allows you to add properties to types, including those that are based on a calculation
- **AliasProperty** Allows you to define an alias for a property
- **ScriptMethod** Allows you to define an action to take on an object

In custom Types.ps1xml files, you can define these extensions using XML elements, and there are many examples available in the $pshome directory. These extensions also can be added dynamically at the prompt or in your scripts. For example, a ScriptProperty is a type of object member that uses a block of code to process or extract information related to an object. The basic syntax is

```
$ObjectName | add-member -membertype scriptproperty -name Name -value
{CodeBlock}
```

Because the –Name and –Value parameters are position sensitive, you don't have to specify them explicitly. Knowing this, consider the following example and sample output:

```
$proc = get-process powershell;

$proc | add-member -Type scriptproperty "UpTime" {return ((date) -
($this.starttime))};

$proc | select Name, @{name='Uptime'; Expression={"{0:n0}" -f
$_.UpTime.TotalMinutes}};
```

```
Name                                                        Uptime
----                                                        ------
powershell                                                     242
```

Here, you obtain a process object for any Powershell.exe processes running on the computer. You then use the Add-Member cmdlet to extend the standard process object by adding a ScriptProperty. The script block defined in the Script-Property is used to calculate the time that a process has been running. Then you get the process object and format its output to include the process name and new Uptime property. Using a regular expression, you convert the output value of the Uptime property to a value in minutes. The result is as shown.

What you don't see happening here is that the first time you assign a value to $proc, you are adding a collection of process objects. You then generate a second collection of process objects because you use the Add-Member cmdlet to wrap the original Process objects in a new PSObject instance that includes the new property you've defined.

While a ScriptProperty extends an object, an AliasProperty simply makes it easier to work with an object. To see how, let's access the C: drive using the Get-PSDrive cmdlet and then create a new PSDriveInfo object so that we can access information about the C: drive. Here's an example:

```
$myDrive = get-psdrive C
$myDriveInfo = New-Object System.IO.DriveInfo $myDrive
```

Now that you have an object you can work with, you can display information about the C: drive simply by typing **$myDriveInfo**. The output you see provides information about the drive, its status, its size, and its free space, and it will be similar to the following:

```
Name               : C:\
DriveType          : Fixed
DriveFormat        : NTFS
IsReady            : True
AvailableFreeSpace : 302748798976
TotalFreeSpace     : 302748798976
TotalSize          : 490580373504
RootDirectory      : C:\
VolumeLabel        :
```

Although the default format is a list, you can also view the information in table format, such as when you are working with multiple drives. When you type **$myDriveInfo | format-table –property ***, the output you get isn't pretty (unless you have a very wide console window). To clean up the output, you might want to create aliases for properties, such as AvailableFreeSpace, TotalFreeSpace, and RootDirectory. You can do this using the Add-Member cmdlet as well. The basic syntax is

```
$ObjectName | add-member -membertype aliasproperty -name AliasName -value
PropertyName
```

where *ObjectName* is the name of the object you are working with, *AliasName* is the new alias for the property, and *PropertyName* is the original name of the property, such as

```
$myDriveInfo | add-member -membertype aliasproperty -name Free -value
AvailableFreeSpace

$myDriveInfo | add-member -membertype aliasproperty -name Format -value
DriveFormat
```

You can access an alias property as you would any other property. For example, to display the value of the AvailableFreeSpace property, you can type either

```
$myDriveInfo.AvailableFreeSpace
```

or

```
$myDriveInfo.Free
```

You can use alias properties in formatted output as well. An example is shown in the following command and sample output:

```
$myDriveInfo | format-table -property Name, Free, Format


Name                                    Free      Format
----                                    ----      ------
C:\                             302748483584        NTFS
```

You use ScriptMethod extensions to define additional methods for an object. The basic syntax is

```
$ObjectName | add-member -membertype scriptmethod -name Name
 -value {CodeBlock}
```

Because the –Name and –Value parameters are position sensitive, you don't have to specify them explicitly. Knowing this, consider the following example:

```
$myDrive = get-psdrive C

$myDrive | add-member -membertype scriptmethod -name Remove
 -value { $force = [bool] $args[0]
 if ($force) {$this | Remove-PSDrive }
 else {$this | Remove-PSDrive -Confirm}
}
```

Here you define a Remote method for a PSDrive object. If you call the method without passing any argument values, PowerShell prompts you to confirm that you want to remove the drive from the current session. If you call the method and pass $true or 0 (zero) as the first argument, PowerShell removes the drive from the current session without requiring confirmation.

Digging Deeper into Objects

To dig a bit deeper into objects, let's look at the $host object. As discussed in the "Configuring Windows PowerShell Console Properties" section in Chapter 1, "Introducing Windows PowerShell," you can use the PowerShell console's Properties dialog box to specify the options, fonts, layouts, and colors to use. The $host object also gives you access to the underlying user interface, which can be either the PowerShell console or the PowerShell application.

To view the current settings of the $host object, type the following command:

```
$host.ui.rawui | format-list -property *
```

The output you see will be similar to the following:

```
ForegroundColor       : DarkYellow
BackgroundColor       : DarkMagenta
CursorPosition        : 0,1050
WindowPosition        : 0,1001
CursorSize            : 25
BufferSize            : 120,3000
WindowSize            : 120,50
MaxWindowSize         : 120,95
MaxPhysicalWindowSize : 240,95
eyAvailable           : False
WindowTitle           : Windows PowerShell V2
```

In the output, you see a number of properties, including the following:

- ForegroundColor, which sets the color of the prompt and text
- BackgroundColor, which sets the background color of the window
- WindowTitle, which sets the name of the PowerShell window

To work with the PowerShell window, you must obtain a reference to the $host object. The easiest way to do this is to store the $host object in a variable, such as

```
$myHostWin = $host.ui.rawui
```

After you have a reference to an object, you can work with the object through the available properties and methods. You can set the foreground or background color to any of the following default color values:

- Black, DarkBlue, DarkGreen, DarkCyan
- DarkRed, DarkMagenta, DarkYellow, Gray
- DarkGray, Blue, Green, Cyan
- Red, Magenta, Yellow, White

To do so, reference the host window object with the property name and the desired value, such as

```
$myHostWin.ForegroundColor = "White"
```

or

```
$myHostWin.BackgroundColor = "DarkGray"
```

Similarly, you can use the WindowTitle property to specify the title for the window. Here's an example:

```
$myHostWin.WindowTitle = "PowerShell on $env.computername"
```

Here, you set the window title to a value based on the computer name. Thus, if you are logged on to TechPC32, the window title is set to

```
PowerShell on TechPC32
```

Take a look back at the output values for the properties of the $host object. Several of properties have values separated by commas. This tells you the value is an array of subproperties. To view the subproperties of a property, you can examine that property separately and format the output as a list. For example, to examine the subproperties of CursorPosition, you can type the following command:

```
$host.ui.rawui.CursorPosition | format-list -property *
```

The output will look similar to the following:

```
X : 0
Y : 2999
```

This tells you the CursorPosition property has two subproperties: X and Y. You reference subproperties of properties by extending the dot notation as shown in these examples:

```
$host.ui.rawui.CursorPosition.X
```

or

```
$host.ui.rawui.CursorPosition.Y
```

If you continue examining subproperties of properties, you'll find both Cursor-Position and WindowPosition have X and Y subproperties. You'll also find that BufferSize, WindowSize, MaxWindowSize, and MaxPhysicalWindowSize have Width and Height properties.

After you know what the subproperties are, you can examine their values in the same way you examine the values of standard properties. However, in this case the subproperties cannot be set directly; you must create an instance of the $host object using the New-Object cmdlet and then modify the properties of the object instance.

This means you must first get a reference to the $host object as shown here:

```
$myHost = $host.ui.rawui
```

Then you create a new object instance and set the desired subproperties on the new instance as shown here:

```
$myHostWindowSize = New-Object
System.Management.Automation.Host.Size(150,100)
```

In this example, you dynamically set the host window size. The first value passed is the desired width. The second value passed is the desired height.

Working with COM and .NET Framework Objects

The Component Object Model (COM) and the .NET Framework are two object models you'll work with frequently in PowerShell. Although many applications provide scripting and administrative objects through COM, .NET Framework and even PowerShell cmdlets are becoming increasingly prevalent.

Creating and Using COM Objects

You can create instances of COM objects using the New-Object cmdlet. The basic syntax is

```
New-Object [-Set AssocArray] [-Strict] [-ComObject] String
```

When creating the object, set the –ComObject parameter to the object's programmatic identifier (ProgID). Most well-known COM objects can be used within PowerShell, including those for Windows Script Host (WSH). The following example creates a shortcut on your desktop:

```
$WshShell = New-Object -ComObject WScript.Shell
$scut = $WshShell.CreateShortcut("$Home\Desktop\PowerShellHome.lnk")
$scut.TargetPath = $PSHome
$scut.Save()
```

This shortcut is called *PowerShellHome*, and it links to the $PSHome directory.

TIP **After you've attached to a COM, you can use tab expansion to view available options. For example, if $a is your object, type $a. and then press Tab or Shift+Tab to browse available methods and properties.**

Beyond WSH, there are many other COM objects you can use. Table 6-4 lists some of these by their ProgID.

TABLE 6-4 Common COM Objects for Use with Windows PowerShell

PROGID	DESCRIPTION
Access.Application	Accesses Microsoft Office Access
CEnroll.Cenroll	Accesses certificate enrollment services
Excel.Application	Accesses Microsoft Office Excel
Excel.Sheet	Accesses worksheets in Excel
HNetCfg.FwMgr	Accesses Windows Firewall

TABLE 6-4 Common COM Objects for Use with Windows PowerShell

PROGID	DESCRIPTION
InternetExplorer.Application	Accesses Internet Explorer
MAPI.Session	Accesses Messaging Application Programming Interface (MAPI) sessions
Messenger.MessengerApp	Accesses Windows Messenger
Microsoft.Update.AutoUpdate	Accesses the autoupdate schedule for Microsoft Update
Microsoft.Update.Installer	Allows you to install updates from Microsoft Update
Microsoft.Update.Searches	Allows you to search for updates from Microsoft Update
Microsoft.Update.Session	Accesses the update history for Microsoft Update
Microsoft.Update.SystemInfo	Accesses system information for Microsoft Update
Outlook.Application	Accesses Microsoft Office Outlook
OutlookExpress.MessageList	Allows for automation of e-mail in Microsoft Office Outlook Express
PowerPoint.Application	Accesses Microsoft Office PowerPoint
Publisher.Application	Accesses Microsoft Office Publisher
SAPI.SpVoice	Accesses the Microsoft Speech application programming interface (API)
Scripting.FileSystemObject	Accesses the computer's file system
SharePoint.OpenDocuments	Accesses Microsoft SharePoint Services
Shell.Application	Accesses the Windows Explorer shell
Shell.LocalMachine	Accesses information about the Windows shell on the local computer
SQLDMO.SQLServer	Accesses the management features of Microsoft SQL Server
WMPlayer.OCX	Accesses Windows Media Player
Word.Application	Accesses Microsoft Office Word
Word.Document	Accesses documents in Word

To show you how easy it is to work with COM objects, I'll work through a series of basic examples with Windows Explorer, Internet Explorer, and Excel. The following example creates an instance of the Windows Explorer shell and then uses its Windows() method to display the location name of all open instances of Windows Explorer and Internet Explorer:

```
$shell = new-object -comobject shell.application
$shell.windows() | select-object locationname
```

```
Data
Computer
Network
Robert Stanek's Bugville Critters
Robert Stanek - Ruin Mist: The Lost Ages
Windows Nation: Home of Technology Author William Stanek
```

By piping the output to Select-Object LocationName, you display the value of the LocationName property for each shell object. Windows Explorer windows are listed by name or folder, such as Computer or Network. Internet Explorer windows are listed by Web page title. With Internet Explorer 7 and later, you get a listing for each page opened in a tabbed window as well. You get details about both Windows Explorer and Internet Explorer because both applications use the Windows Explorer shell.

If you want to know all the properties available for each shell object, pipe the output to Select-Object without specifying properties to display, as shown in this example and sample output:

```
$shell = new-object -comobject shell.application
$shell.windows() | select-object
```

```
Application           : System.__ComObject
Parent                : System.__ComObject
Container             :
Document              : mshtml.HTMLDocumentClass
TopLevelContainer     : True
Type                  : HTML Document
Left                  : 959
Top                   : 1
Width                 : 961
Height                : 1169
LocationName          : Windows Nation: Home of Tech Author William Stanek
LocationURL           : http://www.williamstanek.com/
Busy                  : False
Name                  : Windows Internet Explorer
HWND                  : 854818
FullName              : C:\Program Files\Internet Explorer\iexplore.exe
Path                  : C:\Program Files\Internet Explorer\
Visible               : True
```

```
StatusBar            : True
StatusText           : Done
ToolBar              : 1
MenuBar              : True
FullScreen           : False
ReadyState           : 4
Offline              : False
Silent               : False
RegisterAsBrowser    : False
RegisterAsDropTarget : True
TheaterMode          : False
AddressBar           : True
Resizable            : True
```

REAL WORLD Some COM objects have a .NET Framework wrapper that connects them to the .NET Framework. Because the behavior of the wrapper might be different from the behavior of the normal COM object, New-Object has a –Strict parameter to warn you about wrappers. When you use this flag, PowerShell displays a warning message to tell you that you are not working with a standard COM object. The COM object is still created, however.

The following example opens Internet Explorer to *www.williamstanek.com*:

```
$iexp = new-object -comobject "InternetExplorer.Application"
$iexp.navigate("www.williamstanek.com")
$iexp.visible = $true
```

Here, you create a new COM object for Internet Explorer. The new object has the same properties as those for the shell window listed previously. You use the Navigate() method to set the location to browse and the Visible property to display the window. To see a list of all methods and properties you can work with, enter the example and then type **$iexp | get-member**. You can call any method listed as shown in the example. You can modify properties that you can get and set.

The following example accesses the Microsoft Speech API and talks to you:

```
$v = new-object -comobject "SAPI.SPVoice"
$v.speak("Well, hello there. How are you?")
```

Here, you create a new COM object for the Speech API. You use the Speak() method to say something. To see a list of all methods and properties you can work with, enter the example and then enter **$v | get-member**. You can call any method listed as shown in the example. You can modify any property that you can get and set.

The following example works with Microsoft Excel:

```
$a = New-Object -comobject "Excel.Application"
$a.Visible = $True
$wb = $a.workbooks.add()
$ws = $wb.worksheets.item(1)

$ws.cells.item(1,1) = "Computer Name"
$ws.cells.item(1,2) = "Location"
$ws.cells.item(1,3) = "OS Type"
$ws.cells.item(2,1) = "TechPC84"
$ws.cells.item(2,2) = "5th Floor"
$ws.cells.item(2,3) = "Windows Vista"

$a.activeworkbook.saveas("c:\data\myws.xls")
```

Here, you create a new COM object for Excel and then you display the Excel window by setting the Visible property. When you instantiate the Excel object, you have a number of methods and properties available for working with the Excel application and a number of related subobjects that represent workbooks, worksheets, and individual table cells. To view the default values for properties of the Excel object, enter the example and then enter **$a**. To view the methods and properties available for working with the top-level Excel application object, enter **$a | get-member**.

After you create the Excel object, you add a workbook to the application window by using the Add() method of the Workbooks object. This creates a Workbook object, which also has methods and properties as well as a related Worksheets object array. To view the default values for properties of the Workbook object, enter **$wb**. To view the methods and properties available for working with the Workbook object, type **$wb | get-member**.

Next, you specify that you want to work with the first worksheet in the workbook you just created. You do this by using the Item() method of the Worksheets object array. This creates a Worksheet object, which also has methods and properties as well as a related Cells object array. To view the default values for properties of the Worksheet object, enter **$ws**. To view the methods and properties available for working with the Worksheet object, enter **$ws | get-member**.

Once you've created a worksheet, you can add data to the worksheet. You do this by using the Item() method of the Cells object array. When you call the Item() method, you specify the column and row position of the cell you want to write to and then specify the value you want. To view the default values for properties of the Cells object, enter **$ws.cells**. To view the methods and properties available for working with the Cells object, enter **$ws.cells | get-member**.

Individual table cells are represented by Cell objects. To view the default values for properties of the cell in column 1 row 1, enter **$ws.cells.item(1,1)**. To view the methods and properties available for working with the Cell object in column 1 row 1, enter **$ws.cells.item(1,1) | get-member**.

Working with .NET Framework Classes and Objects

The .NET Framework is so tightly integrated with PowerShell that it is difficult to talk about PowerShell and not talk about .NET as well. We've used .NET classes and .NET objects in this and other chapters.

One way to instantiate and use a .NET Framework object is to make a direct invocation to a static class. To do this, you enclose the class name in square brackets, insert two colon characters, and then add a method or property call. This is the same technique we previously used to work with instances of [System.Datetime], [System.Math], and other classes.

The following example creates an instance of the [System.Environment] class and gets the current directory:

```
[system.environment]::CurrentDirectory
```

```
C:\data\scripts\myscripts
```

> ***TIP*** **You can use tab expansion to view static members of a .NET Framework class. Type the class name in brackets, type :: and then press Tab or Shift+Tab to browse available methods and properties.**

You also can create a reference to an instance of a .NET Framework object using the New-Object cmdlet. The basic syntax is

```
New-Object [-Set AssocArray] [-TypePath Strings] [[-ArgumentList]
Objects] [-TypeName] String
```

The following example creates a reference object for the Application log through the System.Diagnostic.Eventlog object:

```
$log = new-object -type system.diagnostics.eventlog -argumentlist
application
```

```
Max(K) Retain OverflowAction        Entries Name
------ ------ --------------        ------- ----
20,480      0 OverwriteAsNeeded      45,061 application
```

> ***TIP*** **After you've attached to a .NET Framework class instance, you can use tab expansion to view instance members. For example, if you store the object in $log, you type $log, type a dot (.), and then press Tab or Shift+Tab to browse available methods and properties.**

Although we've looked at many .NET Framework classes in this chapter, there are many more available. Table 6-5 lists some of these by their class name.

TABLE 6-5 Common .NET Framework Objects for Use with Windows PowerShell

CLASS	DESCRIPTION
Microsoft.Win32.Registry	Provides Registry objects for working with root keys
Microsoft.Win32.RegistryKey	Represents keys in the registry
System.AppDomain	Represents the environment where applications execute
System.Array	Provides interaction with arrays
System.Console	Represents the standard input, output, and error streams for the console
System.Convert	Provides static methods and a property for converting data types
System.Datetime	Represents a datetime value
System.Diagnostics.Debug	Provides methods and properties for debugging
System.Diagnostics.EventLog	Provides interaction with Windows event logs
System.Diagnostics.Process	Provides interaction with Windows processes
System.Drawing.Bitmap	Represents pixel data for images
System.Drawing.Image	Provides methods and properties for working with images
System.Environment	Provides information about the working environment and platform
System.Guid	Represents a globally unique identifier (GUID)
System.IO.Stream	Represents IO streams
System.Management.Automation.PowerShell	Represents a PowerShell object to which you can add notes, properties, and so on
System.Math	Provides static methods and properties for performing mathematical functions
System.Net.Dns	Provides interaction with Domain Name System (DNS)
System.Net.NetworkCredential	Provides credentials for network authentication

TABLE 6-5 Common .NET Framework Objects for Use with Windows PowerShell

CLASS	DESCRIPTION
System.Net.WebClient	Provides interaction with the Web client
System.Random	Represents a random number generator
System.Reflection.Assembly	Represents .NET Framework assemblies so that you can load and work with them
System.Security.Principal.WellKnownSidType	Represents security identifiers (SIDs)
System.Security.Principal.WindowsBuiltInRole	Specifies built-in roles
System.Security.Principal.WindowsIdentity	Represents a Windows user
System.Security.Principal.WindowsPrincipal	Allows checking of a user's group membership
System.Security.SecureString	Represents secure text that is encrypted for privacy
System.String	Provides interaction with strings
System.Text.RegularExpressions.Regex	Represents immutable regular expressions
System.Threading.Thread	Provides interaction with threads
System.Type	Represents type declarations
System.Uri	Represents uniform resource identifiers (URIs)
System.Windows.Forms.FlowLayoutPanel	Represents a layout panel
System.Windows.Forms.Form	Represents a window or dialog box in an application

Some .NET Framework objects require that related .NET Framework assemblies be loaded before you can use them. Assemblies are simply sets of files, which can include dynamic-link libraries (DLLs), EXE files, and other resources that the .NET Framework object needs to work properly. You'll know that a .NET Framework object requires an assembly because PowerShell will throw an error if the assembly is not loaded, such as

```
Unable to find type [system.drawing.image]: make sure that the assembly
containing this type is loaded.
At line:1 char:23
```

```
+ [system.drawing.image] <<<< |get-member -static
    + CategoryInfo          : InvalidOperation: (system.drawing.
image:String)
[], RuntimeException
    + FullyQualifiedErrorId : TypeNotFound
```

The solution is to use the [Reflection.Assembly] class to load the required assemblies. One way to do this is with the LoadWithPartialName() method of the Reflection.Assembly class. The syntax is

```
[Reflection.Assembly]::LoadWithPartialName("ClassName")
```

where *ClassName* is the name of the .NET Framework class that completes the requirement. For example, you can use the System.Drawing.Bitmap class to convert a GIF image to JPEG. Because this class requires the assemblies of the System.Windows.Forms class, you must load the related assemblies before you can convert an image.

When you load a reflection assembly, PowerShell confirms this and displays the related output automatically as shown in this example:

```
[Reflection.Assembly]::LoadWithPartialName("System.Windows.Forms")
```

```
GAC    Version        Location
---    -------        --------
True   v2.0.50727     C:\Windows\assembly\GAC_MSIL\System.Windows.Forms
\2.0.0.0__b77a5c561934e089\System.Windows.For...
```

This output is important. The True value for GAC tells you the assembly loaded successfully. The Version value tells you the specific version of .NET Framework the assembly uses. The location tells you the location in the operating system.

When you call a reflection assembly, I recommend formatting the output as a list as shown in this example:

```
[Reflection.Assembly]::LoadWithPartialName("System.Windows.Forms") |
format-list
```

```
CodeBase : file:///C:/Windows/assembly/GAC_MSIL/System.Windows.Forms/
2.0.0.0__b77a5c561934e089/System.Windows.Forms.dll
EntryPoint :
EscapedCodeBase : file:///C:/Windows/assembly/GAC_MSIL/System.Windows.
Forms/2.0.0.0__b77a5c561934e089/System.Windows.Forms.dll
FullName  : System.Windows.Forms, Version=2.0.0.0, Culture=neutral,
PublicKeyToken=b77a5c561934e089
GlobalAssemblyCache    : True
```

```
HostContext              : 0
ImageFileMachine         :
ImageRuntimeVersion      : v2.0.50727
Location                 : C:\Windows\assembly\GAC_MSIL\System.Windows.
Forms\2.0.0.0__b77a5c561934e089\System.Windows.Forms.dll
ManifestModule           : System.Windows.Forms.dll
MetadataToken            :
PortableExecutableKind :
ReflectionOnly           : False
```

This listing gives you important additional details about the assembly you just loaded, including the simple text name, version number, culture identifier, and public key. All of this information is listed as the FullName entry. If you copy the FullName entry exactly, beginning with the simple text name, you have the full load string you need to use the Load() method. Because the Load() method is the preferred way to load assemblies and the LoadWithPartialName() method is deprecated, this will help you prepare for when you can no longer use the LoadWithPartialName() method.

To continue the example, after you've loaded the [System.Windows.Forms] class, you can convert a GIF image in the current directory to JPEG using the following statements:

```
$image = New-Object System.Drawing.Bitmap myimage.gif

$image.Save("mynewimage.jpg","JPEG")
```

Here, you get an image called MyImage.gif in the current directory and then convert the image to JPEG format. You can substitute any GIF image and add an image path as necessary. While you are working with the image, you can view its width, height, and other properties by entering **$image**. You can view methods for working with the image by entering **$image | get-member**.

Working with WMI Objects and Queries

Computers running Windows XP and later versions of Windows support Windows Management Instrumentation (WMI). WMI is a management framework that you can use to query a computer to determine its attributes. For example, you can create a WMI query to determine the operating system running on a computer or the amount of available memory. WMI queries by themselves are helpful, especially when used in scripts.

You can use WMI queries to examine settings based on just about any measurable characteristic of a computer, including

- Amount of memory installed
- Available hard disk space

- Processor type or speed
- Network adapter type or speed
- Operating system version, service pack level, or hotfix
- Registry key or key value
- System services that are running

You create WMI queries using the WMI Query Language. The basic syntax is

```
Select * from WMIObjectClass where Condition
```

In this syntax, *WMIObjectClass* is the WMI object class you want to work with, and *Condition* is the condition you want to evaluate. The Select statement returns objects of the specified class. A condition has three parts:

- The name of the object property you are examining
- An operator, such as = for equals, > for greater than, or < for less than
- The value to evaluate

Operators can also be defined by using –Is or –Like. The –Is operator is used to exactly match criteria. The –Like condition is used to match a keyword or text string within a value. In the following example, you create a query to look for computers running Windows Vista:

```
Select * from Win32_OperatingSystem where Caption like "%Vista%"
```

The Win32_OperatingSystem class tracks the overall operating system configuration. The Win32_OperatingSystem class is one of two WMI object classes that you'll use frequently. The other is Win32_ComputerSystem. The Win32_ComputerSystem class tracks the overall computer configuration.

In Windows PowerShell, you can use the Get-WMIObject cmdlet to get a WMI object that you want to work with. The basic syntax is

```
Get-WmiObject -Class WMIClass -Namespace NameSpace -ComputerName
ComputerName
```

where *WMIClass* is the WMI class you want to work with, *NameSpace* sets the namespace to use within WMI, and *ComputerName* sets the name of the computer to work with.

When working with WMI, you should work with the root namespace, as specified by setting the –Namespace parameter to root/cimv2. By using the –Computer parameter, you can specify the computer you want to work with. If you want to work with the local computer, use a dot (.) instead of a computer name. By redirecting the object to Format-List *, you can list all the properties of the object and their values.

Following this, you can examine the Win32_OperatingSystem object and its properties to obtain summary information regarding the operating system configuration of a computer by typing the following command at the Windows PowerShell prompt:

```
Get-WmiObject -Class Win32_OperatingSystem -Namespace root/cimv2
 -ComputerName . | Format-List *
```

To save the output in a file, simply redirect the output to a file. In the following example, you redirect the output to a file in the working directory named os_save.txt:

```
Get-WmiObject -Class Win32_OperatingSystem -Namespace root/cimv2
-ComputerName . | Format-List * > os_save.txt
```

The detailed operating system information tells you a great deal about the operating system running on the computer. The same is true for computer configuration details, which can be obtained by typing the following command at a Windows PowerShell prompt:

```
Get-WmiObject -Class Win32_ComputerSystem -Namespace root/cimv2
-ComputerName . | Format-List *
```

In addition to targeting operating system or computer configuration properties, you might want to target computers based on the amount of disk space and file system type. In the following example, you target computers that have more than 100 megabytes (MB) of available space on the C, D, or G partition:

```
get-wmiobject -query 'Select * from Win32_LogicalDisk where (Name = "C:"
OR Name = "D:"  OR Name = "G:" ) AND DriveType = 3 AND FreeSpace
> 104857600 AND FileSystem = "NTFS"'
```

In the preceding example, *DriveType = 3* represents a local disk, and *FreeSpace* units are in bytes (100 MB = 104,857,600 bytes). The partitions must be located on one or more local fixed disks, and they must be running the NTFS file system. Note that while PowerShell understands storage units in MB, KB, or whatever, the WMI query language does not.

In Windows PowerShell, you can examine all the properties of the Win32_LogicalDisk object by typing the following command at the Windows PowerShell prompt:

```
Get-WmiObject -Class Win32_LogicalDisk -Namespace root/cimv2
-ComputerName . | Format-List *
```

As you'll see, there are many properties you can work with, including Compressed, which indicates whether a disk is compressed. Table 6-6 provides an overview of these and other important WMI object classes.

TABLE 6-6 WMI Classes Commonly Used with Windows PowerShell

WMI CLASS	DESCRIPTIONS
Win32_BaseBoard	Represents the motherboard
Win32_BIOS	Represents the attributes of the computer's firmware
Win32_BootConfiguration	Represents the computer's boot configuration
Win32_CacheMemory	Represents cache memory on the computer
Win32_CDROMDrive	Represents each CD-ROM drive configured on the computer
Win32_ComputerSystem	Represents a computer system in a Windows environment
Win32_Desktop	Represents the common characteristics of a user's desktop
Win32_DesktopMonitor	Represents the type of monitor or display device connected to the computer
Win32_DiskDrive	Represents each physical disk drive on a computer
Win32_DiskPartition	Represents each partitioned area of a physical disk
Win32_DiskQuota	Tracks disk space usage for NTFS volumes
Win32_Environment	Represents a system environment setting on a computer
Win32_LogicalDisk	Represents each logical disk device used for data storage
Win32_LogonSession	Provides information about the current logon session
Win32_NetworkAdapter	Represents each network adapter on the computer
Win32_NetworkAdapter-Configuration	Represents the configuration of each network adapter on the computer
Win32_NetworkConnection	Represents an active network connection
Win32_OperatingSystem	Represents the working environment for the operating system

TABLE 6-6 WMI Classes Commonly Used with Windows PowerShell

WMI CLASS	DESCRIPTIONS
Win32_OSRecoveryConfiguration	Represents recovery and dump files
Win32_PageFileUsage	Represents the page file used for handling virtual memory swapping
Win32_PhysicalMemory	Represents each DIMM of physical memory configured on the computer
Win32_PhysicalMemoryArray	Represents the total memory configuration of the computer by capacity and number of memory devices
Win32_Printer	Represents each configured print device on the computer
Win32_PrinterConfiguration	Represents configuration details for print devices
Win32_PrintJob	Represents active print jobs generated by applications
Win32_Processor	Represents each processor or processor core on the computer
Win32_QuickFixEngineeering	Represents updates that have been applied to the computer
Win32_Registry	Represents the Windows registry
Win32_SCSIController	Represents each SCSI controller on the computer
Win32_Service	Represents each service configured on the computer
Win32_Share	Represents each file share configured on the computer
Win32_SoundDevice	Represents the computer's sound device

Using the techniques I discussed previously, you can examine the properties of any or all of these objects in Windows PowerShell. If you do, you will find that Win32_PhysicalMemoryArray has a MaxCapacity property that tracks the total physical memory in kilobytes. Knowing this, you can easily create a WMI query to look for computers with 256 MB of RAM or more. The WMI query to handle the task is the following:

```
if (get-wmiobject -query "Select * from Win32_PhysicalMemoryArray where
MaxCapacity > 262000") {write-host $env:computername}
```

```
CORPC87
```

I used the value 262000 because there are 262,144 kilobytes in 256 MB, and we want the computer to have at least this capacity. Now if you add this statement to a job running on remote computers as discussed in Chapter 4, "Using Sessions, Jobs, and Remoting," you can search across the enterprise to find computers that meet your specifications.

To display a complete list of WMI objects, type the following command at the Windows PowerShell prompt:

```
Get-WmiObject -list -Namespace root/cimv2 -ComputerName . | Format-List name
```

Because the list of available objects is so long, you'll definitely want to redirect the output to a file. In the following example, you redirect the output to a file in the working directory called FullWMIObjectList.txt:

```
Get-WmiObject -list -Namespace root/cimv2 -ComputerName . |
Format-List name > FullWMIObjectList.txt
```

Rather than viewing all WMI classes, you might want to see only the Win32 WMI classes. To view only the Win32 WMI classes, use the following command:

```
Get-WmiObject -list | where {$_.name -like "*Win32_*"}
```

CHAPTER 7

Managing Computers with Commands and Scripts

PowerShell scripts are text files containing the commands you want to execute. These are the same commands you normally type at the PowerShell prompt. However, rather than type the commands each time you want to use them, you create a script to store the commands for easy execution.

Although scripts are useful, you'll more often work with PowerShell directly at the PowerShell prompt. You can create some extensive one-liners that'll let you do just about anything, and if one line won't suffice, you can type multiple lines of commands just as you would in a script. Additionally, if you want to copy examples from a document, the PowerShell console allows you to copy and paste a series of commands in the same way as you copy and paste a single command. The only difference is that with a series of commands, PowerShell executes each command separately.

Getting More from Your Scripts and Profiles

Because scripts contain standard text characters, you can create and edit scripts using any standard text editor as well as the PowerShell Integrated Scripting Environment (ISE). When you type commands, be sure to place each command or group of commands that should be executed together on a new line or to separate commands with a semicolon. Both techniques ensure proper execution of the commands. When you have finished creating a PowerShell script, save the script file using the .ps1 extension. In most cases, you'll be able to save scripts only to restricted areas of the file system if you start the PowerShell ISE or your text editor as an administrator.

When you save a script, you can execute it as if it were a cmdlet or external utility: simply type the path to the script, type the name of the script, and press Enter. When you do this, PowerShell reads the script file and executes its commands one by one. It stops executing the script when it reaches the end of the file. Any output from the script is written to the PowerShell console, unless you explicitly specify otherwise.

Don't forget that your PowerShell profiles are some of the most powerful scripts you can create. Your profiles can contain aliases, functions, and variables that you can use at any time. When you are logged on locally, the profiles in $pshome and $home affect you. When you are using remoting, the profiles in $pshome and $home on the remote computer affect you.

Listing 7-1 shows an example profile. This profile defines several functions and several aliases. The Prompt function modifies the prompt so that it always shows the current path and the computer name. The GetWinRm function gets the status of the Windows Remote Management service. The GetS function lists configured services by their status, such as Running or Stopped. The Inventory function lists the properties of the Win32_OperatingSystem. Three aliases provide keystroke shortcuts to functions: gr for GetWinRm, gs for GetS, and inv for Inventory.

LISTING 7-1 An Example Profile

```
function prompt {"PS $(get-location) [$env:computername]> "}

new-alias gr getwinrm
new-alias gs gets
new-alias inv inventory
function getwinrm {
   get-service -name winrm | format-list
}

function gets {param ($status)
   get-service | where { $_.status -eq $status}
}

function inventory {param ($name = ".")
   get-wmiobject -class win32_operatingsystem -namespace root/cimv2 `
    -computername $name | format-list *
}
```

> ***NOTE*** **The third line from the bottom includes a back apostrophe (`). As discussed in previous chapters, this character tells PowerShell the command is continued on the next line. If you have trouble typing a line with a continuation character, simply type the divided lines as a single line without the back apostrophe (`).**

You are able to use variables, aliases, and functions in profiles because they are loaded into the global working environment. As you get used to using the additional elements you've created, you'll increasingly want them to be available whenever you are logged on and working with Windows. In some cases, you'll be able to copy your profiles to the computers you work with, such as with servers you manage, and you'll then be able to take advantage of the features you've built into your profile. However, copying your profile to every possible computer you'll work with in the enterprise isn't practical. In these cases, you still can take advantage of your profile if you prepare ahead of time.

To prepare, you need to modify a copy of your profile so that its elements are declared as global explicitly. Listing 7-2 shows how you can accomplish this for the sample profile created previously. Next, you need to save the modified profile in a location that will be accessible on other computers you work with, such as a network share. Finally, on the computer you are working with, you can load the script into the global environment by running it. Be sure to specify the full path to the script, such as \\FileServer84\DataShare\wrstanek\profile.ps1.

LISTING 7-2 Example of a Modified Profile

```
function global:prompt {"PS $(get-location) [$env:computername]> "}

new-alias gr getwinrm -scope global
new-alias gs gets -scope global
new-alias inv inventory -scope global

function global:getwinrm {
   get-service -name winrm | format-list
}

function global:gets {param ($status)
   get-service | where { $_.status -eq $status}
}

function global:inventory {param ($name = ".")
   get-wmiobject -class win32_operatingsystem -namespace root/cimv2 -
computername $name | format-list *
}
```

Keep in mind that execution policy must be set to allow you to run scripts from remote resources. If execution policy requires remote scripts to be signed, you need to add a signature to the script before you can run it. Additionally, before PowerShell runs the script, you will likely see a security warning similar to the following:

```
Security Warning
Run only scripts that you trust. While scripts from the Internet can be
useful, this script can potentially harm your computer. Do you want to
run \\192.168.1.252\wrs\profileold.ps1?
[D] Do not run  [R] Run once  [S] Suspend  [?] Help (default is "D"):
```

To proceed and run the script, you need to type **R** and press Enter. For more information about execution policy and scripting signing, see the "Using Scripts" section in Chapter 1, "Introducing Windows PowerShell."

Creating Transcripts

The PowerShell console includes a transcript feature to help you record all your activities at the prompt. As of this writing, you cannot use this feature in the PowerShell application. Commands you use with transcripts include the following:

- **Start-Transcript** Initializes a transcript file and then creates a record of all subsequent actions in the PowerShell session

```
Start-Transcript [[-path] FilePath] [-force] [-noClobber] [-append]
```

- **Stop-Transcript** Stops recording actions in the session and finalizes the transcript

```
Stop-Transcript
```

You tell PowerShell to start recording your activities using the Start-Transcript cmdlet. This cmdlet creates a text transcript that includes all commands that you type at the prompt and all the output from these commands that appears on the console. The basic syntax for Start-Transcript is

```
Start-Transcript [[-path] FilePath]
```

where *FilePath* specifies an alternate save location for the transcript file. Although you cannot use wildcards when you set the path, you can use variables. The directories in the path must exist or the command fails.

> ***NOTE*** **If you do not specify a path, Start-Transcript uses the path in the value of the $Transcript global variable. If you have not created this variable, Start-Transcript stores the transcript in the $Home\[My]Documents directory as a PowerShell_transcript.*TimeStamp*.txt file, where *TimeStamp* is a date-time stamp.**

Use the –Force parameter to override restrictions that prevent the command from succeeding. For example, –Force will override the read-only attribute on an existing file. However, –Force will not modify security or change file permissions.

By default, if a transcript file exists in the specified path, Start-Transcript overwrites the file without warning. Use the –noClobber parameter to stop PowerShell from overwriting an existing file. Alternatively, use the –Append parameter to add the new transcript to the end of an existing file.

When you want to stop recording the transcript, you can either exit the console or type **Stop-Transcript**. The Stop-Transcript cmdlet requires no additional parameters.

REAL WORLD When you start a transcript, PowerShell initializes the transcript file by inserting a header similar to the following:

```
**********************
Windows PowerShell Transcript Start
Start time: 20100211134826
Username  : CPANDL\Bubba
Machine   : TECHPC85 (Microsoft Windows NT 6.0.6001
Service Pack 1)
**********************
Transcript started, output file is C:\Users\Bubba\Documents\
PowerShell_transcript.20100211134826.txt
```

This header specifies the time the transcript was started, the user who started the transcript, the computer for which the transcript was created, and the full path to the transcript file. Note that the user name is provided in DOMAIN\UserName or MachineName\UserName format and that the machine information includes the Windows version and service pack. This information is helpful when you are troubleshooting, because it enables you to know if the script is running in the wrong user context or against a computer running an incompatible version of Windows. When you stop a transcript, PowerShell inserts a footer similar to the following:

```
**********************
Windows PowerShell Transcript End
End time: 20090211134958
**********************
```

This footer specifies the time the transcript was stopped. The difference between the start time and the stop time is the elapsed run time for a script or the total troubleshooting/work time when you are working at the prompt.

Creating Transactions

A transaction is a block of commands that are managed as a unit where either all the commands are successful and completed, or all the commands are undone and rolled back because one or more commands failed. You can use transactions when you want to be sure that every command in a block of commands is successful and to avoid leaving the computer in a damaged or unpredictable state.

Understanding Transactions

Whether you are working with relational databases, distributed computing environments, or PowerShell, transactions are some of the most powerful commands you can work with. Why? Because transactions ensure that changes are applied only when appropriate, and when you encounter any problems, the changes are undone and the original working environment is restored.

To restore the working environment, transacted commands must keep track of changes that were made as well as the original content and values. Because of this, commands must be designed specifically to support transactions, and not all commands can or do support transactions. In PowerShell, support for transactions must be implemented at two levels:

- **Provider** Providers that provide cmdlets must be designed to support transactions.
- **Cmdlet** Individual cmdlets, implemented on compliant providers, must be designed to support transactions.

In the core PowerShell environment, with Windows Vista or later, the only core component that supports transactions is the Registry provider. On this provider, the Item-related cmdlets support transactions, including New-Item, Set-Item, Clear-Item, Copy-Item, Move-Item, and Remove-Item. You can also use the System.Management .Automation.TransactedString class to include expressions in transactions on any version of Windows that supports Windows PowerShell. Other providers can be updated to support transactions, and you can look for compliant providers by typing the following command:

```
get-psprovider | where {$_.Capabilities -like "*transactions*"}
```

At their most basic, transactions work like this:

1. You start a transaction.
2. You perform transacted commands.
3. You commit or undo transacted commands.

Transactions also can have subscribers. A subscriber is a sequence of transacted commands that is handled as a subunit within an existing transaction. For example, if you are using PowerShell to work with a database, you might want to start a transaction prior to changing data in the database. Then you might want to create subtransactions for each data set you are manipulating. Because the success or failure of each subtransaction determines the success or failure of the entire transaction, you must commit each subtransaction separately before you commit the primary transaction.

Cmdlets you can use with transactions include the following:

- **Get-Transaction** Gets an object that represents the current active transaction in the session or the last transaction if there is no active transaction. This allows you to view the rollback preference, the subscriber count, and the status of the transaction.

  ```
  Get-Transaction
  ```

- **Complete-Transaction** Commits an active transaction, which finalizes the transaction and permanently applies any related changes. If the transaction includes multiple subscribers, you must type one

Complete-Transaction command for every dependent subscriber to commit the transaction fully.

```
Complete-Transaction
```

- **Start-Transaction** Starts a new independent transaction or joins an existing transaction as a dependent subscriber. The default rollback preference is Error. Although there is no default time-out for transactions started at the command line, the default timeout for transactions started in a script is 30 minutes.

```
Start-Transaction [-Independent] [-RollbackPreference {Error |
TerminatingError | Never}] [-Timeout Minutes]
```

- **Undo-Transaction** Rolls back the active transaction, which undoes any related changes and restores the original working environment. If the transaction includes multiple subscribers, the Undo-Transaction command rolls back the entire transaction for all subscribers.

```
Undo-Transaction
```

- **Use-Transaction** Adds a script block to the active transaction, enabling transacted scripting of compliant .NET Framework objects, such as instances of the System.Management.Automation.TransactedString class. You cannot use noncompliant objects in a transacted script block. To enter the active transaction, you must use the –UseTransaction parameter. Otherwise, the command is ineffective.

```
Use-Transaction [-UseTransaction] [-TransactedScript] ScriptBlock
```

REAL WORLD Cmdlets that support transactions have a –UseTransaction parameter. As changes are made to PowerShell, you can find cmdlets that support transactions by typing the following command: **get-help * -parameter UseTransaction**. If a cmdlet has this parameter, the cmdlet supports transactions. Note that default cmdlets, such as the Item cmdlets with the Registry provider, might not be listed in the help documents as having the –UseTransaction parameter.

When you use transactions to modify a computer's configuration, keep in mind the data that is affected by the transaction is not changed until you commit the transaction. However, other commands that are not part of the transaction could make the same changes, and this could affect the working environment. Although most transactional systems, such as relational databases, have a feature that locks data while you are working on it, PowerShell does not have a lock feature.

In each PowerShell session, only one independent transaction can be active at a time. If you start a new, independent transaction while a transaction is in progress, the new transaction becomes the active transaction, and you must complete the new transaction before making any changes to the original transaction. You complete transactions by committing or rolling back changes.

With a successful transaction, all the changes made by the commands are committed and applied to the working environment. With an unsuccessful transaction, all the changes made by the commands are undone, and the working environment is restored to its original state. By default, transactions are rolled back automatically if any command in the transaction generates an error.

Using Transactions

To start a new independent transaction or join an existing transaction as a dependent subscriber, you type **start-transaction** at the PowerShell prompt or in a script. By default, if you use Start-Transaction while a transaction is in progress, the existing transaction object is reused, and the subscriber count is incremented by one. You can think of this as joining the original transaction. To complete a transaction with multiple subscribers, you must type a Complete-Transaction command for each subscriber.

> ***NOTE*** **PowerShell supports subscribers to transactions to accommodate environments when a script contains a transaction that calls another script that contains its own transaction. Because the transactions are related, they should be rolled back or committed as a unit.**

Start-Transaction supports three parameters: –Independent, –RollbackPreference, and –Timeout. The –Independent parameter applies only when a transaction is already in progress in the session. If you use the –Independent parameter, a new transaction is created that can be completed or undone without affecting the original transaction. However, because only one transaction can be active at a time, you must complete or roll back the new transaction before resuming work with the original transaction.

In the following example and sample output, you start a transaction with automatic rollback set to Never and a timeout value of 30 minutes:

```
start-transaction -rollbackpreference "never" -timeout 30
```

```
Suggestion [1,Transactions]: Once a transaction is started, only commands
that get called with the -UseTransaction flag become part of that
transaction.
```

By adding the –RollbackPreference parameter, you can specify whether a transaction is automatically rolled back. Valid values are

- **Error** Transactions are rolled back automatically if any command in the transaction generates a terminating or nonterminating error. This is the default.

- **TerminatingError** Transactions are rolled back automatically if any command in the transaction generates a terminating error.
- **Never** Transactions are never rolled back automatically.

You can use the –Timeout parameter to specify the maximum time, in minutes, that a transaction can be active. When the timeout expires, the transaction is automatically rolled back. By default, there is no timeout for transactions started at the command line. When transactions are started by a script, the default timeout is 30 minutes.

After you've started a transaction, you can perform transacted commands in two ways. You can

- Add script blocks to the active transaction with Use-Transaction.
- Add an individual command to the active transaction using the command's –UseTransaction parameter.

PowerShell executes the script blocks and commands as you add them to the transaction, taking appropriate action if errors are encountered or if the timeout value is reached. You can obtain information about the transaction using Get-Transaction as shown in this example and sample output:

```
get-transaction
```

```
RollbackPreference   SubscriberCount   Status
------------------   ---------------   ------
Never                3                 Active
```

Here, Get-Transaction shows you the rollback preference is Never, the subscriber count is 3, and the status of the transaction is Active.

If PowerShell doesn't automatically roll back the transaction, because of errors or a timeout expiration, you can manually commit or roll back the transaction. To commit the transaction, you type **complete-transaction** once for each subscriber. To undo a transaction completely for all subscribers, you type **undo-transaction**.

Consider the following example:

```
start-transaction

cd hkcu:\Software
new-item MyKey -UseTransaction
new-itemproperty -path MyKey -Name Current -value "Windows PowerShell" `
-UseTransaction

complete-transaction
```

Here, you start a transaction so that you can work safely with the registry. You access the HKCU\Software hive and create a new key called MyKey. Then you add a value to this key. As long as these operations did not generate an error, the transaction continues to be active, and you then apply the changes by completing the transaction.

Common Elements in Scripts

Now that we've discussed how to work with scripts, let's look at common elements you'll use in scripts, including

- Comments
- Initializing statements
- Conditional statements
- Control loops

Using Comments and Initializing Statements

Most scripts begin with comments that specify what a script is for and how it is used. PowerShell supports two types of comments:

- Single-line comments that begin with #. PowerShell interprets everything from the begin-comment mark to the end of the line as a comment. Here is an example:

```
$myVar = "$env:computername" #Get the computer name
```

> **NOTE** Because values in strings are interpreted differently and # is not interpreted as a special character in a string, you can use # in single-quoted and double-quoted strings, and # will not be handled as the beginning of a comment.

- Multiple-line comments that begin with the <# delimiter and end with the #> delimiter. If you have a begin-comment delimiter, you must have a matching end-comment delimiter. PowerShell interprets everything between the begin and end comment tags as a comment. Here is an example:

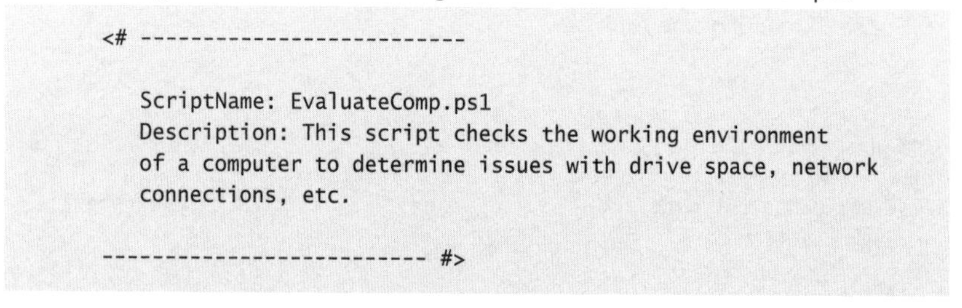

```
<# ------------------------

   ScriptName: EvaluateComp.ps1
   Description: This script checks the working environment
   of a computer to determine issues with drive space, network
   connections, etc.

------------------------ #>
```

Every script you create should have comments that include the following details:

- When the script was created and last modified
- Who created the script

- What the script is used for
- How to contact the script creator
- Whether and where the script output is stored

Not only are the answers to the questions of who, what, how, where, and when important for ensuring that the scripts you create can be used by other administrators, they can also help you remember what a particular script does, especially if weeks or months have passed since you last worked with the script. An example of a script that uses comments to answer these questions is shown as Listing 7-3.

LISTING 7-3 Sample Script Header

```
<# -------------------------
   ScriptName: CheckDNS.ps1
   Creation Date: 2/28/2010
   Last Modified: 3/15/2010
   Author: William R. Stanek
   E-mail: williamstanek@aol.com
   *************************
   Description: Checks DNS and IP configuration.
   *************************
   Files: Stores output in c:\data\checkdns.txt.

------------------------- #>
```

REAL WORLD **Keep in mind that you can also use comments to**

- **Insert explanatory text within scripts, such as documentation on how a function works.**
- **Prevent a command from executing. On the command line, add # before the command to comment it out.**
- **Hide part of a line from interpretation. Add # within a line to block interpretation of everything that follows the # character.**

After you add a header to your script, you might want to initialize the console so that the working environment appears the same way every time. For example, you might want to use Cls (or Clear-Host) to clear the console window and reset the screen buffer, and use the Start-Transcript cmdlet to record all output to a transcript file. If you start a transcript, be sure to add a Stop-Transcript cmdlet at the end of your script to end the transcript session.

You also might want your script to initialize the PowerShell window by setting the window size, text color, and window title. Here is an example:

```
if ($host.name -eq "ConsoleHost") {
$size=New-Object System.Management.Automation.Host.Size(120,80);
$host.ui.rawui.WindowSize=$size }
```

```
$myHostWin = $host.ui.rawui
$myHostWin.ForegroundColor = "Blue"
$myHostWin.BackgroundColor = "Yellow"
$myHostWin.WindowTitle = "Working Script"
```

Here, you get an instance of the System.Management.Automation.Host object so that you can set the window size to 120 lines high by 80 characters wide if you are working with the PowerShell console. Then you use properties of the $host.ui.rawui object to specify that you want to use blue text on a yellow background and a window title of Working Script. For more information on these object instances, see the "Digging Deeper into Functions" and "Digging Deeper into Objects" sections in Chapter 6, "Mastering Aliases, Functions, and Objects."

NOTE When you dynamically reset the size of the PowerShell console, you must keep in mind the current display resolution and the console's configured dimensions. You shouldn't set the width and height of the console so that it is larger than the display size. You'll get an error if you try to set the width of the console so that it is greater than the buffer size. Because resizing the window won't work with the PowerShell application, you may want to check the value of the $Host.Name property to ensure that you are working with the console and not the PowerShell ISE. $Host.Name is set to "Windows PowerShell ISE Host" for the PowerShell application and "ConsoleHost" for the PowerShell console.

When you are initializing the script, you also want to ensure the following:

- The script will run on a computer with a compatible version of PowerShell.
- The host application is indeed Windows PowerShell.
- Required PowerShell snap-ins, providers, and modules are available.

PowerShell includes a #Requires statement that you can use to validate the PowerShell version, the host application, and the availability of snap-ins. Using #Requires statements, you can do the following:

- Verify the PowerShell version, where *N* is the version number and *n* is the optional revision number. To verify the PowerShell version is 2.0 or later, use *2* or *2.0*.

```
#requires -Version N[.n]

#requires -version 2
#requires -version 2.0
```

- Verify the host application ID, where *ShellID* is the identifier for the host application. To verify the host application is the PowerShell console or PowerShell ISE, use a value of *Microsoft.PowerShell*.

```
#requires -ShellId ShellId

#requires -ShellId "Microsoft.PowerShell"
```

- Verify a specified snap-in—or, optionally, a specified version of the snap-in—is loaded in the current session, where *PSSnapIn* is the snap-in identifier and the optional *N* and *.n* values set the required version.

```
#requires -PsSnapIn PsSnapIn [-Version N[.n]]

#requires -PsSnapIn ADRMS.PS.Admin -Version 2
```

Whenever you use #Requires statements, the script runs only if the computer meets the criteria set in the #Requires statements. For additional discussion on this topic, see the "Navigating Windows PowerShell Extensions" section in Chapter 3, "Managing Your Windows PowerShell Environment."

As with most cmdlets and external utilities, you can pass arguments to scripts when you start them. You use arguments to set special parameters in a script or to pass along information needed by the script. Each argument should follow the script name and be separated by a space (and enclosed in quotation marks if necessary). In the following example, a script named Check-Computer in the current working directory is passed the arguments FileServer26 and Extended:

```
.\check-computer fileserver26 extended
```

Each value passed along to a script can be examined using the $args array. You reference the first argument using $args[0], the second using $args[1], and so on. The script name itself is represented by the $MyInvocation.MyCommand.Name property. The full file path to the script is represented by the $MyInvocation.MyCommand.Path property.

> ***NOTE*** **Because PowerShell stores arguments in an array, there is no limit to the number of arguments you can pass to a script. Further, regardless of the number of arguments you use, the last argument is always represented by $args[$arg.length - 1], and the total number of arguments used is represented by $args.count. If no arguments are passed to a script, the argument count is zero.**

Using Conditional Statements

Now that you know how to work with and initialize scripts, let's look at the selection statements used to control the flow of execution based upon conditions known only at run time. These statements include:

- If...Else, to execute a block of statements if a condition is matched (true or false) and to otherwise execute a second block of statements.
- If...ElseIf...Else, to execute a block of statements if a condition is matched (true or false). Otherwise, it's used to execute a second block of statements if a second condition is matched. Finally, it's used to execute a third block of statements if neither of the previous conditions is met.

- If Not, to execute a statement when a condition is false. Otherwise, the statement is bypassed.
- Switch, to perform a series of three or more conditional tests.

Using If, If...Else, and If...ElseIf...Else

Although some of the previous examples in this book used conditional execution, we haven't discussed the syntax for these statements. If your background doesn't include programming, you probably will be surprised by the power and flexibility of these statements.

The If statement is used for conditional branching. It can be used to route script execution through two different paths. Its basic syntax is

```
if (condition) {codeblock1} [else {codeblock2}]
```

Here, each code block can contain a single command or multiple commands. The condition is any expression that returns a Boolean value of True or False when evaluated. The Else clause is optional, meaning you can also use the following syntax:

```
if (condition1) {codeblock1}
```

The If statement works like this: If the condition is true, codeblock1 is executed. Otherwise, codeblock2 is executed (if the Else clause is provided). In no case will both the If and Else clauses be executed. Frequently, the expression used to control If statements involves a test for equality. In fact, the most basic type of string comparison is when you compare two strings using the equality operator (=), such as

```
if (stringA = stringB) {codeblock}
```

Here, you are performing a literal comparison of the strings; if they are identical, the related code block is executed. This syntax works for literal strings but is not ideal for use in scripts. Parameters, property values, and arguments might contain spaces, or there might be no value at all for a variable. In this case, you might get an error if you perform literal comparisons. Instead, use the comparison operators to perform more advanced comparisons, such as –eq, –like, –match, or –contains.

To learn about other advanced techniques, consider the following example and sample output:

```
if ($args.count -eq 0) {throw "No arguments passed to script"}
else {write-host "You passed args to the script"}
```

```
No arguments passed to script
At C:\Users\Bubba\dat.ps1:8 char:24
+ if ($args.count) {throw <<<<  "No arguments passed to script"}
```

```
    + CategoryInfo          : OperationStopped: (No arguments passed to
script:String) [], RuntimeException
    + FullyQualifiedErrorId : No arguments passed to script
```

Here, if you don't pass any arguments to the script, the script throws an error. Because the default error action for PowerShell is to halt execution, this is an effective way to stop processing a script when expected conditions are not met. The Else condition applies when you pass arguments to the script, and in this example, "You passed args to the script" is written to the output.

Alternatively, if a script requires an argument, such as a computer name, you could use the If...Else construct to catch the missing argument and prompt the user to enter it using the Read-Host cmdlet as shown in this example and sample output:

```
if ($args.count -eq 0) {
   $compName = read-host "Enter the name of the computer to check"
} else {
   $compName = $args[0]
}
```

```
Enter the name of the computer to check: FileServer84.cpandl.com
```

Here, if you don't type an argument, the Read-Host cmdlet prompts you and then stores the value you specify in the $compName variable. Otherwise, the $compName variable is set to the value of the first argument you pass to the script.

Using any of the logical operators, listed previously in Table 5-7, you can check two conditions. In the following example, the If condition is met only when the conditions on either side of the logical AND are true:

```
if (($args.count -ge 1) -and ($args[0] -eq "Check")) {
   write-host "Performing system checks..."
  } else {
   write-host "Script will not perform system checks..."
}
```

```
.\check-sys.ps1 Check
Performing system checks...
```

PowerShell also allows you to use If...ElseIf...Else constructs to execute a block of statements if a condition is met. Otherwise, it allows you to execute a second block of statements if a second condition is met. Finally, it allows you to execute a third block of statements if neither of the previous conditions is met. The basic syntax is

```
if (condition1) {action1} elseif (condition2) {action2} else {action3}
```

The following example uses the If...ElseIf...Else construct to perform actions depending on the value of the first argument passed to the script:

```
if (($args.count -ge 1) -and ($args[0] -eq "Check")) {
   write-host "Performing system checks..."
  } elseif (($args.count -ge 1) -and ($args[0] -eq "Test")) {
   write-host "Performing connectivity tests..."
} else {
   write-host "Script will not perform system checks or tests."
}
```

```
.\check-sys.ps1 Test
Performing connectivity tests...
```

When you want to execute a statement only if a condition is false, you can use If Not. The basic syntax is

```
if (!condition) {codeblock1} [else {codeblock2}]
```

or

```
if (-not (condition)) {codeblock1} [else {codeblock2}]
```

Here PowerShell evaluates the condition. If it is false, PowerShell executes the statements in codeblock1. Otherwise, codeblock1 doesn't execute, and PowerShell proceeds to codeblock2, if present. The Else clause is optional, meaning you can also use the following syntax:

```
if (!condition) {codeblock1}
```

Consider the following example:

```
if (!$args.count -ge 1) {
   read-host "Enter the name of the computer to check"
}
```

Here you execute the code block when the argument count is not greater than or equal to one (meaning the argument count is zero).

TIP **A nested If is an If statement within an If statement. Nested Ifs are common in programming, and PowerShell scripting is no exception. When you nest If statements, you place the required If...Else or If...ElseIf...Else construct with its subconditions and subcodeblocks inside the code block of the original If...Else or If...ElseIf...Else construct.**

Using Switch

Checking for multiple conditions using If...ElseIf...Else constructs is a lot of work for you and for PowerShell. An easier way to check three or more conditions is to use Switch constructs. Using Switch, you can check multiple conditions in a way that is clear and easy to understand. You can also add a default code block that is executed if none of the other conditions are met.

The basic syntax for a Switch construct is

```
switch (pipeline_expression) {

   value1 { codeblock1 }
   value2 { codeblock2 }
   value3 { codeblock3 }
  . . .
   valueN { codeblockN }
   default { default_codeblock}
```

The Switch construct is essentially an extended series of If statements that get the condition to test from a pipeline value you provide. If a value in the pipeline matches a specified value, the related code block is executed. After the code block is executed, PowerShell exits the switch. If there are additional values in the pipeline to process, PowerShell evaluates those values, each in turn, in the same way.

> ***NOTE*** **Each Switch construct can have only one default. If there is more than one default clause, an error results.**

Switch constructs can be used with any valid data type. If the value to check is an array of numbers, strings, or objects, each element is evaluated in order against the switch conditions, starting with element 0. At least one element must be present that meets at least one condition, or PowerShell generates an error. In the following example and sample output, you define an array called $myValue, assign four values, and then process the values through a Switch construct:

```
$myValue = 4, 5, 6, 0

switch ($myValue) {
   0 { write-host "The value is zero."}
   1 { write-host "The value is one."}
   2 { write-host "The value is two."}
   3 { write-host "The value is three."}
   default { write-host "The value doesn't match expected parameters."}
}
```

```
The value doesn't match expected parameters.
The value doesn't match expected parameters.
The value doesn't match expected parameters.
The value is zero.
```

This processing approach is the same one PowerShell uses if you insert continue clauses as the last statement in every code block. Rather than have PowerShell continue processing with the next value in the pipeline, you might want PowerShell to stop processing any additional values in the pipeline. To do this, you can add the break statement whenever you want PowerShell to exit the Switch construct. Typically, you add a break statement as the last statement in a code block. Thus, the basic syntax becomes

```
switch (pipeline) {

   value1 { codeblock1 break}
   value2 { codeblock2 break}
   value3 { codeblock3 break}
  . . .
   valueN { codeblockN break}
   default { default_codeblock}
```

In the following example, you use break statements to break out of the Switch construct:

```
$myError = "Green", "Red", "Yellow", "Green"

switch ($myError) {
   "Red" { write-host "A critical error occurred. Break."; break}
   "Yellow" { write-host "A warning occurred. Break."; break}
   "Green" { write-host "No error occurred yet. No break." }
   default { write-host "The values don't match expected parameters."}
}
```

```
No error occurred yet. No break.
A critical error occurred. Break.
```

By default, when you use Switch, PowerShell does not consider the letter case and looks for exact matches only. To control what determines matches, you can add the following flags:

- **–regex** Matches string values against a regular expression. If the value you are testing is not a string, this option is ignored. Don't use it with the –wildcard and –exact flags.
- **–wildcard** Matches string values using wildcards. Indicates that the match clause, if a string, is treated as a wildcard string. If the value you are testing is not a string, this option is ignored. Don't use it with the –regex and –exact flags.
- **–exact** Performs an exact match of string values. If the value you are testing is not a string, this option is ignored. Don't use it with the –regex and –exact flags.

- **–casesensitive** Performs a case-sensitive match. If the value you are testing is not a string, this option is ignored.
- **–file** Takes input from a file rather than a statement. Each line of the file is read as a separate element and passed through the switch block, starting with the first line of the file. At least one element must be present that meets at least one condition, or PowerShell generates an error.

The following example switches based on the status of a service you specify by name in the first argument or when prompted:

```
if (!$args.count -ge 1) {
   $rh = read-host "Enter the name of the service to check"
   $myValue = get-service $rh
} else {
   $myValue = get-service $args[0]
}

$serName = $myValue.Name

switch -wildcard ($myValue.Status) {
   "S*" { write-host "The $serName service is stopped."}
   "R*" { write-host "The $serName service is running."}
   "P*" { write-host "The $serName service is paused."}
   default { write-host "Check the service."}
}
```

```
Enter the name of the service to check: w32time
The W32Time service is running.
```

Using Control Loops

When you want to execute a command or a series of commands repeatedly, you use control loops. A *loop* is a method for controlling the logical flow and execution of commands. In PowerShell, you can perform controlled looping in several ways, including

- For looping
- ForEach looping
- While looping
- Do While looping
- Do Until looping

You can create a basic loop using the For statement. You use For loops to execute a code block for a specific count. The structure of For loops is as follows:

```
for (countStartValue; condition; countNextValue) { CodeBlockToRepeat }
```

where *countStartValue* is a statement that initializes the counter that controls the For loop, *condition* is a statement that specifies what value the counter must reach to stop looping, and *countNextValue* is a statement that sets the next value for the counter. Note that the elements in parentheses are separated with semicolons and that the next value for the counter is set after each iteration (and not before iteration begins).

You can set the next value for the counter using any assignment operator. In the following example and sample output, you initialize the counter to 1, loop as long as the counter is less than or equal to 10, and increment the counter by 1 after each iteration:

```
for ($c=1; $c -le 10; $c++){write-host $c}
```

```
1
2
3
4
5
6
7
8
9
10
```

In the following example and sample output, you initialize the counter to 10, loop as long as the counter is greater than or equal to 0, and decrement the counter by 1 after each iteration:

```
for ($c = 10; $c -ge 0; $c--) {Write-Host $c}
```

```
10
9
8
7
6
5
4
3
2
1
0
```

You can just as easily increment or decrement the counter by twos, threes, or more as shown in these examples:

```
for ($c=1; $c -le 100; $c += 2){write-host $c}
for ($c=1; $c -le 100; $c += 3){write-host $c}

for ($c = 20; $c -ge 0; $c -= 2) {Write-Host $c}
for ($c = 20; $c -ge 0; $c -= 3) {Write-Host $c}
```

Another type of loop is a ForEach loop. With ForEach loops, you iterate through each element in a collections of items. Although you can work with other types of collections, you'll more typically work with collections of items in an array.

ForEach loops are similar to standard For loops. The key difference is that the number of elements in the collection determines the number of times you go through the loop. The basic syntax is

```
ForEach ( Item in Collection) { CodeBlockToRepeat }
```

where *Item* is a variable that PowerShell creates automatically when the ForEach loop runs, and *Collection* is the collection of items to iterate through. The collection can come directly from the pipeline. In the following example and sample output, you perform an action against each process in a collection of processes:

```
foreach ($p in get-process) {
    if ($p.handlecount -gt 500) {
        Write-Host $p.Name, $p.pm }
}
```

```
aolsoftware 14766080
csrss 1855488
csrss 22507520
explorer 34463744
```

Here, every running process is examined. The If statement checks for processes with greater than 500 file handles and lists their name and private memory set. This technique can help you find processes that are using a lot of resources on the computer.

In the following example and sample output, you perform an action against each file in a collection of files:

```
if (!$args.count -ge 1) {
    $path = read-host "Enter the name of the base directory to check"
} else {
    $path = $args[0]
}
```

```
foreach ($file in Get-ChildItem -path $path -recurse) {
    if ($file.length -gt 1mb) {
      $size = [Math]::Round($file.length/1MB.ToString("F0"))
      Write-Host $file, $size, $file.lastaccesstime }
}
```

```
A Catalog Section 1.pdf 8095845 11/23/2009 8:10:16 PM
A Catalog Section 2.pdf 12021788 11/23/2009 8:10:16 PM
```

Here, every file in a specified base directory and its subdirectories is examined. The If statement looks for files with a file size greater than 1 MB and lists their name, size in MB, and last access time. This technique can help you find large files that haven't been accessed in a long time.

> ***TIP*** **With For and ForEach loops, you'll sometimes want to break out of the loop before iterating through all of the possible values. To break out of a loop ahead of schedule, you can use the Break statement. The best place for this statement is within the code blocks for If, If...Else, and If...ElseIf...Else constructs.**

Sometimes you'll want to execute a code segment while a condition is met. To do this, you use While looping. The structure of this loop is as follows:

```
while (condition) {CodeBlockToRepeat}
```

With the While statement, the loop is executed as long as the condition is met. To break out of the loop, you must change the condition at some point within the loop. Here is an example of a While loop that changes the status of the condition:

```
$x = 0
$continuetoggle = $true
while ($continuetoggle) {
   $x = $x + 1
   if ($x -lt 5) {write-host "x is less than 5."}
   elseif ($x -eq 5) {write-host "x equals 5."}
   else { write-host "exiting the loop."
     $continuetoggle = $false }
}
```

```
X is less than 5.
X is less than 5.
X is less than 5.
X is less than 5.
X equals 5.
Exiting the loop.
```

By placing the condition at the top of the loop, you ensure that the loop is executed only if the condition is met. In the previous example, this means the loop won't be executed at all if continueToggle is set to False beforehand.

However, sometimes you want to execute the loop at least once before you check the condition. To do this, you can use the Do While construct, which places the condition test at the bottom of the loop, as in the following example:

```
do {CodeBlockToRepeat} while (condition)
```

In the following example, the code block is processed at least once before the condition is checked:

```
$x = 0
$continuetoggle = $true
do { $x = $x + 1
   if ($x -lt 5) {write-host "x is less than 5."}
   elseif ($x -eq 5) {write-host "x equals 5."}
   else { write-host "exiting the loop."
      $continuetoggle = $false }
}
while ($continuetoggle)
```

```
X is less than 5.
X is less than 5.
X is less than 5.
X is less than 5.
X equals 5.
Exiting the loop.
```

The final type of control loop available in PowerShell is the Do Until loop. With Do Until, you execute a loop until a condition is met instead of while a condition is met. As with Do While, you place the condition test at the end of the loop. The basic syntax is

```
do {CodeBlockToRepeat} until (condition)
```

The following loop is executed one or more times until the condition is met:

```
do {
   $cont = read-host "Do you want to continue? [Y/N]"
} until ($cont -eq "N")
```

```
Do you want to continue? [Y/N]: y
Do you want to continue? [Y/N]: y
Do you want to continue? [Y/N]: n
```

CHAPTER 8

Managing Roles, Role Services, and Features

When you are working with Windows Server 2008 or later, you have many more configuration options than when you are working with Windows Vista, Windows 7, or later. After you've installed a server running Windows Server 2008 or later, you can manage the server configuration by installing and configuring the following components:

- **Server roles** Server roles are related sets of software components that allow servers to perform specific functions for users and other computers on networks. A server can be dedicated to a single role, such as File Services, or a server can have multiple roles.
- **Role services** Role services are software components that provide the functionality of server roles. While some server roles have a single function and installing the role installs this function, most server roles have multiple, related role services and you are able to choose which role services to install.
- **Features** Features are software components that provide additional functionality. Features are installed and removed separately from roles and role services. A computer can have multiple features installed or none, depending on its configuration.

Normally, you manage roles, role services, and features using ServerManagerCmd, which is a command-line administration tool, and Server Manager, which is a graphical administration tool. However, when you are working with Windows PowerShell 2.0 or later, you can manage roles, role services, and features by importing the Server-Manager module into the PowerShell console.

Server Manager Essentials

When you want to manage server configuration using PowerShell, you need to import the ServerManager module. Not only can you use this module's cmdlets to add or remove roles, role services, and features, but you can use this module's cmdlets to view the configuration details and status for these software components. You can add the Import statement to your profile and scripts to ensure the ServerManager module is available as shown in this example:

```
import-module servermanager
```

The ServerManager module is available on Windows Server 2008. The Server-Manager module has several advantages over Server Manager version 6.0 and Server Manager version 6.1, which are included in Windows Server 2008 and Windows Server 2008 Release 2, respectively. The ServerManager module as implemented in PowerShell allows concurrent instances to add or remove components at the same time. This gives PowerShell an advantage over Server Manager version 6.1, which allows only one instance of either ServerManagerCmd or Server Manager to work at a time. Although updates to Server Manager, ServerManagerCmd, or both might remove this restriction, the usefulness of concurrent instances remains the same: you are able to run multiple Server Manager sessions simultaneously. For example, you can add roles in one Server Manager session while you are removing features in a different Server Manager session.

REAL WORLD **You can add supplemental components to Windows Server 2008 or later as downloads from the Microsoft Web site, including Windows Media Server 2008 and Windows SharePoint Server 2008. To make supplemental components available for installation and configuration in the Server Manager environment, download the installer package or packages from the Microsoft Web site. Typically, these are provided as a set of Microsoft Update Standalone Package (.msu) files. Afterward, double-click each installer package to register it for use.**

Server Manager Commands

Whenever you work with the ServerManager module you should use an elevated administrator PowerShell console. You can manage roles, role services, and features using the following cmdlets:

- **Get-WindowsFeature** Lists the server's current state with regard to roles, role services, and features.

```
Get-WindowsFeature [[-Name] ComponentNames] [-LogPath LogFile.txt]
```

- **Add-WindowsFeature** Installs the named role, role service, or feature. The –IncludeAllSubFeature parameter allows you to install all subordinate role services and features of the named component.

```
Add-WindowsFeature [-Name] ComponentNames [-IncludeAllSubFeature]
[-LogPath LogFile.txt] [-Restart] [-Concurrent]
```

- **Remove-WindowsFeature** Removes the named role, role service, or feature.

```
Remove-WindowsFeature [-Name] ComponentNames [-LogPath LogFile.txt]
[-Restart] [-Concurrent]
```

When applicable, you can

- Use the –LogPath parameter to log error details to a named log file as an alternative to the default logging used.
- Use the –Restart parameter to restart the computer automatically (if restarting is necessary to complete the operation).
- Use the –Concurrent parameter to allow concurrent instances to add or remove components at the same time.
- Use the –WhatIf parameter to display the operations that would be performed if the command were executed.

The parameter values that you can use include:

- **ComponentNames** Identifies the roles, role services, or features to work with by their name (not their display name). The –Name parameter matches actual component names and not display names. With Get-WindowsFeature, you can use wildcard characters. With Add-WindowsFeature and Remove-WindowsFeature, you can use pipelining to get the required input names from another command, such as Get-WindowsFeature.
- **LogFile.txt** Sets the path and name of the text file to which log error details should be written.

Most installable roles, role services, and features have a corresponding component name that identifies the component so that you can manipulate it from the PowerShell prompt. This also is true for supplemental components you've made available by downloading and installing their installer packages from the Microsoft Web site.

Available Roles and Role Services

Table 8-1 provides a hierarchical listing of the component names associated with roles, related role services, and related subcomponents. When you are installing a role, you can use the –IncludeAllSubFeature parameter to install all the subordinate role services and features listed under the role. When you are installing a role service, you can use the –IncludeAllSubFeature parameter to install all the subordinate features listed under the role service.

NOTE **In the following table, a notation of [1] indicates a new or revised role for Windows Server 2008 R2 or later. A notation of [2] indicates a role that is no longer available.**

TABLE 8-1 Component Names for Key Roles and Role Services

COMPONENT NAME	ROLE	SERVICE	FEATURE
AD-Certificate	Active Directory Certificate Services		
ADCS-Cert-Authority		Certification Authority	
ADCS-Web-Enrollment		Certification Authority Web Enrollment	
ADCS-Online-Cert		Online Responder	
ADCS-Device-Enrollment		Network Device Enrollment Service	
ADCS-Enroll-Web-Svc		Certificate Enrollment Web Service	
ADCS-Enroll-Web-Pol		Certificate Enrollment Policy Web Service	
AD-Domain-Services	Active Directory Domain Services (AD DS)		
ADDS-Domain-Controller		Active Directory Domain Controller	
ADDS-Identity-Mgmt		Identity Management for UNIX	
ADDS-NIS			Server for Network Information Services (NIS)
ADDS-Password-Sync			Password Synchronization
ADDS-IDMU-Tools			Administration Tools
AD-Federation-Services	Active Directory Federation Services (AD FS)		
ADFS-Federation		Federation Service	
ADFS-Proxy		Federation Service Proxy	
ADFS-Web-Agents		AD FS Web Agents	
ADFS-Claims			Claims-Aware Agent
ADFS-Windows-Token			Windows Token-Based Agent
ADLDS	Active Directory Lightweight Directory Services (AD LDS)		
ADRMS	Active Directory Rights Management Services		
ADRMS-Server		Active Directory Rights Management Services Server	
ADRMS-Identity		Identity Federation Support	
DHCP	Dynamic Host Configuration Protocol (DHCP) Server		

TABLE 8-1 Component Names for Key Roles and Role Services

COMPONENT NAME	ROLE	SERVICE	FEATURE
DNS	Domain Name System (DNS) Server		
Fax	Fax Server		
File-Services	File Services		
FS-FileServer		File Server	
FS-DFS		Distributed File System	
FS-DFS-Namespace			DFS Namespace
FS-DFS-Replication			DFS Replication
FS-Resource-Manager		File Server Resource Manager	
FS-NFS-Services		Services for Network File System (NFS)	
FS-Search-Service		Windows Search Service	
FS-Win2003-Services		Windows Server 2003 File Services	
FS-Replication			File Replication Service[2]
FS-Indexing-Service			Indexing Service
FS-BranchCache		BranchCache for Remote Files[1]	
Hyper-V	Hyper-V		
NPAS	Network Policy and Access Services		
NPAS-Policy-Server		Network Policy Server	
NPAS-RRAS-Services		Routing and Remote Access Services	
NPAS-RRAS			Remote Access Service
NPAS-Routing			Routing
NPAS-Health		Health Registration Authority	
NPAS-Host-Cred		Host Credential Authorization Protocol	
Print-Services	Print and Document Services[1]		
Print-Server		Print Server	
Print-LPD-Service		LPD Service	
Print-Internet		Internet Printing	
Print-Scan-Server		Distributed Scan Management Server[1]	
Remote-Desktop-Services	Remote Desktop Services[1]		
RDS-RD-Server		Remote Desktop Server[1]	

TABLE 8-1 Component Names for Key Roles and Role Services

COMPONENT NAME	ROLE	SERVICE	FEATURE
RDS-Licensing		Remote Desktop (RD) Services Licensing[1]	
RDS-Connection-Broker		RD Connection Broker[1]	
RDS-Gateway		RD Gateway[1]	
RDS-Web-Access		RD Web Access[1]	
RDS-Virtualization		RD Virtualization[1]	
WDS	Windows Deployment Services		
WDS-Deployment		Deployment Server	
WDS-Transport		Transport Server	
OOB-WSUS	Windows Server Update Services[1]		

Available Features

Table 8-2 provides a hierarchical listing of the component names associated with features and related subfeatures. When you are installing a feature, you can use the –IncludeAllSubFeature parameter to install all the subordinate second-level and third-level features listed under the feature. When you are installing a second-level feature, you can use the –IncludeAllSubFeature parameter to install all the subordinate third-level features listed under the second-level feature.

> ***NOTE*** **An asterisk following the feature command indicates that the feature has unlisted subordinate features that generally are installed together by adding the parameter –IncludeAllSubFeature. A notation of [1] indicates a new or revised feature for Windows Server 2008 R2 or later. A notation of [2] indicates a feature no longer available. A notation of [3] indicates a feature integrated with the operating system.**

TABLE 8-2 Component Names for Key Features and Subfeatures

COMPONENT NAME	FEATURE	SECOND-LEVEL FEATURE	THIRD-LEVEL FEATURE
NET-Framework*	.NET Framework 3.5.1 Features[1]		
BitLocker*	BitLocker Drive Encryption		
BITS	Background Intelligent Transport Services (BITS) Server Extensions		
BranchCache	BranchCache[1]		
CMAK	Connection Manager Administration Kit		
Desktop-Experience	Desktop Experience		

TABLE 8-2 Component Names for Key Features and Subfeatures

COMPONENT NAME	FEATURE	SECOND-LEVEL FEATURE	THIRD-LEVEL FEATURE
DAMC	Direct Access Management Console[1]		
Failover-Clustering	Failover Clustering		
GPMC	Group Policy Management Console		
Ink-Handwriting*	Ink and Handwriting Services[1]		
Internet-Print-Client	Internet Printing Client		
ISNS	Internet Storage Name Server		
LPR-Port-Monitor	LPR Port Monitor		
MSMQ*	Message Queuing		
Multipath-IO	Multipath I/O		
NLB	Network Load Balancing		
PNRP	Peer Name Resolution Protocol		
qWave	Quality Windows Audio Video Experience		
Remote-Assistance	Remote Assistance		
RDC	Remote Differential Compression		
RSAT	Remote Server Administration Tools		
RSAT-Role-Tools	Role Administration Tools		
RSAT-ADCS*		Active Directory Certificate Services Tools	
RSAT-AD-Tools		AD DS and AD LDS Tools	
RSAT-ADDS*			Active Directory Domain Services Tools
RSAT-ADLDS			Active Directory Lightweight Directory Services Tools
RSAT-AD-PowerShell			Active Directory PowerShell snap-in[1]
RSAT-RMS		Active Directory Rights Management Services Tools	
RSAT-DHCP		DHCP Server Tools	

TABLE 8-2 Component Names for Key Features and Subfeatures

COMPONENT NAME	FEATURE	SECOND-LEVEL FEATURE	THIRD-LEVEL FEATURE
RSAT-DNS-Server		DNS Server Tools	
RSAT-Fax		Fax Server Tools	
RSAT-File-Services*		File Services Tools	
RSAT-NPAS*		Network Policy and Access Services Tools	
RSAT-Print-Services		Print Services Tools	
RSAT-RDS*		Remote Desktop Services Tools[1]	
RSAT-UDDI		Universal Description, Discovery, and Integration (UDDI) Services Tools[2]	
RSAT-Web-Server		Web Server (Internet Information Services, IIS) Tools	
RSAT-WDS		Windows Deployment Services Tools	
RSAT-Hyper-V		Hyper-V Tools	
RSAT-Feature-Tools		Feature Administration Tools	
RSAT-BitLocker*			BitLocker Drive Encryption Tools[1]
RSAT-BITS-Server			BITS Server Extensions Tools
RSAT-Clustering			Failover Clustering Tools
RSAT-NLB			Network Load Balancing Tools
RSAT-SMTP			Simple Mail Transfer Protocol (SMTP) Server Tools
RSAT-WINS			Windows Internet Naming Service (WINS) Server Tools
Removable-Storage	Removable Storage Manager[2]		
RPC-over-HTTP-Proxy	RPC over HTTP Proxy		

TABLE 8-2 Component Names for Key Features and Subfeatures

COMPONENT NAME	FEATURE	SECOND-LEVEL FEATURE	THIRD-LEVEL FEATURE
Simple-TCPIP	Simple TCP/IP Services		
SMTP-Server	Simple Mail Transfer Protocol (SMTP) Server		
SNMP-Services*	Simple Network Management Protocol Services		
Storage-Mgr-SANS	Storage Manager for SANs		
Subsystem-UNIX-Apps	Subsystem for UNIX-Based Applications		
Telnet-Client	Telnet Client		
Telnet-Server	Telnet Server		
TFTP-Client	Trivial File Transfer Protocol (TFTP) Client		
Biometric-Framework	Windows Biometric Framework[1]		
Windows-InternalDB	Windows Internal Database		
PowerShell	Windows PowerShell[3]		
Backup-Features	Windows Server Backup Features		
Backup		Windows Server Backup	
Backup-Tools		Command-Line Tools	
Migration	Windows Server Migration Tools[1]		
WSRM	Windows System Resource Manager		
WinRM-IIS-Ext	WinRM IIS Extension		
WINS-Server	WINS Server		
Wireless-Networking	Wireless Local Area Network (LAN) Service		
XPS-Viewer	XML Paper Specification (XPS) Viewer		

Checking Installed Roles, Role Services, and Features

Before modifying a server's configuration, you check its current configuration and carefully plan how adding or removing a role, role service, or feature will affect a server's overall performance. Although you typically want to combine complementary roles, doing so increases the workload on the server, so you need to optimize the server hardware accordingly.

At a standard or elevated PowerShell prompt, you can determine the roles, role services, and features that are installed on a server by typing **Get-WindowsFeature**. Get-WindowsFeature then lists the configuration status of each available role, role service, and feature. Installed roles, role services, and features are highlighted and marked as being installed. In the output, roles and role services are listed before features as shown in the following example and sample output:

```
get-windowsfeature
```

```
Display Name                                            Name
-----------                                             ----
[ ] Active Directory Certificate Services              AD-Certificate
    [ ] Certification Authority                         ADCS-Cert-Authority
    [ ] Certification Authority Web Enrollment          ADCS-Web-Enrollment
    [ ] Online Responder                                ADCS-Online-Cert
    [ ] Network Device Enrollment Service               ADCS-Device-Enrollment
    [ ] Certificate Enrollment Web Service              ADCS-Enroll-Web-Svc
    [ ] Certificate Enrollment Policy Web Service       ADCS-Enroll-Web-Pol
[X] Active Directory Domain Services                    AD-Domain-Services
    [X] Active Directory Domain Controller              ADDS-Domain-Controller
    [X] Identity Management for UNIX                    ADDS-Identity-Mgmt
        [X] Server for Network Information Services      ADDS-NIS
        [X] Password Synchronization                    ADDS-Password-Sync
        [X] Administration Tools                        ADDS-IDMU-Tools
[X] Active Directory Federation Services                AD-Federation-Services
    [X] Federation Service                              ADFS-Federation
    [X] Federation Service Proxy                        ADFS-Proxy
    [X] AD FS Web Agents                                ADFS-Web-Agents
        [X] Claims-aware Agent                          ADFS-Claims
        [X] Windows Token-based Agent                   ADFS-Windows-Token
[ ] Active Directory Lightweight Directory Services      ADLDS
[X] Active Directory Rights Management Services         ADRMS
    [X] Active Directory Rights Management Server       ADRMS-Server
    [X] Identity Federation Support                     ADRMS-Identity

. . .

[X] .NET Framework 3.5.1 Features                       NET-Framework
    [X] .NET Framework 3.5.1                            NET-Framework-Core
    [X] WCF Activation                                  NET-Win-CFAC
        [X] HTTP Activation                             NET-HTTP-Activation
        [X] Non-HTTP Activation                         NET-Non-HTTP-Activ
[ ] Background Intelligent Transfer Service (BITS)    BITS
    [ ] Compact Server                                  BITS-LWDLServer
    [ ] IIS Server Extension                            BITS-IIS-Ext
[ ] BitLocker Drive Encryption                          BitLocker
```

You can use wildcard characters to review the status for a subset of components by name. For example, if you want to check the status of only Active Directory–related components, you can enter **Get-WindowsFeature -name ad*** or **Get-WindowsFeature ad***.

In addition to helping you determine at a glance what components are installed, Get-WindowsFeature can help you document a server's configuration. To do this, you can save the output in a file as standard text using the redirection symbol (>) as shown in this example:

```
Get-WindowsFeature > ServerConfig03-21-2010.txt
```

In this example, you save the output to a text file named ServerConfig03-21-2010.txt.

Installing Roles, Role Services, and Features

The ServerManager module is the PowerShell component you use to install roles, role services, and features. Roles, role services, and features can be dependent on other roles, role services, and features. When you install roles, role services, and features, Server Manager prompts you to install any additional roles, role services, or features that are required.

Adding Roles, Role Services, and Features

At an elevated command prompt, you can install roles, role services, and features by typing **add-windowsfeature *ComponentName***, where *ComponentName* is the name of the component to install, as listed in Table 8-1 or Table 8-2. You can install subordinate components by including the –IncludeAllSubFeature parameter as shown in the following example and sample output:

```
add-windowsfeature fs-dfs -IncludeAllSubFeature
```

```
Success   Restart Needed   Exit Code   Feature Result
-------   --------------   ---------   -------------
True      No               Success     {DFS Replication, DFS Namespaces}
```

Here, you install the Distributed File System role service as well as the subordinate DFS Namespaces and DFS Replication role services. As PowerShell works, you see a Start Installation progress bar. When the installation is complete, you see the result. The output for a successful installation should look similar to the example.

As you can see, the output specifies whether the installation was successful, whether a restart is needed, an exit code, and a list of the exact changes made. The exit code can be different from the Success status. For example, if the components you specify are already installed, the exit code is NoChangeNeeded, as shown in this example and sample output:

```
add-windowsfeature -name net-framework -includeallsubfeature
```

```
Success   Restart Needed   Exit Code        Feature Result
-------   --------------   ---------        -------------
True      No               NoChangeNeeded   {}
```

Here, you see that Add-WindowsFeature was successful but didn't actually make any changes. The Feature Result shows no changes as well.

Add-WindowsFeature allows you to specify component names by getting the input from the output of another command. Consider the following example and sample output:

```
get-windowsfeature bits* | add-windowsfeature
```

```
WARNING: [Installation] Succeeded: [Background Intelligent Transfer
Service (BITS)] Compact Server. You must restart this server to finish
the installation process.
Success   Restart Needed   Exit Code               Feature Result
-------   --------------   ---------               -------------
True      Yes              SuccessRestartRequired  { BITS-LWDLServer,
BITS-IIS-Ext }
```

Here, Add-WindowsFeature gets the list of components to install from the Get-WindowsFeature cmdlet. You install the Background Intelligent Transfer Service (BITS) role service as well as the subordinate Compact Server and IIS Server Extension role services. Because you must restart the server to complete the installation of BITS, you see a warning message as well as results.

If a restart is required to complete an installation, you can have the Add-WindowsFeature cmdlet restart the computer by including the –Restart parameter. Also note that a pending restart can prevent you from adding or removing other components. You'll see a related error message as well as the standard output:

```
Add-WindowsFeature: Please restart the computer before trying to install
more roles/features.

Success   Restart Needed   Exit Code              Feature Result
-------   --------------   ---------              -------------
False     Yes              FailedRestartRequired  { }
```

Handling Configuration Errors and Other Issues

Some components cannot be installed from the command line. If you try to install one of these components, you'll see a warning as shown in the following example and sample output:

```
get-windowsfeature ad-fe* | add-windowsfeature
```

```
WARNING: Installation of 'Active Directory Federation Services' is not
supported on the command line. Skipping . . .
Success   Restart Needed   Exit Code         Feature Result
-------   --------------   ---------         -------------
True      No               NoChangeNeeded    { }
```

To test the installation prior to performing the actual operation, you can use the –WhatIf parameter. If you are trying to install components that are already installed, you see a message in the output stating no changes were made, such as

```
get-windowsfeature ad-d* | add-windowsfeature -whatif
```

```
What if: Checking if running in 'WhatIf' Mode.
Success   Restart Needed   Exit Code        Feature Result
-------   --------------   ---------        -------------
True      No               NoChangeNeeded   {}
```

If an error occurs and Add-WindowsFeature is not able to perform the operation specified, you see an error. Generally, error text is shown in red and includes an error flag and error text as shown in the following example output:

```
The term 'add-windowsfeature' is not recognized as a cmdlet, function,
operable program, or script file. Verify the term and try again.
At line:1 char:19
+ add-windowsfeature <<<<  fs-dfs
    + CategoryInfo          : ObjectNotFound: (add-windowsfeature:String)
[], CommandNotFoundException
    + FullyQualifiedErrorId : CommandNotFoundException
```

This error indicates that PowerShell doesn't recognize the Add-WindowsFeature cmdlet. You see this error if you forget to import the ServerManager module using the command import-module servermanager.

Another common error you'll see occurs when you don't use an elevated administrator PowerShell prompt:

```
Add-WindowsFeature: Because of security restrictions imposed by User
Account Control you must run Add-WindowsFeature in a Windows PowerShell
session opened with elevated rights.
```

To resolve this problem, right-click the PowerShell shortcut on the menu and select Run As Administrator. This opens an administrator PowerShell prompt.

When you install components, Add-WindowsFeature writes extended logging information to %SystemRoot%\logs\servermanager.log. This logging information details every operation performed by Add-WindowsFeature. You can write the detailed information to an alternate location by including the –LogPath parameter. In this example, you write the logging information to C:\logs\install.log:

```
add-windowsfeature BITS -IncludeAllSubFeature -LogPath
c:\logs\install.log
```

Finally, because PowerShell returns the output as an object, you can pass the output object along the pipeline as necessary. You also can apply alternative formatting to the output, such as list formatting, as shown in this example and sample output:

```
get-windowsfeature net-* | add-windowsfeature | format-list *
```

```
Success       : True
RestartNeeded : No
FeatureResult : { }
ExitCode      : NoChangeNeeded
```

Uninstalling Roles, Role Services, and Features

The ServerManager module is the PowerShell component you use to uninstall roles, role services, and features. Roles, role services, and features can be dependent on other roles, role services, and features. If you try to remove a required component of an installed role, role service, or feature, Server Manager warns that you cannot remove the component unless you also remove the other role, role service, or feature.

Removing Roles, Role Services, and Features

At an elevated command prompt, you can uninstall roles, role services, and features by typing **remove-windowsfeature *ComponentName***, where *ComponentName* is the name of the component to uninstall as listed in Table 8-1 or Table 8-2. When you uninstall a top-level component, subordinate components are automatically uninstalled as well. Consider the following example and sample output:

```
remove-windowsfeature net-framework
```

```
WARNING: [Removal] Succeeded: [Background Intelligent Transfer Service
(BITS)] Compact Server. You must restart this server to finish the
removal process.
Success   Restart Needed   Exit Code               Feature Result
-------   --------------   ---------               -------------
True      Yes                SuccessRestartRequired {Compact Server, IIS
Server Extension}
```

Here, you uninstall the BITS role service as well as the subordinate Compact Server and IIS Server Extension role services. As PowerShell works, you see a Start Removal progress bar. When the removal is complete, you see the result. The output for a successful removal should look similar to the example. Because you must restart the server to complete the removal of BITS, you see a warning message as well as results.

If a restart is required to complete a removal, you can have the Remove-WindowsFeature cmdlet restart the computer by including the –Restart parameter. As with installation, you can test the removal prior to performing the actual operation using the –WhatIf parameter. If you are trying to remove components that aren't installed, you see a note stating no changes were made, such as

```
remove-windowsfeature net-framework -whatif
```

```
What if: Checking if running in 'WhatIf' Mode.
Success   Restart Needed   Exit Code       Feature Result
-------   --------------   ---------       -------------
True      No               NoChangeNeeded  {}
```

Remove-WindowsFeature allows you to specify component names by getting the input from the output of another command. Consider following example and sample output:

```
get-windowsfeature fs-* | remove-windowsfeature
```

```
Success   Restart Needed   Exit Code    Feature Result
-------   --------------   ---------    -------------
True      No               Success      {DFS Replication, DFS Namespaces}
```

Here, Remove-WindowsFeature gets the list of components to remove from the Get-WindowsFeature cmdlet. You uninstall the Distributed File System role service as well as the subordinate role services.

Handling Removal Errors and Other Issues

If an error occurs and Remove-WindowsFeature is not able to perform the operation specified, you see an error. The errors you see are similar to those for adding components.

In some cases, you might not be able to uninstall a component. Typically, this occurs because a component is required by or depended on by another role, role service, or feature. Consider the following example and sample output:

```
get-windowsfeature fs-* | remove-windowsfeature
```

```
Remove-WindowsFeature : DFS Replication and DFS Namesspace cannot be
removed from a domain controller.

Success   Restart Needed   Exit Code      Feature Result
-------   --------------   ---------      --------------
False     No               Failed         {}
```

Here, you try to uninstall the Distributed File System role service as well as the subordinate role services on a domain controller. However, you are unable to remove these role services because they are required on domain controllers.

During the removal process, Remove-WindowsFeature writes extended logging information to %SystemRoot%\logs\servermanager.log. As with the installation process, you can write the detailed information to an alternate location by including the –logPath parameter. Here is an example:

```
remove-windowsfeature net-framework -logpath c:\logs\uninstall.log
```

CHAPTER 9

Inventorying and Evaluating Windows Systems

Often when you are working with a user's computer or a remote server, you'll want to examine the working environment and computer configuration details. For example, you might want to know who is logged on, the current system time, or what accounts are available locally. You might also want to know what processor and how much RAM are installed. To do this and much more, you can take an inventory of your computers.

While you are inventorying your computers, you also might want to evaluate the hardware configuration and determine whether there are issues that need your attention. For example, if a computer's primary disk is getting low in free space or a computer has little available memory, you'll want to note this at the least and possibly take preventative measures.

Getting Basic System Information

Sometimes when you are working with a computer, you won't know basic information, such as the name of the computer, the logon domain, or the current user. This can happen when you get called to support a computer in another department within your organization and when you are working remotely. Items that help you quickly gather basic user and system information include the following:

- **$env:computername** Displays the name of the computer

```
$env:computername
```

- **$env:username** Displays the name of the user currently logged on to the system, such as wrstanek

```
$env:username
```

- **$env:userdomain** Displays the logon domain of the current user, such as CPANDL

```
$env:userdomain
```

- **Get-Date** Displays the current system date or current system time

```
Get-Date [-Date] DateTime
Get-Date -DisplayHint [Date | Time]
```

- **Set-Date** Sets the current system date or current system time

```
Set-Date [-Date] DateTime
Set-Date [-Adjust] TimeChange
```

- **Get-Credential** Gets a credential needed for authentication

```
Get-Credential [-Credential] Credential
```

Determining the Current User, Domain, and Computer Name

Often, you can obtain the basic information you need about the working environment from environment variables. The most common details you might need to know include the name of the computer, the identity of the current user, and the logon domain.

You can obtain the user, domain, and computer name information by using $env:username, $env:userdomain, and $env:computername, respectively. In the following example and sample output, you write this information to the console:

```
write-host "Domain: $env:userdomain 'nUser: $env:username 'nComputer:
$env:computername"
```

```
Domain: CPANDL
User: wrstanek
Computer: TECHPC76
```

Here, the user is wrstanek, the computer is TechPC76, and the user's logon domain is CPANDL.

A faster alternative that provides even more information about the working environment is to list all available environment variables and their values as shown in this example and sample output:

```
get-childitem env:
```

```
Name                           Value
----                           -----
ALLUSERSPROFILE                C:\ProgramData
APPDATA                        C:\Users\WilliamS\AppData\Roaming
CommonProgramFiles             C:\Program Files\Common Files
COMPUTERNAME                   TECHPC125
ComSpec                        C:\Windows\system32\cmd.exe
FP_NO_HOST_CHECK               NO
HOMEDRIVE                      C:
HOMEPATH                       \Users\WilliamS
LOCALAPPDATA                   C:\Users\WilliamS\AppData\Local
LOGONSERVER                    \\ENGPC42
NUMBER_OF_PROCESSORS           4
OS                             Windows_NT
Path                           C:\Windows\system32;C:\Windows;
PATHEXT                       .COM;.EXE;.BAT;.CMD;.VBS; JS;.PSC1
PROCESSOR_ARCHITECTURE         x86
PROCESSOR_IDENTIFIER           x86 Family GenuineIntel
PROCESSOR_LEVEL                6
PROCESSOR_REVISION             0f07
ProgramData                    C:\ProgramData
ProgramFiles                   C:\Program Files
PSMODULEPATH                   C:\Windows\System32\WindowsPowerShell;
PUBLIC                         C:\Users\Public
SystemDrive                    C:
SystemRoot                     C:\Windows
TEMP                           C:\Users\WilliamS\AppData\Local\Temp
USERDOMAIN                     ENGPC42
USERNAME                       WilliamS
USERPROFILE                    C:\Users\WilliamS
```

Determining and Setting the Date and Time

You can get the current date and time using Get-Date. To use Get-Date, simply type the cmdlet name at the PowerShell prompt and press Enter. The output of Get-Date is the current date and time as shown in the following example and sample output:

```
get-date
```

```
Tuesday, March 16, 2010 10:40:51 AM
```

If you want only the current date or current time, use the –DisplayHint parameter. While the output of Get-Date –DisplayHint Date is the current date—such as Tuesday, March 16, 2010—the output of Get-Date –DisplayHint Time is the current time, such as 10:40:51 AM. Here is an example and sample output:

```
get-date -displayhint time
```

```
10:40:51 AM
```

To set the date, time, or both, you must use an elevated administrator PowerShell prompt. Simply follow Set-Date with the desired date and time enclosed in quotation marks.

You enter the current date in MM-DD-YY format, where *MM* is for the two-digit month, *DD* is for the two-digit day, and *YY* is for the two-digit year, such as typing **03-20-10** for March 20, 2010, as shown in the following example:

```
set-date "03-20-10"
```

You enter the current time in HH:MM or HH:MM:SS format, where *HH* is for the two-digit hour, *MM* is for the two-digit minute, and *SS* is for the two-digit second. If you enter the time without designating AM for A.M. or PM for P.M., the time command assumes you are using a 24-hour clock, where hours from 00 to 11 indicate A.M. and hours from 12 to 23 indicate P.M. The following example sets the time to 3:30 P.M.:

```
set-date "3:30 PM"
```

You can set the date and time at the same time. All of the following examples set the date and time to March 20, 2010, 3:30 P.M.:

```
set-date "03-20-10 03:30 PM"
set-date "03-20-10 03:30:00 PM"
set-date "03-20-10 15:30:00"
```

You also can adjust the time forward or backward using the –Adjust parameter. Type **Set-Date -Adjust** followed by the time adjustment. Specify the time change in HH:MM:SS format. The following example sets the time ahead 30 minutes:

```
set-date -adjust 00:30:00
```

To adjust the time backward, use a minus sign (–) to indicate that you want to subtract time. The following example sets the time back one hour:

```
set-date -adjust -01:00:00
```

TIP The Get-Date cmdlet returns a DateTime object. Before you experiment with setting the date and time, store the current date and time in a variable by typing **$date = get-date**. When you are done testing, restore the date and time by typing **set-date $date**. Then adjust the time as necessary to get the current time exactly.

Specifying Authentication Credentials

When you are working with some cmdlets and objects in PowerShell that modify system information, you might need to specify a credential for authentication. Whether in a script or at the prompt, the easiest way to do this is to use Get-Credential to obtain a Credential object and save the result in a variable for later use. Consider the following example:

```
$cred = get-credential
```

When PowerShell reads this command, PowerShell prompts you for a user name and password and then stores the credentials provided in the $cred variable. It is important to point out that the credentials prompt is displayed simply because you typed **Get-Credential**.

You also can specify that you want the credentials for a specific user in a specific domain. In the following example, you request the credentials for the TestUser account in the DevD domain:

```
$cred = get-credential -credential devd\testuser
```

A Credential object has UserName and Password properties that you can work with. Although the user name is stored as a regular string, the password is stored as a secure, encrypted string. Knowing this, you can reference the user name and password stored in $cred as follows:

```
$user = $cred.username
$password = $cred.password
```

Examining the System Configuration and the Working Environment

Sometimes when you are working with a computer, you'll want to obtain detailed information on the system configuration or the operating system. With mission-critical systems, you might want to save or print this information for easy reference. Items that help you gather detailed system information include the following:

- **Get-HotFix** Gets information about service packs and updates applied to the local computer or specified computers. Use –Id to look for a specific hotfix by its identifier. Use –Description to get hotfixes by type.

```
Get-HotFix [[-Id | -Description] HotFixes] {AddtlParams}

AddtlParams=
 [-Credential Credential] [-ComputerName ComputerName1, ComputerName2,
...]
```

- **Win32_ComputerSystem** Lists detailed information about the local computer or a specified computer.

```
Get-Wmiobject -Class Win32_ComputerSystem [-ComputerName
ComputerName1, ComputerName2, ...] [-Credential Credential] |
format-list *
```

- **Win32_OperatingSystem** Lists detailed information about the operating system installed on the local computer or a specified computer.

```
Get-Wmiobject -Class Win32_OperatingSystem [-ComputerName
ComputerName1, ComputerName2, ...] [-Credential Credential] |
format-list *
```

- **Win32_UserAccount** Lists the user accounts created or available on a computer, which can include local user accounts and domain user accounts.

```
Get-Wmiobject -Class Win32_UserAccount [-ComputerName
ComputerName1, ComputerName2, ...] [-Credential Credential] |
format-list Caption, Name, Domain, FullName, SID
```

- **Win32_Group** Lists the groups created or available on a computer, which can include local user accounts and domain user accounts.

```
Get-Wmiobject -Class Win32_Group [-ComputerName ComputerName1,
ComputerName2, ...] [-Credential Credential] | format-list Caption,
Name, Domain, SID
```

To use these commands on a local computer, simply type the commands on a single line using the syntax shown.

Determining Windows Updates and Service Packs

With Get-HotFix, you can use the –ComputerName parameter to specify computers to examine in a comma-separated list as shown in this example:

```
get-hotfix -ComputerName fileserver84, dcserver32, dbserver11
```

However, to access remote computers, you'll often need to provide credentials, and you can do this using the –Credential parameter. Note that although you can provide credentials for remote connections, you typically won't be able to provide credentials for working with the local computer (and this is why you need to start with an elevated, administrator prompt if required). The following example shows how you can prompt directly for a required credential:

```
get-hotfix -Credential (get-credential) -ComputerName fileserver84,
dcserver32, dbserver11
```

You also can use a stored credential as shown in this example:

```
$cred = get-credential
get-hotfix -Credential $cred -ComputerName fileserver84, dcserver32,
dbserver11
```

Because you'll often work with the same remote computers, you might want to get the names of the remote computers from a file. To do this, enter each computer name on a separate line in a text file and save this text file to a location where you can always access it, such as a network share. Then get the content from the file as your input to the –ComputerName parameter as shown in this example:

```
get-hotfix -Credential (get-credential) -ComputerName (get-content
c:\data\servers.txt)
```

Or get it as shown in this example and sample output:

```
$comp = get-content c:\data\servers.txt
$cred = get-credential
get-hotfix -Credential $cred -ComputerName $comp
```

```
Source        Description       HotFixID      InstalledBy           InstalledOn
------        -----------       --------      -----------           -----------
TECHPC75                          {026C2636-...                       12/19/2009
12:00:00 AM
TECHPC75                          {AFB4DC8C-...                       10/22/2010
12:00:00 AM
TECHPC75        Update           KB937286      TECHPC75\wrstanek     10/15/2010
3:50:09 AM
TECHPC75        Software Update  928439        TECHPC75\wrstanek      4/18/2010
4:10:35 PM
TECHPC75        Security Update  KB925902      NT AUTHORITY\SYSTEM    4/17/2010
4:57:48 PM
TECHPC75        Update           KB929399      NT AUTHORITY\SYSTEM    4/17/2010
4:57:48 PM
TECHPC75        Update           KB929777      NT AUTHORITY\SYSTEM    4/17/2010
4:57:48 PM
```

Here, you are getting a list of hotfixes on a specified set of remote computers using credentials you entered when prompted. Each hotfix is listed by

- **Source** Shows the name of the source computer.
- **Description** Shows the type of hotfix. Types of hotfixes include software update, security update, and service pack. Hotfixes also can be listed simply as *update* or *hotfix*.
- **HotFixID** Shows the identifier for the hotfix, which can be a globally unique identifier (GUID), an update identification number, or a knowledge base identification number.
- **InstalledBy** Shows the name of the user who installed the update. If a specific user name is listed, this user installed the update or the update was installed on behalf of the user when the user was logged on. If the user is listed as NT AUTHORITY\SYSTEM, the update was automatically installed by Windows Update.
- **InstalledOn** Shows the date and time the update was installed.

Using the –Id and –Description parameters, you can look for hotfixes with a specific identifier or a specific descriptive type. In the following example and sample output, you look for service packs installed on the local computer:

```
get-hotfix -description "Service Pack"
```

```
Source        Description     HotFixID     InstalledBy           InstalledOn
------        -----------     --------     -----------           -----------
TECHPC16      Service Pack    KB936330     TECHPC16\CharleneD    10/15/2008
2:18:22 AM
```

When you are trying to determine the update status of computers throughout the enterprise, you can take this idea a step further by logging the output or by tracking computers that don't have a particular update installed. For example, if KB936330 is a new service pack that you want to ensure is installed on specific computers, you can type the name of each computer to check on a separate line in a text file and store this list in a file named computers.txt. Next, you can use Get-HotFix to check each of these computers and log your findings. One approach is shown in the following example:

```
$comp = get-content c:\data\computers.txt
$comp | foreach { if (!(get-hotfix -id KB936330 -computername $_)) { add-
content $_ -path log.txt }}
```

Here, you retrieve a list of computer names and store each computer name as an item in an array called $comp, and then you use a ForEach loop to take an action on each item (computer name) in the array. That action is an If Not test that executes Get-HotFix for each computer. As a result, if a computer does not have the required hotfix, you write the computer's name to a file called log.txt in the current working directory. When you use $_ in this way, it refers to the current item in a specified array, which in this case is the name of a computer.

Obtaining Detailed System Information

When inventorying computers in the enterprise, you'll also want to use the Win32_OperatingSystem and Win32_ComputerSystem classes. You use the Win32_OperatingSystem object and its properties to obtain summary information regarding the operating system configuration, as shown in the following example and partial output:

```
Get-WmiObject -Class Win32_OperatingSystem | Format-List *
```

```
Status                          : OK
Name                          : Microsoft® Windows Server® 2008 Enterprise
                                |C:\Windows|\Device\Harddisk1\Partition1
FreePhysicalMemory              : 679172
FreeSpaceInPagingFiles          : 3749368
FreeVirtualMemory               : 2748020
BootDevice                      : \Device\HarddiskVolume2
BuildNumber                     : 7000
BuildType                       : Multiprocessor Free
Caption                         : Microsoftr Windows Server 2008
CodeSet                         : 1252
CountryCode                     : 1
```

When you are working with Win32_OperatingSystem, some of the most important information includes the following:

- The amount of free physical memory and free virtual memory, which are tracked in the TotalVisibleMemorySize and TotalVirtualMemorySize properties, respectively.
- The boot device, system directory, build number, build type, and operating system type, which are tracked in the BootDevice, SystemDirectory, BuildNumber, BuildType, and Caption properties, respectively.
- The encryption level and operating system architecture, which are tracked in the EncryptionLevel and OSArchitecture properties, respectively.
- The last boot-up time, which is tracked in the LastBootUp time property.

The TotalVisibleMemorySize and TotalVirtualMemorySize are shown in kilobytes. To quickly convert the values provided to megabytes, copy each value separately, paste it at the PowerShell prompt, and then type **/1kb**. For example, if the TotalVisibleMemorySize is 3403604, you type **3403604/1kb** and the answer is 3323.832 MB.

NOTE Are you wondering why I didn't use **/1mb** to get a value in megabytes? The value of the kb constant is 1024. The value of the mb constant is 1048576. If a value is in bytes, you can type **/1mb** to convert the value to megabytes. However, if the value is in kilobytes already, you must divide by 1024 to convert the value to megabytes.

Knowing this, you can obtain and store the memory values in megabytes using the following technique:

```
$os = get-wmiobject -class win32_operatingsystem
$AvailMemInMB = $os.totalvisiblememorysize/1kb
$VirtualMemInMB = $os.totalvirtualmemorysize/1kb
```

Whether you are at the PowerShell prompt or working in a script, the $AvailMemInMB and $VirtualMemInMB variables are then available for your use.

The boot device, system device, system directory, and build information provide essential information about the configuration of the operating system. You can use this information to determine the physical disk device on which Windows is installed, the actual directory in the file system, the type of build as either single or multiprocessor, and the exact operating system version installed.

Knowing this, you can obtain and store the related information using the following technique:

```
$os = get-wmiobject -class win32_operatingsystem
$BootDevice = $os.bootdevice
$SystemDevice = $os.systemdevice
$SystemDirectory = $os.systemdirectory
$BuildType = $os.buildtype
$OSType = $os.caption
```

You can then work with these values as necessary. For example, if you want to perform an action only when Windows Vista is installed, you can use the following technique:

```
$os = get-wmiobject -class win32_operatingsystem
$OSType = $os.caption

if ($OSType -match "Vista") {
   #Vista is installed; run the commands in this code block
} else {
   #Vista is not installed; run these commands instead
}
```

Using the LastBootUpTime property of the Win32_OperatingSystem object, you can determine how long a computer has been running since it was last started. To do this, you perform a comparison of the current date and time with the date and time stored in the LastBootUpTime property. However, because the value stored in this property is a string rather than a DateTime object, you must first convert the string value to a DateTime object using the ConvertToDateTime() method. An example and sample output follows:

```
$date = get-date
$os = get-wmiobject -class win32_operatingsystem
$uptime = $os.ConvertToDateTime($os.lastbootuptime)
write-host ($date - $uptime)
```

```
09:20:57.2639083
```

Here, you store the current date and time in the $date variable; then you use Get-WmiObject to get the Win32_OperatingSystem object. Next, you use the ConvertToDateTime() method to convert the string value in the LastBootUpTime property to a DateTime object. Finally, you perform a comparison of the current date and the boot date and display the difference. In this example, the computer has been running about 9 hours and 20 minutes.

You use the Win32_ComputerSystem object and its properties to obtain summary information regarding the computer configuration as shown in the following example and partial output:

```
Get-WmiObject -Class Win32_ComputerSystem | Format-List *
```

```
AdminPasswordStatus         : 1
BootupState                 : Normal boot
ChassisBootupState          : 3
KeyboardPasswordStatus      : 2
PowerOnPasswordStatus       : 1
PowerSupplyState            : 3
PowerState                  : 0
FrontPanelResetStatus       : 2
ThermalState                : 3
Status                      : OK
Name                        : CORPSERVER84
```

With the Win32_ComputerSystem object, there is a great deal of useful information about the computer and its configuration. Some of the most important information includes the following:

- The boot-up state and status of the computer, which are tracked in the BootUpState and Status properties, respectively.
- The name, DNS host name, domain, and domain role, which are tracked in the Name, DNSHostName, Domain, and DomainRole properties, respectively.
- The system type and total physical memory, which are tracked in the properties SystemType and TotalPhysicalMemory, respectively. Note that the total memory available is shown in bytes, not kilobytes.

The boot-up state and status can help you decide whether you want to modify the configuration of a computer, which is helpful when you are working with a remote computer and you don't know its current status. In the following example, you perform one block of commands if the computer is in a normal state and another block of commands if the computer is in a different state:

```
$cs = get-wmiobject -class win32_computersystem
$BootUpState = $cs.bootupstate

if ($BootUpState -match "Normal") {
   "Computer is in a normal state, so run these commands."
} else {
   "Computer not in a normal state, so run these commands instead."
}
```

A computer's name and domain information also can help you decide whether you want to work with the computer. For example, although you might want to reconfigure desktops and laptops, you might not want to reconfigure servers and domain controllers. To help you avoid modifying computers of a specific type inadvertently, you can perform actions based on a computer's role as shown in this example:

```
$cs = get-wmiobject -class win32_computersystem
$DomainRole = $cs.domainrole

switch -regex ($DomainRole) {
  [0-1] { "This computer is a workstation." }
  [2-3] { "This computer is a server but not a domain controller."}
  [4-5] { "This computer is a domain controller."}
  default { "Unknown value."}
}
```

In the shift to 64-bit computing, you might want to track which computers in the enterprise support 64-bit operating systems, which computers are already running 64-bit operating systems, or both. To determine whether a computer has a 64-bit operating system installed already, you can use the OSArchitecture property of the Win32_OperatingSystem object. To determine whether a computer supports a 64-bit operating system, you can use the Name and Description properties of the Win32_Processor object.

You can type the name of each computer to check on a separate line in a text file and store this list in a file called computers.txt.

Next, you can use Get-WmiObject to check each of these computers and log your findings. One approach is shown in the following example:

```
$comp = get-content computers.txt

#Get list of computers that don't have 64-bit OS installed
```

```
$comp | foreach {
  $os = get-wmiobject -class win32_operatingsystem -computername $_
  $OSArch = $os.osarchitecture
  if (!($OSArch -match "32-bit")) { add-content $_ -path next.txt }
}

#Determine which computers without 64-bit OS can have 64-bit OS
$comp2 = get-content next.txt
$comp2 | foreach {
  $ps = get-wmiobject -class win32_processor -computername $_
  $SystemType = $ps.description
  if ($SystemType -like "*x64*") { add-content $_ -path final.txt }
}
```

Here, you retrieve a list of computer names from a file called computers.txt in the current working directory and store each computer name as an item in an array called $comp. Then you use a ForEach loop to take an action on each item (computer name) in the array. As a result, if a computer has a 32-bit operating system installed, you write the computer's name to a file called next.txt in the current working directory. When you use $_ in this way, it refers to the current item in a specified array, which in this case is the name of a computer.

In the final series of commands, you retrieve the list of computers that don't have 64-bit operating systems installed and store each computer name as an item in an array called $comp2. Then you use a ForEach loop to take an action on each item (computer name) in the array. As a result, if a computer is capable of having a 64-bit operating system installed, you write the computer's name to a file called final.txt in the current working directory. The result is a quick but clean approach to inventorying your computers. Any computer listed in final.txt is capable of having a 64-bit operating system but currently has a 32-bit operating system.

Determining Available Users and Groups

As part of your inventory of computers in the enterprise, you'll often want to know what users and groups have been created and are available. One way to examine users and groups is to use the Win32_UserAccount and Win32_Group classes. As shown in the following example and sample output, Win32_UserAccount lists user accounts by name, domain, and more:

```
Get-Wmiobject -Class Win32_UserAccount | format-list Caption,Name,Domain
```

```
Caption : TECHPC76\Administrator
Name : Administrator
Domain : TECHPC76

Caption : TECHPC76\Barney
Name : Barney
Domain : TECHPC76
```

Here, you are working with the local computer. If the user or group was created on the local computer, the computer name is set as the domain. Otherwise, the Active Directory domain name is set as the domain.

You can use the –ComputerName parameter to specify the remote computer or computers that you want to work with and –Credential to specify credentials required for authentication. To see how these could be used, consider the following example:

```
$cred = get-credential
$comp = get-content c:\data\computers.txt
$comp | foreach { Get-Wmiobject -Class Win32_UserAccount `
-ComputerName $_ -Credential $cred }
```

Here, you prompt the user for a credential and store the credential in the $cred variable. Then you retrieve a list of computer names and store each computer name as an item in an array called $comp. Afterward, you use a ForEach loop to take an action on each item (computer name) in the array. That action is to list the user accounts available on the computer.

> ***TIP*** **You can enter these commands at the PowerShell prompt or use them in scripts. At the prompt, enter each command separately. In a script, place each command on a separate line. Either way works and will yield the same results. For continued lines, you might find it easier to enter the divided lines as a single line. If you do, don't forget to remove the continuation character (`).**

Because some scheduled tasks and backup processes require a computer to have a specific local user or group available, you might want to determine whether computers have this user or group. One way to do this is shown in the following example:

```
$comp = get-content computers.txt

#Get list of computers that don't have the BackUpUser account
$comp | foreach {

 $Global:currentc = $_
 $ua = get-wmiobject -class win32_useraccount -computername $_

 $ua | foreach {
  $user = $_.name
  if ($user -eq "sqldb") {add-content $currentc -path valid.txt}
  }
}
```

Here, you retrieve a list of computer names from a file called computers.txt in the current working directory and store each computer name as an item in an array called $comp. Then you use a ForEach loop to take an action on each item (computer name) in the $comp array. First, you store the current computer name in a global variable so that you can access it later. Then you retrieve objects representing all the user accounts on the computer and store these in an array called $ua. Next, you use a second ForEach loop to take action on each item (group object) in the $ua array. As a result, if a computer has a group called SqlDb, you write the computer's name to a file called valid.txt in the current working directory.

Because we are using direct matching, you can use the –Filter parameter of the Get-WmiObject to get only the user account you are looking for in the first place. The –Filter parameter works like a Where clause in a WMI query. Here is an example of the revised code:

```
$comp = get-content computers.txt

#Get list of computers that don't have the BackUpUser account
$comp | foreach {
if (get-wmiobject -class win32_useraccount -computername $_ -filter `
"Name='sqldb'") { add-content $_ -path valid.txt }
}
```

Note the syntax for the Where clause in the string passed to the –Filter parameter. Because you use double quotes to enclose the string, you must use single quotes to match a specific property value.

You can work with Win32_Group in much the same way. Although this is a quick and easy way to inventory users and groups, you'll want to use the Active Directory cmdlets to work with and manage users and groups. Other useful Win32 classes for inventorying computers include Win32_BIOS, Win32_NetworkAdapterConfiguration, Win32_PhysicalMemory, Win32_Processor, and Win32_LogicalDisk.

Evaluating System Hardware

When you are working with computers in the enterprise, you'll often need to obtain detailed configuration information for hardware components. This configuration information will help you evaluate hardware to ensure it is functioning properly and help you diagnose and resolve difficult issues, such as hardware malfunctions and improper configurations.

Checking Firmware Versions and Status

A computer's firmware can be the source of many hardware problems. The firmware must be configured properly and should be kept current with the latest revision.

You can use Win32_BIOS to examine the status, version, language, and manufacturer of a computer's BIOS firmware. When you are trying to determine whether a computer's BIOS is up to date, look at the SMBIOSBIOSVersion information. An example and sample output using WIN32_BIOS follow:

```
get-wmiobject win32_bios | format-list * |
Out-File -append -filepath save.txt
```

```
__PATH              : \\ENGPC42\root\cimv2:Win32_BIOS.Name="Default
                      System BIOS",SoftwareElementID="Default
                      System BIOS",SoftwareElementState=3,
                      TargetOperatingSystem=0,Version="GATEWA - 11d"
Status              : OK
Name                : Default System BIOS
SMBIOSPresent       : True
BIOSVersion         : {GATEWA - 11d}
CurrentLanguage     : enUS
Manufacturer        : Intel Corp.
SMBIOSBIOSVersion   : LA97510J.15A.0285.2007.0906.0226
```

To help keep your computers current, you might want to inventory the firmware versions that are installed and determine whether computers need a firmware update. The SMBIOSBIOSVersion property provides the value you can use to do this. In the following example, you retrieve the BIOS version for a group of computers and store the computer name and BIOS version in a file called bioscheck.txt:

```
$comp = get-content computers.txt

#Store BIOS version for each computer
$comp | foreach {
 $bios = get-wmiobject -class win32_bios -computername $_
 $BiosVersion = $bios.SMBIOSBIOSVersion
 add-content ("$_ $BiosVersion") -path bioscheck.txt
}
```

If your organization has standardized its computers, you might want to determine whether the BIOS version for a group of computers is up to date. One way to do this is to check to see if the current BIOS version is installed and log information about computers that have a different BIOS version, as shown in this example:

```
$comp = get-content computers.txt

$comp | foreach {
 $bios = get-wmiobject -class win32_bios -computername $_
 $BiosVersion = $bios.SMBIOSBIOSVersion
 if (!($BiosVersion -match "LA97510J.15A.0285.2007.0906.0226")) {
   add-content ("$_ $BiosVersion") -path checkfailed.txt }
}
```

Checking Physical Memory and Processors

Few things affect a computer's performance more than the physical memory and processors that are installed. You'll want to ensure computers have adequate memory and processors to support their daily tasks.

You can use Win32_PhysicalMemory to get detailed information for each individual DIMM of memory on a computer as well as status indicators that could indicate problems. A DIMM is a group of memory chips on a card handled as a single unit.

Many computers have an even number of memory card banks, such as two or four. A computer's memory cards should all have the same data width and speed. An example and sample output using Win32_PhysicalMemory follow:

```
get-wmiobject Win32_PhysicalMemory | format-list *  |
Out-File -append -filepath save.txt
```

```
__PATH : \\ENGPC42\root\cimv2:Win32_PhysicalMemory.Tag="Physical Memory
0"
BankLabel             : CHAN A DIMM 0
Capacity              : 1073741824
Caption               : Physical Memory
DataWidth             : 64
Description           : Physical Memory
DeviceLocator         : J6H1
FormFactor            : 8
HotSwappable          :
InstallDate           :
InterleaveDataDepth   : 1
InterleavePosition    : 1
Manufacturer          : 0xAD00000000000000
MemoryType            : 21
Model                 :
Name                  : Physical Memory
Speed                 : 667
Status                :
Tag                   : Physical Memory 0
TotalWidth            : 64
TypeDetail            : 128
Version               :
```

The BankLabel entry shows the channel and DIMM number, such as CHAN A DIMM 0. Capacity is shown in bytes. To quickly convert the value provided to megabytes, copy the value and paste it at the PowerShell prompt and then type **/1mb**, such as **1073741824/1mb**.

The Status entry tells you the current error status. The error status can help you identify a malfunctioning DIMM. The error status also can help you identify a DIMM that is not valid for the computer.

REAL WORLD Windows Vista and later versions of Windows have built-in features to help you identify and diagnose problems with memory. If you suspect a computer has a memory problem that isn't being automatically detected, you can run the Windows Memory Diagnostics utility by completing the following steps:

1. Click Start, type **mdsched.exe** in the Search box, and then press Enter.
2. Choose whether to restart the computer and run the tool immediately or schedule the tool to run at the next restart.
3. Windows Memory Diagnostics runs automatically after the computer restarts and performs a standard memory test automatically. If you want to perform fewer or more tests, press F1, use the Up and Down arrow keys to set the Test Mix as Basic, Standard, or Extended, and then press F10 to apply the desired settings and resume testing.
4. When testing is completed, the computer restarts automatically. You'll see the test results when you log on.

Note also that if a computer crashes because of failing memory, and Windows Memory Diagnostics detects this, you are prompted to schedule a memory test the next time the computer is restarted.

The total memory capacity is the sum of the capacity of all memory banks on the computer. As discussed in Chapter 6, "Mastering Aliases, Functions, and Objects," the Win32_PhysicalMemoryArray class has a MaxCapacity property that tracks the total physical memory in kilobytes as well as a MemoryDevices property that tracks the number of memory banks.

You can use Win32_Processor to get detailed information about each processor on a computer. When you are working with processors, note the clock speed, data width, deviceID, and cache details as well as the number of cores and number of logical processor. A single processor might have multiple processor cores, and each of those processor cores might have a logical representation. Processor cache usually is shown in kilobytes. While most desktop computers have only L2 cache, many servers will have L3 and additional cache. An example and sample output using Win32_Processor follow:

```
get-wmiobject Win32_Processor | format-list *  |
Out-File -append -filepath save.txt
```

```
__PATH : \\ENGPC42\root\cimv2:Win32_Processor.DeviceID="CPU0"
CpuStatus                      : 1
CreationClassName              : Win32_Processor
CurrentClockSpeed              : 2660
CurrentVoltage                 : 16
DataWidth                      : 64
Description                    : x64 Family 6 Model 15 Stepping 7
DeviceID                       : CPU0
ErrorCleared                   :
```

```
ErrorDescription            :
ExtClock                    : 266
Family                      : 190
InstallDate                 :
L2CacheSize                 : 4096
L2CacheSpeed                :
L3CacheSize                 : 0
L3CacheSpeed                : 0
LastErrorCode               :
Level                       : 6
LoadPercentage              : 2
Manufacturer                : GenuineIntel
MaxClockSpeed               : 2660
Name                        : Intel(R) Core(TM)2 Quad CPU    @ 2.66GHz
NumberOfCores               : 4
NumberOfLogicalProcessors   : 4
PowerManagementCapabilities :
PowerManagementSupported    : False
ProcessorId                 : BFEBFBFF000006F7
ProcessorType               : 3
Revision                    : 3847
Role                        : CPU
SocketDesignation           : LGA 775
Status                      : OK
```

In the output, note the ErrorCleared, ErrorDescription, and Status properties. These properties can help you identify a malfunctioning processor. Note error details or error conditions that are shown, and take corrective action as appropriate. For example, if a processor has an error status that restarting the computer doesn't resolve, you might need to service the motherboard, the processor, or both. In some cases, updating the motherboard firmware can resolve intermittent errors.

Checking Hard Disks and Partitions

Hard disks are used to store data. Computers need enough disk space to accommodate the operating system files, the working environment, and user data. To ensure proper performance, hard disks need ample free space as well because this ensures housekeeping tasks and disk cleanup activities can be performed automatically as necessary.

WMI provides several Win32 classes for working with disk drives. Using Win32_DiskDrive, you can work with physical drives, including both fixed hard drives and USB reader devices. If you want to see only a computer's fixed hard disks, you can filter on the media type as shown in the following example and sample output:

```
get-wmiobject -class win32_diskdrive -filter '
"MediaType='Fixed hard disk media'"
```

```
Partitions : 2
DeviceID   : \\.\PHYSICALDRIVE0
Model      : ST3500630AS
Size       : 500105249280
Caption    : ST3500630AS


Partitions : 1
DeviceID   : \\.\PHYSICALDRIVE1
Model      : ST3500630AS
Size       : 500105249280
Caption    : ST3500630AS
```

The computer in this example has two fixed hard drives. PhysicalDrive0 has two disk partitions. PhysicalDrive1 has one disk partition.

If you filter the output by the device ID or caption, you can get information that is more detailed for individual fixed hard drives. In the following example and sample output, you examine a fixed hard drive by its caption:

```
get-wmiobject -class win32_diskdrive -filter "Caption='ST3500630AS'" |
format-list *
```

```
ConfigManagerErrorCode      : 0
LastErrorCode               :
NeedsCleaning               :
Status                      : OK
DeviceID                    : \\.\PHYSICALDRIVE0
StatusInfo                  :
Partitions                  : 2
BytesPerSector              : 512
ConfigManagerUserConfig     : False
DefaultBlockSize            :
Index                       : 0
InstallDate                 :
InterfaceType               : SCSI
SectorsPerTrack             : 63
Size                        : 500105249280
TotalCylinders              : 60801
TotalHeads                  : 255
TotalSectors                : 976768065
TotalTracks                 : 15504255
TracksPerCylinder           : 255
Caption                     : ST3500630AS
CompressionMethod           :
ErrorCleared                :
ErrorDescription            :
ErrorMethodology            :
FirmwareRevision            : 3.AA
```

```
Manufacturer                  : (Standard disk drives)
MediaLoaded                   : True
MediaType                     : Fixed hard disk media
Model                         : ST3500630AS
Name                          : \\.\PHYSICALDRIVE0
SCSIBus                       : 0
SCSILogicalUnit               : 0
SCSIPort                      : 0
SCSITargetId                  : 0
```

As you can see, the detailed information tells you the exact configuration of the physical device, including:

- The number of bytes per sector, sectors per track, and tracks per cylinder.
- The interface type, such as SCSI or IDE.
- The size in bytes. Divide the value by 1gb to get the size in gigabytes.
- The total number of cylinders, heads, sectors, and tracks.
- The bus, logical unit, port, and target ID.

In the output, note the ErrorCleared, ErrorDescription, ErrorMethodology, and Status properties. These properties can help you identify a malfunctioning disk. Note error details or error conditions that are shown, and take corrective action as appropriate. For example, if a processor has an error status that restarting the computer doesn't resolve, you might need to service the hardware controller, the hard disk, or both. In some cases, updating the controller firmware can resolve intermittent errors.

You can use Win32_DiskPartition to obtain partitioning details for each fixed hard disk on the computer. The partitions correspond exactly to how you've partitioned fixed hard disks using Disk Management. As shown in the following example and sample output, each partition of each fixed hard disk is accessible:

```
get-wmiobject -class win32_diskpartition
```

```
NumberOfBlocks   : 18603207
BootPartition    : False
Name             : Disk #0, Partition #0
PrimaryPartition : True
Size             : 9524841984
Index            : 0

NumberOfBlocks   : 958164795
BootPartition    : True
Name             : Disk #0, Partition #1
PrimaryPartition : True
Size             : 490580375040
Index            : 1
```

```
NumberOfBlocks   : 976768002
BootPartition    : False
Name             : Disk #1, Partition #0
PrimaryPartition : True
Size             : 500105217024
Index            : 0
```

The key information you need to know is listed as part of the standard output, so you might not need to view the extended properties. In this example, the computer has two fixed hard disks: Disk 0 and Disk 1. Disk 0 has two partitions: Partition 0 and Partition 1. Disk 1 has one partition: Partition 0. Because partition size is shown in bytes, you can divide the value listed by 1gb to get the size of the partition in gigabytes.

Windows represents formatted disk partitions as logical disks. The WMI object you can use to work with logical disks is Win32_LogicalDisk, which you can use to get detailed information for each logical disk on a computer. However, note that removable disks, CD/DVD drives, and paths assigned drive letters are also represented as logical disks. You can distinguish among these elements using the Description property. Values you'll see include:

- CD-ROM Disc, for CD/DVD drives
- Removable Disk, for removable disks
- Local Fixed Disk, for fixed hard drives

When you are working with the logical representation of partitions on fixed hard disks, note the device ID, compression status, file system type, free space, size, and supported options. DeviceID shows the drive designator, such as C:. An example and sample output using Win32_LogicalDisk follow:

```
get-wmiobject -class win32_logicaldisk -filter "name='c:'" |
format-list * | Out-File -append -filepath save.txt
```

```
Status                        :
Availability                  :
DeviceID                      : C:
StatusInfo                    :
Access                        : 0
BlockSize                     :
Caption                       : C:
Compressed                    : False
ConfigManagerErrorCode        :
ConfigManagerUserConfig       :
CreationClassName             : Win32_LogicalDisk
Description                   : Local Fixed Disk
DriveType                     : 3
FileSystem                    : NTFS
```

```
FreeSpace                     : 298870042624
InstallDate                   :
LastErrorCode                 :
MaximumComponentLength        : 255
MediaType                     : 12
Name                          : C:
NumberOfBlocks                :
QuotasDisabled                : True
QuotasIncomplete              : False
QuotasRebuilding              : False
Size                          : 490580373504
SupportsDiskQuotas            : True
SupportsFileBasedCompression  : True
SystemCreationClassName       : Win32_ComputerSystem
SystemName                    : ENGPC42
VolumeDirty                   : False
VolumeName                    :
VolumeSerialNumber            : 008EA097
```

The FreeSpace and Size properties are shown in bytes. To quickly convert the value provided to gigabytes, copy the value, paste it at the PowerShell prompt, and then type **/1gb**, such as **302779912192/1gb**. Here is an example and sample output:

```
$dr = get-wmiobject -class win32_logicaldisk -filter "name='c:'"
$free = [Math]::Round($dr.freespace/1gb)
$capacity = [Math]::Round($dr.size/1gb)

write-host $dr.name "on" $dr.systemname
write-host "Disk Capacity: $capacity"
write-host "Free Space: $free"
```

```
C: on ENGPC42
Disk Capacity: 457
Free Space: 278
```

Checking and Managing Device Drivers

Computers can have all sorts of hardware devices installed on and connected to them. Because all of these devices require device drivers to operate properly, you'll often want to know detailed information about a particular device's driver. For example, you might want to know whether the device driver is:

- Enabled or disabled.
- Running or stopped.
- Configured to start automatically.

The Win32 class for working with device drivers is Win32_SystemDriver. Using Win32_SystemDriver, you can obtain detailed configuration and status information on any device driver configured for use on a computer. You can examine device drivers by device display name using the DisplayName property, by state using the State property, or by start mode using the StartMode property. The display name for a device and its driver is the same as the one shown in Device Manager.

In the following example, you use the DisplayName property to check the RAID controller on a computer:

```
get-wmiobject -class win32_systemdriver | where-object '
{$_.displayname -like "*raid c*"} | format-list *
```

```
Status                  : OK
Name                    : iaStor
State                   : Running
ExitCode                : 0
Started                 : True
ServiceSpecificExitCode : 0
AcceptPause             : False
AcceptStop              : True
Caption                 : Intel RAID Controller
CreationClassName       : Win32_SystemDriver
Description             : Intel RAID Controller
DesktopInteract         : False
DisplayName             : Intel RAID Controller
ErrorControl            : Normal
InstallDate             :
PathName                : C:\Windows\system32\drivers\iastor.sys
ServiceType             : Kernel Driver
StartMode               : Boot
StartName               :
SystemCreationClassName : Win32_ComputerSystem
SystemName              : ENGPC42
TagId                   : 25
Site                    :
Container               :
```

Generally, State is shown as either Running or Stopped. Knowing this, you can check for device drivers in either state as shown in the following example and sample output:

```
get-wmiobject -class win32_systemdriver -filter "state='Running'"
```

```
DisplayName : Microsoft ACPI Driver
Name        : ACPI
State       : Running
Status      : OK
```

```
Started     : True

DisplayName : Ancillary Function Driver for Winsock
Name        : AFD
State       : Running
Status      : OK
Started     : True
```

The start mode can be set as:

- **Boot** Used for boot device drivers
- **Manual** Used for device drivers that are started manually
- **Auto** Used for device drivers that are started automatically
- **System** Used for system device drivers

Using StartMode for your filter, you can list boot device drivers as shown in the following example:

```
get-wmiobject -class win32_systemdriver -filter "startmode='Boot'"
```

The Win32_SystemDriver class provides a number of methods for managing system drivers. These methods include:

- **Change()** Changes the device driver configuration. It accepts the following parameters in the following order: DisplayName, PathName, ServiceType-Byte, ErrorControlByte, StartMode, DesktopInteractBoolean, StartName, StartPassword, LoadOrderGroup, LoadOrderGroupDependenciesArray, and ServiceDependenciesArray.

  CAUTION **Modifying devices at the PowerShell prompt is not something you should do without careful forethought. PowerShell lets you make changes that will make your computer unbootable. Before you make any changes to devices, you should create a system restore point as discussed in Chapter 12, "Managing and Securing the Registry." You also might want to consider performing a full backup of the computer.**

- **ChangeStartMode()** Changes the start mode of the device driver. It accepts a single parameter, which is the start mode to use. Valid values are boot, manual, auto, or system.

  CAUTION **Before you change the start mode of a device driver, ensure the driver supports this start mode. You also should ensure that the start mode won't affect the computer's ability to start.**

- **Delete()** Deletes the device driver (if the device is in a state that allows this). Deleting the device driver doesn't prevent the device from being used. To prevent the device from being used, you should disable it instead. If you delete a device driver without disabling a device, Windows will, in most cases, detect and reinstall the device the next time the computer is started. As part of troubleshooting, you can sometimes delete a device's driver to force Windows to reinstall the device.

CAUTION **Exercise extreme caution if you plan to delete device drivers using PowerShell. PowerShell will not warn you if you are making harmful changes to your computer.**

- **InterrogateService()** Connects to the device using the device driver. If the return value is zero, WMI was able to connect to and interrogate the device using the device driver. If the return value isn't zero, WMI encountered a problem while trying to communicate with the device using the device driver. If the device is stopped or paused, this method always returns an error status.
- **PauseService()** Pauses the device, which might be necessary during troubleshooting or diagnostics. Devices that can be paused indicate this when the AcceptPause property is set to True for their device drivers. Further, you can pause only a device that is in a state where pausing is permitted.
- **ResumeService()** Resumes the device after it has been paused.
- **StopService()** Stops the device, which might be necessary during troubleshooting or diagnostics. Devices that can be stopped indicate this when the AcceptStop property is set to True for their device drivers. Further, you can stop only a device that is in a state where stopping is permitted.
- **StartService()** Starts a stopped device, including devices that are configured for manual start up.

If you want to change the start mode for a device driver, you can use the ChangeStartMode() method to specify the desired start mode. The basic syntax is

```
$driverObject.ChangeStartMode(StartMode)
```

where *$driverObject* is a reference to a Win32_SystemDriver object, and *StartMode* is the desired start mode entered as a string value, as shown in this example and sample output:

```
$d = get-wmiobject -class win32_systemdriver | where-object '
{$_.displayname -like "creative audio*"}
$d.changestartmode("auto")
```

```
__GENUS          : 2
__CLASS          : __PARAMETERS
__SUPERCLASS     :
__DYNASTY        : __PARAMETERS
__RELPATH        :
__PROPERTY_COUNT : 1
```

```
__DERIVATION     : {}
__SERVER         :
__NAMESPACE      :
__PATH           :
ReturnValue      : 0
```

Here, you set the start mode to Auto for a Creative Audio device. The return value in the output is what you want to focus on. A return value of 0 (zero) indicates success. Any other return value indicates an error. Typically, errors occur because you aren't using an elevated administrator PowerShell prompt, you haven't accessed the correct device driver, or the device isn't in a state in which it can be configured. Keep in mind that if you alter the configuration of required device drivers, you might not be able to start the computer. Because of this, don't make any changes to device drivers without careful planning and forethought.

Digging In Even More

Want to really dig in and explore what's available on a computer? Enter the following command as a single line to list every available .NET type:

```
[System.AppDomain]::CurrentDomain.GetAssemblies() |
Foreach-Object { $_.GetTypes() }
```

You can expand on this idea by creating a function and then calling this function with various filters to find specific .NET types. The code for a ListType function follows:

```
function ListType() {
  [System.AppDomain]::CurrentDomain.GetAssemblies() |
  Foreach-Object { $_.GetTypes() }
}
```

To list all .NET types, you can call the ListType function without any filters, as shown in this example:

```
ListType
```

You can view specific .NET types if you check for names that are like a specified value. For example, to list all .NET types with "parser" as part of the name, you could enter

```
ListType | ? { $_.Name -like "*parser*" }
```

To learn more about a .NET type, you can look at the constructors for the type. The following example lists the constructors for all .NET types with "parser" as part of the name:

```
ListType | ? { $_.Name -like "*parser*" } |
 % { $_.GetConstructors() }
```

Pretty cool. However, not every .NET type is loaded for use. Therefore, to use a .NET type you find, you might need to load it before you use it.

Another cool trick is to examine the available COM objects on a computer. COM objects are registered in the registry, and by exploring the appropriate registry branches, you can find COM objects that are registered for use on the computer. A function for checking the registry follows:

```
function ListProgID {
  param()
  $paths = @("REGISTRY::HKEY_CLASSES_ROOT\CLSID")
  if ($env:Processor_Architecture -eq "amd64") {
    $paths+="REGISTRY::HKEY_CLASSES_ROOT\Wow6432Node\CLSID" }
  Get-ChildItem $paths -include VersionIndependentPROGID -recurse |
  Select-Object @{
    Name='ProgID'
    Expression={$_.GetValue("")}
  }, @{
    Name='Type'
    Expression={
      if ($env:Processor_Architecture -eq "amd64") { "Wow6432" }
      else { "32-bit" }
    }
  }
}
```

Here, you check the processor architecture on the computer. If the computer is running a 32-bit operating system, you look under HKEY_CLASSES_ROOT\CLSID for 32-bit COM objects. If the computer is running a 64-bit operating system, you look under HKEY_CLASSES_ROOT\CLSID for 32-bit COM objects and under HKEY_CLASSES_ROOT\Wow6432Node\CLSID for additional COM objects. You then list the registered COM objects by their progID and type.

To use this function to list all COM objects by their ProgID and type, you could enter the following command:

```
ListProgID
```

You can view specific COM objects if you check for names that are like a specified value. For example, to list all COM objects with "Microsoft" as part of the name, you could enter

```
ListProgID | Where-Object { $_.ProgID -like "*Microsoft*" }
```

Have fun; there's a lot here to explore. For more information on objects, .NET types, and COM objects, see "Working with Objects" and "Working with COM and .NET Framework Objects" in Chapter 6.

CHAPTER 10

Managing File Systems, Security, and Auditing

In this chapter, you'll learn techniques for managing file systems and security—and there's a lot more flexibility to this than most people realize. You can create, copy, move, and delete individual directories and files. You can read and write files, and you also can append data to files and clear the contents of files. You can examine and set access control lists on directories and files, and you also can take ownership of directories and files. Moreover, because you are working with Windows PowerShell, it's just as easy to manipulate multiple directories and files matching specific parameters you specify as it is to work with individual directories and files.

Managing PowerShell Drives, Directories, and Files

You can use PowerShell to manage drives, directories, and files. The core set of features for performing related procedures were discussed previously in the "Using Providers" section in Chapter 3, "Managing Your PowerShell Environment," and include the FileSystem provider, the cmdlets for working with data stores listed in Table 3-4, and the cmdlets for working with provider drives listed in Table 3-5.

Adding and Removing PowerShell Drives

Using the Get-PSDrive cmdlet, you can view the PowerShell drives that currently are available. As the following example and sample output shows, this includes actual drives and the resources PowerShell lets you work with as if they were drives:

```
get-psdrive
```

```
Name       Provider     Root
----       --------     ----
Alias      Alias
C          FileSystem   C:\
cert       Certificate  \
D          FileSystem   D:\
E          FileSystem   E:\
Env        Environment
F          FileSystem   F:\
Function   Function
G          FileSystem   G:\
HKCU       Registry     HKEY_CURRENT_USER
HKLM       Registry     HKEY_LOCAL_MACHINE
I          FileSystem   I:\
J          FileSystem   J:\
K          FileSystem   K:\
L          FileSystem   L:\
M          FileSystem   M:\
N          FileSystem   N:\
O          FileSystem   O:\
P          FileSystem   P:\
Q          FileSystem   Q:\
Variable   Variable
W          FileSystem   W:\
WSMan      WSMan
X          FileSystem   X:\
Y          FileSystem   Y:\
Z          FileSystem   Z:\
```

NOTE **To query multiple computers, use the Invoke-Command cmdlet as discussed in Chapter 4, "Using Sessions, Jobs, and Remoting." Here is an example:**

```
invoke-command -computername Server43, Server27, Server82
-scriptblock { get-psdrive }
```

You can change the working location to any of these drives using Set-Location. Simply follow the cmdlet name with the desired drive or path relative to a drive, such as

```
set-location c:
```

or

```
set-location c:\logs
```

When you switch drives using only the drive designator, PowerShell remembers the working path, allowing you to return to the previous working path on a drive simply by referencing the drive designator. See the "Navigating and Using Provider Drives" section in Chapter 3 for more information.

You can use the New-PSDrive cmdlet to create a PowerShell drive that is mapped to a location in a data store, which can include a shared network folder, local directory, or registry key. The drive acts as a shortcut and is available only in the current PowerShell console. For example, if you frequently work with the C:\Data\Current\History\Files directory, you might want to create a new drive to quickly reference this location. When you create a drive, you specify the alias to the drive using the –Name parameter, the provider type using the –PSProvider parameter, and the root path using the –Root parameter, as shown in this example:

```
new-psdrive -name hfiles -psprovider filesystem -root c:\data\current\
history\files
```

Here, you create a drive called *hfiles* as a FileSystem type to act as a shortcut to C:\Data\Current\History\Files. You can switch to this drive by typing **set-location hfiles:**. As long as you have the appropriate permissions to create drives, the creation process should be successful. A common error you might see occurs when a like-named drive already exists.

Because the drive exists only in the current PowerShell session, the drive ceases to exist when you exit the PowerShell console. You also can remove a drive using Remove-PSDrive. Although you can remove drives you added to the console, you cannot delete Windows drives or mapped network drives created by using other methods.

NOTE You can create a drive that maps to registry locations as well. If you do, the PSProvider type to reference is registry. Type **get-psprovider** to list all available provider types.

Creating and Managing Directories and Files

In PowerShell, you work with directories and files in much the same way. You view directories and files using Get-ChildItem as shown in many previous examples. To create directories and files, you use New-Item. The basic syntax is

```
new-item -type [Directory | File] -path Path
```

where you specify the type of item you are creating as either *Directory* or *File* and then use *Path* to specify where the directory or file should be created. When you create a directory or file, New-Item displays results that confirm the creation process. In the following example, you create a C:\Logs\Backup directory, and the resulting output confirms that the directory was successfully created:

```
new-item -type directory -path c:\logs\backup
```

```
    Directory: C:\logs
Mode                LastWriteTime     Length Name
----                -------------     ------ ----
d----         2/18/2009   4:54 PM            backup
```

NOTE To create directories and files on remote computers, use the Invoke-Command cmdlet as discussed in Chapter 4. Here is an example:

```
invoke-command -computername Server43, Server27, Server82
-scriptblock { new-item -type directory -path c:\logs\backup }
```

As long as you have the appropriate permissions to create a directory or file in the specified location, the creation process should be successful. The New-Item cmdlet even creates any required subdirectories for you automatically. In this example, if the C:\Logs directory doesn't exist, PowerShell creates this directory and then creates the Backup subdirectory. When you create a file, PowerShell creates an empty file with no contents.

Using similar procedures, you can copy, move, rename, and delete directories and files.

Copying Directories and Files

You can copy directories and files using Copy-Item. The basic syntax for directories and their contents is

```
copy-item SourcePath DestinationPath -recurse
```

where *SourcePath* is the path to the directory to copy, and *DestinationPath* is where you'd like to create a copy of the directory. In the following example, you copy the C:\Logs directory (and all its contents) to C:\Logs_Old:

```
copy-item c:\logs c:\logs_old -recurse
```

The command will create the Logs_Old directory if it does not already exist. The basic syntax for copying files is

```
copy-item PathToSourceFile DestinationPath
```

where *PathToSourceFile* is the path to the file or files to copy, and *DestinationPath* is where you'd like to create a copy of the file or files. In the following example, you copy all the .txt files in the C:\Logs directory to C:\Logs_Old:

```
copy-item c:\logs\*.txt c:\logs_old
```

As long as you have the appropriate permissions, you should be able to copy directories and files. You can use Copy-Item to copy resources across volumes as shown in the following example:

```
copy-item c:\logs d:\logs_old -recurse
```

Moving Directories and Files

You can move directories and files using Move-Item. The basic syntax is

```
move-item SourcePath DestinationPath
```

where *SourcePath* is the current path to the directory or file, and *DestinationPath* is the new path for the directory or file. When you move a directory or file, Move-Item displays an error that indicates failure but doesn't display any output to indicate success. In the following example, you move the C:\Logs directory (and all its contents) to C:\Backup\Logs:

```
move-item c:\logs c:\backup\logs
```

The following command moves all the .txt files in the C:\Logs directory to C:\Backup\Logs:

```
move-item c:\logs\*.txt c:\backup\logs
```

As long as you have the appropriate permissions, you should be able to move directories and files. However, some caveats apply. Because you cannot use Move-Item to move resources across volumes, the source and destination path must have identical roots. If files in a directory are in use, a file is in use, or a directory is shared, you won't be able to move the directory or file.

Renaming Directories and Files

To rename directories and files, you use the Rename-Item cmdlet. Rename-Item has the following syntax:

```
rename-item OriginalNamePath NewName
```

where *OriginalNamePath* is the full path to the directory or file, and *NewName* is the new name for the directory or file. In the following example, you rename Log1.txt in the C:\Logs directory as Log1_hist.txt:

```
rename-item c:\logs\log1.txt log1_hist.txt
```

As long as you have the appropriate permissions, you should be able to rename directories and files. However, if files in a directory are in use, a file is in use, or a directory is shared, you won't be able to rename the directory or file.

Deleting Directories and Files

You can delete directories and files using the Remove-Item cmdlet. Remove-Item has the following syntax:

```
remove-item NamePath [-force]
```

where *NamePath* is the full path to the directory or file that you want to remove, and *–Force* is an optional parameter to force the removal of a directory or file. In the following example, you delete the D:\Logs_Old directory (and all its contents):

```
remove-item d:\logs_old
```

As long as you have the appropriate permissions, you should be able to remove directories and files. However, if files in a directory are in use, a file is in use, or a directory is shared, you won't be able to remove the directory or file. Additionally, if a directory or file is marked Read-Only, Hidden, or System, you'll have to use the –Force parameter to remove it.

Working with File Contents

Often when you are working with computers, you'll want to create your own configuration and inventory records or logs to record your activities. PowerShell makes this easy by providing a simple set of commands for reading the contents of files and writing new contents to files.

Commands for Managing File Contents

Commands that help you access file resources include the following:

- **Get-Content** Displays the contents of files in a specified location. Use –Force to force access to a hidden, system, or read-only file. Use –TotalCount to specify the number of lines in each matching file to display. Use –Include to limit the matches to files meeting specific criteria. Use –Exclude to omit specified files. Both –Include and –Exclude accept wildcard characters.

```
Get-Content [-LiteralPath | -Path] FilePath {AddtlParams}

AddtlParams=
[-Credential Credential] [-Delimiter String] [-Encoding Encoding]
[-Exclude FilesToExclude] [-Force] [-Include FilesToInclude]
[-TotalCount Count]
```

REAL WORLD Many PowerShell cmdlets accept –Path and –LiteralPath parameters. Both parameters specify the path to an item. However, unlike –Path, the value of –LiteralPath is used exactly as it is typed. This means no characters are interpreted as wildcards. If a path includes actual escape characters, enclose them in single quotation marks because this tells PowerShell not to interpret any characters as escape sequences.

- **Set-Content** Overwrites the contents of files in a specified location. Use –Force to force access to a hidden, system, or read-only file. Specify the content to write using the –Value parameter or by pipelining input from another command. Use –Include to limit the matches to files meeting specific criteria. Use –Exclude to omit specified files. Both –Include and –Exclude accept wildcard characters.

```
Set-Content [-LiteralPath | -Path] FilePath [-Value Content]
{AddtlParams}

AddtlParams=
[-Credential Credential] [-Encoding Encoding] [-Exclude
FilesToExclude] [-Force] [-Include FilesToInclude]
```

- **Add-Content** Adds contents to files in a specified location. Use –Force to force access to a hidden, system, or read-only file. Specify the content to write using the –Value parameter or by pipelining input from another command.

```
Add-Content [-LiteralPath | -Path] FilePath [-Value NewContent]
{AddtlParams}

AddtlParams=
[-Credential Credential] [-Encoding Encoding] [-Exclude
FilesToExclude] [-Force] [-Include FilesToInclude]
```

- **Clear-Content** Clears the contents of files in a specified location. Use –Force to force access to a hidden, system, or read-only file. Use –Include to limit the matches to files meeting specific criteria.

```
Add-Content [-LiteralPath | -Path] FilePath {AddtlParams}

AddtlParams=
[-Credential Credential] [-Exclude FilesToExclude] [-Force]
[-Include FilesToInclude]
```

Reading and Writing File Content

By default, Get-Content searches the current directory for a file you specify by name or by partial name using wildcards and then displays its contents as text. This means you can quickly display the contents of any text-based file at the prompt simply by typing **Get-Content** followed by the name of a file in the current directory. The following example gets the log1.txt file in the current directory:

```
get-content log1.txt
```

To display the contents of a file in a specified path, type the full path to the file. The following example gets the log1.txt file in the C:\Logs directory:

```
get-content c:\logs\log1.txt
```

If you use wildcards, you can display the contents of any files that match the wildcard criteria. The following example displays the contents of any file in the C:\Logs directory that begins with "log":

```
get-content c:\logs\log*
```

To restrict wildcard matches to specific types of files, use the –Include parameter. To exclude specific files or types of files, use the –Exclude parameter. For example, to match only files with the .txt and .log extension, you can enter

```
get-content -include *.txt, *.log -path c:\logs\log*
```

Alternatively, to exclude .xml files and match all other files beginning with "log", you can enter

```
get-content -exclude *.xml -path c:\logs\log*
```

Additionally, if you want to see only the first few lines of matching files, use –TotalCount to specify the number of lines in each matching file to display. The following example displays the first 10 lines of each matching file:

```
get-content -totalcount 10 -path c:\logs\log*
```

Other cmdlets for working with the contents of files include Set-Content, Add-Content, and Clear-Content. Set-Content overwrites the contents of one or more files in a specified location with content you specify. Add-Content adds content you specify to the end of one or more files in a specified location. Clear-Content removes the contents of files in a specified location. Because Clear-Content does not delete the files, this results in files with no contents (empty files).

Accessing Security Descriptors

As an administrator, some of the most important tasks you perform have to do with configuring and maintaining file-system security. PowerShell makes this easy by providing a simple set of commands for viewing and configuring security descriptors. If you save a transcript of your work or use a script to perform the work, you can easily duplicate your efforts on one computer on other computers in the enterprise.

Commands for Working with Security Descriptors

Commands that help you access file resources include the following:

- **Get-Acl** Gets objects that represent the security descriptor of a file, registry key, or any other resource with a provider that supports the concept of security descriptors. Use –Audit to get the audit data for the security descriptor from the access control list.

```
Get-Acl [-Path] FilePaths {AddtlParams}

AddtlParams=
[-Audit] [-Exclude FilesToExclude] [-Include FilesToInclude]
```

- **Set-Acl** Changes the security descriptor of a file, registry key, or any other resource with a provider that supports the concept of security descriptors. Use –AclObject to set the desired security settings.

```
Set-Acl [-Path] FilePaths [-Aclobject] Security {AddtlParams}

AddtlParams=
[-Exclude FilesToExclude] [-Include FilesToInclude]
```

NOTE **On NTFS file system volumes, access permissions control access to files and directories. If you do not have appropriate access permissions, you will not be able to work with files and directories.**

Getting and Setting Security Descriptors

Whenever you are working with system resources—such as directories, files, or registry keys—you might want to view or modify a resource's security descriptor. Use Get-Acl with the –Path parameter to specify the path to resources you want to work with. As with Get-Content, you can use wildcard characters in the path and also include or exclude files using the –Include and –Exclude parameters.

Get-Acl returns a separate object containing the security information for each matching file. By default, Get-Acl displays the path to the resource, the owner of the resource, and a list of the access control entries on the resource. The access control list is controlled by the resource owner. To get additional information—including the security group of the owner, a list of auditing entries, and the full security descriptor as an SDDL (Security Descriptor Definition Language) string—format the output as a list as shown in the following example and sample output:

```
get-acl c:\windows\system32\windowspowershell | format-list
```

```
Path: Microsoft.PowerShell.Core\FileSystem::
C:\windows\system32\windowspowershell
Owner  : NT AUTHORITY\SYSTEM
Group  : NT AUTHORITY\SYSTEM
Access : NT SERVICE\TrustedInstaller Allow  FullControl
         NT SERVICE\TrustedInstaller Allow  268435456
         NT AUTHORITY\SYSTEM Allow  FullControl
         NT AUTHORITY\SYSTEM Allow  268435456
         BUILTIN\Administrators Allow  FullControl
         BUILTIN\Administrators Allow  268435456
         BUILTIN\Users Allow  ReadAndExecute, Synchronize
         BUILTIN\Users Allow  -1610612736
         CREATOR OWNER Allow  268435456
Audit  :
Sddl   : O:SYG:SYD:AI(A;ID;FA;;;S-1-5-80-956008885-3418522649-1831038044-
1853292631-2271478464)(A;CIIOID;GA;;;S-1-5-80-956008885-3418522649-
1831038044-1853292631-2271478464)(A;ID;FA;;;SY) (A;OICIIOID;GA;;;SY)
(A;ID;FA;;;BA)(A;OICIIOID;GA;;;BA)(A;ID;0x1200a9;;;BU)(A;OICIIOID;GXGR;;;
BU)(A;OICIIOID;GA;;;CO)
```

Here, Get-Acl returns a DirectorySecurity object representing the security descriptor of the C:\Windows\System32\WindowsPowerShell directory. The result is then sent to the Format-List cmdlet.

You can work with files in the same way. Here is an example:

```
get-acl -include *.txt, *.log -path c:\logs\log* | format-list
```

Here, Get-Acl returns FileSecurity objects representing the security descriptors of each matching file. The results are then sent to the Format-List cmdlet.

You can work with any properties of security objects separately, including:

- **Owner** Shows the owner of the resource
- **Group** Shows the primary group the owner is a member of
- **Access** Shows the access control rules on the resource
- **Audit** Shows the auditing rules on the resource
- **Sddl** Shows the full security descriptor as an SDDL string

NOTE FileSecurity and DirectorySecurity objects have additional properties that aren't displayed as part of the standard output. To see these properties, send the output to Format-List *. You'll then see the following note and script properties: PSPath (the PowerShell path to the resource), PSParentPath (the PowerShell path to the parent resource), PSChildName (the name of the resource), PSDrive (the PowerShell drive on which the resource is located), AccessToString (an alternate representation of the access rules on the resource), and AuditToString (an alternate representation of the audit rules on the resource).

You can use the objects that Get-Acl returns to set the security descriptors on other system resources, including directories, files, and registry keys. To do this, you'll want to do the following:

1. Open an elevated administrator PowerShell prompt.
2. Obtain a single security descriptor object for a resource that has the security settings you want to use.
3. Use the security descriptor object to establish the desired security settings for another resource.

When you are setting security descriptors in PowerShell, it is a best practice either to specify exactly what you are including, what you are excluding, or both, or to specify only a single resource to modify. Previously, we were working with a log file named log1.txt in the C:\Logs directory. If this log file has a security descriptor that you want to apply to another file, you can do this as shown in the following example:

```
set-acl -path c:\logs\log2.txt -aclobject (get-acl c:\logs\log1.txt)
```

Here you use the security descriptor on log1.txt to set the security descriptor for log2.txt.

You can easily extend this technique. In this example, you use the security descriptor on log1.txt to set the security descriptor for all other .txt and .log files in the C:\Logs directory:

```
$secd = get-acl c:\logs\log1.txt
set-acl -include *.txt, *.log -path c:\logs\* -aclobject $secd
```

To include files in subdirectories, you need to use Get-ChildItem to obtain reference objects for all the files you want to work with. Here is an example:

```
$s = get-acl c:\logs\log1.txt
gci c:\logs -recurse -include *.txt, *.log -force | set-acl -aclobject $s
```

Here, *gci* is an alias for Get-ChildItem. You obtain the security descriptor for log1.txt. Next you get a reference to all .txt and .log files in the C:\Logs directory and all subdirectories. Finally, you use the security descriptor on log1.txt to set the security descriptor for all these files.

If you want to work with directories rather than files, you need to limit the results returned by Get-ChildItem. For files and directories, each resource object returned by Get-ChildItem includes a Mode property as shown in the following example and sample output:

```
get-childitem c:\
```

```
    Directory: C:\
Mode                LastWriteTime     Length Name
----                -------------     ------ ----
d----         6/20/2008   1:20 PM            Backup
d----         2/19/2008  10:57 AM            cabs
d----        12/18/2008   9:16 AM            Documents
-a---         9/18/2006   2:43 PM         24 autoexec.bat
-ar-s         2/29/2008   9:53 AM       8192 BOOTSECT.BAK
-a---         9/18/2006   2:43 PM         10 config.sys
```

The valid values for modes are the following:

- d (directory)
- a (archive)
- r (read-only)
- h (hidden)
- s (system)

Therefore, if you want to work only with directories, you can look for resources where the mode contains a *d* or is like *d**, for example,

```
where-object {$_.mode -like "d*"}
```

In addition, if you want to work only with files, you can use

```
where-object {$_.mode -notlike "d*"}
```

Knowing this, you can copy the security descriptor on C:\Data to C:\Logs and all its subdirectories as shown in this example:

```
gci c:\logs -recurse -force | where-object {$_.mode -like "d*"} |
set-acl -aclobject (get-acl c:\data)
```

Alternatively, you can copy the security descriptor on C:\Data\key.txt to all files in C:\Logs and all its subdirectories, as shown here:

```
gci c:\logs -recurse -force | where-object {$_.mode -notlike "d*"} |
set-acl -aclobject (get-acl c:\data\key.txt)
```

NOTE For these examples to work, the directories and files must exist. If you want to try these examples on your computer, create the C:\Data and C:\Logs directories and then add several .txt files to these directories, including a file called key.txt.

Working with Access Rules

As you can see, it is fairly easy and straightforward to copy security descriptors from one resource to another—and more importantly, the same techniques apply to any type of resource that has security descriptors, whether you are working with files, directories, registry keys, or whatever. If you want to create your own security descriptors, we'll have to dig deeper into the security object model. In this model, access control rules, such as security descriptors, are represented as objects. The Access property of security objects is defined as a collection of authorization rules. With directories and files, these rules have the following object type:

System.Security.AccessControl.FileSystemAccessRule

You can view the individual access control objects that apply to a resource in several ways. One way is to get a security descriptor object and then list the contents of its Access property as shown in the following example and sample output:

```
$s = get-acl c:\logs
$s.access
```

```
FileSystemRights  : FullControl
AccessControlType : Allow
IdentityReference : BUILTIN\Administrators
IsInherited       : True
InheritanceFlags  : None
PropagationFlags  : None

FileSystemRights  : ReadAndExecute, Synchronize
AccessControlType : Allow
IdentityReference : BUILTIN\Users
IsInherited       : True
InheritanceFlags  : ContainerInherit, ObjectInherit
PropagationFlags  : None

FileSystemRights  : Modify, Synchronize
AccessControlType : Allow
IdentityReference : NT AUTHORITY\Authenticated Users
IsInherited       : True
InheritanceFlags  : None
PropagationFlags  : None
```

Here you get the DirectorySecurity object for the C:\Logs directory and then display the contents of its Access property. Although each value listed is an access rule object, you cannot work with each access rule object separately. Note the following in the output:

- **FileSystemRights** Shows the file system rights being applied
- **AccessControlType** Shows the access control type as Allow or Deny
- **IdentityResource** Shows the user or group to which the rule applies
- **IsInherited** Specifies whether the access rule is inherited
- **InheritanceFlags** Shows the way inheritance is being applied
- **PropagationFlags** Specifies whether the access rule will be inherited

Another way to work with each access rule object separately is to use a ForEach loop as shown in this example:

```
$s = get-acl c:\logs

foreach($a in $s.access) {

 #work with each access control object

 if ($a.identityreference -like "*administrator*") {$a | format-list *}
}
```

```
FileSystemRights  : FullControl
AccessControlType : Allow
IdentityReference : BUILTIN\Administrators
IsInherited       : True
InheritanceFlags  : None
PropagationFlags  : None
```

Here, you examine each access rule object separately, which allows you to take action on specific access rules. In this example, you look for access rules that apply to administrators.

As an administrator, you'll often want to perform similar searches to find files and folders that aren't configured to allow access that might be required to perform backups or other administrative tasks. Previously, we discussed using Get-ChildItem to work with directories and files. For directories and files, each resource object returned by Get-ChildItem includes a Mode property that you can use to work with either directories or files. In the following example and sample output, you list every directory and file on drive C that doesn't allow administrators full control:

```
$resc = gci c:\ -recurse -force | where-object {$_.mode -notlike "*hs*"}

foreach($r in $resc) {
  $s = get-acl $r.FullName
  $found = $false

  foreach($a in $s.access) {
   if (($a.identityreference -like "*administrator*") -and `
       ($a.filesystemrights -eq "fullcontrol")) {
           if ($a.accesscontroltype -eq "allow") { $found = $true }
   }
  }

  if (-not $found) { write-host $r.FullName}
}
```

```
C:\logs\backup
C:\logs\backup2
C:\logs\logs
C:\logs\data.ps1
C:\logs\log1.txt
C:\logs\log2.txt
C:\logs\log3.txt
C:\logs\log4.txt
C:\logs\backup\backup
C:\logs\backup\backup\b2
```

Here, you should run the code using an elevated administrator PowerShell prompt. The $resc variable stores a collection of objects that includes all files and directories on C:\, except for files and directories marked as Hidden or System. Using a ForEach loop, you then examine each related resource object. First, you get the access control list for the object by referencing the full name of the object. Then you initialize the $found variable to False so that you can use this variable to track whether a file has the access rights you are looking for.

In the second ForEach loop, you examine each access control object associated with a particular file or folder. If a resource allows administrators full control, you set $found to True. Because you are checking the status of three properties, you use a logical AND to check two properties first. If those properties are both set as expected, you check the third property to see if it is True also. Finally, if $found is not True (meaning it's False), you write the full name of the file or folder to the output. The result is a list of all files and folders that are not configured so that all administrators have full control.

Configuring File and Directory Permissions

On NTFS volumes, you can assign two types of access permissions to files and directories: Basic and Special. These permissions grant or deny access to users and groups.

Setting Basic Permissions

The basic permissions you can assign to directories and files are shown in Table 10-1 and Table 10-2. These permissions are made up of multiple special permissions. Note the rule flag for each permission because this is the value you must reference when creating an access rule.

TABLE 10-1 Basic Folder Permissions

PERMISSION	DESCRIPTION	RULE FLAG
Full Control	This permission permits reading, writing, changing, and deleting files and subdirectories. If a user has Full Control over a folder, she can delete files in the folder regardless of the permission on the files.	FullControl
Modify	This permission permits reading and writing to files and subdirectories, and it allows deletion of the folder.	Modify
List Folder Contents	This permission permits viewing and listing files and subdirectories as well as executing files; it's inherited by directories only.	Synchronize
Read & Execute	This permission permits viewing and listing files and subdirectories as well as executing files; it's inherited by files and directories.	ReadAnd-Execute
Write	This permission permits adding files and subdirectories.	Write
Read	This permission permits viewing and listing files and subdirectories.	Read

TABLE 10-2 Basic File Permissions

PERMISSION	DESCRIPTION	RULE FLAG
Full Control	This permission permits reading, writing, changing, and deleting the file.	FullControl
Modify	This permission permits reading and writing of the file; it allows deletion of the file.	Modify
Read & Execute	This permission permits viewing and accessing the file's contents as well as executing the file.	ReadAnd-Execute
Write	This permission permits writing to a file. Giving a user permission to write to a file but not to delete it doesn't prevent the user from deleting the file's contents.	Write
Read	This permission permits viewing or accessing the file's contents. Read is the only permission needed to run scripts. Read access is required to access a shortcut and its target.	Read

When you are configuring basic permissions for users and groups, you can specify the access control type as either Allowed or Denied. If a user or group should be granted an access permission, you allow the permission. If a user or group should be denied an access permission, you deny the permission.

You configure basic permissions for resources using access rules. Access rules contain collections of arrays that define

- The user or group to which the rule applies.
- The access permission that applies.
- The allow or deny status.

This means regardless of whether you are adding or modifying rules, the basic syntax for an individual access rule is

```
"UserOrGroupName", "ApplicablePermission", "ControlType"
```

where *UserOrGroupName* is the name of the user or group to which the access rule applies, *ApplicablePermission* is the basic permission you are applying, and *Control-Type* specifies the allow or deny status. User and group names are specified in COMPUTER\Name or DOMAIN\Name format. In the following example, you grant full control to BackupOpUser:

```
"BackupOpUser", "FullControl", "Allow"
```

When you are working with folders, you can use the basic syntax to configure permissions for folders. You also can use an expanded syntax to configure permissions for a folder and its contents. The expanded syntax for an access rule is

```
"UserOrGroupName", "ApplicablePermission", "InheritanceFlag",
"PropagationFlag","ControlType"
```

where UserOrGroupName is the name of the user or group to which the access rule applies, ApplicablePermission is the basic permission you are applying, Inheritance-Flag controls inheritance, PropagationFlag controls propagation of inherited rules, and ControlType specifies the type of access control. In the following example, you grant full control to DeploymentTesters and apply inheritance to the folder and all its subfolders:

```
"BackupOpUser", "FullControl", "ContainerInherit", "None", "Allow"
```

With the inheritance flag, you can specify one of the following flag values:

- **None** The access rule is not inherited by child objects.
- **ContainerInherit** The access rule is inherited by subfolders (child container objects).
- **ObjectInherit** The access rule is inherited by files (child objects).
- **ContainerInherit, ObjectInherit** The access rule is inherited by files and subfolders (child objects and child container objects).

With the propagation flag, you can specify the following flag values:

- **None** The access rule is propagated without modification.
- **InheritOnly** The access rule is propogated to immediate child and child container objects.
- **NoPropagateInherit** The access rule applies to child objects and to child container objects but not to child objects of child container objects.
- **NoPropagateInherit, InheritOnly** The access rule applies to child container objects.

You add access rules to a resource using either the SetAccessRule() method or the AddAccessRule() method of the access control object. You remove access rules from a resource using the RemoveAccessRule() method of the access control object. As discussed previously, access rules are defined as having the System.Security.Access-Control.FileSystemAccessRule type.

The easiest way to add and remove access rules is to

1. Get an access control object. This object can be the one that applies to the resource you want to work with or one that applies to a resource that has the closest access control permissions to those you want to use.
2. Create one or more instances of the System.Security.AccessControl.File-SystemAccessRule type, and store the desired permissions in these object instances.
3. Call AddAccessRule() or RemoveAccessRule() to add or remove access rules as necessary. These methods operate on the access control object you retrieved in the first step.

4. To apply the changes you've made to an actual resource, you must apply the access control object to a specified resource.

Consider the following example:

```
$acl = get-acl c:\logs
$perm = "cpandl\dev","fullcontrol","allow"
$r = new-object system.security.accesscontrol.filesystemaccessrule $perm
$acl.addaccessrule($r)
$acl | set-acl c:\logs
```

Here, you get the access control object on C:\Logs. You store the values for an access rule in a variable called $perm and then create a new instance of the FileSystem-AccessRule type for this access rule. The Dev group in the Cpandl domain must exist to create the access rule. To add the permission to the access control object you retrieved previously, you call its AddAccessRule() method. Although you could have created additional permissions and added or removed these, you didn't in this example. Finally, you applied the access control object to a specific resource using Set-Acl.

You can easily extend the previous examples to apply to multiple directories and files as shown in the following example:

```
$acl = get-acl c:\logs
$perm = "room5\test","fullcontrol","allow"
$r = new-object system.security.accesscontrol.filesystemaccessrule $perm
$acl.addaccessrule($r)

$resc = gci c:\logs -recurse -force
foreach($f in $resc) {

   write-host $f.fullname
   $acl | set-acl $f.FullName
}
```

```
C:\logs\backup
C:\logs\backup2
C:\logs\logs
C:\logs\data.ps1
C:\logs\log1.txt
C:\logs\log2.txt
C:\logs\log3.txt
C:\logs\log4.txt
C:\logs\backup\backup
C:\logs\backup\backup\b2
```

Here, you apply an access control list with a modified permission set to every subdirectory of C:\Logs and every file in C:\Logs and its subdirectories. The Test group on the local computer (named Room5) must exist to create the access rule. In the output, you list the names of the directories and files you've modified. This helps you keep track of the changes.

Setting Special Permissions

The special permissions you can assign to directories and files are shown in Table 10-3. Because special permissions are combined to make the basic permissions, they are also referred to as *atomic permissions*. As with basic permissions, note the rule flag for each permission because this is the value you must reference when creating an access rule. When an item has two rule flags, you need to reference only one or the other to set the related special permission.

TABLE 10-3 Special Permissions

PERMISSION	DESCRIPTION	RULE FLAG
Traverse Folder/ Execute File	Traverse Folder lets you directly access a folder even if you don't have explicit access to read the data it contains. Execute File lets you run an executable file.	Traverse, ExecuteFile
List Folder/Read Data	List Folder lets you view file and folder names. Read Data lets you view the contents of a file.	ListDirectory, ReadData
Read Attributes	Lets you read the basic attributes of a file or folder. These attributes include Read-Only, Hidden, System, and Archive.	ReadAttributes
Read Extended Attributes	Lets you view the extended attributes (named data streams) associated with a file. These include Summary fields, such as Title, Subject, and Author, as well as other types of data.	ReadExtendedAttributes
Create Files/Write Data	Create Files lets you put new files in a folder. Write Data allows you to overwrite existing data in a file (but not add new data to an existing file because this is covered by Append Data).	CreateFiles, WriteData

TABLE 10-3 Special Permissions

PERMISSION	DESCRIPTION	RULE FLAG
Create Folders/ Append Data	Create Folders lets you create subfolders within folders. Append Data allows you to add data to the end of an existing file (but not to overwrite existing data because this is covered by Write Data).	CreateFolders, AppendData
Write Attributes	Lets you change the basic attributes of a file or folder. These attributes include Read-Only, Hidden, System, and Archive.	WriteAttributes
Write Extended Attributes	Lets you change the extended attributes (named data streams) associated with a file. These include Summary fields, such as Title, Subject, and Author, as well as other types of data.	WriteExtendedAttributes
Delete Subfolders and Files	Lets you delete the contents of a folder. If you have this permission, you can delete the subfolders and files in a folder even if you don't specifically have Delete permission on the subfolder or file.	DeleteSubdirectoriesAnd-Files
Delete	Lets you delete a file or folder. If a folder isn't empty and you don't have Delete permission for one of its files or subfolders, you won't be able to delete it. You can do this only if you have the Delete Subfolders and Files permission.	Delete
Read Permissions	Lets you read all basic and special permissions assigned to a file or folder.	ReadPermissions
Change Permissions	Lets you change basic and special permissions assigned to a file or folder.	ChangePermissions

TABLE 10-3 Special Permissions

PERMISSION	DESCRIPTION	RULE FLAG
Take Ownership	Lets you take ownership of a file or folder. By default, administrators can always take ownership of a file or folder and can also grant this permission to others.	TakeOwnership

Tables 10-4 and 10-5 show how special permissions are combined to make the basic permissions for files and folders.

TABLE 10-4 Special Permissions for Folders

SPECIAL PERMISSIONS	FULL CONTROL	MODIFY	READ & EXECUTE	LIST FOLDER CONTENTS	READ	WRITE
Traverse Folder/Execute File	X	X	X	X		
List Folder/Read Data	X	X	X	X	X	
Read Attributes	X	X	X	X	X	
Read Extended Attributes	X	X	X	X	X	
Create Files/Write Data	X	X				X
Create Folders/Append Data	X	X				X
Write Attributes	X	X				X
Write Extended Attributes	X	X				X
Delete Subfolders and Files	X					
Delete	X	X				
Read Permissions	X	X	X	X	X	X
Change Permissions	X					
Take Ownership	X					

TABLE 10-5 Special Permissions for Files

SPECIAL PERMISSIONS	FULL CONTROL	MODIFY	READ & EXECUTE	READ	WRITE
Traverse Folder/Execute File	X	X	X		
List Folder/Read Data	X	X	X	X	
Read Attributes	X	X	X	X	
Read Extended Attributes	X	X	X	X	
Create Files/Write Data	X	X			X
Create Folders/Append Data	X	X			X
Write Attributes	X	X			X
Write Extended Attributes	X	X			X
Delete Subfolders and Files	X				
Delete	X	X			
Read Permissions	X	X	X	X	X
Change Permissions	X				
Take Ownership	X				

You configure special permissions for directories and files in the same way as basic permissions. You add access rules to a resource using either the SetAccessRule() method or the AddAccessRule() method of the access control object. You remove access rules from a resource using the RemoveAccessRule() method of the access control object.

Consider the following example:

```
$acl = get-acl c:\logs
$p1 = "cpandl\dev","executefile","allow"
$r1 = new-object system.security.accesscontrol.filesystemaccessrule $p1
$acl.addaccessrule($r1)

$p2 = "cpandl\dev","listdirectory","allow"
$r2 = new-object system.security.accesscontrol.filesystemaccessrule $p2
$acl.addaccessrule($r2)

$acl | set-acl c:\logs
```

Here, you get the access control object on C:\Logs. After you define an access rule and store the related values in $p1, you create a new instance of the FileSystem-AccessRule type and add the permission to the access control object by calling the

AddAccessRule() method. After you define a second access rule and store the related values in $p2, you create a new instance of the FileSystemAccessRule type and add the permission to the access control object by calling the AddAccessRule() method. Finally, you apply the access control object to a specific resource using Set-Acl. The Dev group in the Cpandl domain must exist to create the access rules.

Taking Ownership

In Windows, the file or directory owner isn't necessarily the file or directory's creator. Instead, the file or directory owner is the person who has direct control over the file or directory. File or directory owners can grant access permissions and give other users permission to take ownership of a file or directory.

The way ownership is assigned initially depends on where the file or directory is being created. By default, the user who created the file or directory is listed as the current owner. Ownership can be taken or transferred in several ways. Any administrator can take ownership. Any user or group with the Take Ownership permission can take ownership. Any user who has the Restore Files And Directories right, such as a member of the Backup Operators group, can take ownership as well. Any current owner can transfer ownership to another user as well.

You can take ownership using a file or directory using the SetOwner() method of the access control object. The easiest way to take ownership is to

1. Get an access control object for the resource you want to work with.
2. Get the IdentityReference for the user or group that will take ownership. This user or group must already have permission on the resource (as discussed previously).
3. Call SetOwner to specify that you want the user or group to be the owner.
4. Apply the changes you've made to the resource.

Consider the following example:

```
$acl = get-acl c:\logs
$found = $false
foreach($rule in $acl.access) {
 if ($rule.identityreference -like "*administrators*") {
   $global:ref = $rule.identityreference; $found = $true; break}
}

if ($found) {
 $acl.setowner($ref)
 $acl | set-acl c:\logs
}
```

Here, you get the access control object on C:\Logs. You then examine each access rule on this object, looking for the one that applies to the group you want to work with. If you find a match, you set $ref to the IdentityReference for this group, change

$found to $true, and then break out of the ForEach loop. After you break out of the loop, you check to see if $found is True. If it is, you set the ownership permission on the access control object you retrieved previously and then apply the access control object to C:\Logs using Set-Acl.

Configuring File and Directory Auditing

You can use auditing to track what's happening on your computers. Auditing collects information related to resource usage, such as a file or directory audit. Any time an action occurs that you've configured for auditing, the action is written to the system's security log, where it's stored for your review. The security log is accessible from Event Viewer. For most auditing changes, you need to be logged on using an account that's a member of the Administrators group, or you need to be granted the Manage Auditing And Security Log right in Group Policy.

Auditing policies are essential to ensure the security and integrity of your systems. Just about every computer system on the network should be configured with some type of auditing. You can set auditing policies for directories and files using auditing rules.

Audit rules contain collections of arrays that define

- The user or group to which the rule applies.
- The permission usage that is audited.
- The type of auditing.

This means regardless of whether you are adding or modifying rules, the basic syntax for an individual audit rule is

```
"UserOrGroupName", "PermissionAudited", "AuditType"
```

where *UserOrGroupName* is the name of the user or group to which the audit rule applies, *PermissionAudited* is the basic or special permission you are tracking, and *AuditType* specifies the type of auditing. Use Success to track successful use of a specified permission. Use Failure to track failed use of a specified permission. Use None to turn off auditing of the specified permission. Use Both to track both failure and success.

As with security permissions, user and group names are specified in COMPUTER\Name or DOMAIN\Name format. In the following example, you track users in the Cpandl domain who are trying to access the resource but fail to do so because they don't have sufficient access permissions:

```
"CPANDL\USERS", "ReadData", "Failure"
```

When you are working with folders, you can use the basic syntax to configure auditing for folders. You also can use an expanded syntax to configure auditing for a folder and its contents. The expanded syntax for an access rule is

```
"UserOrGroupName", "PermissionAudited", "InheritanceFlag",
"PropagationFlag","AuditType"
```

where UserOrGroupName is the name of the user or group to which the access rule applies, PermissionAudited is the basic or special permission you are tracking, InheritanceFlag controls inheritance, PropagationFlag controls propagation of inherited rules, and AuditType specifies the type of auditing. In the following example, you apply an auditing rule to a resource as well as the files and subfolders it contains:

```
"CPANDL\USERS", "ReadData", "ContainerInherit", "None", "Failure"
```

With the inheritance flag, you can specify one of the following flag values:

- **None** The access rule is not inherited by child objects.
- **ContainerInherit** The access rule is inherited by subfolders (child container objects).
- **ObjectInherit** The access rule is inherited by files (child objects).
- **ContainerInherit, ObjectInherit** The access rule is inherited by files and subfolders (child objects and child container objects).

With the propagation flag, you can specify the following flag values:

- **None** The access rule is propagated without modification.
- **InheritOnly** The access rule is propogated to immediate child and child container objects.
- **NoPropagateInherit** The access rule applies to child objects and to child container objects but not to child objects of child container objects.
- **NoPropagateInherit, InheritOnly** The access rule applies to child container objects.

You add audit rules to a resource using either the SetAuditRule() method or the AddAuditRule() method of the access control object. You remove audit rules from a resource using the RemoveAuditRule() method of the access control object. Audit rules are defined as having the System.Security.AuditControl.FileSystemAuditRule type.

The easiest way to add and remove audit rules is to do the following:

1. Get an access control object. This object can be the one that applies to the resource you want to work with or one that applies to a resource that has the closest audit control permissions to those you want to use.
2. Create one or more instances of the System.Security.AuditControl.FileSystem-AuditRule type, and store the desired auditing settings in these object instances.
3. Call AddAuditRule() or RemoveAuditRule() to add or remove audit rules as necessary. These methods operate on the access control object you retrieved in the first step.
4. Apply the changes you've made to an actual resource.

Consider the following example:

```
$acl = get-acl d:\data
$audit = "cpandl\users","readdata","failure"
$r = new-object system.security.accesscontrol.filesystemauditrule $audit
$acl.addauditrule($r)
$acl | set-acl d:\data
```

Here, you get the access control object on D:\Data. You store the values for an audit rule in a variable called $audit, and then you create a new instance of the FileSystemAuditRule type with this auditing rule. The Users group in the Cpandl domain must exist to create the auditing rule. To add the auditing setting to the access control object you retrieved previously, you call its AddAuditRule() method. Although you could have created additional auditing rules and added or removed these, you didn't in this example. Finally, you apply the access control object to a specific resource using Set-Acl.

You can easily extend the previous examples to apply to multiple directories and files as shown in the following example:

```
$acl = get-acl d:\data
$audit = "cpandl\users","readdata","failure"
$r = new-object system.security.accesscontrol.filesystemauditrule $audit
$acl.addauditrule($r)

$resc = gci d:\data -recurse -force
foreach($f in $resc) {

  write-host $f.fullname
  $acl | set-acl $f.FullName
}
```

```
D:\data\backup
D:\data\backup\historydat.txt
D:\data\logs\datlog.log
D:\data\data.ps1
D:\data\transcript1.txt
D:\data\transcript2.txt
D:\data\backup\backup
```

Here, you apply an auditing rule to every subdirectory of D:\Data and every file in D:\Data and its subdirectories. In the output, you list the names of the directories and files you've modified. This helps you keep track of the changes. The Users group in the Cpandl domain must exist to create the auditing rule.

CHAPTER 11

Managing Shares, Printers, and TCP/IP Networking

As an administrator, you enable networked computers to communicate and share resources using the basic networking features built into Windows. You use TCP/IP to enable network communications. You use network shares and printers to share resources across the enterprise.

Managing Network Shares

When you share a directory or a drive, you make all its files and subdirectories available to a specified set of users. You can enable network shares only on disks formatted with NTFS. When you do, two sets of permissions determine who has access to shared files: NTFS permissions and share permissions. Together, these permissions let you control who has access to shared files and the level of access assigned. You do not need to move the files you are sharing.

With network shares, share permissions are used only when a user attempts to access a file or directory from a different computer on the network, whereas access permissions are always used, whether the user is logged on to the console or using a remote system to access the file or directory over the network. When data is accessed remotely, first the share permissions are applied, and then the access permissions are applied. When data is accessed locally, only access permissions apply.

TIP A computer's sharing configuration determines whether directories and drives can be shared. You can access Network And Sharing Center to configure these settings by clicking Start and then clicking Network. On the Explorer toolbar, click Network And Sharing Center.

Getting Information About Shares

Shared resources are managed differently from drives or other types of file system resources. To work with shares in Windows PowerShell, you use the Win32_Share class. By typing **Get-Wmiobject -Class Win32_Share**, you can view the shares that are available as shown in this example and sample output:

```
get-wmiobject -class win32_share
```

```
Name            Path                                  Description
----            ----                                  -----------
ADMIN$          C:\Windows                            Remote Admin
C$              C:\                                   Default share
D$              D:\                                   Default share
E$              E:\                                   Default share
HP3505-PCL6     HP CLJ CP3505 PCL6,LocalsplOnly       HP CLJ CP3505
IPC$            Remote IPC
print$          C:\Windows\system32\spool\drivers     Printer Driver
W$              W:\                                   Default share
```

Shares have a number of properties that you can view and manage. To view the properties of a particular share, limit the results using a Windows Management Instrumentation (WMI) query or a Where-Object match expression. In the following example and sample output, you examine the properties of the C$ share:

```
get-wmiobject -class win32_share | where-object {$_.Name -eq "C$"} |
format-list *
```

```
Status           : OK
Type             : 2147483648
Name             : C$
__GENUS          : 2
__CLASS          : Win32_Share
__SUPERCLASS     : CIM_LogicalElement
__DYNASTY        : CIM_ManagedSystemElement
__RELPATH        : Win32_Share.Name="C$"
__PROPERTY_COUNT : 10
__DERIVATION     : {CIM_LogicalElement, CIM_ManagedSystemElement}
__SERVER         : TECHPC89
__NAMESPACE      : root\cimv2
__PATH           : \\TECHPC89\root\cimv2:Win32_Share.Name="C$"
AccessMask       :
```

```
AllowMaximum     : True
Caption          : Default share
Description      : Default share
InstallDate      :
MaximumAllowed   :
Path             : C:\
Scope            : System.Management.ManagementScope
Options          : System.Management.ObjectGetOptions
ClassPath        : \\TECHPC89\root\cimv2:Win32_Share
Properties       : {AccessMask, AllowMaximum, Caption, Description...}
SystemProperties : {__GENUS, __CLASS, __SUPERCLASS, __DYNASTY...}
Qualifiers       : {dynamic, Locale, provider, UUID}
Site             :
Container        :
```

NOTE To query multiple computers, use the –ComputerName parameter of the Get-Wmiobject cmdlet. Here is an example:

```
get-wmiobject -class win32_share -computername Server43,
Server27, Server82
```

The Type property specifies the type of share. Values you'll see include the following:

- **0** Disk Share
- **1** Print Share
- **2** Device Share
- **3** IPC Share
- **2147483648** Administrative Disk Share
- **2147483649** Administrative Print Share
- **2147483650** Administrative Device Share
- **2147483651** Administrative IPC Share

Changing Share Settings

At an elevated administrator PowerShell prompt, you can modify several settings on a share, including the maximum number of allowed users and the description. The MaxAllow property controls the maximum number of simultaneous connections to the share. The Description property describes the purpose of the share.

You set the MaxAllow and Description properties using the SetShareInfo() method of the Win32_Share object. The basic syntax is

```
$shareObject.setShareInfo(MaxAllow,Description)
```

where *$shareObject* is a reference to a Win32_Share object, *MaxAllow* is the desired maximum number of users, and *Description* is the desired description. Set the maximum number of users with a value between 1 and 2,147,483,647. Use a value of 0 to allow an unlimited number of users.

You also can set the Name, Path Caption, Description, and MaximumAllowed values using the related properties.

You can reference a Win32_Share object by storing the object in a variable. A quick way to specify a WMI query is to use the –Filter parameter. This parameter specifies a Where clause to use as a filter. In the following example, you get a reference to the Logs share and store the related object in the $share variable:

```
$share = get-wmiobject -class win32_share -filter "name='logs'"
```

Note the syntax for the Where clause in the string passed to the –Filter parameter. The share must exist or the value won't be set. Because you use double quotes to enclose the string, you must use single quotes to match a specific property value. After you have a reference to the Win32_Share object, you can call the SetShareInfo() method to set the desired values. An example and sample output follow:

```
$share = get-wmiobject -class win32_share -filter "name='logs'"
$share.setShareInfo(255,"Logging Share")
```

```
__GENUS          : 2
__CLASS          : __PARAMETERS
__SUPERCLASS     :
__DYNASTY        : __PARAMETERS
__RELPATH        :
__PROPERTY_COUNT : 1
__DERIVATION     : {}
__SERVER         :
__NAMESPACE      :
__PATH           :
ReturnValue      : 2
```

The return value in the output is what you want to focus on. A return value of 0 indicates success. Any other return value indicates an error. Here, the return value of 2 indicates an Access Denied error, which can occur if you forget to use an administrator prompt or don't have the correct privileges to manage the share.

You can store the return value in a variable and then process the results. Here's an example with sample output:

```
$share = get-wmiobject -class win32_share -filter "name='logs'"
$results = $share.setShareInfo(255,"Logging Share")
write-host $results.returnvalue
```

```
0
```

Here, you obtain a reference to the Logs share. You then set the maximum number of users to 255 and the description to Logging Share. To verify the change, you store the results in a variable and display the return value.

Creating Shares

At an elevated administrator PowerShell prompt, you can create shares using a static Create() method of the Win32_Share class. The basic syntax is

```
$shareObject.Create(FolderPath, ShareName, ShareType, MaxAllow,Description)
```

where *$shareObject* is a reference to a Win32_Share object, *FolderPath* is the path to the share, *ShareName* is the name of the share, *ShareType* is a valid type indicator, *MaxAllow* is the desired maximum number of users, and *Description* is the desired description. As long as you have the appropriate permissions, PowerShell should be able to create the share. A common error you might see occurs when a like-named share already exists.

The easiest way to create a class instance for Win32_Share is to use the [wmiclass] alias as shown in this example:

```
$share = [wmiclass]"Win32_Share"
```

After you've created a class instance, you can create the share.

```
$share.Create("c:\data", "Data", 0, 255,"Data Share")
```

The format and values of the returned results are the same as those for the SetShareInfo() method. A return value of 0 indicates success. Any other return value indicates an error. A complete example and sample output follow:

```
$share = [wmiclass]"Win32_Share"
$results = $share.Create("c:\data", "Data", 0, 0,"Data Share")
write-host $results.returnvalue
```

```
0
```

Here, you obtain a reference to the Win32_Share class. You then create a Data share mapped to C:\Data. You specify the share type as a disk share and allow an unlimited number of users to connect to the share. To verify the change, you store the results in a variable and display the return value.

> ***NOTE*** **After you create a share, you'll want to set the share permissions. By default, the share is created so that the implicit group Everyone has Read access and no other groups or users have access.**

Deleting Shares

At an elevated administrator PowerShell prompt, you can delete a share using the Delete() method of a Win32_Share object. The basic syntax is

```
$shareObject.delete()
```

where *$shareObject* is a reference to a Win32_Share object that you want to delete. As with the other methods, the Delete() method returns results that indicate success or failure. The format and values are the same as those discussed previously.

You can delete the Data share created previously as shown in the following example and sample output:

```
$share = get-wmiobject -class win32_share -filter "name='data'"
$results = $share.delete()


write-host $results.returnvalue
```

```
0
```

Managing Printers

As an administrator, you need to do two main things to allow users throughout a network to access print devices connected to a Windows computer: you need to set up a print server, and you need to use the print server to share print devices on the network. A print server provides a central location for sharing printers on a network. When many users require access to the same printers, you should configure print servers in the domain. With Windows Server 2008 and later, you must specifically configure a server to be a print server.

Two types of print devices are used on a network: *local print devices* and *network print devices*. A local print device is a print device that's physically attached to the user's computer and employed only by the user who is logged on to that computer. A network print device is a print device that's set up for remote access over the network. This can be a print device attached directly to a print server or a print device attached directly to the network through a network interface card (NIC).

A print server is a workstation or server configured to share one or more printers. These printers can be physically attached to the computer or the network. A limit on the number of allowed connections is the disadvantage to using a workstation operating system over a server operating system. With Windows Server 2008 or later, on the other hand, you don't have to worry about operating system–enforced connection limits.

The print server's primary job is to share the print device out to the network and to handle print spooling. The main advantages of print servers are that the printer will have a centrally managed print queue and you don't have to install printer drivers on client systems.

You don't have to use a print server, however. You can connect users directly to a network-attached printer. When you do this, the network printer is handled much like a local printer attached directly to the user's computer. The key differences are that multiple users can connect to the printer and that each user has a different print queue. Each print queue is managed separately, which can make administration and problem resolution difficult.

Getting Information About Printers

In PowerShell, you use the Win32_Printer class to work with printers. By typing **Get-Wmiobject -Class Win32_Printer**, you can view the printers that are available as shown in this example and sample output:

```
get-wmiobject -class win32_printer
```

```
Location      : 18th Floor
Name          : HP CLJ CP3505 PCL6
PrinterState  : 131072
PrinterStatus : 1
ShareName     : HP3505-PCL6
SystemName    : PrinterServer08

Location      : 17th Floor
Name          : magicolor 2300 DL
PrinterState  : 0
PrinterStatus : 3
ShareName     : Color2300
SystemName    : PrintServer21
```

NOTE To query multiple computers, use the –ComputerName parameter of the Get-WmiObject cmdlet. Here is an example:

```
get-wmiobject -class win32_printer -computername EngPC45,
TechPC15, EngPC82
```

Printers have a number of properties that you can view and manage. To view the properties of a particular printer, limit the results using a WMI query or a Where-Object match expression. In the following example and partial output, you examine the properties of the printer shared as HP3505-PCL6:

```
get-wmiobject -class win32_printer -filter "ShareName='HP3505-PCL6'" |
format-list *
```

```
Status                      : OK
Name                        : HP CLJ CP3505 PCL6
__GENUS                     : 2
__CLASS                     : Win32_Printer
__SUPERCLASS                : CIM_Printer
__DYNASTY                   : CIM_ManagedSystemElement
__RELPATH                   : Win32_Printer.DeviceID="HP CLJ CP3505 PCL6"
__PROPERTY_COUNT            : 86
__DERIVATION                : {CIM_Printer, CIM_LogicalDevice, CIM_
LogicalElement, CIM_ManagedSystemElement}
__SERVER                    : TECHPC87
__NAMESPACE                 : root\cimv2
__PATH                      : \\TECHPC87\root\cimv2:Win32_Printer.
DeviceID="HP CLJ CP3505 PCL6"
Attributes                  : 588
Availability                :
AvailableJobSheets          :
AveragePagesPerMinute       : 0
Capabilities                : {4, 2, 3, 5}
CapabilityDescriptions      : {Copies, Color, Duplex, Collate}
Caption                     : HP CLJ CP3505 PCL6
Description                 :
DetectedErrorState          : 5
DeviceID                    : HP CLJ CP3505 PCL6
Direct                      : False
DoCompleteFirst             : True
DriverName                  : HP Color LaserJet CP3505 PCL 6
```

To check the TCP/IP configuration of a network printer, you use the Win32_TcpIpPrinterPort class. Type **Get-Wmiobject -Class Win32_TcpIpPrinterPort**, and you can view all the TCP/IP printer ports that are configured, as shown in this example and sample output:

```
get-wmiobject -class win32_tcpipprinterport
```

```
__GENUS                 : 2
__CLASS                 : Win32_TCPIPPrinterPort
__SUPERCLASS            : CIM_ServiceAccessPoint
__DYNASTY               : CIM_ManagedSystemElement
__RELPATH               : Win32_TCPIPPrinterPort.Name="192.168.0.90"
__PROPERTY_COUNT        : 17
__DERIVATION            : {CIM_ServiceAccessPoint, CIM_LogicalElement,
CIM_ManagedSystemElement}
__SERVER                : TECHPC87
```

```
__NAMESPACE              : root\cimv2
__PATH                   : \\TECHPC87\root\cimv2:Win32_TCPIPPrinterPort.
Name="192.168.0.90"
ByteCount                :
Caption                  :
CreationClassName        : Win32_TCPIPPrinterPort
Description              :
HostAddress              : 192.168.0.90
InstallDate              :
Name                     : 192.168.0.90
PortNumber               : 9100
Protocol                 : 1
Queue                    :
SNMPCommunity            :
SNMPDevIndex             :
SNMPEnabled              : False
Status                   :
SystemCreationClassName  : Win32_ComputerSystem
SystemName               :
Type                     :
```

NOTE To query multiple computers, use the –ComputerName parameter of the Get-WmiObject cmdlet. Here is an example:

```
get-wmiobject -class win32_tcpipprinterport -computername
EngPC45, TechPC15, EngPC82
```

```
D
```

Checking Printer Drivers

Many standard printer drivers are installed by default on computers running the Windows operating system. Windows stores printer drivers in the %SystemRoot%\Inf folder. In this folder, printer drivers are stored in files beginning with Prn, and you'll find driver definition files with the .pnf extension as well as driver files with the .inf extension. Knowing this, you can write a command to examine the print drivers that are available on a computer. An example and sample output follow:

```
get-childitem ((get-item env:systemroot).value + "\inf") -exclude *.pnf |
where-object {$_.name -match "prn"} | format-list Fullname
```

```
D FullName : C:\Windows\inf\prnao001.inf
FullName : C:\Windows\inf\prnbr001.inf
FullName : C:\Windows\inf\prnca001.inf
```

Here, you use the Get-ChildItem cmdlet to get files in the %SystemRoot%\Inf folder. You search for files that begin with Prn while excluding files that end with .pnf. You use Get-Item Env:Systemroot to retrieve the value of the %SystemRoot% environment variable, and then you add its string value to "\Inf," resulting in a full file path, such as C:\Windows\Inf.

Managing Printer Connections

As I write this, PowerShell 2.0 is not ideally suited for the tasks of creating and managing printer connections—even if you go through WMI to do it. My preferred workaround is to access Windows Script Host (WSH) via the Component Object Model (COM). To do this, you can create an instance of the WScript.Network object via COM and then use its related methods to work with printers. Note that if you are configuring printers for a particular user, you should log on as the user or modify permissions later as appropriate for the user.

The default printer is the primary printer for a user. This printer is used whenever a user prints a document and doesn't select a specific destination printer. You can set a default printer using the SetDefaultPrinter() method of the WScript.Network object. This method automatically updates the user's profile to use the default printer.

When you set the default printer, you must specify either the printer's name or the share path, such as **"HP CLJ CP3505 PCL6"** or **"\\PrintServer72\ColorPrinter03"**. Here is an example:

```
$wn = New-Object -ComObject WScript.Network
$wn.SetDefaultPrinter("\\PrintServer72\ColorPrinter03")
```

You can manage connections to network printers in much the same way as you manage connections to network drives. You map printer connections using the AddWindowsPrinterConnection() method of the WScript.Network object. You remove printer connections using the RemovePrinterConnection() method of the WScript.Network object.

The AddWindowsPrinterConnection() method expects to be passed the path to the network printer, such as

```
$wn = New-Object -ComObject WScript.Network
$wn.AddWindowsPrinterConnection("\\PrintServer72\ColorPrinter03")
```

After you call AddWindowsPrinterConnection(), WSH attempts to connect to the print server and validate that the printer is available. If WSH can connect to the print server and the printer is valid, Windows creates the printer connection and automatically transfers the appropriate print drivers from the print server to the local computer.

When you are finished working with a network printer, you might want to remove the connection. To do this, you can use the RemovePrinterConnection() method. Specify the local name of the printer you want to disconnect, like this:

```
$wn = New-Object -ComObject WScript.Network
$wn.RemovePrinterConnection("HP CLJ CP3505 PCL6")
```

Managing TCP/IP Networking

Windows PowerShell provides a dynamic environment for working with TCP/IP configurations. If you want to install networking on a computer, you must install TCP/IP networking and a network adapter. Windows uses TCP/IP as the default wide area network (WAN) protocol.

Normally, networking is installed during Windows setup. You can also install TCP/IP networking through local area connection properties. Windows computers support IP version 4 (IPv4) addressing and IP version 6 (IPv6) addressing.

Getting Information About Network Adapters

A local area connection is created automatically if a computer has a network adapter and is connected to a network. If a computer has multiple network adapters and is connected to a network, you'll have one local area connection for each adapter. If no network connection is available, you should connect the computer to the network or create a different type of connection.

Computers use IP addresses to communicate over TCP/IP. Windows provides the following ways to configure IP addressing:

- **Manually** IP addresses that are assigned manually are called *static IP addresses*. Static IP addresses are fixed and don't change unless you change them. You usually assign static IP addresses to Windows servers, and when you do this, you need to configure additional information to help the server navigate the network.
- **Dynamically** A Dynamic Host Configuration Protocol (DHCP) server (if one is installed on the network) assigns dynamic IP addresses at startup, and the addresses might change over time. Dynamic IP addressing is the default configuration.
- **Alternatively (IPv4 only)** When a computer is configured to use DHCPv4 and no DHCPv4 server is available, Windows Server 2008 assigns an alternate private IP address automatically. By default, the alternate IPv4 address is in the range from 169.254.0.1 to 169.254.255.254, with a subnet mask of 255.255.0.0. You can also specify a user-configured alternate IPv4 address, which is particularly useful for laptop users.

You can use Win32_NetworkAdapter and Win32_NetworkAdapterConfiguration objects to examine the configuration of each network adapter on a computer. While Win32_NetworkAdapter stores basic information for each network adapter, Win32_NetworkAdapterConfiguration stores the detailed configuration for each adapter. Knowing this, you might be tempted to use only Win32_NetworkAdapterConfiguration.

However, most computers have a large number of pseudoadapters. As a result, if you don't know the specific adapter you want to examine, you're going to get lots of extraneous information. Therefore, the technique you want to use is this:

1. Use Win32_NetworkAdapter to get the index value of a specific adapter. On most computers, the primary network adapter has a network connection ID of Local Area Connection.
2. Use Win32_NetworkAdapterConfiguration with a Where clause or filter that gets the information for a specific adapter. The configuration details provide complete information on the TCP/IP configuration of the adapter as well as the media access control (MAC) address of the adapter, which you need in order to make reservations on a DHCP server.

Knowing this, you can get the configuration for a computer's primary adapter as shown in the following example and sample output:

```
$na = get-wmiobject Win32_NetworkAdapter -filter `
"NetConnectionID='Local Area Connection'"

$index = $na.index
get-wmiobject Win32_NetworkAdapterConfiguration -filter "Index=$index"
```

```
__PATH : \\ROOM5\root\cimv2:Win32_NetworkAdapterConfiguration.Index=4
DHCPLeaseExpires             : 20090129095440.000000-480
Index                        : 4
Description                  : Intel(R) PRO/1000 PM Network Connection
DHCPEnabled                  : True
DHCPLeaseObtained            : 20090128095440.000000-480
DHCPServer                   : 192.168.1.1
DNSDomain                    :
DNSDomainSuffixSearchOrder   :
DNSEnabledForWINSResolution  : False
DNSHostName                  : TechPC242
DNSServerSearchOrder         : {68.87.78.177, 68.77.75.78, 68.77.79.176}
DomainDNSRegistrationEnabled : False
FullDNSRegistrationEnabled   : True
IPAddress                    : {192.168.1.104, fe80::7330:2226:ee62:2312}
IPConnectionMetric           : 1
IPEnabled                    : True
IPFilterSecurityEnabled      : False
WINSEnableLMHostsLookup      : True
WINSHostLookupFile           :
```

```
WINSPrimaryServer             :
WINSScopeID                   :
WINSSecondaryServer           :
DatabasePath                  : %SystemRoot%\System32\drivers\etc
DeadGWDetectEnabled           :
DefaultIPGateway              : {192.168.1.1}
DefaultTOS                    :
DefaultTTL                    :
ForwardBufferMemory           :
GatewayCostMetric             : {0}
IGMPLevel                     :
InterfaceIndex                : 7
IPPortSecurityEnabled         :
IPSecPermitIPProtocols        : {}
IPSecPermitTCPPorts           : {}
IPSecPermitUDPPorts           : {}
IPSubnet                      : {255.255.255.0, 64}
MACAddress                    : 89:76:FF:D4:D6:35
MTU                           :
NumForwardPackets             :
TcpipNetbiosOptions           : 0
TcpMaxConnectRetransmissions :
TcpMaxDataRetransmissions     : 5
TcpNumConnections             :
TcpWindowSize                 :
Scope                         : System.Management.ManagementScope
```

From this information, you can determine the computer's

- IPv4 and IPv6 addresses.
- IPv4 subnet mask.
- Default IP gateway.
- MAC address.
- DNS domain.
- DNS domain suffix search order.
- DNS server search order.
- Domain DNS registration status.
- DHCP status.
- DHCP lease.
- DHCP server.

With Win32_NetworkAdapter, you also can use the value of the NetConnection-Status property to check for connected adapters because all connected adapters are in use and active. This ensures you check the configuration of all active adapt-ers on a computer. The value you are looking for is 2. Knowing this, you can get configuration details for each connected adapter using the technique shown in this example and sample output:

```
$na = get-wmiobject Win32_NetworkAdapter -filter "NetConnectionStatus=2"

$na | foreach {
   $index = $_.index
   get-wmiobject Win32_NetworkAdapterConfiguration -filter "Index=$index"
}
```

```
DHCPEnabled      : True
IPAddress        : {192.168.10.152}
DefaultIPGateway : {192.168.10.1}
DNSDomain        :
ServiceName      : elexpress
Description      : Intel(R) PRO/1000 PM Network Connection
Index            : 4
```

A complete list of values for the NetConnectionStatus and their meaning are as follows: 0 (disconnected), 1 (connecting), 2 (connected), 3 (disconnecting), 4 (hardware not present), 5 (hardware disabled), 6 (hardware malfunction), 7 (media disconnected), 8 (authenticating), 9 (authentication succeeded), and 10 (authentication failed).

In the following example, you check for and display the state of the local area connection:

```
$na = get-wmiobject Win32_NetworkAdapter -filter "NetConnectionID='Local
Area Connection'"
$status = $na.NetConnectionStatus
switch -regex ($status) {
 [0] { "Disconnected." }
 [1] { "Connecting." }
 [2] { "Connected. The connection is active." }
 [3] { "Disconnecting." }
 [4-6] { "Hardware is disabled, malfunctioning or not present. Check and
enable hardware."}
 [7] { "Media is disconnected; connect the network cable."}
 [8-9] { "Authenticating."}
 [10] { "Authentication failed."}
}
```

```
Connected. The connection is active.
```

Configuring Static IP Addressing

When you assign a static IP address, you need to tell the computer the IP address you want to use, the subnet mask for this IP address, and, if necessary, the default gateway to use for internetwork communications. An IP address is a numeric identifier for a computer. IP addressing schemes vary according to how your network is configured, but they're normally assigned based on a particular network segment.

IPv6 addresses and IPv4 addresses are very different. With IPv6, the first 64 bits represent the network ID, and the remaining 64 bits represent the network interface. With IPv4, a variable number of the initial bits represent the network ID, and the rest of the bits represent the host ID. For example, if you're working with IPv4 and a computer on the network segment 192.168.1.0 with a subnet mask of 255.255.255.0, the first three bits represent the network ID, and the address range you have available for computer hosts is from 192.168.1.1 to 192.168.1.254. In this range, the address 192.168.1.255 is reserved for network broadcasts.

If you're on a private network that is indirectly connected to the Internet, you should use private IPv4 addresses. Table 11-1 summarizes private network IPv4 addresses.

TABLE 11-1 Private IPv4 Network Addressing

PRIVATE NETWORK ID	SUBNET MASK	NETWORK ADDRESS RANGE
10.0.0.0	255.0.0.0	10.0.0.0–10.255.255.255
172.16.0.0	255.240.0.0	172.16.0.0–172.31.255.255
192.168.0.0	255.255.0.0	192.168.0.0–192.168.255.255

All other IPv4 network addresses are public and must be leased or purchased. If the network is connected directly to the Internet and you've obtained a range of IPv4 addresses from your Internet service provider, you can use the IPv4 addresses you've been assigned.

When you are working with an elevated administrator PowerShell prompt, you can use the methods Win32_NetworkAdapterConfiguration provides to change a computer's TCP/IP configuration. Computers that have directly assigned IP addresses are said to use static IP addressing. Win32_NetworkAdapterConfiguration provides methods and properties for working with static IP addressing. Useful properties include the following:

- **DNSDomain** Specifies the DNS suffix for the connection that overrides the default DNS names already configured for use. Normally the entry is blank.
- **DNSDomainSuffixSearchOrder** Specifies the DNS suffixes to use for the connection and their search order. DNS suffixes are used to resolve unqualified computer names. Normally, this entry includes the parent domain as the first entry, which means the DNS suffix for the parent domain is added to unqualified computer names.

- **DNSEnabledForWINSResolution** Specifies whether DNS can be used for resolving Windows Internet Naming Service (WINS) lookups. By default, this is normally set to False.
- **DNSServerSearchOrder** Specifies IP addresses of DNS servers in the order in which they should be used.
- **DomainDNSRegistrationEnabled** Specifies whether IP addresses for this connection are registered in DNS under the DNS suffix provided for the connection. By default, this is normally set to False.
- **FullDNSRegistrationEnabled** Specifies whether IP addresses for this connection are registered in DNS under the computer's fully qualified domain name. By default, this is normally set to True.

Useful methods include the following:

- **SetDNSDomain()** Sets the DNS domain suffix for the connection. This overrides the default DNS names already configured for use. This method accepts a string value that specifies the suffix to use.
- **SetDNSServerSearchOrder()** Sets the IP addresses of DNS servers in the order in which they should be used. This method accepts a string or array of strings that sets the IP addresses of the DNS servers to use.
- **SetDynamicDNSRegistration()** Enables automatic registration of IP addresses used for this connection. The IP addresses are registered in DNS under the computer's fully qualified domain name. This method accepts a Boolean value of $True or $False.
- **SetGateways()** Sets the IP addresses and metric of gateways to use. Accepts a string or array of strings containing gateway IP addresses as the first value. This method accepts an integer or array of integers specifying the metric as the second parameter.
- **SetWINSServer()** Sets the IP addresses of WINS servers in the order in which they should be used. This method accepts a string or array of strings that sets the IP addresses of the WINS servers to use.

If a computer uses dynamic or static IP addressing and you want to change the TCP/IP configuration, you can use the EnableStatic() method to enable static IP addressing and specify the IP addresses and subnet masks to use. The basic syntax is

```
$nacObject.EnableStatic(IPAddress,SubnetMask)
```

where *$nacObject* is a reference to a Win32_NetworkAdapterConfiguration object, *IPAddress* is the desired IP address entered as a string, and *SubnetMask* is the desired subnet mask entered as a string value, as shown in this example and sample output:

```
$na = get-wmiobject Win32_NetworkAdapter -filter `
"NetConnectionID='Local Area Connection'"
$index = $na.index
```

```
$nac = get-wmiobject Win32_NetworkAdapterConfiguration -filter `
"Index=$index"

$nac.EnableStatic("192.168.1.100","255.255.255.0")
```

```
__GENUS            : 2
__CLASS            : __PARAMETERS
__SUPERCLASS       :
__DYNASTY          : __PARAMETERS
__RELPATH          :
__PROPERTY_COUNT   : 1
__DERIVATION       : {}
__SERVER           :
__NAMESPACE        :
__PATH             :
ReturnValue        : 0
```

Here, you set an IP address of 192.168.1.100 and a subnet mask of 255.255.255.0. The return value in the output is what you want to focus on. A return value of 0 indicates success. Any other return value indicates an error. Typically, errors occur because you aren't using an elevated administrator PowerShell prompt or haven't accessed the correct network adapter.

If a computer uses default gateways that are not set by DHCP, you can use the SetGateways() method to specify the gateways to use by IP address and metric. When you assign multiple gateways, Windows uses the gateway metric to determine which gateway to use first. The basic syntax is

```
$nacObject.SetGateways(DefaultIPGateway,Metric)
```

where *$nacObject* is a reference to a Win32_NetworkAdapterConfiguration object, *DefaultIPGateway* is the desired gateway address entered as a string value or an array of strings, and *Metric* is the desired gateway metric entered as an integer value or an array of integer values. In the following example, you set a default gateway address of 192.168.1.1 and a metric of 1:

```
$nac.SetGateways("192.168.1.1",1)
```

As before, a return value of 0 indicates success. Any other return value indicates an error. This is true for all the examples in this section.

In the following example, you set three default gateways, each with a different metric:

```
$g = "192.168.1.1", "192.168.2.1", "192.168.3.1"
$m = 1,2,3
$nac.setgateways($g,$m)
```

If a computer uses DNS servers that are not set by DHCP, you can use the SetDNSServerSearchOrder() method to specify the DNS servers to use by IP address. The basic syntax is

```
$nacObject.SetDNSServerSearchOrder(DNSServerIPAddresses)
```

where *$nacObject* is a reference to a Win32_NetworkAdapterConfiguration object, and *DNSServerIPAddresses* are the IP addresses for the DNS servers to use entered as a string or an array of strings. In the following example, you specify the IP address of the primary and secondary DNS servers:

```
$dns = "10.10.10.52", "10.10.10.68"
$nac.SetDNSServerSearchOrder($dns)
```

Configuring Dynamic IP Addressing

Computers can have IP addresses that are dynamically assigned by DHCP servers. When an IP address is given to a client by a server, the client is said to have a lease on the IP address. The term *lease* is used because the assignment is not permanent. The DHCP server sets the duration of the lease when the lease is granted.

Win32_NetworkAdapterConfiguration provides methods and properties for working with dynamic IP addressing. Useful properties include the following:

- **DHCPEnabled** Specifies whether the adapter uses DHCP. If True, you can use DHCPLeaseObtained to determine when a computer obtains the lease on the IP address assigned by DHCP.
- **DHCPServer** Specifies the IP addressees of DHCP servers.
- **DHCPLeaseObtained** Specifies when the computer obtains the lease on the IP address assigned by DHCP. The value is specified as a DateTime string.
- **DHCPLeaseExpires** Specifies when the lease on the IP address expires. The value is specified as a DateTime string.

Useful methods include the following:

- **EnableDHCP()** Enables DHCP on the selected adapter. This method requires no parameters.
- **ReleaseDHCPLease()** Releases the DHCP lease and related addressing information. This method requires no parameters.
- **RenewDHCPLease()** Releases the DHCP lease and then renews it. This method requires no parameters.

When you have a reference to a Win32_NetworkAdapterConfiguration object for a connection that uses DHCP, you can use the properties of this object to view DHCP-related information. An example and sample output follow:

```
$na = get-wmiobject Win32_NetworkAdapter -filter `
"NetConnectionID='Local Area Connection'"
$index = $na.index
```

```
$nac = get-wmiobject Win32_NetworkAdapterConfiguration -filter `
"Index=$index"

$nac | format-list DHCPLeaseExpires, DHCPEnabled, DHCPLeaseObtained, `
DHCPServer
```

```
DHCPLeaseExpires              : 20090220080155.000000-480
DHCPEnabled                   : True
DHCPLeaseObtained             : 20090219080155.000000-480
DHCPServer                    : 192.168.1.1
```

To convert the DateTime strings to a more readable form, you can use the ConvertToDateTime() method as shown in this example and sample output:

```
$na = get-wmiobject Win32_NetworkAdapter -filter `
"NetConnectionID='Local Area Connection'"
$index = $na.index
$nac = get-wmiobject Win32_NetworkAdapterConfiguration -filter `
"Index=$index"

$gotlease = $nac.ConvertToDateTime($nac.dhcpleaseobtained)
$explease = $nac.ConvertToDateTime($nac.dhcpleaseexpires)

write-host ("DHCP Lease Obtained: $gotlease")
write-host ("DHCP Lease Expires: $explease")
```

```
DHCP Lease Obtained: 02/19/2009 14:42:56
DHCP Lease Expires: 02/20/2009 14:42:56
```

> ***NOTE*** **If the adapter you are working with uses static IP addressing, the previous example will not work, and you'll get multiple errors in the output. The reason for this is that the DHCP values are set to Null and cannot be converted to DateTime objects.**

You manage a computer's dynamic IP addressing configuration at an elevated administrator PowerShell prompt. When you have a reference to a Win32_NetworkAdapterConfiguration object, you can use the EnableDHCP() method to enable DHCP. As shown in the following example and sample output, all you need to do is call EnableDHCP() on the Win32_NetworkAdapterConfiguration object:

```
$na = get-wmiobject Win32_NetworkAdapter -filter `
"NetConnectionID='Local Area Connection'"
$index = $na.index
$nac = get-wmiobject Win32_NetworkAdapterConfiguration -filter `
"Index=$index"

$nac.EnableDHCP()
```

```
__GENUS            : 2
__CLASS            : __PARAMETERS
__SUPERCLASS       :
__DYNASTY          : __PARAMETERS
__RELPATH          :
__PROPERTY_COUNT   : 1
__DERIVATION       : {}
__SERVER           :
__NAMESPACE        :
__PATH             :
ReturnValue        : 0
```

Here, you enable DHCP on the local area connection. A return value of 0 indicates success. Any other return value indicates an error. Typically, errors occur because you aren't using an elevated administrator PowerShell prompt or haven't accessed the correct network adapter.

When you are working with a Win32_NetworkAdapterConfiguration object, you can release or renew the adapter's DHCP lease by calling ReleaseDHCPLease() or RenewDHCPLease() as appropriate. In the following example, you renew the lease on the local area connection:

```
$na = get-wmiobject Win32_NetworkAdapter -filter `
"NetConnectionID='Local Area Connection'"
$index = $na.index
$nac = get-wmiobject Win32_NetworkAdapterConfiguration -filter `
"Index=$index"

$nac.RenewDHCPLease()
```

Configuring Windows Firewall

Windows Firewall is included with Windows XP with Service Pack 2 and later versions of the Windows operating system. When you are configuring Windows systems, you'll often want to determine whether Windows Firewall is enabled or disabled and then either enable or disable the firewall as appropriate. You might also want to determine what firewall ports are open or closed and then either open or close ports as appropriate. In PowerShell, you can easily perform these basic firewall management tasks.

Viewing and Managing Windows Firewall Settings

Windows Firewall supports three types of profiles:

- **Domain** The profile applicable when a computer is connected to a domain.
- **Private** The profile applicable when a computer is a member of a workgroup or connected to a home network.
- **Public** The profile applicable when a computer is connected to a public network.

You manage Windows Firewall using the HNetCfg.FwMgr COM object. You can create an instance of this object so that you can work with Windows Firewall, as shown in the following example:

```
$firewall = new-object -com HNetCfg.FwMgr
```

Although you can view Windows Firewall settings at a standard PowerShell prompt, you must access an elevated administrator PowerShell prompt to change most firewall settings. As shown in the following example and sample output, the top-level firewall object has several methods and properties you can use:

```
$firewall = new-object -com HNetCfg.FwMgr
$firewall | get-member
```

```
   TypeName: System.__ComObject#{f7898af5-cac4-4632-a2ec-da06e5111af2}

Name               MemberType Definition
----               ---------- ----------
IsIcmpTypeAllowed  Method     void IsIcmpTypeAllowed (NET_FW_IP_VERSION
IsPortAllowed      Method     void IsPortAllowed (string, NET_FW_IP_VERSION
RestoreDefaults    Method     void RestoreDefaults ()
CurrentProfileType Property   NET_FW_PROFILE_TYPE_ CurrentProfileType ()
LocalPolicy        Property   INetFwPolicy LocalPolicy () {get}
```

Calling the RestoreDefaults() method on the firewall object restores the default settings as shown in this example:

```
$firewall = new-object -com HNetCfg.FwMgr
$firewall.restoredefaults()
```

Accessing the CurrentProfileType property displays the current profile type: 0 (Private), 1 (Public), or 2 (Domain). This is shown in the following example and sample output:

```
$firewall = new-object -com HNetCfg.FwMgr
$firewall.currentprofiletype
```

```
1
```

Most of the time, you'll want to work with the LocalPolicy property, which returns an object representing the local firewall policy. Using this object, you can get objects representing the current, active profile or any specific firewall profile by name.

You use the CurrentProfile property of the Local Firewall Policy object to get the current, active profile, as shown in this example and sample output:

```
$firewall = new-object -com HNetCfg.FwMgr
$current = $firewall.localpolicy.currentprofile
$current | format-list *
```

```
Type                                        : 1
FirewallEnabled                             : False
ExceptionsNotAllowed                        : False
NotificationsDisabled                       : False
UnicastResponsesToMulticastBroadcastDisabled : False
RemoteAdminSettings                         : System.__ComObject
IcmpSettings                                : System.__ComObject
GloballyOpenPorts                           : {Intel(R) Viiv(TM) Media}
Services                                    : {File and Printer Sharing}
AuthorizedApplications                      : {Roxio Upnp Service, SPCM}
```

You use the GetProfileByType() method of the Local Firewall Policy object to get a specific profile, as shown in the following example and sample output:

```
$firewall = new-object -com HNetCfg.FwMgr
$private = $firewall.localpolicy.getprofilebytype(0)
$private | format-list *
```

```
Type                                        : 0
FirewallEnabled                             : True
ExceptionsNotAllowed                        : False
NotificationsDisabled                       : True
UnicastResponsesToMulticastBroadcastDisabled : True
RemoteAdminSettings                         : System.__ComObject
IcmpSettings                                : System.__ComObject
GloballyOpenPorts                           : {Intel(R) Viiv(TM) Media}
Services                                    : {File and Printer Sharing}
AuthorizedApplications                      : {Roxio Upnp Service, SPCM}
```

Regardless of whether you are working with the current profile or a profile of a specific type, you have the following properties available:

- **AuthorizedApplications** Returns a collection of objects representing applications authorized to communicate through the firewall. By accessing individual objects in the collection, you control authorized applications. Properties can be viewed or set by their name as shown in the following example and sample output:

```
$firewall = new-object -com HNetCfg.FwMgr
$apps = $firewall.localpolicy.currentprofile.authorizedapplications
foreach ($a in $apps) {$a}
```

```
Name                 : Roxio Upnp Service
ProcessImageFileName : C:\Program Files\Roxio\Easy Media Creator 8\
Digital Home\RoxUpnpServer.exe
IpVersion            : 2
Scope                : 0
RemoteAddresses      : *
Enabled              : True
```

- **ExceptionsNotAllowed** Displays or controls whether firewall exceptions are allowed. This property accepts a Boolean value.

```
$firewall = new-object -com HNetCfg.FwMgr
$cp = $firewall.localpolicy.currentprofile
$cp.exceptionsnotallowed = $True
write-host $cp.exceptionsnotallowed
```

```
True
```

- **FirewallEnabled** Displays or controls whether the firewall is enabled. This property accepts a Boolean value.

```
$firewall = new-object -com HNetCfg.FwMgr
$cp = $firewall.localpolicy.currentprofile
$cp.firewallenabled = $True
write-host $cp.firewallenabled
```

```
True
```

- **GloballyOpenPorts** Returns a collection of objects representing open ports. By accessing individual objects in the collection, you control open ports. Properties can be viewed or set by their name as shown in the following example and sample output:

```
$firewall = new-object -com HNetCfg.FwMgr
$oports = $firewall.localpolicy.currentprofile.globallyopenports
foreach ($o in $oports) {$o}
```

```
Name            : Adobe Version Cue CS3 Server
IpVersion       : 2
Protocol        : 6
Port            : 50901
Scope           : 0
RemoteAddresses : *
Enabled         : True
BuiltIn         : False
```

- **IcmpSettings** Returns a collection of objects representing Internet Control Message Protocol (ICMP) settings. By accessing individual objects in the collection, you control ICMP settings.

```
$firewall = new-object -com HNetCfg.FwMgr
$icmpsettings = $firewall.localpolicy.currentprofile.icmpsettings
foreach ($i in $icmpsettings) {$i}
```

```
AllowOutboundDestinationUnreachable : False
AllowRedirect                       : False
AllowInboundEchoRequest             : False
AllowOutboundTimeExceeded           : False
AllowOutboundParameterProblem       : False
AllowOutboundSourceQuench           : False
AllowInboundRouterRequest           : False
AllowInboundTimestampRequest        : False
AllowInboundMaskRequest   .         : False
AllowOutboundPacketTooBig           : True
```

- **NotificationsDisabled** Displays or controls whether notifications are disabled. When notifications are enabled, messages are displayed to the user when a program is blocked from receiving inbound connections. This property accepts a Boolean value.

```
$firewall = new-object -com HNetCfg.FwMgr
$cp = $firewall.localpolicy.currentprofile
$cp.notificationsdisabled = $True
write-host $cp.notificationsdisabled
```

```
True
```

- **RemoteAdminSettings** Returns a collection of objects representing remote administration settings. By accessing individual objects in the collection, you control these settings.

```
$firewall = new-object -com HNetCfg.FwMgr
$ras = $firewall.localpolicy.currentprofile.remoteadminsettings
foreach ($r in $ras) {$r | format-list *}
```

```
IpVersion          : 2
Scope              : 1
RemoteAddresses : LocalSubnet
Enabled            : False
```

- **UnicastResponsesToMulticastBroadcastDisabled** Displays or controls whether unicast responses are disabled. When unicast responses are enabled, Windows Firewall allows unicast responses to multicast or broadcast network traffic. This property accepts a Boolean value.

```
$firewall = new-object -com HNetCfg.FwMgr
$cp = $firewall.localpolicy.currentprofile
$cp.unicastresponsestomulticastbroadcastdisabled = $True
write-host $cp.unicastresponsestomulticastbroadcastdisabled
```

```
True
```

- **Type** Displays the type of profile you are working with as 0 (Private), 1 (Public), or 2 (Domain).

```
$firewall = new-object -com HNetCfg.FwMgr
$cp = $firewall.localpolicy.currentprofile
write-host $cp.type
```

```
1
```

Adding and Removing Firewall Ports

At an elevated administrator PowerShell prompt, you can open and close firewall ports using the Add() and Remove() methods accessible via the HNetCfg.FWOpenPort COM object. To add a port, you create a reference to this COM object and then define the settings for the port as shown in this example:

```
$PROTOCOL_TCP = 6
$firewall = new-object -com HNetCfg.FwMgr
$port = new-object -com HNetCfg.FWOpenPort

$port.name = "Web Services"
$port.port = 8080
$port.protocol = $PROTOCOL_TCP

$firewall.localpolicy.currentprofile.globallyopenports.Add($port)
```

The port name is a descriptive value for anyone who reviews the firewall settings. The port number is the TCP or UDP port to open on the firewall. The protocol is the specific TCP or UDP protocol that will be used.

After you create a port, you can verify the settings using the GloballyOpenPorts property of the applicable profile. Here is an example and sample output:

```
$firewall = new-object -com HNetCfg.FwMgr
$oports = $firewall.localpolicy.currentprofile.globallyopenports
$oports | where-object {$_.name -eq "Web Services"}
```

```
Name            : Web Services
IpVersion       : 2
Protocol        : 6
Port            : 8080
Scope           : 0
RemoteAddresses : *
Enabled         : True
BuiltIn         : False
```

To remove a port, you create a reference to the HNetCfg.FWOpenPort COM object and then identify the port to remove by its port address and protocol identifier as shown in this example:

```
$PROTOCOL_TCP = 6
$firewall = new-object -com HNetCfg.FwMgr
$cp = $firewall.localpolicy.currentprofile
$cp.globallyopenports.Remove(8080, $PROTOCOL_TCP)
```

You can verify that the port was removed using the same technique you use to verify that a port was added. If you can no longer find the port by its name, the port was removed successfully.

CHAPTER 12

Managing and Securing the Registry

The Windows registry stores configuration settings. Using the Registry provider built into Windows PowerShell, you can view, add, delete, compare, and copy registry entries. Because the Windows registry is essential to the proper operation of the operating system, make changes to the registry only when you know how these changes will affect the system. You should perform all registry changes within the context of a transaction. Transactions were discussed in the "Creating Transactions" section in Chapter 7, "Managing Computers with Commands and Scripts." With transactions, you can do the following:

1. Use Start-Transaction to start a transaction before you modify the registry.
2. Make changes and then verify your changes.
3. Use Stop-Transaction to finalize your changes or Undo-Transaction to roll back your changes.

After you finalize a transaction using Stop-Transaction, you can no longer undo your changes. Additionally, transactions won't help you identify changes that will cause problems with the computer and its installed components and applications. Therefore, before you edit the registry in any way, you should create a system restore point. This way, if you make a mistake, you can recover the registry and the system.

CAUTION Improperly modifying the Windows registry can cause serious problems. If the registry becomes corrupted, you might have to reinstall the operating system. Double-check the commands you use. Make sure that they do exactly what you intend.

Understanding Registry Keys and Values

The Windows registry stores configuration settings for the operating system, applications, users, and hardware. Registry settings are stored as keys and values, which are placed under a specific root key controlling when and how the keys and values are used.

Table 12-1 lists the registry root keys you can work with in PowerShell as well as a description and the reference name you use to refer to the root key when working with the Registry provider. Under the root keys, you'll find the main keys that control system, user, application, and hardware settings. These keys are organized into a tree structure, with folders representing keys. Within these folders are the registry keys that store important service configuration settings and their subkeys.

TABLE 12-1 Keys in the Windows Registry

ROOT KEY	REFERENCE NAME	DESCRIPTION
HKEY_CURRENT_USER	HKCU	Stores configuration settings for the current user.
HKEY_LOCAL_MACHINE	HKLM	Stores system-level configuration settings.
HKEY_CLASSES_ROOT	HKCR	Stores configuration settings for applications and files. It also ensures that the correct application is opened when a file is accessed.
HKEY_USERS	HKU	Stores default-user and other-user settings by profile.
HKEY_CURRENT_CONFIG	HKCC	Stores information about the hardware profile being used.

Keys that you want to work with must be designated by their folder path. For example, under HKLM\SYSTEM\CurrentControlSet\Services, you'll find folders for all services installed on the system. Values associated with the DNS key in this folder path allow you to work with the Domain Name System (DNS) service and its configuration settings.

Key values are stored as a specific data type. Table 12-2 provides a summary of the main data types used with keys.

TABLE 12-2 Registry Key Values and Data Types

DATA TYPE	DESCRIPTION	REFERENCE NAME	EXAMPLE
REG_BINARY	Identifies a binary value. Binary values are stored using base2 (0 or 1 only) but are displayed and entered in hexadecimal (base16) format.	Binary	01 00 14 80 90 00 00 9C 00
REG_DWORD	Identifies a binary data type in which 32-bit integer values are stored as four byte-length values in hexadecimal.	Dword	0x00000002
REG_EXPAND_SZ	Identifies an expandable string value, which is usually used with directory paths.	Expandstring	%SystemRoot%\dns.exe
REG_MULTI_SZ	Identifies a multiple-string value.	Multistring	Tcpip Afd RpcSc
REG_NONE	Identifies data without a particular type. This data is written as binary values but is displayed and entered in hexadecimal (base16) format.	None	23 45 67 80
REG_QWORD	Identifies a binary data type in which 64-bit integer values are stored as eight byte-length values in hexadecimal.	Qword	0x0000EA3FC
REG_SZ	Identifies a string value containing a sequence of characters.	String	DNS Server

Navigating the Registry

The core set of features for performing related procedures was discussed previously in the "Using Providers" section in Chapter 3, "Managing Your Windows PowerShell Environment," and include the Registry provider, the cmdlets for working with data stores listed in Table 3-4, and the cmdlets for working with provider drives listed in Table 3-5. As long as you know the key path and understand the available key data types, you can use the Registry provider to view and manipulate keys in a variety of ways.

By default, only the HKLM and HKCU root keys are available in PowerShell. To make other root keys available, you can register them as new PowerShell drives. The following example shows how to register HKCR, HKU, and HKCC:

```
new-psdrive -name hkcr -psprovider registry -root hkey_classes_root
new-psdrive -name hku -psprovider registry -root hkey_users
new-psdrive -name hkcc -psprovider registry -root hkey_current_config
```

Now you can directly access these additional root keys. For example, if you want to access HKCC, you type

```
set-location hkcc:
```

You can access keys and values in any Registry location using Set-Location. For example, if you want to change the location to HKLM, you type

```
set-location hklm:
```

You can then work with registry keys and values in HKLM. Locations under HKLM (or any other root key) are navigated in the same way you navigate directory paths. If you are working with HKLM, for example, you can use Set-Location (or CD) to change to HKLM\SYSTEM\CurrentControlSet\Services by typing

```
set-location system\currentcontrolset\services
```

Alternatively, to access HKLM and start in this location in the first place, you can type

```
set-location hklm:\system\currentcontrolset\services
```

NOTE **If you specify a nonexistent path, key, or value, an error message is displayed. Typically, it reads:** `Cannot find _________ because it does not exist.`

When you are working with a Registry location and want to view the available keys, type **get-childitem** (or **dir**) as shown in the following example and sample output:

```
set-location hklm:\system\currentcontrolset\services
get-childitem
```

```
    Hive: HKEY_LOCAL_MACHINE\system\currentcontrolset\services

SKC  VC Name                           Property
---  -- ----                           --------
  2   0 .NET CLR Data                  {}
  2   0 .NET CLR Networking            {}
  2   0 .NET Data Provider for Oracle  {}
  2   0 .NET Data Provider for SqlS... {}
  1   0 .NETFramework                  {}
  2   7 ACPI                           {Tag, DisplayName, Group...}
  1   7 Adobe LM Service               {Description, DisplayName...}
  1   6 Adobe Version Cue CS2          {DisplayName, Type, Start...}
  1   7 Adobe Version Cue CS3          {Type, Start, ErrorControl...}
```

The following information is provided in this output:

- SKC shows the subkey count under the named key.
- VC shows the value count, which is the number of values under the named key.
- Name shows the name of the subkey.
- Property lists the names of properties for the named key.

To learn more about navigating the registry, let's focus on the APCI key. In this example, you know ACPI has a number of named property values. You can list these property values by typing **get-itemproperty** as shown in the following example and sample output:

```
set-location hklm:\system\currentcontrolset\services\acpi
get-itemproperty .
```

```
PSPath       : Microsoft.PowerShell.Core\Registry::HKEY_LOCAL_MACHINE\
system\currentcontrolset\services\acpi
PSParentPath : Microsoft.PowerShell.Core\Registry::HKEY_LOCAL_MACHINE\
system\currentcontrolset\services
PSChildName  : acpi
PSDrive      : HKLM
PSProvider   : Microsoft.PowerShell.Core\Registry
Tag          : 1
DisplayName  : Microsoft ACPI Driver
Group        : Boot Bus Extender
ImagePath    : system32\drivers\acpi.sys
ErrorControl : 3
Start        : 0
Type         : 1
```

You don't have to access a location to view its properties. The value you provide to Get-Item Property is a path. In the previous example, the dot (.) refers to the current working location. If you were working with another drive or location, you could enter the full path to the key to get the same results, as shown in this example:

```
get-itemproperty hklm:\system\currentcontrolset\services\acpi
```

Continuing this example, you know there are two source keys and seven key values under ACPI. If you access ACPI, you can list the two source keys by typing **get-childitem** (or **dir**) as shown in this example and sample output:

```
set-location hklm:\system\currentcontrolset\services\acpi
get-childitem
```

```
    Hive: HKEY_LOCAL_MACHINE\system\currentcontrolset\services\acpi

SKC  VC Name                           Property
---  -- ----                           --------
  1   2 Parameters                     {AMLIMaxCTObjs,
WHEAOSCImplemented}
  0   3 Enum                           {0, Count, NextInstance}
```

As with Get-ItemProperty, Get-ChildItem also accepts a path. This means you can use Get-ChildItem and enter the full path to the key to get the same results shown in the previous example:

```
get-childitem hklm:\system\currentcontrolset\services\acpi
```

If you access the enum key under ACPI, you'll find several properties, including Count and NextInstance. Although you can use Get-ChildItem to view the values of all related properties, you'll more typically want to view and work with individual property values. To do this, get the properties and store the results in a variable. This allows you to then view and work with properties individually as shown in the following example and sample output:

```
$p = get-itemproperty hklm:\system\currentcontrolset\services\acpi\enum
$p.count
```

```
1
```

Alternatively, you can read registry values by referencing the full path and name of the property value that you want to examine. The basic syntax is

```
get-itemproperty [-path] KeyPath [-name] ValueName
```

where *KeyPath* is the path of the key you want to examine and *ValueName* is an optional parameter that specifies a specific key value. Here is an example with sample output:

```
get-itemproperty hklm:\system\currentcontrolset\services\acpi\enum count
```

```
PSPath       : Microsoft.PowerShell.Core\Registry::HKEY_LOCAL_MACHINE\
system\currentcontrolset\services\acpi\enum
PSParentPath : Microsoft.PowerShell.Core\Registry::HKEY_LOCAL_MACHINE\
system\currentcontrolset\services\acpi
PSChildName  : enum
PSDrive      : HKLM
PSProvider   : Microsoft.PowerShell.Core\Registry
Count        : 1
```

As you can see, the output includes path, drive, and provider values as well as the value of the property you are examining. You can filter the output so that you see only the property value using Format-List, as shown in the following example:

```
get-itemproperty hklm:\system\currentcontrolset\services\acpi\enum `
count | format-list -property count
```

```
Count        : 1
```

NOTE To work with the registry on remote computers, use the Invoke-Command cmdlet as discussed in Chapter 4, "Using Sessions, Jobs, and Remoting." Here is an example:

```
invoke-command -computername Server43, Server27, Server82 `
-scriptblock { get-itemproperty `
hklm:\system\currentcontrolset\services\acpi\enum }
```

Alternatively, you can establish remote sessions using the New-PSSession cmdlet and then run individual commands against each computer automatically. Here is an example:

```
$s = new-PSSession -computername Server43, Server27, Server82
invoke-command -session $s -scriptblock {get-itemproperty `
hklm:\system\currentcontrolset\services\acpi\enum}
```

Managing Registry Keys and Values

When you are working with the Registry provider, you have many Item and Item-Property cmdlets available for managing registry keys and values. You'll use these cmdlets to create, copy, move, rename, and delete registry items.

Creating Registry Keys and Values

You can easily add subkeys and values to the Windows registry using PowerShell. To create keys, you use the New-Item cmdlet. To create key values, you use the New-ItemProperty cmdlet. The basic syntax for creating a key is

```
new-item [-type registrykey] [-path] Path
```

where you can optionally specify the type of item you are creating as Registrykey and then use *Path* to specify where the key should be created. When you create a registry key, New-Item displays results that confirm the creation process. In the following example, you create an HKCU:\Software\Test key, and the resulting output confirms that the key was successfully created:

```
new-item -type registrykey -path hkcu:\software\test
```

```
    Hive: HKEY_CURRENT_USER\software
SKC  VC Name                           Property
---  -- ----                           --------
  0   0 test                           {}
```

> **NOTE** To create keys and set key values on remote computers, use the Invoke-Command cmdlet as discussed in Chapter 4. Here is an example:
>
> ```
> invoke-command -computername Server43, Server27, Server82 `
> -scriptblock { new-item hkcu:\software\test }
> ```

As long as you have the appropriate permissions to create the key in the specified location, the creation process should be successful. If the key already exists, however, you'll see an error stating the following: "A key at this path already exists."

The basic syntax for creating a key value is

```
new-itemproperty [-path] Path [-name] Name [-type Type] [-value Value]
```

where *Path* is the path to an existing registry key, *Name* is the name of the value, *Type* is the value type, and *Value* is the value to assign. Permitted value types are listed by their reference name in Table 12-2. As the table shows, valid types include Binary, Dword, Expandstring, Multistring, None, and String.

When you create a key value, New-ItemProperty displays results that confirm the creation process. In the following example, you create a string value called Data under the HKCU:\Software\Test key, and the resulting output confirms that the key value was successfully created:

```
new-itemproperty -path hkcu:\software\test Data -type "string" `
-value "Current"
```

```
PSPath       : Microsoft.PowerShell.Core\Registry::HKEY_CURRENT_USER\
software\test
PSParentPath : Microsoft.PowerShell.Core\Registry::HKEY_CURRENT_USER\
software
PSChildName  : test
PSDrive      : HKCU
PSProvider   : Microsoft.PowerShell.Core\Registry
Data         : Current
```

As long as you have the appropriate permissions to create the key in the specified location, the creation process should be successful. If the key value already exists, however, you'll see an error stating the following: "The property already exists."

Copying Registry Keys and Values

You can copy registry keys using Copy-Item. The basic syntax is

```
copy-item SourcePath DestinationPath
```

where *SourcePath* is the path to the registry key to copy and *DestinationPath* is where you'd like to create a copy of the registry. In the following example, you copy the HKCU:\Software\Test key (and all its contents) to HKLM:\Software\Dev:

```
copy-item hkcu:\software\test hklm:\software\dev
```

As long as you have the appropriate permissions, you should be able to copy registry keys. When you copy a key, Copy-ItemProperty displays an error that indicates failure but doesn't display any output to indicate success.

You can copy registry values using Copy-ItemProperty. The basic syntax is

```
copy-itemproperty [-path] SourcePath [-destination] DestinationPath [-name]
KeyValueToCopy
```

where *SourcePath* is the current path to the key value, *DestinationPath* is the new path for the copy of the key value, and *KeyValueToCopy* identifies the key value you want to copy. In the following example, you copy the Data value from the HKCU:\Software\Test key to the HKLM:\Software\Dev key:

```
copy-itemproperty -path hkcu:\software\test -destination `
hklm:\software\dev -name data
```

As long as you have the appropriate permissions and the source value exists, you should be able to copy the key value. You can use Copy-ItemProperty to copy multiple key values. Use comma-separated values or wildcard characters as appropriate.

Moving Registry Keys and Values

You can move keys and their associated values using Move-Item. The basic syntax is

```
move-item SourcePath DestinationPath
```

where *SourcePath* is the current path to the key and *DestinationPath* is the new path to the key. When you move a key, Move-Item displays an error that indicates failure but doesn't display any output to indicate success. In the following example, you move the HKCU:\Software\Test key (and all its contents) to the HKCU:\Software\Test2 key:

```
move-item hkcu:\software\test hkcu:\software\test2
```

As long as you have the appropriate permissions, you should be able to move keys. You can use Move-Item to move keys from one root to another. For example, you can move HKCU:\Software\Test to HKLM:\Software\Test.

You can move key values using Move-ItemProperty. The basic syntax is

```
move-itemproperty [-path] SourcePath [-destination] DestinationPath [-name]
KeyValueToMove
```

where *SourcePath* is the current path to the key value, *DestinationPath* is the new path to the key value, and *KeyValueToMove* identifies the key value you want to move. When you move a key value, Move-ItemProperty displays an error that indicates failure but doesn't display any output to indicate success. In the following example, you move the Data value from the HKCU:\Software\Test key to the HKLM:\Software\Test key:

```
move-itemproperty -path hkcu:\software\test -destination `
hklm:\software\test2 -name data
```

As long as you have the appropriate permissions and the source and destination keys exist, you should be able to move the key value. You can use Move-ItemProperty to move multiple key values. Use comma-separated values or wildcard characters as appropriate.

Renaming Registry Keys and Values

To rename keys, you use the Rename-Item cmdlet. Rename-Item has the following syntax

```
rename-item OriginalNamePath NewName
```

where *OriginalNamePath* is the full path to the key and *NewName* is the new name for the key. In the following example, you rename Test under HKCU:\Software as Test2:

```
rename-item hkcu:\software\test test2
```

As long as you have the appropriate permissions, you should be able to rename keys.

To rename key values, you use the Rename-ItemProperty cmdlet. Rename-ItemProperty has the following syntax

```
rename-item [-path] OriginalNamePath [-name] CurrentName [-newname] NewName
```

where *OriginalNamePath* is the full path to the key value and *NewName* is the new name for the key value. In the following example, you rename Data under the HKCU:\Software\Test key as EntryType:

```
rename-itemproperty -path hkcu:\software\test2 -name data `
-newname entrytype
```

As long as you have the appropriate permissions, you should be able to rename keys.

Deleting Registry Keys and Values

You can delete registry keys using the Remove-Item cmdlet. Remove-Item has the following syntax

```
remove-item NamePath [-Force]
```

where *NamePath* is the full path to the registry key that you want to remove, and –Force is an optional parameter to force the removal of the key. In the following example, you delete the HKCU:\Software\Test2 key (and all its contents):

```
remove-item hkcu:\software\test2
```

As long as you have the appropriate permissions, you should be able to remove registry keys.

You can delete key values using the Remove-ItemProperty cmdlet. Remove-ItemProperty has the following syntax

```
remove-itemproperty [-Path] KeyPath [-Name] ValueName [-Force]
```

where *KeyPath* is the full path to the registry key that contains the value that you want to remove, *ValueName* is the name of the value to remove, and –Force is an optional parameter to force the removal of the key value. In the following example, you delete the Data value for the HKCU:\Software\Test key:

```
remove-itemproperty -path hkcu:\software\test -name data
```

As long as you have the appropriate permissions, you should be able to remove key values.

Comparing Registry Keys

You can compare registry entries and values between and among computers or between two different keys on the same system. Performing registry comparisons is useful in the following situations:

- When you are trying to troubleshoot service and application configuration issues.

  At such times, it is useful to compare the registry configurations between two different systems. Ideally, these systems include one registry that appears to be configured properly and one that you suspect is misconfigured. You can then perform a comparison of the configuration areas that you suspect are causing problems.

- When you want to ensure that an application or service is configured the same way on multiple systems.

  Here you use one system as the basis for testing the other system configurations. Ideally, the basis system is configured exactly as expected before you start comparing its configuration with other systems.

To see how you can compare registry values across computers, consider the following example and sample output:

```
$c1 = "techpc18"
$c2 = "engpc25"

$p = invoke-command -computername $c1 -scriptblock { get-itemproperty `
hklm:\system\currentcontrolset\services\acpi\enum }

$h = invoke-command -computername $c2 -scriptblock { get-itemproperty `
hklm:\system\currentcontrolset\services\acpi\enum }

if ($p = $h) {write-host $True} else {
write-host "Computer: $c1"
write-host $p

write-host "Computer: $c2"
write-host $h}
```

```
True
```

When you run these commands at an elevated administrator PowerShell prompt and the remote computers are configured for remoting, you get a comparison of the specified keys on both computers. If the keys have the same values, PowerShell writes True to the output as shown. Otherwise, PowerShell writes the values associated with each key on each computer, allowing you to see where there are differences.

You can easily extend this comparison technique so that you can compare the values on a computer you know is configured correctly with multiple computers in the enterprise that you want to check. An example and sample output follow:

```
$clist = "techpc18", "techpc25", "techpc36"
$src = "engpc25"

$ps = invoke-command -computername $clist -scriptblock { `
get-itemproperty hklm:\system\currentcontrolset\services\acpi\enum }

$h = invoke-command -computername $src -scriptblock { get-itemproperty `
hklm:\system\currentcontrolset\services\acpi\enum }

$index = 0

foreach ($p in $ps) {

if ($p = $h) {write-host $clist[$index] "same as $src" } else {
write-host "Computer:" $clist[$index]
write-host $p

write-host "Computer: $src"
write-host $h

$index++}
}
```

```
techpc18 same as engpc25
techpc25 same as engpc25
techpc36 same as engpc25
```

Here, you check the registry on multiple target computers and compare key values with a source computer. If a target computer has different values for the key compared, you list the target computer's values followed by the source computer's values. This allows you to see where there are differences.

Viewing and Managing Registry Security Settings

As an administrator, you'll sometimes need to view and manage security settings in the registry. In PowerShell, these tasks are accomplished using Get-Acl and Set-Acl. The syntax for these commands is as follows:

- **Get-Acl** Gets objects that represent the security descriptor of registry keys. Use –Audit to get the audit data for the security descriptor from the access control list.

```
Get-Acl [-Path] KeyPaths {AddtlParams}

AddtlParams=
[-Audit] [-Exclude KeysToExclude] [-Include KeysToInclude]
```

- **Set-Acl** Changes the security descriptor of registry keys. Use –Aclobject to specify the desired security settings.

```
Set-Acl [-Path] KeyPaths [-Aclobject] Security {AddtlParams}

AddtlParams=
[-Exclude KeysToExclude] [-Include KeysToInclude]
```

Whenever you are working with registry keys, you might want to view or modify the security descriptor. Use Get-Acl with the –Path parameter to specify the path to resources you want to work with. You can use wildcard characters in the path, and you can also include or exclude keys using the –Include and –Exclude parameters.

Getting and Setting Registry Security Descriptors

Get-Acl returns a separate object containing the security information for each matching key. By default, Get-Acl displays the path to the resource, the owner of the resource, and a list of the access control entries on the resource. The access control list is controlled by the resource owner. To get additional information, including the security group of the owner, a list of auditing entries, and the full security descriptor as an SDDL (Security Descriptor Definition Language) string, format the output as a list as shown in the following example and sample output:

```
get-acl hklm:\software\test | format-list
```

```
Path:Microsoft.PowerShell.Core\Registry::HKEY_LOCAL_MACHINE\software\test
Owner  : BUILTIN\Administrators
Group  : ENGPC18\None
Access : BUILTIN\Users Allow  ReadKey
         BUILTIN\Users Allow  -2147483648
         BUILTIN\Administrators Allow  FullControl
         BUILTIN\Administrators Allow  268435456
         NT AUTHORITY\SYSTEM Allow  FullControl
         NT AUTHORITY\SYSTEM Allow  268435456
         CREATOR OWNER Allow  268435456
Audit  :
Sddl   : O:BAG:S-1-5-21-3603280705-3559929044-3306537903-
513D:AI(A;ID;KR;;;BU)(A;CIIOID;GR;;;BU)(A;ID;KA;;;BA)(A;CIIOID;GA;;;BA)
(A;ID;KA;;;SY)(A;CIIOID;GA;;;SY)(A;CIIOID;GA;;;CO)
```

NOTE You can view and manage registry security on remote computers using any of the remoting techniques discussed in Chapter 4. Here is an example:

```
invoke-command -computername Server16, Server12, Server18 `
-scriptblock { get-acl hklm:\software\test | format-list }
```

Here, Get-Acl returns a RegistrySecurity object representing the security descriptor of the HKLM:\Software\Test key. The result is then sent to the Format-List cmdlet. You can work with any properties of security objects separately, including the following:

- **Owner** Shows the owner of the resource
- **Group** Shows the primary group the owner is a member of
- **Access** Shows the access control rules on the resource
- **Audit** Shows the auditing rules on the resource
- **Sddl** Shows the full security descriptor as an SDDL string

NOTE RegistrySecurity objects have additional properties that aren't displayed as part of the standard output. To see these properties, send the output to Format-List *. You'll then see the following note and script properties: PSPath (the PowerShell path to the resource), PSParentPath (the PowerShell path to the parent resource), PSChildName (the name of the resource), PSDrive (the PowerShell drive on which the resource is located), AccessToString (an alternate representation of the access rules on the resource), and AuditToString (an alternate representation of the audit rules on the resource).

You can use the objects that Get-Acl returns to set the security descriptors on registry keys. To do this, open an elevated administrator PowerShell prompt, obtain a single security descriptor object for a registry key that has the security settings you want to use, and then use the security descriptor object to establish the desired security settings for another registry key. An example and sample output follow:

```
set-acl -path hkcu:\software\dev -aclobject (get-acl hklm:\software\test)
```

Here you use the security descriptor on HKLM:\Software\Test to set the security descriptor for HKCU:\Software\Dev.

You can easily extend this technique. In this example, you use the security descriptor on HKLM:\Software\Test to set the security descriptor for subkeys directly under the HKCU:\Software\Dev key:

```
$secd = get-acl hklm:\software\test
set-acl -path hkcu:\software\dev\* -aclobject $secd
```

To include keys in subpaths, you need to use Get-ChildItem to obtain reference objects for all the keys you want to work with. Here is an example:

```
$s = get-acl hklm:\software\test
gci hkcu:\software\dev -recurse -force | set-acl -aclobject $s
```

Here, *gci* is an alias for Get-ChildItem. You obtain the security descriptor for HKLM:\Software\Test. Next you get a reference to all subpaths of HKCU:\Software\Dev. Finally, you use the security descriptor on HKLM:\Software\Test to set the security descriptor for these subkeys.

Working with Registry Access Rules

To create your own security descriptors, you need to work with access control rules. The Access property of security objects is defined as a collection of authorization rules. With registry keys, these rules have the following object type:

System.Security.AccessControl.RegistryAccessRule

One way to view the individual access control objects that apply to a registry key is shown in this example and sample output:

```
$s = get-acl hklm:\software\test
$s.access
```

```
RegistryRights    : FullControl
AccessControlType : Allow
IdentityReference : ENGPC72\Bubba
IsInherited       : True
InheritanceFlags  : ContainerInherit, ObjectInherit
PropagationFlags  : None

RegistryRights    : FullControl
AccessControlType : Allow
IdentityReference : NT AUTHORITY\SYSTEM
IsInherited       : True
InheritanceFlags  : ContainerInherit, ObjectInherit
PropagationFlags  : None
RegistryRights    : FullControl

RegistryRights    : FullControl
AccessControlType : Allow
IdentityReference : BUILTIN\Administrators
IsInherited       : True
InheritanceFlags  : ContainerInherit, ObjectInherit
PropagationFlags  : None
```

Here you get the RegistrySecurity object for the HKLM:\Software\Test key and then display the contents of its Access property. Although each value listed is an access rule object, you cannot work with each access rule object separately. Note the following in the output:

- **RegistryRights** Shows the registry rights being applied
- **AccessControlType** Shows the access control type as Allow or Deny
- **IdentityReference** Shows the user or group to which the rule applies

- **IsInherited** Specifies whether the access rule is inherited
- **InheritanceFlags** Shows the way inheritance is being applied
- **PropagationFlags** Specifies whether the access rule will be inherited

Another way to work with each access rule object separately is to use a ForEach loop as shown in this example:

```
$s = get-acl hklm:\software\test

foreach($a in $s.access) {

 #work with each access control object

 if ($a.identityreference -like "*administrator*") {$a | format-list *}
}
```

```
RegistryRights    : FullControl
AccessControlType : Allow
IdentityReference : BUILTIN\Administrators
IsInherited       : True
InheritanceFlags  : ContainerInherit, ObjectInherit
PropagationFlags  : None
```

Here, you examine each access rule object separately, which allows you to take action on specific access rules. In this example, you look for access rules that apply to administrators.

Configuring Registry Permissions

You can assign two types of access permissions to registry keys: basic and special. These permissions grant or deny access to users and groups.

The basic permissions you can assign to registry keys are shown in Table 12-3. The basic permissions are made up of multiple special permissions. Note the rule flag for each permission, because this is the value you must reference when creating an access rule.

TABLE 12-3 Basic Registry Permissions

PERMISSION	DESCRIPTION	RULE FLAG
Full Control	This permission permits reading, writing, changing, and deleting registry keys and values.	FullControl
Read	This permission permits reading registry keys and their values.	ReadKey, ExecuteKey
Write	This permission permits reading and writing registry keys and their values.	WriteKey

When you are configuring basic permissions for users and groups, you can specify the access control type as either Allowed or Denied. If a user or group should be granted an access permission, you allow the permission. If a user or group should be denied an access permission, you deny the permission.

You configure basic permissions for resources using access rules. Access rules contain collections of arrays that define:

- The user or group to which the rule applies.
- The access permission that applies.
- The Allow or Deny status.

This means regardless of whether you are adding or modifying rules, the basic syntax for an individual access rule is

```
"UserOrGroupName", "ApplicablePermission", "ControlType"
```

where *UserOrGroupName* is the name of the user or group to which the access rule applies, *ApplicablePermission* is the basic permission you are applying, and *ControlType* specifies the Allow or Deny status. User and group names are specified in COMPUTER\Name or DOMAIN\Name format. In the following example, you grant full control to DeploymentTesters:

```
"DeploymentTesters", "FullControl", "Allow"
```

The expanded syntax for an access rule is

```
"UserOrGroupName", "ApplicablePermission", "InheritanceFlag",
"PropagationFlag", "ControlType"
```

where *UserOrGroupName* is the name of the user or group to which the access rule applies, *ApplicablePermission* is the basic permission you are applying, *Inheritance-Flag* controls inheritance, *PropagationFlag* controls propagation of inherited rules, and *ControlType* specifies the type of access control. In the following example, you grant full control to DeploymentTesters and apply inheritance to the key and all its subkeys:

```
"DeploymentTesters", "FullControl", "ContainerInherit", "None", "Allow"
```

With the inheritance flag, you can specify one of the following flag values:

- **None** The access rule is not inherited by subkeys of the current key.
- **ContainerInherit** The access rule is inherited by child container objects.
- **ObjectInherit** The access rule is inherited by child leaf objects.

Because all registry keys are containers, the only inheritance flag that is meaningful for registry keys is the ContainerInherit flag for InheritanceFlags. If this flag is not used, the propagation flags are ignored, and only the key you are working with is affected. If you use the ContainerInherit flag, the rule is propagated according to the propagation flags.

With the propagation flag, you can specify the following flag values:

- **None** The access rule is propagated without modification. This means the rule applies to subkeys, subkeys with child keys, and subkeys of child keys.
- **InheritOnly** The access rule is propagated to container and leaf child objects. This means the rule applies to subkeys with child keys and subkeys of child keys; the rule does not apply to subkeys of the key.
- **NoPropagateInherit** The access rule applies to its child objects. This means the rule applies to subkeys of the key and subkeys with child keys but not to subkeys of child keys.
- **NoPropagateInherit, InheritOnly** The access rule applies to containers. This means the rule applies to subkeys with child keys but not to subkeys of child keys or to subkeys of the key.

You add access rules to a resource using either the SetAccessRule() method or the AddAccessRule() method of the access control object. You remove access rules from a resource using the RemoveAccessRule() method of the access control object. As discussed previously, access rules are defined as having the System.Security .AccessControl.RegistryAccessRule type.

The easiest way to add and remove access rules is to follow these steps:

1. Get an access control object. This object can be the one that applies to the registry key you want to work with or one that applies to a registry key that has the closest access control permissions to those you want to use.
2. Create one or more instances of the System.Security.AccessControl .RegistryAccessRule type, and store the desired permissions in these object instances.
3. Call AddAccessRule() or RemoveAccessRule() to add or remove access rules as necessary. These methods operate on the access control object you retrieved in the first step.
4. To apply the changes you've made to an actual registry key, you must apply the access control object to a specified resource.

Consider the following example:

```
$acl = get-acl hklm:\software\test
$perm = "cpandl\deploymenttesters","fullcontrol","allow"
$r = new-object system.security.accesscontrol.registryaccessrule $perm
$acl.addaccessrule($r)
$acl | set-acl hkcu:\software\dev
```

Here, you get the access control object on HKLM:\Software\Test. You store the values for an access rule in a variable called $perm and then create a new instance of the RegistryAccessRule type for this access rule. To add the permission to the access control object you retrieved previously, you call its AddAccessRule() method. Although you could have created additional permissions and added or removed these, you didn't in this example. Finally, you applied the access control object to a specific resource using Set-Acl.

You can easily extend the previous examples to apply to multiple registry keys as shown in the following example:

```
$acl = get-acl hklm:\software\test
$perm = "cpandl\devtesters","fullcontrol","allow"
$r = new-object system.security.accesscontrol.registryaccessrule $perm
$acl.addaccessrule($r)

$resc = gci hkcu:\software\test -force
foreach($f in $resc) {

  write-host $f.pspath
  $acl | set-acl $f.pspath
}
```

```
Microsoft.PowerShell.Core\Registry::HKEY_CURRENT_USER\software\test\Dt\IO
Microsoft.PowerShell.Core\Registry::HKEY_CURRENT_USER\software\test\Queue
Microsoft.PowerShell.Core\Registry::HKEY_CURRENT_USER\software\test\Stats
```

Here, you apply an access control list with a modified permission set to every subkey of HKCU:\Software\Test. In the output, you list the names of the keys you've modified. This helps you keep track of the changes.

The special permissions you can assign to registry keys are shown in Table 12-4. As with basic permissions, note the rule flag for each permission, because this is the value you must reference when creating an access rule.

TABLE 12-4 Special Permissions

PERMISSION	DESCRIPTION	RULE FLAG
Query Values	Allows the user or group to read the values within a key.	QueryValues
Set Value	Allows the user or group to set the values within a key.	SetValue
Create Subkey	Allows the user or group to create subkeys under the selected key.	CreateSubKey
Enumerate Subkeys	Allows the user or group to list the subkeys under a key.	EnumerateSubKeys
Notify	Allows the user or group to get notifications for changes that occur in a key.	Notify
Create Link	Allows the user or group to create links from one key to another key.	CreateLink

TABLE 12-4 Special Permissions

PERMISSION	DESCRIPTION	RULE FLAG
Delete	Allows the user or group to delete the key, subkeys, and values associated with the key. Delete permission must apply on the key and on all the key's subkeys in order for a user or group to delete a registry key.	Delete
Write DAC	Allows the user or group to change the key's security permissions.	ChangePermissions
Take Ownership	Allows the user or group to modify ownership of a key.	TakeOwnership
Read Control	Allows the user or group to read the key's security permissions.	ReadPermissions

Table 12-5 shows how special permissions are combined to make the basic permissions for registry keys.

TABLE 12-5 Combining Special Permissions

PERMISSION	FULL CONTROL	READ	WRITE
Query Values	X	X	
Set Value	X		X
Create Subkey	X		X
Enumerate Subkeys	X	X	
Notify	X	X	
Create Link	X		
Delete	X		
Write DAC	X		
Write Owner	X		
Read Control	X	X	X

You configure special permissions for registry keys in the same way as basic permissions. You add access rules to a resource using either the SetAccessRule() method or the AddAccessRule() method of the access control object. You remove access rules from a resource using the RemoveAccessRule() method of the access control object.

Consider the following example:

```
$acl = get-acl hklm:\software\test
$p1 = "cpandl\dev","queryvalues","allow"
$r1 = new-object system.security.accesscontrol.registryaccessrule $p1
$acl.addaccessrule($r1)

$p2 = "cpandl\dev","enumeratesubkeys","allow"
$r2 = new-object system.security.accesscontrol.registryaccessrule $p2
$acl.addaccessrule($r2)

$acl | set-acl hklm:\software\test
```

Here, you get the access control object on the HKLM:\Software\Test key. This key must exist for the example to work. After you define an access rule and store the related values in $p1, you create a new instance of the RegistryAccessRule type and add the permission to the access control object by calling the AddAccessRule() method. After you define a second access rule and store the related values in $p2, you create a new instance of the RegistryAccessRule type and add the permission to the access control object by calling the AddAccessRule() method. Finally, you apply the access control object to a specific resource.

Taking Ownership of Registry Keys

You can take ownership using a registry key using the SetOwner() method of the access control object. The easiest way to take ownership is to complete the following steps:

1. Get an access control object for the registry you want to work with.
2. Get the IdentityReference for the user or group that will take ownership. This user or group must already have permission on the registry key.
3. Call SetOwner to specify that you want the user or group to be the owner.
4. Apply the changes you've made to the registry key.

Consider the following example:

```
$acl = get-acl hklm:\software\test
$found = $false
foreach($rule in $acl.access) {
 if ($rule.identityreference -like "*administrators*") {
   $global:ref = $rule.identityreference; $found = $true; break}
}

if ($found) {
 $acl.setowner($ref)
 $acl | set-acl hklm:\software\test
}
```

Here, you get the access control object on HKLM:\Software\Test. You then examine each access rule on this object, looking for the one that applies to the group you want to work with. If you find a match, you set $ref to the IdentityReference for this group, change $found to $true, and then break out of the ForEach loop. After you break out of the loop, you check to see if $found is True. If it is, you set the ownership permission on the access control object you retrieved previously and then apply the access control object to HKLM:\Software\Test using Set-Acl.

Auditing the Registry

Access to the registry can be audited, as can access to other areas of the operating system. Auditing allows you to track which users access the registry and what they're doing. All the permissions listed previously in Tables 12-1 and 12-2 can be audited. However, you usually limit what you audit to only the essentials to reduce the amount of data that is written to the security logs and to reduce the resources used to track registry usage.

Before you can enable auditing of the registry, you must enable the auditing function on the computer you are working with. You can do this either through the server's local policy or through the appropriate Group Policy object. The policy that controls auditing is Computer Configuration\Windows Settings\Security Settings \Local Policies\Audit Policy.

After auditing is enabled for a computer, you can configure how you want auditing to work for the registry. This means configuring auditing for each key you want to track. Thanks to inheritance, this doesn't mean you have to go through every key in the registry and enable auditing for it. Instead, you can select a root key or any subkey to designate the start of the branch for which you want to track access, and then ensure the auditing settings are inherited for all subkeys below it. (Inheritance is the default setting.)

You can set auditing policies for registry keys using auditing rules. Auditing rules contain collections of arrays that define the following:

- The user or group to which the rule applies
- The permission usage that is audited
- The inheritance flag specifying whether the audit rule applies to subkeys of the current key
- The propagation flag specifying how an inherited audit rule is propagated to subkeys of the current key
- The type of auditing

This means regardless of whether you are adding or modifying rules, the basic syntax for an individual audit rule is

```
"UserOrGroupName", "PermissionAudited", "InheritanceFlag",
"PropagationFlag", "AuditType"
```

where *UserOrGroupName* is the name of the user or group to which the audit rule applies, *PermissionAudited* is the basic or special permission you are tracking, *InheritanceFlag* controls inheritance, *PropagationFlag* controls propagation of inherited rules, and *AuditType* specifies the type of auditing.

With the inheritance flag, you can specify one of the following flag values:

- **None** The audit rule is not inherited by subkeys of the current key.
- **ContainerInherit** The audit rule is inherited by child container objects.
- **ObjectInherit** The audit rule is inherited by child leaf objects.

Because all registry keys are containers, the only inheritance flag that is meaningful for registry keys is the ContainerInherit flag for InheritanceFlags. If this flag is not used, the propagation flags are ignored, and only the key you are working with is affected. If you use the ContainerInherit flag, the rule is propagated according to the propagation flags.

With the propagation flag, you can specify the following flag values:

- **None** The audit rule is propagated without modification. This means the rule applies to subkeys, subkeys with child keys, and subkeys of child keys.
- **InheritOnly** The audit rule is propagated to container and leaf child objects. This means the rule applies to subkeys with child keys and subkeys of child keys; the rule does not apply to subkeys of the key.
- **NoPropagateInherit** The audit rule applies to its child objects. This means the rule applies to subkeys of the key and subkeys with child keys but not to subkeys of child keys.
- **NoPropagateInherit, InheritOnly** The audit rule applies to containers. This means the rule applies to subkeys with child keys but not to subkeys of child keys or to subkeys of the key.

With audit type, use Success to track successful use of a specified permission, Failure to track failed use of a specified permission, and None to turn off auditing of the specified permission. Use Both to track success and failure.

As with security permissions, user and group names are specified in COMPUTER\Name or DOMAIN\Name format. In the following example, you track users in the

CPANDL domain who are trying to query key values but fail to do so because they don't have sufficient access permissions:

```
"CPANDL\USERS", "QueryValues", "ContainerInherit", "None", "Failure"
```

You add audit rules to a resource using either the SetAuditRule() method or the AddAuditRule() method of the access control object. You remove audit rules from a resource using the RemoveAuditRule() method of the access control object. Audit rules are defined as having the System.Security.AuditControl.RegistryAuditRule type.

The easiest way to add and remove audit rules is to complete these steps:

1. Get an access control object. This object can be the one that applies to the registry key you want to work with or one that applies to a registry key that has the closest audit control permissions to those you want to use.
2. Create one or more instances of the System.Security.AuditControl .RegistryAuditRule type, and store the desired auditing settings in these object instances.
3. Call AddAuditRule() or RemoveAuditRule() to add or remove audit rules as necessary. These methods operate on the access control object you retrieved in the first step.
4. Apply the changes you've made to an actual resource.

Consider the following example:

```
$acl = get-acl hklm:\software\test
$audit = "cpandl\users","queryvalues","containerinherit","none","failure"
$r = new-object system.security.accesscontrol.registryauditrule $audit
$acl.addauditrule($r)
$acl | set-acl hklm:\software\test
```

Here, you get the access control object on HKLM:\Software\Test. You store the values for an audit rule in a variable called $audit, and then you create a new instance of the RegistryAuditRule type with this auditing rule. To add the auditing setting to the access control object you retrieved previously, you call its AddAuditRule() method. Although you could have created additional auditing rules and added or removed these, you didn't in this example. Finally, you applied the access control object to a registry key using Set-Acl.

You can easily extend the previous examples to apply to multiple registry keys as shown in the following example:

```
$acl = get-acl hklm:\software\test
$audit = "cpandl\users","queryvalues","containerinherit","none","failure"
$r = new-object system.security.accesscontrol.registryauditrule $audit
$acl.addauditrule($r)

$resc = gci hkcu:\software\test -recurse -force
foreach($f in $resc) {

  write-host $f.pspath
  $acl | set-acl $f.pspath
}
```

```
Microsoft.PowerShell.Core\Registry::HKEY_CURRENT_USER\software\test\Dt\IO
Microsoft.PowerShell.Core\Registry::HKEY_CURRENT_USER\software\test\Queue
Microsoft.PowerShell.Core\Registry::HKEY_CURRENT_USER\software\test\Stats
```

Here, you apply an auditing rule to every subkey of HKCU:\Software\Test. In the output, you list the names of the registry keys you've modified. This helps you keep track of the changes.

CHAPTER 13

Monitoring and Optimizing Windows Systems

Windows PowerShell can help you to identify and track system problems, monitor applications and services, and maintain system security. When systems slow down, behave erratically, or experience other problems, you might want to look to the event logs to identify the potential source of the problem. Once you've identified problem sources or issues, you can perform maintenance or preventative tasks to resolve or eliminate them. Using performance monitoring, you can watch for adverse conditions and take appropriate action to resolve them.

Managing Windows Events and Logs

In Windows, an event is any significant occurrence in the operating system that requires users or administrators to be notified. Events are recorded in the Windows event logs and provide important historical information to help you monitor systems, maintain system security, solve problems, and perform diagnostics. It's not just important to sift regularly through the information collected in these logs, it is essential. Administrators should closely monitor the event logs of every business server and ensure that workstations are configured to track important system events. On servers, you want to ensure that systems are secure, that applications and services are operating normally, and that the server isn't experiencing errors that could hamper performance. On workstations, you want to ensure that the events you need to maintain systems and resolve problems are being logged and that the logs are accessible to you as necessary.

Working with Event Logs

The Windows service that manages event logging is called the Windows Event Log service. When this service is started, Windows logs important information. The logs available on a system depend on the system's role and the services installed. Two general types of log files are used:

- **Windows Logs** Logs that the operating system uses to record general system events related to applications, security, setup, and system components
- **Applications and Services Logs** Logs that specific applications and services use to record application-specific or service-specific events

Logs you might see include the following:

- **Application** This log records significant incidents associated with specific applications. For example, Microsoft Exchange Server logs events related to mail exchange, including events for the information store, mailboxes, and service states. By default, this log is stored in %SystemRoot%\System32\Winevt\Logs\Application.evtx.
- **DFS Replication** On domain controllers using DFS replication, this log records file replication activities on the system, including events for service status and control, scanning data in system volumes, and managing replication sets. By default, this log is stored in %SystemRoot%\System32\Winevt\Logs\DFS Replication.Evtx.
- **Directory Service** On domain controllers, this log records incidents from Active Directory Domain Services (AD DS), including events related to directory startup, global catalogs, and integrity checking. By default, this log is stored in %SystemRoot%\System32\Winevt\Logs\Directory Service.Evtx.
- **DNS Server** On Domain Name System (DNS) servers, this log records DNS queries, responses, and other DNS activities. By default, this log is stored in %SystemRoot%\System32\Winevt\Logs\DNS Server.Evtx.
- **File Replication Service** This log records file replication activities on the system. By default, this log is stored in %SystemRoot%\System32\Winevt\Logs\File Replication Service.Evtx.
- **Forwarded Events** When event forwarding is configured, this log records forwarded events from other servers. The default location is %SystemRoot%\System32\Winevt\Logs\FordwardedEvents.Evtx.
- **Hardware Events** When hardware subsystem event reporting is configured, this log records hardware events reported to the operating system. The default location is %SystemRoot%\System32\Winevt\Logs\Hardware-Event.Evtx.
- **Microsoft\Windows** A group of logs that track events related to specific Windows services and features. Logs are organized by component type and event category.

- **Security** This log records events related to security, such as logon/logoff, privilege use, and resource access. By default, this log is stored in %SystemRoot%\System32\Winevt\Logs\Security.Evtx.

> ***TIP*** **To gain access to security logs, users must be granted the user right named Manage Auditing And Security Log. By default, members of the administrators group have this user right. You can learn more about assigning user rights in the "Configuring User Rights Policies" section in Chapter 10, "Creating User and Group Accounts," of the *Windows Server 2008 Administrator's Pocket Consultant* (Microsoft Press, 2008).**

- **Setup** This log records events logged by the operating system or its components during setup and installation. The default location is %SystemRoot%\System32\Winevt\Logs\Setup.Evtx.
- **System** This log records events from the operating system or its components, such as the failure of a service to start, driver initialization, system-wide messages, and other messages that relate to the system. By default, this log is stored in %SystemRoot%\System32\Winevt\Logs\System.Evtx.
- **Windows PowerShell** This log records activities related to the use of Windows PowerShell. The default location is %SystemRoot%\System32\Winevt\Logs\Windows PowerShell.Evtx.

Events range in severity from informational messages to general warnings to serious incidents such as critical errors and failures. The category of an event is indicated by its event level. Event levels include:

- **Information** Indicates an informational event has occurred, which is generally related to a successful action.
- **Warning** Indicates a general warning. Warnings are often useful in preventing future system problems.
- **Error** Indicates a critical error, such as a DHCPv6 address configuration problem.
- **Critical** Indicates a critical error, such as the computer rebooting after a power loss or crash.
- **Audit Success** Indicates the successful execution of an action that you are tracking through auditing, such as privilege use.
- **Audit Failure** Indicates the failed execution of an action that you are tracking through auditing, such as failure to log on.

> ***TIP*** **Of the many event types, the two you'll want to monitor closely are warnings and errors. Whenever these types of events occur and you're unsure of the reason, you should take a closer look to determine whether you need to take further action.**

In addition to having a level, each event has the following common properties associated with it:

- **Computer** Identifies the computer that caused the event to occur.
- **Data** Any data or error code output by the event.
- **Date and Time** Specifies the date and time the event occurred.
- **Description** Provides a detailed description of the event and can include details about where to find more information with which to resolve or handle an issue. This field is available when you double-click a log entry in Event Viewer.
- **Event ID** Details the specific event that occurred with a numeric identifier. Event IDs are generated by the event source and used to uniquely identify the event.
- **Log Name** Specifies the name of the log in which the event was entered.
- **Source** Identifies the source of the event, such as an application, service, or system component. The event source is useful for pinpointing the cause of an event.
- **Task Category** Specifies the category of the event, which is sometimes used to further describe the related action. Each event source has its own event categories. For example, with the security source, categories include logon/logoff, privilege use, policy change, and account management.
- **User** Identifies the user account that caused the event to be generated. Users can include special identities, such as Local Service, Network Service, and Anonymous Logon, as well as actual user accounts. The user account can also be listed as N/A to indicate that a user account is not applicable in this particular situation.

The GUI tool you use to manage events is Event Viewer. You can start this tool by typing **eventvwr** at the PowerShell prompt for the local computer or **eventvwr *ComputerName***, where *ComputerName* is the name of the remote computer whose events you want to examine. As with most GUI tools, Event Viewer is easy to use, and you might want to continue to use it for certain management tasks.

PowerShell provides several commands for working with the event logs, including the following:

- **Get-WinEvent** Gets events from event logs and event tracing log files on the local computer or specified remote computers. It is supported only on Windows Vista, Windows Server 2008, and later versions of Windows.

```
Get-WinEvent [-ListLog] LogNames {BasicParams}
Get-WinEvent [-ListProvider] ProviderNames {BasicParams}

Get-WinEvent [-Path] LogFilePath {BasicParams} {AddtlParams}
Get-WinEvent [-LogName] LogName {BasicParams} {AddtlParams}
Get-WinEvent [-ProviderName] Name {BasicParams} {AddtlParams}
Get-WinEvent -FilterHashTable Values {BasicParams} {AddtlParams}
```

```
{BasicParams}
[-ComputerName ComputerName] [-Credential CredentialObject]

{AddtlParams}
[-FilterXPath XPathQuery] [-Oldest] [-MaxEvents NumEvents]
```

REAL WORLD **XPath queries help you create custom or filtered views of event logs, allowing you to quickly and easily find events that match specific criteria. Because XPath queries can be used on any compatible system, you can re-create custom and filtered views on other computers simply by running the query on a target computer.**

- **Clear-EventLog** Deletes all entries from specified event logs on the local computer or specified remote computers.

```
Clear-EventLog [[-ComputerName] ComputerNames] [-LogName] LogNames
```

- **Get-EventLog** Gets a list of the event logs or the events in a specified event log on local or remote computers.

```
Get-EventLog [-List] [-ComputerName ComputerNames] [-AsString]

Get-EventLog [-ComputerName ComputerNames] [-LogName] LogName
[-AsBaseObject] [-After DateTime] [-Before DateTime]
[-EntryType EntryTypes] [-Index IndexValues] [[-InstanceID] ID]
[-Message Message] [-Newest NumEvents] [-Source Sources]
[-UserName UserNames]
```

- **Limit-EventLog** Configures limits on event log size and event retention for specified logs on specified computers.

```
Limit-EventLog [-ComputerName ComputerNames] [-MaximumKiloBytes
MaxSize] [-OverFlowAction {DoNotOverwrite | OverwriteAsNeeded |
OverwriteOlder] [-Retention MinDays] [-LogName] LogNames
```

- **Show-EventLog** Displays the event logs of the local computer or a remote computer in Event Viewer.

```
Show-EventLog [[-ComputerName] ComputerName]
```

NOTE **You can use Get-Event, Wait-Event, and Remove-Event to work with the PowerShell event log. When you are creating your own event logs, you can use New-EventLog, Register-ObjectEvent, Register-EngineEvent, Unregister-Event, Get-EventSubscriber, and Register-WmiEvent.**

Monitoring system events isn't something you should do haphazardly. Rather, it is something you should do routinely and thoroughly. With servers, you will want to examine event logs at least once a day. With desktop computers, you will want to examine logs on specific computers as necessary, such as when a user reports a problem.

Viewing and Filtering Event Logs

You can obtain detailed information from the event logs using either Get-EventLog or Get-WinEvent. Get-EventLog is handy for its versatility and simplicity. Use Get-WinEvent when you want to apply complex filters, such as those based on XPath queries or hashtable strings. If you don't use complex filters, you really don't need Get-WinEvent.

The basic syntax for Get-EventLog is

```
get-eventlog "LogName" [-computername ComputerNames]
```

where *LogName* is the name of the log you want to work with—such as "Application," "System," or "Directory Service"—and *ComputerNames* are the names of remote computers you want to work with. In this example, you examine the Application log:

```
get-eventlog "Application" -computername fileserver87, dbserver23
```

> ***NOTE*** **Technically, the quotation marks are necessary only when the log name contains a space, as is the case with the DNS Server, Directory Service, and File Replication Service logs.**

The output of this query will look similar to the following:

```
Index  Time          EntryType   Source          InstanceID Message
-----  ----          ---------   ------          ---------- -------
22278  Feb 27 10:54 Information DQLWinService            0 The description
for Event ID '0' in Source 'DQL
22277  Feb 27 10:49  Information DQLWinService            0 The description
for Event ID '0' in Source 'DQL
```

As you can see, the output shows the Index, Time, EntryType, Source, InstanceID, and Message properties of events. The Index is the position of the event in the event log. The Time is the time the event was written. The EntryType shows the category of the event. The Source shows the source of the event. The InstanceID shows the specific event that occurred with a numeric identifier (and is the same as the EventID field in the event logs). The Message shows the description of the event.

Because the index is the position of the event in the log, this example lists events 22,277 and 22,278. By default, Get-EventLog returns every event in the specified event log from newest to oldest. In most cases, this is simply too much information, and you'll need to filter the events to get a usable amount of data. One way to filter the event logs is to specify that you want to see details about only the newest events. For example, you might want to see only the 50 newest events in a log.

Using the –Newest parameter, you can limit the return to the newest events. The following example lists the 50 newest events in the security log:

```
get-eventlog "security" -newest 50
```

One of the key reasons for using Get-EventLog is its ability to group and filter events in the result set. When you group events by type, you can more easily separate informational events from critical, warning, and error events. When you group by source, you can more easily track events from specific sources. When you group by event ID, you can more easily correlate the recurrence of specific events.

You can group events by Source, EventId, EntryType, and TimeGenerated using the following technique:

1. Get the events you want to work with, and store them in a variable, such as

    ```
    $e = get-eventlog -newest 100 -logname "application"
    ```

2. Use the Group-Object cmdlet to group the event objects by a specified property. In this example, you group by EventType:

    ```
    $e | group-object -property eventtype
    ```

Another way to work with events is to sort them according to a specific property. You can sort by Source, EventId, EntryType, or TimeGenerated using the following technique:

1. Get the events you want to work with, and store them in a variable, such as

    ```
    $e = get-eventlog -newest 100 -logname "application"
    ```

2. Use the Sort-Object cmdlet to sort the event objects by a specified property. In this example, you sort by EntryType:

    ```
    $e | sort-object -property entrytype
    ```

Typically, you won't want to see every event generated on a system. More often, you will want to see only warnings or critical errors, and that is precisely what filters are for. Using filters, you can include only events that match the criteria you specify. To do this, you search the EntryType property for occurrences of the word *error*. Here is an example:

1. Get the events you want to work with, and store them in a variable, such as

    ```
    $e = get-eventlog -newest 500 -logname "application"
    ```

2. Use the Where-Object cmdlet to search for specific text in a named property of the event objects stored in $e. In this example, you match events with the Error entry type:

```
$e | where-object {$_.EntryType -match "error"}
```

With the –Match parameter, the Where-Object cmdlet uses a search algorithm that is not case-sensitive, meaning you can type **Error**, **error**, or **ERROR** to match error events. You can also search for warning, critical, and information events. Because Where-Object considers partial text matches to be valid, you don't want to enter the full entry type. You can also search for **warn**, **crit**, or **info**, such as

```
$e = get-eventlog -newest 100 -logname "application"
$e | where-object {$_.EntryType -match "warn"}
```

You can use Where-Object with other event object properties as well. The following example searches for event sources containing the text *User Profile Service*:

```
$e = get-eventlog -newest 500 -logname "application"
$e | where-object {$_.Source -match "User Profile Service"}
```

The following example searches for event ID *1530*:

```
$e = get-eventlog -newest 500 -logname "application"
$e | where-object {$_.EventID -match "1530"}
```

Sometimes, you'll want to find events that occurred before or after a specific date, and you can do this using the –Before and –After parameters. The –Before parameter gets only the events that occur before a specified date and time. The –After parameter gets only the events that occur after a specified date and time.

In the following example, you get all of the errors in the System log that occurred in July 2010:

```
$Jun30 = get-date 6/30/10
$Aug1 = get-date 8/01/10

get-eventlog -log "system" -entrytype Error -after $jun30 -before $aug1
```

In the following example, you get all of the errors in the System log that occurred in the last seven days:

```
$startdate = (get-date).adddays(-7)
get-eventlog -log "system" -entrytype Error -after $startdate
```

You can automate the event querying process by creating a script that obtains the event information you want to see and then writes it to a text file. Consider the following example:

```
$e = get-eventlog -newest 100 -logname "system" $e | where-object
{$_.EntryType -match "error"} > \\FileServer18\www\currentlog.txt


$e = get-eventlog -newest 100 -logname "application" $e | where-object
{$_.EntryType -match "error"} >> \\FileServer18\www\currentlog.txt


$e = get-eventlog -newest 100 -logname "security" $e | where-object
{$_.EntryType -match "error"} >> \\FileServer18\www\currentlog.txt
```

Here, you are examining the system, application, and security event logs and writing any resulting output to a network share on FileServer18. If any of the named logs have error events among the 100 most recent events in the logs, the errors are written to the CurrentLog.txt file. Because the first redirection is overwrite (>) and the remaining entries are append (>>), any existing Currentlog.txt file is overwritten each time the script runs. This ensures that only current events are listed. To take the automation process a step further, you could create a scheduled task that runs the script each day or at specific intervals during the day.

Setting Log Options

Log options allow you to control the size of the event logs as well as how logging is handled. By default, event logs are set with a maximum file size. Then, when a log reaches this limit, events are overwritten to prevent the log from exceeding the maximum file size.

You use Limit-EventLog to set log options. The basic syntax is

```
Limit-EventLog [-ComputerName ComputerNames] [-LogName] LogNames Options
```

Here *ComputerNames* are the names of the computers you are configuring, *LogNames* sets the logs to modify, and *Options* includes one or more of the following:

- **–MaximumSize** Sets the maximum size in bytes of a log file. The size must be in the range 64 KB to 4 GB, in increments of 64 KB. Make sure that the drive containing the operating system has enough free space for the maximum log size you select. Most log files are stored in the %SystemRoot%\System32\Winevt\Logs directory by default.
- **–OverFlowAction** Sets the event log wrapping mode. The options are DoNotOverwrite, OverwriteAsNeeded, and OverwriteOlder. With DoNotOverwrite, the computer generates error messages telling you the event log is full when the maximum file size is reached. With OverwriteAsNeeded, each new entry overwrites the oldest entry when the maximum file size is reached,

and there are no limitations. With OverwriteOlder, new events overwrite only events older than the value specified by the Retention property when the maximum file size is reached. If there are no events older than the minimum retention value, the computer generates error messages telling you events cannot be overwritten.

- **–Retention** Sets the minimum number of days that an event must remain in the event log.

In the following example, you configure the system log with a maximum size of 4096 KB, an overflow action of OverwriteOlder, and a minimum retention period of seven days:

```
limit-eventlog -maximumsize 4096kb -overflowaction overwriteolder
-retention 7 -logname system
```

If you are configuring multiple computers, you can use the –ComputerName property to specify the computer names. Or you can get the list of computer names from a text file as shown in the following example:

```
limit-eventlog -computername (get-content c:\data\clist.txt)
-maximumkilobytes 4096 -overflowaction overwriteolder -retention 7
-logname system
```

Here, you get the list of remote computers to manage from a file called CList.txt in the C:\Data directory.

Archiving and Clearing Event Logs

On key systems such as domain controllers and application servers, you'll want to keep several months' worth of event logs. However, it usually isn't practical to set the maximum log size to accommodate this. Instead, you should allow Windows to periodically archive the event logs, or you should manually archive the event logs. Logs can be archived in four formats:

- Event files (.evtx) format, for access in Event Viewer
- Tab-delimited text (.txt) format, for access in text editors or word processors or for import into spreadsheets and databases
- Comma-delimited text (.csv) format, for import into spreadsheets or databases
- XML (.xml) format, for saving as a structured Extensible Markup Language (XML) file.

The best format to use for archiving is the .evtx format. Use this format if you plan to review old logs in the Event Viewer. However, if you plan to review logs in other applications, you might need to save the logs in a tab-delimited or comma-delimited format. With the tab-delimited or comma-delimited format, you sometimes need to edit the log file in a text editor for the log to be properly interpreted. If you have saved the log in the .evtx format, you can always save another copy in the tab-delimited or comma-delimited format later by doing another Save As after opening the archive in the Event Viewer.

Windows creates log archives automatically when you select the event log-wrapping mode Archive The Log When Full, Do Not Overwrite Events. This mode is set in Event Viewer.

You can create a log archive manually by following these steps:

1. In Event Viewer, you should see a list of event logs. Right-click the event log you want to archive, and select Save Events As from the shortcut menu.
2. In the Save As dialog box, select a directory and type a log file name.
3. In the Save As Type dialog box, Event Files (*.evtx) is the default file type. Select a log format as appropriate and then choose Save.
4. If the Display Information dialog box is displayed, choose the appropriate display options and then click OK.

If you plan to archive logs regularly, you might want to create an archive directory. This way you can easily locate the log archives. You should also name the log file so that you can easily determine the log file type and the period of the archive. For example, if you're archiving the system log file for January 2010, you might want to use the file name System Log January 2010.

When an event log is full and you want to clear it, you can do so using Clear-EventLog. The basic syntax is

```
Clear-EventLog [-ComputerName ComputerNames] [-LogName] LogNames
```

Here *ComputerNames* are the names of the computers you are configuring and *LogNames* sets the logs to clear, such as

```
clear-eventlog system
```

Writing Custom Events to the Event Logs

Whenever you work with automated scripts, scheduled tasks, or custom applications, you might want those scripts, tasks, or applications to write custom events to the event logs. For example, if a script runs normally, you might want to write an informational event in the application log that specifies this so that it is easier to determine that the script ran and completed normally. Similarly, if a script doesn't run normally and generates errors, you might want to log an error or warning event in the application log so that you'll know to examine the script and determine what happened.

Windows PowerShell includes built-in logging features that log events to the PowerShell event log. You can view events in this log using Get-EventLog. You control logging using the following environment variables, which must be set in the appropriate profile or profiles to be applicable:

- **$LogCommandHealthEvent** Determines whether errors and exceptions in command initialization and processing are logged
- **$LogCommandLifecycleEvent** Determines whether PowerShell logs the starting and stopping of commands and command pipelines and security exceptions in command discovery
- **$LogEngineHealthEvent** Determines whether PowerShell logs errors and failures of sessions
- **$LogEngineLifecycleEvent** Determines whether PowerShell logs the opening and closing of sessions
- **$LogProviderHealthEvent** Determines whether PowerShell logs provider errors, such as read and write errors, lookup errors, and invocation errors
- **$LogProviderLifecycleEvent** Determines whether PowerShell logs adding and removing of PowerShell providers

If you set a logging variable to $True, the related events are logged in the PowerShell log. Use a value of $False to turn off logging.

You can create custom events using the Eventcreate utility. Custom events can be logged in any available log except the security log, and they can include the event source, ID, and description you want to use. The syntax for Eventcreate is as follows:

```
eventcreate /l LogName /so EventSource /t EventType /id EventID
/d EventDescr
```

- **LogName** Sets the name of the log to which the event should be written. Use quotation marks if the log name contains spaces, as in "DNS Server."

  TIP **Although you cannot write custom events to the security log, you can write custom events to the other logs. Start by writing a dummy event using the event source you want to register for use with that log. The initial event for that source will be written to the application log. You can then use the source with the specified log and your custom events.**

- **EventSource** Specifies the source to use for the event, and can be any string of characters. If the string contains spaces, use quotation marks, as in "Event Tracker." In most cases, you'll want the event source to identify the application, task, or script that is generating the error.

  REAL WORLD **Carefully plan the event source you want to use before you write events to the logs using those sources. Each event source you use must be unique and cannot have the same name as an existing source used by an installed service or application. Further, you shouldn't use event source names used by Windows roles, role services, or features. For example, you shouldn't use DNS, W32Time, or Ntfrs as sources because these sources are used by Windows Server 2008.**

Additionally, once you use an event source with a particular log, the event source is registered for use with that log on the specified system. For example, you cannot use "EventChecker" as a source in the application log and in the system log on FILESERVER82. If you try to write an event using "EventChecker" to the system log after writing a previous event with that source to the application log, you will see the following error message: "ERROR: Source already exists in 'Application' log. Source cannot be duplicated."

- **EventType** Sets the event type as Information, Warning, or Error. Audit Success and Audit Failure event types are not valid; these events are used with the security logs, and you cannot write custom events to the security logs.
- **EventID** Specifies the numeric ID for the event, and can be any value from 1 to 1,000. Before you assign event IDs haphazardly, you might want to create a list of the general events that can occur and then break these down into categories. You can then assign a range of event IDs to each category. For example, events in the 100s could be general events, events in the 200s could be status events, events in the 500s could be warning events, and events in the 900s could be error events.
- **EventDescr** Sets the description for the event, and can be any string of characters. Be sure to enclose the description in quotation marks.

Eventcreate runs by default on the local computer with the permissions of the user who is currently logged on. As necessary, you can also specify the remote computer whose tasks you want to query and the Run As permissions using ***/S Computer* /u [*Domain*\]*User* [/P *Password*]**, where *Computer* is the remote computer name or IP address, *Domain* is the optional domain name in which the user account is located, *User* is the name of the user account whose permissions you want to use, and *Password* is the optional password for the user account.

To see how you can use Eventcreate, consider the following examples:

CREATE AN INFORMATION EVENT IN THE APPLICATION LOG WITH THE SOURCE EVENT TRACKER AND EVENT ID 209:

```
eventcreate /l "application" /t information /so "Event Tracker"
/id 209 /d "evs.bat script ran without errors."
```

CREATE A WARNING EVENT IN THE SYSTEM LOG WITH THE SOURCE CUSTAPP AND EVENT ID 511:

```
eventcreate /l "system" /t warning /so "CustApp" /id 511
/d "sysck.exe didn't complete successfully."
```

CREATE AN ERROR EVENT IN THE SYSTEM LOG ON FILESERVER18 WITH THE SOURCE "SYSMON" AND EVENT ID 918:

```
eventcreate /s FileServer18 /l "system" /t error /so "SysMon"
/id 918 /d "sysmon.exe was unable to verify write operation."
```

Creating and Using Saved Queries

For Windows Vista, Windows Server 2008, and later, Microsoft significantly enhanced Event Viewer's filtering and query capabilities. Because of these enhancements, Event Viewer now supports XPath queries for creating custom views and filtering event logs. XPath is a non-XML language used to identify specific parts of XML documents. Event Viewer uses XPath expressions that match and select elements in a source log and copy them to a destination log to create a custom or filtered view.

When you are creating a custom or filtered view in Event Viewer, you can copy the XPath query and save it to an Event Viewer Custom View file. By running this query again, you can re-create the custom view or filter on any computer running Windows Vista or Windows Server 2008. For example, if you create a filtered view of the application log that helps you identify a problem with SQL Server, you can save the related XPath query to a Custom View file so that you can create the filtered view on other computers in your organization.

Event Viewer creates several filtered views of the event logs for you automatically. Filtered views are listed under the Custom Views node. When you select the Administrative Events node, you see a list of all errors and warnings for all logs. When you expand the Server Roles node and then select a role-specific view, you see a list of all events for the selected role.

You can create and save your own custom view by following these steps:

1. Start Event Viewer by clicking Event Viewer on the Administrative Tools menu.
2. Select the Custom Views node. In the Actions pane or on the Action menu, click Create Custom View.
3. In the Create Custom View dialog box, use the Logged list to select the included time frame for logged events. You can choose to include events from Anytime, Last Hour, Last 12 Hours, Last 24 Hours, Last 7 Days, or Last 30 Days. You also can specify a custom range.
4. Use the Event Level check boxes to specify the level of events to include. Select Verbose to get additional detail.
5. You can create a custom view for either a specific set of logs or a specific set of event sources:
   - Use the Event Logs list to select event logs to include. You can select multiple event logs by selecting their related check boxes. If you select specific event logs, all other event logs are excluded.
   - Use the Event Sources list to select event sources to include. You can select multiple event sources by selecting their related check boxes. If you select specific event sources, all other event sources are excluded.
6. Optionally, use the User and Computer(s) boxes to specify users and computers that should be included. If you do not specify the users and computers to be included, events generated by all users and computers are included.

7. Click the XML tab to display the related XPath query.
8. Click OK to close the Create Custom View dialog box. In the Save Filter To Custom View dialog box, type a name and description for the custom view.
9. Select where to save the custom view. By default, custom views are saved under the Custom View node. You can create a new node by clicking New Folder, typing the name of the new folder, and then clicking OK.
10. Click OK to close the Save Filter To Custom View dialog box. You should now see a filtered list of events.
11. Right-click the custom view and then select Export Custom View. Use the Save As dialog box to select a save location and enter a file name for the Event Viewer Custom View file.

The Custom View file contains the XPath query that was displayed on the XML tab previously. Members of the Event Log Readers group, administrators, and others with appropriate permissions can run the query to view events on remote computers using the following syntax:

```
eventvwr ComputerName /v: QueryFile
```

Here *ComputerName* is the name of the remote computer whose events you want to examine and *QueryFile* is the name or full path to the Custom View file containing the XPath query, such as

```
eventvwr fileserver18 /v: importantevents.xml
```

When Event Viewer starts, you'll find the custom view under the Custom Views node.

Managing System Services

Services provide key functions to workstations and servers. To manage system services on local and remote systems, you use the following commands:

- **Get-Service** Gets information about the services on a local or remote computer, including running and stopped services. You can specify services by their service names or display names, or you can pass in references to service objects to work with.

```
Get-Service [[-Name] ServiceNames] [AddlParams]
Get-Service -DisplayName ServiceNames [AddlParams]
Get-Service [-InputObject ServiceObjects] [AddlParams]

{AddlParams}
[-ComputerName ComputerNames] [-DependentServices] [-Exclude
ServiceNames] [-Include ServiceNames] [-ServicesDependedOn]
```

- **Stop-Service** Stops one or more running services. You can specify services by their service names or display names, or you can pass in references to service objects to work with. Services that can be stopped indicate this because the CanStop property is set to True. Further, you can stop only a service that is in a state where stopping is permitted.

```
Stop-Service [-Name] ServiceNames [AddlParams]
Stop-Service -DisplayName ServiceNames [AddlParams]
Stop-Service [-InputObject ServiceObjects] [AddlParams]

{AddlParams}
[-Include ServiceNames] [-Exclude ServiceNames] [-Force]
[-PassThru]
```

- **Start-Service** Starts one or more stopped services. You can specify services by their service names or display names, or you can pass in references to service objects to work with.

```
Start-Service [-Name] ServiceNames [AddlParams]
Start-Service -DisplayName ServiceNames [AddlParams]
Start-Service [-InputObject ServiceObjects] [AddlParams]

{AddlParams}
[-Include ServiceNames] [-Exclude ServiceNames] [-Force]
[-PassThru]
```

- **Suspend-Service** Suspends (pauses) one or more running services. While paused, a service is still running, but its execution is halted until it is resumed. You can specify services by their service names or display names, or you can pass in references to service objects to work with. Services that can be suspended indicate this because the CanPauseAndContinue property is set to True. Further, you can pause only a service that is in a state where pausing is permitted.

```
Suspend-Service [-Name] ServiceNames [AddlParams]
Suspend-Service -DisplayName ServiceNames [AddlParams]
Suspend-Service [-InputObject ServiceObjects] [AddlParams]

{AddlParams}
[-Exclude ServiceNames] [-Include ServiceNames] [-PassThru]
```

- **Resume-Service** Resumes one or more suspended (paused) services. If you reference a service that is not paused, the control change is ignored. You can specify services by their service names or display names, or you can pass in references to service objects to work with.

```
Resume-Service [-Name] ServiceNames [AddlParams]
Resume-Service -DisplayName ServiceNames [AddlParams]
Resume-Service [-InputObject ServiceObjects] [AddlParams]

{AddlParams}
[-Exclude ServiceNames] [-Include ServiceNames] [-PassThru]
```

- **Restart-Service** Stops and then starts one or more services. If a service is already stopped, it is started. You can specify services by their service names or display names, or you can pass in references to service objects to work with.

```
Restart-Service [-Name] ServiceNames [AddlParams]
Restart-Service -DisplayName ServiceNames [AddlParams]
Restart-Service [-InputObject ServiceObjects] [AddlParams]

{AddlParams}
[-Include ServiceNames] [-Exclude ServiceNames] [-Force]
[-PassThru]
```

- **Set-Service** Changes the properties or status of a service on a local or remote computer. Use the status to change the state of the service.

```
Set-Service [-Name] ServiceName [ | -InputObject ServiceObjects]
[-DisplayName DisplayName] [-Description Description]
[-StartupType {Automatic | Manual | Disabled}]
[-Status {Running | Stopped | Paused}] [-PassThru] [-ComputerName
ComputerNames]
```

- **New-Service** Creates a new Windows service in the registry and in the services database. Pass in a credential if required to create the service.

```
New-Service [-Credential CredentialObject] [-DependsOn
ServiceNames] [-Description Description] [-DisplayName DisplayName]
[-StartupType {Automatic | Manual | Disabled}]
[-Name] Name [-BinaryPathName] PathtoExeFile
```

With some of these commands, you can specify the name of the remote computer whose services you want to work with. To do this, use the –ComputerName parameter and then specify the NetBIOS name, IP address, or fully qualified domain name (FQDN) of the remote computer or computers that you want to work with. In some cases, you might want to specify the local computer as well as a remote computer. To reference the local computer, type the computer name, a dot (.), or "localhost".

Viewing Configured Services

To get a list of all services configured on a system, type **get-service** at the command prompt. Using the –ComputerName parameter, you can specify a remote computer to work with, as shown in the following example and sample output:

```
get-service -computername fileserver86
```

```
Status   Name               DisplayName
------   ----               -----------
Stopped  AppMgmt            Application Management
Running  AudioEndpointBu... Windows Audio Endpoint Builder
Running  Audiosrv           Windows Audio
Running  BFE                Base Filtering Engine
Running  BITS               Background Intelligent Transfer Ser...
Running  Browser            Computer Browser
Stopped  CertPropSvc        Certificate Propagation
```

The –ComputerName parameter accepts multiple name values. You can check the status of services on multiple computers simply by entering the names of the computers to check in a comma-separated list as shown in the following example:

```
get-service -computername fileserver86, dcserver22, printserver31
```

Rather than type computer names each time, you can enter computer names on separate lines in a text file and then get the list of computer names from the text file, as shown in the following example:

```
get-service -computername (get-content c:\data\clist.txt)
```

Here, you get the list of remote computers to check from a file called CList.txt in the C:\Data directory.

When you are looking for a specific service, you can reference the service by its service name or display name. To match partial names, you can use wildcard characters as shown in the following example and sample output:

```
get-service -displayname *browser* -computername fileserver86
```

```
Status   Name               DisplayName
------   ----               -----------
Running  Browser            Computer Browser
```

Here, you look for all services where the display name includes the word *browser*.

Get-Service returns objects representing each service matching the criteria you specify. From previous examples and sample output, you can see that the standard output includes the Status, Name, and DisplayName properties. To view all of the available properties, you need to format the output as a list, as shown in the following example and sample output:

```
get-service -displayname *browser* -computername server12 | format-list *
```

```
Name                : Browser
CanPauseAndContinue : False
CanShutdown         : False
CanStop             : True
DisplayName         : Computer Browser
DependentServices   : {}
MachineName         : Server12
ServiceName         : Browser
ServicesDependedOn  : {LanmanServer, LanmanWorkstation}
ServiceHandle       :
Status              : Running
ServiceType         : Win32ShareProcess
Site                :
Container           :
```

The output shows the exact configuration of the service. As an administrator, you will work with the following properties most often:

- **Name/ServiceName** The abbreviated name of the service. Only services installed on the system are listed here. If a service you need isn't listed, you'll need to install it.
- **DisplayName** The descriptive name of the service.
- **Status** The state of the service as Running, Paused, or Stopped.
- **DependentServices** Services that cannot run unless the specified service is running.
- **ServicesDependedOn** The services this service relies on to operate.
- **Type** The type of service and whether it is a shared process.
- **MachineName** The name of the computer the service is configured on. This property is available only when you use the –ComputerName property.

TIP **When you are configuring services, it is sometimes important to know whether a process runs in its own context or is shared. Shared processes are listed as WIN32SHAREPROCESS. Processes that run in their own context are listed as WIN32OWNPROCESS.**

By default, Get-Service looks at all services regardless of their status. With the Status property, you can work with services in a specific state, such as Stopped or Paused. Consider the following examples:

```
get-service | where-object {$_.status -eq "Running"}
get-service | where-object {$_.status -eq "Stopped"}
```

In the first example, you list all services that are running. In the second example, you list all services that are stopped.

Starting, Stopping, and Pausing Services

As an administrator, you'll often have to start, stop, or pause Windows services. When you are working with an elevated, administrator PowerShell prompt, you can do this using the service-related cmdlets or the methods of the Win32_Service class. Examples using the service cmdlets follow:

START A SERVICE:

```
start-service ServiceName
start-service -displayname DisplayName
get-service ServiceName | start-service
```

PAUSE A SERVICE:

```
suspend-service ServiceName
suspend-service -displayname DisplayName
get-service ServiceName | suspend-service
```

RESUME A PAUSED SERVICE:

```
resume-service ServiceName
resume-service -displayname DisplayName
get-service ServiceName | resume-service
```

STOP A SERVICE:

```
stop-service ServiceName
stop-service -displayname DisplayName
get-service ServiceName | stop-service
```

In this example, *ServiceName* in each case is the abbreviated name of a service, and *DisplayName* is the descriptive name of a service, such as

```
stop-service -displayname "DNS Client"
```

Although Start-Service, Suspend-Service, Resume-Service, and Stop-Service don't support the –ComputerName parameter, you can use the following technique to manage the state of services on remote computers:

```
get-service dnscache -computername engpc18 | stop-service
get-service dnscache -computername engpc18 | start-service
```

```
invoke-command -computername engpc18 -scriptblock {get-service dnscache |
stop-service }
invoke-command -computername engpc18 -scriptblock {get-service dnscache |
start-service }
```

Here, you use Get-Service to get a Service object on a remote computer, and then you manage the service using Start-Service, Suspend-Service, Resume-Service, or Stop-Service as appropriate. Note that these commands report only failure. They won't tell you that the service was already started, stopped, paused, or resumed.

Before you stop or pause a service, you should check to see if the service can be stopped or paused. With Service objects, the properties you can check are CanPauseAndContinue and CanStop. An example and sample output follow:

```
$sname = read-host "Enter service name to stop"
$cname = read-host "Enter computer to work with"

$s = get-service $sname -computername $cname
if ($s.CanStop -eq $True) { $s | stop-service }
```

```
Enter service name to stop : dnscache
Enter computer to work with : engpc85
```

Here, you get the name of the service and computer to work with by prompting the user, and then you get the related Service object. If the service can be stopped, you stop the service. As shown in the following example and sample output, you can easily extend this basic functionality to perform other actions on services:

```
$cname = read-host "Enter computer to work with"
$sname = read-host "Enter service name to work with"

$s = get-service $sname -computername $cname
write-host "Service is:" $s.status -foregroundcolor green

$action = read-host "Specify action [Start|Stop|Pause|Resume]"

switch ($action) {

"start" { $s | start-service }
"stop" { if ($s.CanStop -eq $True) { $s | stop-service } }
"pause" { if ($s.CanPauseAndContinue -eq $True) { $s | pause-service } }
"resume" { $s | resume-service }

}

$su = get-service $sname -computername $cname
write-host "Service is:" $su.status -foregroundcolor green
```

```
Enter computer to work with: techpc12
Enter service name to work with: dnscache
Service is: Running
Specify action [Start|Stop|Pause|Resume]: stop
Service is:  Stopped
```

Here, you get the name of the service and computer to work with by prompting the user, and then you get the related Service object. Next, you display the current status of the service and then get the action to perform on the service. After performing CanStop and CanPauseAndContinue tests if appropriate and taking the appropriate action on the service, you display the updated status of the service.

REAL WORLD **Want to manage services any time you are working with PowerShell? Wrap this code in a function, and add it to your profile. Then you can manage services simply by calling the function. Here is an example:**

```
function ms {
 #Insert code here
}
```

Now any time your profile is loaded and you type ms at the PowerShell prompt, you'll be able to manage services on any computer in the enterprise.

Configuring Service Startup

You can set Windows services to start manually or automatically. You also can turn services off permanently by disabling them. You configure service startup using

```
set-service ServiceName -StartupType Type [-ComputerName ComputerNames]
```

or

```
set-service -displayname DisplayName -StartupType Type [-ComputerName
ComputerNames]
```

where *ServiceName* or *DisplayName* identifies the service to modify, *Type* is the startup type to use, and *ComputerNames* are the names of the computers to work with. The valid startup types are:

- **Automatic** Starts a service at system startup. If the service requires a delayed start, the subtype Automatic (Delayed Start) is assigned automatically.
- **Manual** Allows the service to be started manually by the service control manager when a process invokes the service.
- **Disable** Disables the service to prevent it from being started the next time the computer is started. If the service is running, it will continue to run until the computer is shut down. You can stop the service if necessary.

Following this, you can configure a service to start automatically by using

```
set-service dnscache -startuptype automatic
```

or

```
set-service dnscache -startuptype automatic -computername techpc85
```

Instead of typing a comma-separated list of computer names, you can enter computer names on separate lines in a text file and then get the list of computer names from the text file as shown in the following example:

```
set-service dnscache -startuptype automatic -computername (get-content
c:\data\clist.txt)
```

Here, you get the list of remote computers to work with from a file called CList.txt in the C:\Data directory.

Set-Service also lets you start, stop, and pause services. If you are enabling a service on multiple computers, you also might want to start the service. You can enable and start a service as shown in the following example:

```
set-service w3svc -startuptype automatic -status running
```

If you are disabling a service on multiple computers, you also might want to stop the service. You can disable and stop a service as shown in the following example:

```
set-service w3svc -startuptype disabled -status stopped
```

Managing Service Logon and Recovery Modes

Occasionally, you might need to manage service logon and recovery options. The easiest way to do this is to use the Services Configuration utility. This utility has several subcommands that allow you to work with Windows services. The executable for this utility is sc.exe. Although you normally can type **sc** at the prompt and run this utility, *sc* is a default alias for Set-Content in Windows PowerShell. For this reason, you must type **sc.exe** whenever you work with this utility at the PowerShell prompt.

Configuring Service Logon

Using the SC config command, you can configure Windows services to log on as a system account or as a specific user. To ensure a service logs on as the LocalSystem account, use

```
sc.exe ComputerName config ServiceName obj= LocalSystem
```

where *ComputerName* is the Universal Naming Convention (UNC) name of the computer to work with, and *ServiceName* is the name of the service you are configuring to use the LocalSystem account. If the service provides a user interface that can be manipulated, add the flags **type= interact type= own**, as shown in the following example:

```
sc.exe config vss obj= LocalSystem type= interact type= own
```

or

```
sc.exe \\techpc85 config vss obj= LocalSystem type= interact type= own
```

> **NOTE** You must include a space after the equal sign (=) as shown. If you don't use a space, the command will fail. Note also these commands report only SUCCESS or FAILURE. They won't tell you that the service was already configured in a specified way.

The *type= interact* flag specifies that the service is allowed to interact with the Windows desktop. The type= own flag specifies that the service runs in its own process. In the case of a service that shares its executable files with other services, you use the type= share flag, as shown in this example:

```
sc.exe config dnscache obj= LocalSystem type= interact type= share
```

> **TIP** If you don't know whether a service runs as a shared process or in its own context, you should determine the service's start type using Get-Service.

Services can also log on using named accounts. To do this, use

```
sc.exe config ServiceName obj= [Domain\]User password= Password
```

where *Domain* is the optional domain name in which the user account is located, *User* is the name of the user account whose permissions you want to use, and *Password* is the password of that account. Consider the following example:

```
sc.exe config vss obj= adatum\backers password= TenMen55!
```

Here, you configure Microsoft Visual SourceSafe (VSS) to use the Backers account in the Adatum domain. The output of the command should state SUCCESS or FAILED. The change will fail if the account name is invalid or doesn't exist, or if the password for the account is invalid.

> **NOTE** If a service has been previously configured to interact with the desktop under the LocalSystem account, you cannot change the service to run under a domain account without using the *type= own* flag. The syntax therefore becomes `sc config ServiceName obj= [Domain\]User password= Password type= own`.

Although SC is designed to work with individual computers, you can use the built-in features of Windows PowerShell to modify the way SC works, as shown in the following example:

```
$c = "\\techpc85"
sc.exe $c query dnscache
```

Here, rather than specifying the computer name explicitly, you pass in the computer name as a variable.

You can extend this basic technique to get a list of remote computers to work with from a file. Here is an example:

```
$computers = (get-content c:\data\unclist.txt)
foreach ($c in $computers) { sc.exe $c query dnscache }
```

Here, you get the list of computers to work with from a file called UncList.txt in the C:\Data directory and then execute an SC query for each computer name.

> ***TIP*** **Don't forget that SC requires computer names to be specified using Universal Naming Convention. This means you must type \\\\techpc85 rather than techpc85 in the text file from which computer names are obtained.**

Configuring Service Recovery

Using the SC Qfailure and Failure commands, you can view and configure actions taken when a service fails. For example, you can configure a service so that the service control manager attempts to restart it or to run an application that can resolve the problem.

You can configure recovery options for the first, second, and subsequent recovery attempts. The current failure count is incremented each time a failure occurs. You can also set a parameter that specifies the time that must elapse before the failure counter is reset. For example, you can specify that if 24 hours have passed since the last failure, the failure counter should be reset.

Before you try to configure service recovery, check the current recovery settings using SC Qfailure. The syntax is

```
sc.exe ComputerName qfailure ServiceName
```

where *ComputerName* is the UNC name of the computer to work with, and *ServiceName* is the name of the service you want to work with, such as

```
sc.exe qfailure vss
```

or

```
sc.exe \\techpc85 qfailure vss
```

In the output, the failure actions are listed in the order they are performed. In the following example output, VSS is configured to attempt to restart the service the first and second times the service fails and to restart the computer if the service fails a third time:

```
[SC] QueryServiceConfig2 SUCCESS

SERVICE_NAME: vss
        RESET_PERIOD (in seconds)    : 86400
        REBOOT_MESSAGE               :
        COMMAND_LINE                 :
         FAILURE_ACTIONS             : RESTART -- Delay = 1 milliseconds.
                                       RESTART -- Delay = 1 milliseconds.
                                       REBOOT -- Delay = 1000 milliseconds.
```

NOTE **Windows automatically configures recovery for some critical system services during installation. Typically, these services are configured so that they attempt to restart the service. Services can be configured so that they run programs or scripts as well upon failure.**

The command you use to configure service recovery is SC Failure, and its basic syntax is

```
sc.exe failure ServiceName reset= FailureResetPeriod actions=
RecoveryActions
```

where *ServiceName* is the name of the service you are configuring; *FailureReset-Period* specifies the time, in seconds, that must elapse without failure in order to reset the failure counter; and *RecoveryActions* are the actions to take when failure occurs plus the delay time (in milliseconds) before that action is initiated. The available recovery actions are:

- **Take No Action** (indicated by an empty string "") The operating system won't attempt recovery for this failure but might still attempt recovery of previous or subsequent failures.
- **Restart The Service** Stops and then starts the service after a brief pause.
- **Run A Program** Allows you to run a program or a script in case of failure. The script can be a batch program or a Windows script. If you select this option, set the full file path to the program you want to run, and then set any necessary command-line parameters to pass in to the program when it starts.
- **Reboot The Computer** Shuts down and then restarts the computer after the specified delay time has elapsed.

NOTE When you configure recovery options for critical services, you might want to try to restart the service on the first and second attempts and then reboot the server on the third attempt.

When you work with SC Failure, keep the following in mind:

- The reset period is set in seconds.

  Reset periods are commonly set in multiples of hours or days. An hour is 3,600 seconds, and a day is 86,400 seconds. For a two-hour reset period, for example, you'd use the value 7,200.
- Each recovery action must be followed by the time to wait (in milliseconds) before performing the action.

  For a service restart, you'll probably want to use a short delay, such as 1 millisecond (no delay), 1 second (1,000 milliseconds), or 5 seconds (5,000 milliseconds). For a restart of the computer, you'll probably want to use a longer delay, such as 15 seconds (15,000 milliseconds) or 30 seconds (30,000 milliseconds).
- Enter the actions and their delay times as a single text entry, with each value separated by a forward slash (/).

  For example, you could use the following value: restart/1000/restart/1000/reboot/15000. Here, on the first and second attempts the service is restarted after a 1-second delay, and on the third attempt the computer is rebooted after a 15-second delay.

Consider the following examples:

```
sc.exe failure w3svc reset= 86400 actions=
restart/1/restart/1/reboot/30000
```

Here, on the first and second attempts the service is restarted almost immediately, and on the third attempt the computer is rebooted after a 30-second delay. In addition, the failure counter is reset if no failures occur in a 24-hour period (86,400 seconds). You can also specify a remote computer by inserting the UNC name or IP address as shown in previous examples.

If you use the Run action, you specify the command or program to run using the Command= parameter. Follow the Command= parameter with the full file path to the command to run and any arguments to pass to the command. Be sure to enclose the command path and text in double quotation marks, as in the following example:

```
sc.exe failure w3svc reset= 86400 actions= restart/1/restart/1/run/30000
command= "c:\restart_w3svc.exe 15"
```

Digging Deeper into Service Management

Although the Get-Service cmdlet provides sufficient details to help you perform many administrative tasks, it doesn't provide the detailed information you might need to know to manage the configuration of services. At a minimum, to manage service configuration, you need to know a service's current start mode and start name. The start mode specifies the startup mode of the service, and the start name specifies the account name under which the service will run. A service's start mode can be set to any of the following:

- **Automatic** Indicates the service is started automatically by the service control manager during startup of the operating system.
- **Manual** Indicates the service is started manually by the service control manager when a process calls the StartService method.
- **Disabled** Indicates the service is disabled and cannot be started.

Most services run under one of the following accounts:

- **NT Authority\LocalSystem** LocalSystem is a pseudo account for running system processes and handling system-level tasks. This account is part of the Administrators group on a computer and has all user rights on the computer. If services use this account, the related processes have full access to the computer. Many services run under the LocalSystem account. In some cases, these services have the privilege to interact with the desktop as well. Services that need alternative privileges or logon rights run under the LocalService or NetworkService accounts.
- **NT Authority\LocalService** LocalService is a pseudo account with limited privileges. This account grants access to the local system only. The account is part of the Users group on the computer and has the same rights as the NetworkService account, except that it is limited to the local computer. If services use this account, the related processes don't have access to other computers.
- **NT Authority\NetworkService** NetworkService is a pseudo account for running services that need additional privileges and logon rights on a local system and the network. This account is part of the Users group on the computer and provides fewer permissions and privileges than the LocalSystem account (but more than the LocalService account). Specifically, processes running under this account can interact throughout a network using the credentials of the computer account.

You can obtain the start mode, start name, and other configuration information for services using Windows Management Instrumentation (WMI) and the Win32_Service class. You use the Win32_Service class to create instances of service objects as they are represented in WMI.

You can list all services configured on a computer by typing **get-wmiobject -class win32_service** as shown in the following example and sample output:

```
get-wmiobject -class win32_service |
format-table name, startmode, state, status
```

```
name                    startmode       state          status
----                    ---------       -----          ------
AppMgmt                 Manual          Stopped        OK
AudioEndpointBuilder    Auto            Running        OK
Audiosrv                Auto            Running        OK
BFE                     Auto            Running        OK
BITS                    Auto            Running        OK
Bonjour Service         Auto            Running        OK
Browser                 Auto            Running        OK
CertPropSvc             Manual          Stopped        OK
```

If you want to work with a specific service or examine services with a specific property value, you can add the –Filter parameter. In the following example and sample output, you check the configuration details of the Browser service:

```
get-wmiobject -class win32_service -filter "name='browser'"
```

```
ExitCode  : 0
Name      : Browser
ProcessId : 1136
StartMode : Auto
State     : Running
Status    : OK
```

If you format the output as a list, you'll see additional configuration information including PathName, which specifies the executable that starts the service and any parameters passed to this executable, and StartName, which specifies the account under which the service runs. In the following example and partial output, you examine the properties of the DNS Client service:

```
$s = get-wmiobject -class win32_service -filter "name='dnscache'"
$s | format-list *
```

```
Name                    : Dnscache
Status                  : OK
ExitCode                : 0
DesktopInteract         : False
ErrorControl            : Normal
PathName                : C:\Windows\system32\svchost.exe -k NetworkService
ServiceType             : Share Process
StartMode               : Manual
AcceptPause             : False
```

```
AcceptStop              : True
Caption                 : DNS Client
CheckPoint              : 0
CreationClassName       : Win32_Service
Description             : Caches Domain Name System (DNS) names.
DisplayName             : DNS Client
InstallDate             :
ProcessId               : 1536
ServiceSpecificExitCode : 0
Started                 : True
StartName               : NT AUTHORITY\NetworkService
State                   : Running
SystemCreationClassName : Win32_ComputerSystem
SystemName              : TechPC85
```

Get-WmiObject supports a –ComputerName parameter that lets you specify the remote computer or computers to work with, as shown in these examples:

```
get-wmiobject -class win32_service -computername fileserver86,
dcserver22, printserver31

get-wmiobject -class win32_service -computername (get-content
c:\data\clist.txt)
```

NOTE **When you are working with multiple computers, you can use the SystemName property to help you determine the name of the computer the service is configured on.**

You can work with the properties of Win32_Service objects in much the same way as you work with properties of Service objects. To see a list of all services configured to start automatically, you can type the following command:

```
get-wmiobject -class win32_service -filter "startmode='auto'" |
format-table name, startmode, state, status
```

To view all running services, you can type

```
get-wmiobject -class win32_service -filter "state='running'" |
format-table name, startmode, state, status
```

The Win32_Service class provides a number of methods for managing system services. These methods include:

- **Change()** Changes the configuration of a user-configurable service. This method accepts the following parameters in the following order: DisplayName, PathName, ServiceTypeByte, ErrorControlByte, StartMode, DesktopInteract-Boolean, StartName, StartPassword, LoadOrderGroup, LoadOrderGroup-DependenciesArray, and ServiceDependenciesArray.

CAUTION **Not all services can be reconfigured. Modifying services at the PowerShell prompt is not something you should do without careful forethought. PowerShell will let you make changes that could put your computer in an unstable state. Before you make any changes to services, you should create a system restore point as discussed in Chapter 14, "Fine-Tuning System Performance."**

- **ChangeStartMode()** Changes the start mode of a user-configurable service. This method accepts a single parameter, which is the start mode to use. Valid values are Manual, Automatic, or Disabled.

NOTE **Some services are configured by default to use delayed-start automatic mode. When you are working with Win32_Service, any time you set these services to Automatic, they use delayed-start automatic mode. Additionally, note that disabling a service doesn't stop a running service. It only prevents the service from being started the next time the computer is booted. To ensure that the service is disabled and stopped, disable and then stop the service.**

CAUTION **Before you change the start mode of a service, you should check dependencies and ensure any changes you make won't affect other services.**

- **Delete()** Deletes a user-configurable service (if the service is in a state that allows this). Rather than delete a service, you should consider disabling it. Disabled services no longer run and can easily be enabled if needed in the future. Deleted services, however, must be reinstalled to be used in the future.

CAUTION **Exercise extreme caution if you plan to delete services using PowerShell. PowerShell will not warn you if you are making harmful changes to your computer.**

- **InterrogateService()** Connects to the service using the service control manager. If the return value is zero, the service control manager was able to connect to and interrogate the service using its configured parameters. If the return value wasn't zero, the service control manager encountered a problem while trying to communicate with the service using the configured parameters. If the service is stopped or paused, this method will always return an error status.
- **PauseService()** Pauses the service, which might be necessary during troubleshooting or when performing diagnostics. Services that can be paused indicate this by setting the AcceptPause property to True for their services. Further, you can pause only a service that is in a state where pausing is permitted.
- **ResumeService()** Resumes the service after it has been paused.

- **StopService()** Stops the service, which might be necessary during troubleshooting or when performing diagnostics. Services that can be stopped indicate this by setting the AcceptStop property to True for their services. Further, you can stop only a service that is in a state where stopping is permitted.
- **StartService()** Starts a stopped service, including services that are configured for manual startup.

When you are working with an elevated, administrator PowerShell prompt, you can use these methods to manage system services. For example, you can set Windows services to start manually or automatically. You can also turn them off permanently by disabling them. You configure service startup using the ChangeStartMode() method to specify the desired start mode. The basic syntax is

```
$serviceObject.ChangeStartMode(StartMode)
```

where *$serviceObject* is a reference to a Win32_Service object, and *StartMode* is the desired start mode entered as a string value, as shown in this example and sample output:

```
$s = get-wmiobject -class win32_service -filter "name='dnscache'"
$s.changestartmode("automatic")
```

```
__GENUS          : 2
__CLASS          : __PARAMETERS
__SUPERCLASS     :
__DYNASTY        : __PARAMETERS
__RELPATH        :
__PROPERTY_COUNT : 1
__DERIVATION     : {}
__SERVER         :
__NAMESPACE      :
__PATH           :
ReturnValue      : 0
```

Here, you set the start mode to Automatic. The return value in the output is what you want to focus on. A return value of 0 indicates success. Any other return value indicates an error. Typically, errors occur because you aren't using an elevated, administrator PowerShell prompt, you haven't accessed the correct service, or the service isn't in a state in which it can be configured. Keep in mind that if you alter the configuration of required services, the computer might not work as expected. Because of this, don't make any changes to services without careful planning and forethought.

NOTE **These commands report only SUCCESS or FAILURE. They won't tell you that the service was already started, stopped, or configured in the startup mode you've specified.**

A technique for invoking methods of WMI objects we haven't discussed previously is using a direct invocation using the Invoke-WMIMethod cmdlet. This cmdlet provides a one-line alternative to the two-line technique that requires you to get a WMI object and then invoke its method. For example, instead of using

```
$s = get-wmiobject -class win32_service -filter "name='dnscache'"
$s.stopservice()
```

you can use

```
invoke-wmimethod -path "win32_service.name='dnscache'" -name stopservice
```

Syntax options for Invoke-WmiMethod include the following:

```
Invoke-WmiMethod [-ComputerName [ComputerNames]] [-Credential
[CredentialObject]] [-Name] [MethodName] [-ThrottleLimit [LimitValue]]
[-AsJob]

Invoke-WmiMethod [-InputObject [WMIObject]] [-Name] [MethodName]
[-ThrottleLimit [LimitValue]] [-AsJob]

Invoke-WmiMethod [-Namespace [WMINamespace]] -Path [WMIPath]
[-ArgumentList [Objects] [-Name] [MethodName] [-ThrottleLimit
[LimitValue]] [-AsJob]

Invoke-WmiMethod [-EnableAllPrivileges] [-Authority [Authority]] [-Name]
[MethodName] [-ThrottleLimit [LimitValue]] [-AsJob]

Invoke-WmiMethod [-Locale [Locale]] [-Name] [MethodName] [-ThrottleLimit
[LimitValue]] [-AsJob]
```

You can use the methods of the Win32_Service class and Invoke-WmiMethod to manage services as shown in the following examples:

START A SERVICE:

```
invoke-wmimethod -path "win32_service.name='ServiceName'"
-name startservice

invoke-wmimethod -path "win32_service.displayname='DisplayName'"
-name startservice

get-wmiobject -class win32_service -filter "name='ServiceName'" |
invoke-wmimethod -name startservice
```

PAUSE A SERVICE:

```
invoke-wmimethod -path "win32_service.name='ServiceName'"
-name pauseservice

invoke-wmimethod -path "win32_service.displayname='DisplayName'"
-name pauseservice

get-wmiobject -class win32_service -filter "name='ServiceName'" |
invoke-wmimethod -name pauseservice
```

RESUME A PAUSED SERVICE:

```
invoke-wmimethod -path "win32_service.name='ServiceName'"
-name resumeservice

invoke-wmimethod -path "win32_service.displayname='DisplayName'"
-name resumeservice

get-wmiobject -class win32_service -filter "name='ServiceName'" |
invoke-wmimethod -name resumeservice
```

STOP A SERVICE:

```
invoke-wmimethod -path "win32_service.name='ServiceName'"
-name stopservice

invoke-wmimethod -path "win32_service.displayname='DisplayName'"
-name stopservice

get-wmiobject -class win32_service -filter "name='ServiceName'" |
invoke-wmimethod -name stopservice
```

Before you stop or pause a service, you should check to see if the service can be stopped or paused. With Win32_Service objects, the properties you can check are AcceptPause and AcceptStop.

You can use the techniques discussed previously to work with services when Get-WmiObject returns a single matching Win32_Service object. However, these techniques won't work as expected when Get-WmiObject returns multiple Win32_Service objects. The reason for this is that the objects are stored in an array, and you must specify the instance within the array to work with. One technique for doing so is shown in the following example and partial output:

```
$servs = get-wmiobject -class win32_service |
where-object {$_.name -match "client"}

foreach ($s in $servs) { $s.changestartmode("automatic") }
```

```
ReturnValue      : 0


ReturnValue      : 0


ReturnValue      : 0
```

Here, three Win32_Service objects were returned, and each was set to start automatically. This technique will work when there is only one matching service as well.

Managing Computers

Computers have attributes that you can manage, including names and group memberships. You can add computer accounts to any container or organizational unit (OU) in Active Directory. However, the best containers to use are Computers, Domain Controllers, and any OUs that you've created. The standard Windows tool for working with computer accounts is Active Directory Users And Computers. In Windows PowerShell, you have many commands, each with a specific use. Whether you are logged on to a Windows Vista, Windows Server 2008, or later version of Windows, you can use the techniques discussed in this section to manage computers.

Commands for Managing Computers

Commands you'll use to manage computers in Windows PowerShell include:

- **Add-Computer** Adds computers to a domain or workgroup. You can specify computers by their NetBIOS name, IP address, or fully qualified domain name. To join a domain, you must specify the name of the domain to join. In domains, if a computer doesn't have a domain account, this command also creates the domain account for the computer. A restart is required to complete the join operation. To get the results of the command, use the –Verbose and –PassThru parameters.

```
Add-Computer [-OUPath ADPath] [-Server Domain\ComputerName]
[[-ComputerName] ComputerNames] [-DomainName] DomainName
[-Unsecure] [-PassThru] [-Reboot] [[-Credential] CredentialObject]

Add-Computer [[-ComputerName] ComputerNames] [-WorkGroupName] Name
[-PassThru] [-Reboot] [[-Credential] CredentialObject]
```

- **Remove-Computer** Removes local and remote computers from their current workgroup or domain. When you remove a computer from a domain, Remove-Computer also disables the computer's domain account. A restart is required to complete the unjoin operation. For domain computers, you must provide authentication credentials.

```
Remove-Computer [[-ComputerName] ComputerNames]
[-PassThru] [-Reboot] [[-Credential] CredentialObject]
```

- **Rename-Computer** Renames computers in workgroups and domains. When you rename a computer in a domain, Rename-Computer also changes the name in the computer's domain account. You cannot use Rename-Computer to rename domain controllers. For remote computers, you must provide authentication credentials.

```
Rename-Computer [[-ComputerName] ComputerName] [-NewComputerName]
NewComputerName [-Credential CredentialObject] [-Reboot]
```

- **Restart-Computer** Restarts the operating system on local and remote computers. Use the –Force parameter to force an immediate restart of the computers.

```
Restart-Computer [[-ComputerName] ComputerNames] [-AsJob]
[-Authentication AuthType] [[-Credential] CredentialObject]
[-Force] [-Impersonation ImpType] [-ThrottleLimit Limit]
```

- **Stop-Computer** Shuts down local or remote computers. The –AsJob parameter runs the command as a background job, providing the computers are configured for remoting.

```
Stop-Computer [[-ComputerName] ComputerNames] [-AsJob]
[-Authentication AuthType] [[-Credential] CredentialObject]
[-Force] [-Impersonation ImpType] [-ThrottleLimit Limit]
```

- **Test-Connection** Sends Internet Control Message Protocol (ICMP) echo request packets (pings) to one or more remote computers, and returns the responses. As long as ICMP is not blocked by a firewall, this can help you determine whether a computer can be contacted across an IP network. You can specify both the sending and receiving computers. You also can set a time-out and the number of pings.

```
Test-Connection [-Count NumPings] [-Delay DelayBetweenPings]
[-TimeToLive MaxTime] [[-Source] SourceComputers] [-Destination]
DestinationComputers

[-AsJob] [-Authentication AuthType] [-BufferSize Size] [-Credential
CredentialObject] [-Impersonation ImpType] [-ThrottleLimit Limit]
```

You'll usually want to run these commands at an elevated, administrator PowerShell prompt. Regardless, you also might need to provide the appropriate credentials, and you can do this as shown in the following example:

```
$cred = get-credential
add-computer -domainname cpandl-credential $cred
```

When you use Get-Credential, PowerShell prompts you for a user name and password and then stores the credentials provided in the $cred variable. These credentials are then used for authentication.

When you test a connection to a computer, restart a computer, or stop a computer, note the following:

- The –Authentication parameter sets the authentication level for the WMI connection to the computer. The default value is Packet. Valid values are Unchanged (the authentication level is the same as the previous command), Default (Windows Authentication), None (no COM authentication), Connect (Connect-level COM authentication), Call (Call-level COM authentication), Packet (Packet-level COM authentication), PacketIntegrity (Packet Integrity–level COM authentication), and PacketPrivacy (Packet Privacy–level COM authentication).
- The –Impersonation parameter sets the impersonation level to use when establishing the WMI connection. The default value is Impersonate. Valid values are Default (default impersonation), Anonymous (hides the identity of the caller), Identify (allows objects to query the credentials of the caller), and Impersonate (allows objects to use the credentials of the caller).

As you can see, the default authentication technique is to use Packet-level COM authentication, and the default impersonation technique is to use the credentials of the caller. Most of the time, these are what you'll want to use. Occasionally, you might want to use Windows Authentication rather than COM authentication. To do this, set the –Authentication parameter to Default.

Test-Connection is the same as Ping. With Test-Connection, you can determine whether you can connect to a computer by its name or IP address. To test the IPv4 address 192.168.10.55, you use the following command:

```
test-connection 192.168.10.55
```

To test the IPv6 address FEC0::02BC:FF:BECB:FE4F:961D, you use the following command:

```
test-connection FEC0::02BC:FF:BECB:FE4F:961D
```

If you receive a successful reply from Test-Connection, Test-Connection was able to connect to the computer. If you receive a time-out or "Unable to Connect" error, Test-Connection was unable to connect to the computer either because the computer was disconnected from the network, the computer was shut down, or the connection was blocked by a firewall.

Renaming Computer Accounts

Using Rename-Computer, you can easily rename workstations and member servers. If the workstation or member server is joined to a domain, the computer's account is renamed as well. You should not, however, use Rename-Computer to rename domain controllers, servers running Certificate Services, or servers running any other services that require a specific, fixed server name.

You can rename a workstation or member server using the following command syntax:

```
rename-computer -ComputerName ComputerName -NewComputerName NewName
-reboot
```

where *ComputerName* is the current name of the computer, and *NewName* is the new name for the computer. If you are renaming the local computer, you omit the –ComputerName parameter as shown in the following example:

```
rename-computer -NewComputerName TechPC12 -reboot
```

Here, you rename the local computer TechPC12. Because a reboot is required to complete the renaming, you specify that you want to reboot the computer after renaming it. If you need to specify credentials to rename a computer, you can do so as shown in the following example:

```
$cred = get-credential
rename-computer -NewComputerName TechPC12 -credential $cred -reboot
```

Joining Computers to a Domain

Any authenticated user can join a computer to a domain using Add-Computer. If the related computer account hasn't been created, running Add-Computer also creates the computer account. When a computer joins a domain, the computer establishes a trust relationship with the domain. The computer's security identifier is changed to match that of the related computer account in Active Directory, and the computer is made a member of the appropriate groups in Active Directory. Typically, this means the computer is made a member of the Domain Computers group. If the computer is later made a domain controller, the computer will be made a member of the Domain Controllers group instead.

REAL WORLD Before trying to join a computer to a domain, you should verify the computer's network configuration. If the network configuration is not correct, you will need to modify the settings before attempting to join the computer to the domain. Additionally, if the computer account was created previously, only a user specifically delegated permission or an administrator can join the computer to a domain. Users must also have local administrator permissions on the local computer.

When logged on to the computer you want to join to a domain, you can use Add-Computer to simultaneously join a computer to a domain and create a computer account in the domain with the following command syntax:

add-computer -DomainName *DomainName* -reboot

where *DomainName* is the name of the Active Directory domain to join. Because you must reboot the computer to complete the join operation, you typically will want to include the –Reboot parameter. This isn't required, however. If you don't specify the organizational unit to use, the default organizational unit is used. Consider the following example:

```
$cred = get-credential
add-computer -domainname cpandl -credential $cred -reboot
```

Here, you join the local computer to the cpandl.com domain and create the related computer account in the default Computers container. If the computer's name is TechPC85, the full path to this computer object is CN=TechPC85,CN=Computers, DC=cpandl,DC=com.

TIP Add the –PassThru and –Verbose parameters to get detailed results. Additionally, when you join a computer to a domain, you can specify the domain controller to use with the –Server parameter. Specify the server name in *Domain\ComputerName* format, such as CPANDL\DcServer14. If you don't specify the domain controller to use, any available domain controller is used.

Additionally, you can use the –OUPath parameter to specify the distinguished name of the OU into which the computer account should be placed. Consider the following example:

```
$cred = get-credential
add-computer -domainname cpandl -outpath ou=engineering,dc=cpandl,dc=com
-credential $cred -reboot
```

Here, you join the local computer to the cpandl.com domain and create the related computer account in the Engineering OU. If the computer's name is TechPC85, the full path to this computer object is CN=TechPC85,OU=Engineering,DC=cpandl, DC=com.

When running Add-Computer from another computer and connecting to the computer you want to join to a domain, you use the following command syntax:

```
add-computer -DomainName DomainName -computername ComputerNames -reboot
```

where *DomainName* is the name of the Active Directory domain to join and *ComputerNames* is a comma-separated list of computers joining the domain. As before, this command creates the related computer account if necessary and you optionally can use the –OUPath parameter to specify the distinguished name of the OU into which the computer account should be placed.

Consider the following example:

```
$cred = get-credential
add-computer -domainname cpandl -computername EngPC14, EngPC17 -outpath
ou=engineering,dc=cpandl,dc=com -credential $cred -reboot
```

Here, you join EngPC14 and EngPC15 to the cpandl.com domain and create the related computer account in the Engineering OU.

You can read the list of computers to join to a domain from a file as well. Here is an example:

```
add-computer -domainname cpandl -computername (get-content
c:\data\clist.txt)
```

Here, you add the computers listed in the C:\Data\CList.txt file to the cpandl.com domain. If you are renaming the local computer as well as other computers, you can type **"."** or **"localhost"** as the computer name.

Adding Computers to a Workgroup

In addition to using Add-Computer to add computers to domains, you can use Add-Computer to add computers to workgroups. To add the local computer to a specified workgroup, use the following syntax:

```
add-computer -WorkgroupName WorkgroupName -reboot
```

where *WorkgroupName* is the name of the workgroup to join. Because you must reboot the computer to complete the join operation, you typically will want to include the –Reboot parameter. This isn't required, however.

Consider the following example:

```
$cred = get-credential
add-computer -workgroupname testing -credential $cred -reboot
```

Here, you join the local computer to the Testing workgroup. Add the –PassThru and –Verbose parameters to get detailed results.

When running Add-Computer from another computer and connecting to the computer you want to join to a workgroup, you use the following command syntax:

```
add-computer -WorkgroupName WorkgroupName -computername ComputerNames
-reboot
```

where *WorkgroupName* is the name of the workgroup to join, and *ComputerNames* is a comma-separated list of computers joining the domain.

Consider the following example:

```
$cred = get-credential
add-computer -workgroupname testing -computername TestPC11, TestPC12
-credential $cred -reboot
```

Here, you join TestPC11 and TestPC12 to the Testing workgroup.

You can read the list of computers to join to a workgroup from a file as well. Here is an example:

```
add-computer -workgroupname testing -computername (get-content
c:\data\clist.txt)
```

Here, you add the computers listed in the C:\Data\CList.txt file to the Testing workgroup. If you are renaming the local computer as well as other computers, you can type **"."** or **"localhost"** as the computer name.

Removing Computers from Domains and Workgroups

Only authorized users can remove a computer from a domain or workgroup. Removing a computer from a domain disables the computer account in the domain and breaks the trust relationship between the computer and the domain. The computer's security identifier is changed to match that of a computer in a workgroup. The computer then joins the default workgroup, called Workgroup.

You remove computers from a domain or workgroup using Remove-Computer. Consider the following example:

```
$cred = get-credential
remove-computer -credential $cred -reboot
```

Here, you remove the local computer from its current domain or workgroup and make it a member of the default workgroup, Workgroup.

When running Add-Computer from another computer and connecting to the computer you want to manage, you use the following command syntax:

```
remove-computer -computername ComputerNames -reboot
```

where *ComputerNames* is a comma-separated list of computers to remove from domains or workgroups.

Consider the following example:

```
$cred = get-credential
remove-computer -computername TestPC11, TestPC12 -credential $cred
-reboot
```

Here, you remove TestPC11 and TestPC12 from their current domain or workgroup and make them members of the default workgroup, Workgroup.

Managing the Restart and Shutdown of Computers

You'll often find that you need to shut down or restart systems. One way to do this is to run Shutdown-Computer or Restart-Computer at the PowerShell prompt, which you can use to work with both local and remote systems. Another way to manage system shutdown or restart is to schedule a shutdown. Here, you can use the Schtasks utility to specify when shutdown should be run, or you can create a script with a list of shutdown commands for individual systems.

Although Windows systems usually start up and shut down without problems, they can occasionally stop responding during these processes. If this happens, try to determine the cause. Some of the reasons systems might stop responding include the following:

- The system is attempting to execute or is running a startup or shutdown script that has not completed or is itself not responding (and in this case, the system might be waiting for the script to time out).
- A startup initialization file or service might be the cause of the problem and, if so, you might need to troubleshoot startup items using the System Configuration (Msconfig) utility. Disabling a service, startup item, or entry in a startup initialization file might also solve the problem.
- The system might have an antivirus program that is causing the problem. In some cases, the antivirus program might try to scan the floppy disk drive when you try to shut down the system. To resolve this, configure the antivirus software so that it doesn't scan the floppy drive or other drives with removable media on shutdown. You can also try temporarily disabling or turning off the antivirus program.
- Improperly configured sound devices can cause startup and shutdown problems. To determine what the possible source is, examine each of these devices in turn. Turn off sound devices and then restart the computer. If the problem clears up, you have to install new drivers for the sound devices you are using, or you might have a corrupted Start Windows or Exit Windows sound file.
- Improperly configured network cards can cause startup and shutdown problems. Try turning off the network adapter and restarting. If that works, you might need to remove and then reinstall the adapter's driver or obtain a new driver from the manufacturer.

- Improperly configured video adapter drivers can cause startup and shutdown problems. From another computer, remotely log on and try to roll back the current video drivers to a previous version. If that's not possible, try uninstalling and then reinstalling the video drivers.

When logged on to the computer you want to restart or shut down, you can type **restart-computer** or **stop-computer** to restart or shut down the computer, respectively. To force an immediate restart or shutdown, add the –Force parameter.

When running Restart-Computer or Stop-Computer from another computer and connecting to the computer you want to restart or stop, you use the following command syntax:

```
restart-computer -computername ComputerNames
```

or

```
stop-computer -computername ComputerNames
```

where *ComputerNames* is a comma-separated list of computers to restart or stop. As before, you can use the –Force parameter to force a restart or shutdown. You also might need to specify credentials. You can do that as shown in this example:

```
$cred = get-credential
stop-computer -computername TestPC11, TestPC12 -credential $cred
```

Here, you shut down TestPC11 and TestPC12 using specific credentials.

You can read the list of computers to restart or shut down from a file as well. Here is an example:

```
$cred = get-credential
restart-computer -computername (get-content c:\data\clist.txt)
-credential $cred -force
```

Here, you restart the computers listed in the C:\Data\CList.txt file using specific credentials.

Creating and Using System Restore Checkpoints

With System Restore enabled, a computer makes periodic snapshots of the system configuration. These snapshots are called *restore points*. These restore points include Windows settings, lists of programs that have been installed, and so on. If the computer has problems starting or isn't working properly because of a system configuration change, you can use a restore point to restore the system configuration to the point at which the snapshot was made. For example, suppose your system is working fine and then you install a new service pack release for Microsoft Office. Afterward, the computer generates errors, and Office applications won't run. You try to uninstall the update, but that doesn't work, so you decide to run System

Restore. Using System Restore, you can restore the system using a snapshot taken before the update.

System Restore automatically creates several types of restore points. These include the following:

- **Scheduled** Checkpoints scheduled by the operating system and occurring at regular intervals
- **Windows Update** Checkpoints created before applying Windows updates
- **Application Install** Checkpoints created before installing applications
- **Application Uninstall** Checkpoints created before uninstalling applications
- **Device Install** Checkpoints created before installing devices
- **Device Uninstall** Checkpoints created before uninstalling devices

You should create restore points manually before performing an operation that might cause problems on the system.

System Restore manages restore points on a per-drive basis. Each drive with critical applications and system files should be monitored for configuration changes. By default, System Restore is enabled only for the System drive. You can modify the System Restore configuration by turning on monitoring of other drives as needed. If a drive isn't configured for System Restore monitoring, configuration changes are not tracked, and the disk cannot be recovered if problems occur.

In Windows Vista and later desktop versions of Windows, previous versions of files and folders are created automatically as part of a restore point. Any file or folder that was modified since the last restore point is saved and made available as a previous version. The only exceptions are for system files and folders. Previous versions are not available for system folders, such as C:\Windows.

You can use previous versions of files to restore files that were inadvertently modified, deleted, or damaged. When System Restore is enabled on a drive, compliant versions of Windows automatically make daily copies of files and folders that have changed on that drive. You can also create copies of files and folders that have changed by setting a restore point.

NOTE **Protection points are created daily for all drives being monitored by System Restore. However, only versions of files that are actually different from the current version are stored as previous versions. You can enable or disable previous versions on a per-drive basis by enabling or disabling System Restore on that drive. Previous versions are saved as part of a volume's automatically or manually created protection points.**

Commands for Configuring System Restore

At an elevated, administrator PowerShell prompt, you can view and work with System Restore using the following commands:

- **Enable-ComputerRestore** Turns on the System Restore feature on one or more fixed, internal drives. You cannot enable System Restore on external or network drives.

```
Enable-ComputerRestore [-Drive] DriveStrings
```

- **Disable-ComputerRestore** Turns off the System Restore feature on one or more file system drives. As a result, attempts to restore the computer do not affect the specified drive.

```
Disable-ComputerRestore [-Drive] DriveStrings
```

- **Get-ComputerRestorePoint** Gets one or more restore points on the local computer, or displays the status of the most recent attempt to restore the computer.

```
Get-ComputerRestorePoint [-RestorePoint] SequenceNumber
Get-ComputerRestorePoint -LastStatus
```

- **Checkpoint-Computer** Creates a system restore point on the local computer. The –RestorePointType parameter optionally specifies the type of restore point.

```
Checkpoint-Computer [[-RestorePointType] Type] [-Description]
Description
```

- **Restore-Computer** Restores the local computer to the specified system restore point. A restart of the computer is performed to complete the restore. The –RestorePoint parameter specifies the sequence number of the restore point.

```
Restore-Computer [-RestorePoint] SequenceNumber
```

The system process responsible for monitoring configuration and application changes is the System Restore service. This service is configured for automatic startup and runs under the Local System account. System Restore won't work properly if this service isn't running or configured appropriately.

System Restore saves system checkpoint information for all monitored drives and requires at least 300 MB of disk space on the System volume to save restore points. System Restore reserves additional space for restore points as necessary, up to 10 percent of the total disk capacity, but this additional space is always available for user and application storage. System Restore frees up additional space for you as necessary. If System Restore runs out of available space, the operating system overwrites previously created restore points.

Enabling and Disabling System Restore

You can enable System Restore for a volume using Enable-ComputerRestore. The basic syntax is

```
Enable-ComputerRestore [-Drive] DriveStrings
```

With the –Drive parameter, specify one or more drive letters, each followed by a colon and a backslash and enclosed in quotation marks, as shown in the following example:

```
enable-computerrestore -drive "C:\", "D:\"
```

To enable System Restore on any drive, it must be enabled on the system drive, either first or concurrently. When you enable System Restore, restore points are created automatically as discussed previously.

You can disable System Restore for a volume using Disable-ComputerRestore. The basic syntax is

```
Disable-ComputerRestore [-Drive] DriveStrings
```

With the –Drive parameter, specify one or more file system drive letters, each followed by a colon and a backslash and enclosed in quotation marks, as shown in the following example:

```
disable-computerrestore -drive "C:\", "D:\"
```

You cannot disable System Restore on the System volume without disabling System Restore on all other volumes.

Although these commands don't support the –ComputerName parameter, you can use the remoting techniques discussed in Chapter 6, "Mastering Aliases, Functions, and Objects," to invoke System Restore–related commands on remote computers. Here is an example:

```
invoke-command -computername techpc24 -scriptblock
{ enable-computerrestore -drive "C:\", "D:\" }
```

Here, you enable System Restore on the C and D drives of TechPC25.

Creating and Using Checkpoints

You can manually create a restore point by typing **checkpoint-computer** followed by a description of the checkpoint. Consider the following example:

```
checkpoint-computer "Modify PowerShell"
```

Here, you create a "Modify PowerShell" checkpoint. Windows PowerShell displays a progress bar while the restore point is being created. Optionally, you can specify the type of restore point using the –RestorePointType parameter. The default is APPLICATION_INSTALL. Valid values are as follows:

- APPLICATION_INSTALL, for when you are planning to install an application
- APPLICATION_UNINSTALL, for when you are planning to uninstall an application
- DEVICE_DRIVER_INSTALL, for when you are planning to modify device drivers
- MODIFY_SETTINGS, for when you are planning to modify configuration settings

You can use Get-ComputerRestorePoint to list all available restore points or a specific restore point by its sequence number. The sequence number is simply an incremented value that makes it possible to track a specific instance of a restore point.

To list all available restore points, type **get-computerrestorepoint**, as shown in the following example and sample output:

```
get-computerrestorepoint
```

```
CreationTime Description SequenceNumber  EventType RestorePointType
------------ ----------- --------------  ---------  ----------------
1/22/2009 9:56:36 AM   Windows Update     287   BEGIN_SYSTEM_C...
APPLICATION_INSTALL
1/23/2009 11:30:46 AM  Windows Update     288   BEGIN_SYSTEM_C...
APPLICATION_INSTALL
1/23/2009 11:38:24 AM  Windows Update     289   BEGIN_SYSTEM_C...
APPLICATION_INSTALL
```

From the output, you can see restore points are listed by creation time, description, sequence number, event type, and restore point type. Once you identify a restore point that you want to work with, note its sequence number. Using the –RestorePoint parameter, you can get that specific restore point. In this example, you get restore point 289:

```
get-computerrestorepoint 289
```

As each value returned for a restore point is set in a like-named property, you can filter the output of Get-ComputerRestorePoint using Where-Object. In the following example, you get all restore points created in the last three days:

```
$date = (get-date).adddays(-3)
get-computerrestorepoint | where-object {$_.creationtime -gt $date}
```

In the following example, you get restore points with a specific description:

```
get-computerrestorepoint | where-object {$_.description -eq
"Modify PowerShell"}
```

To get restore points by description, you need to know the numeric value that denotes a specific type. These values include the following:

- 0 for application install checkpoints, which include Windows Update check points
- 1 for application uninstall checkpoints
- 7 for scheduled checkpoints
- 10 for device driver install checkpoints
- 12 for modify settings checkpoints

In the following example, you get all restore points for application installs:

```
get-computerrestorepoint | where-object {$_.restorepointtype -eq 0}
```

Recovering from Restore Points

To recover a computer from a restore point, type **restore-computer** followed by the sequence number of the restore point to restore. Use Get-ComputerRestorePoint to display a list of available restore points by their sequence number if necessary. In the following example, you initiate a restore of the computer using restore point 353:

```
restore-computer 353
```

Here, you initiate a restore of EngPC85 to restore point 276:

```
invoke-command -computername engpc85 -scriptblock
{ restore-computer 276 }
```

During the restoration, System Restore shuts down the computer. After the restore is complete, the computer is restarted using the settings from the date and time of the snapshot. After the computer restarts, you can type **get-computer-restorepoint -laststatus** to check the status of the restore operation. Read the message provided to confirm the restore was successful. If the restore was unsuccessful, this is stated explicitly, such as

```
The last restore was interrupted.
```

If Windows isn't working properly after a restore, you can apply a different restore point or reverse the restore operation by repeating this procedure and selecting the restore point that was created automatically before applying the current system state.

CHAPTER 14

Fine-Tuning System Performance

In the previous chapter, I discussed techniques for monitoring and optimizing Windows systems. Monitoring is the process by which systems are regularly checked for problems. Optimization is the process of fine-tuning system performance to maintain or achieve its optimal capacity. Now that you know the essentials for monitoring and optimization, let's dig deeper and look at techniques that you can use to:

- Manage applications, processes, and performance.
- Monitor and maintain a computer's performance.
- Detect and resolve performance issues.

Managing Applications, Processes, and Performance

An important part of every administrator's job is to monitor network systems and ensure that everything is running smoothly—or as smoothly as can be expected, anyway. As you learned in the previous chapter, watching the event logs closely can help you detect and track problems with applications, security, and essential services. Often when you detect or suspect a problem, you'll need to dig deeper to search out the cause of the problem and correct it. If you're fortunate, by pinpointing the cause of a problem, you can prevent it from happening again.

Whenever the operating system or a user starts a service, runs an application, or executes a command, Windows starts one or more processes to handle the related program. Several commands are available to help you manage and monitor programs. These commands include the following:

- **Debug-Process** Debugs one or more processes running on the local computer.

```
Debug-Process [-Id] ProcessIDs | -InputObject Objects | -Name Names
```

- **Get-Process** Lists all running processes by name and process ID. The list includes information on memory usage.

```
Get-Process -Id ProcessIDs | -InputObject Objects | [[-Name] Names]
[-ComputerName ComputerNames] [-FileVersionInfo] [-Module]
```

- **Start-Process** Starts one or more processes on the local computer. To specify the program that runs in the process, enter the path to an executable file or script file. Alternatively, you can specify a file that can be opened in a program, such as a Microsoft Office Word document or Office Excel worksheet. If you specify a nonexecutable file, Start-Process starts the program that is associated with the file by using the default action. Typically, the default action is Open. You can set the action to take using the –Verb parameter.

```
Start-Process [-Verb {Edit|Open|Print|...}] [-WorkingDirectory
DirectoryPath] [[-ArgumentList] Args] [-FilePath] PathToExeOrDoc

[-Credential CredentialObject] [-LoadUserProfile {$True|$False}]
[-NoNewWindow] [-PassThru] [-RedirectStandardError FilePath]
[-RedirectStandardInput FilePath] [-RedirectStandardOutput
FilePath] [-UseNewEnvironment] [-Wait] [-WindowStyle
{Normal|Hidden|Minimized|Maximized}]
```

- **Stop-Process** Stops running processes by name or process ID. Using filters, you can also halt processes by process status, session number, CPU time, memory usage, and more.

```
Stop-Process [-Id] ProcessIDs | -InputObject Objects | -Name Names
[-Force] [-PassThru]
```

- **Wait-Process** Waits for a specified process to be stopped before accepting more input.

```
Wait-Process -Id ProcessIDs | -InputObject Objects | [-Name] Names
[[-TimeOut] WaitTime]
```

In the sections that follow, you'll find detailed discussions on how these commands are used. First, however, let's look at the ways processes are run and the common problems you might encounter when working with them.

Understanding System and User Processes

When you want to examine processes that are running on a local or remote system, you can use Get-Process and other commands. With Get-Process, you can obtain the process ID, status, and other important information about processes running on a system. You also can use filters to include or exclude processes from Get-Process queries. To dig deeper, you can use the Win32_Process and Win32_Service classes.

Generally, processes that the operating system starts are referred to as system processes; processes that users start are referred to as user processes. Most user processes are run in interactive mode. That is, a user starts a process interactively with the keyboard or mouse. If the application or program is active and selected, the related interactive process has control over the keyboard and mouse until you switch control by terminating the program or selecting a different one. When a process has control, it's said to be running "in the foreground."

Processes can also run in the background, independently of user logon sessions. Background processes do not have control over the keyboard, mouse, or other input devices and are usually run by the operating system. Using the Task Scheduler, users can run processes in the background as well, however, and these processes can operate regardless of whether the user is logged on. For example, if Task Scheduler starts a scheduled task while the user is logged on, the process can continue even when the user logs off.

Windows tracks every process running on a system by image name, process ID, priority, and other parameters that record resource usage. The image name is the name of the executable that started the process, such as Msdtc.exe or Svchost.exe. The process ID is a numeric identifier for the process, such as 1160. The base priority is an indicator of how much of the system's resources the process should get relative to other running processes. With priority processing, a process with a higher-priority gets preference over processes with lower priority, and the higher-priority process might not have to wait to get processing time, access memory, or work with the file system. A process with lower priority, on the other hand, usually must wait for a higher-priority process to complete its current task before gaining access to the CPU, memory, or the file system.

In a perfect world, processes would run perfectly and would never have problems. The reality is, however, that problems occur and they often appear when you least want them to. Common problems include the following:

- Processes become nonresponsive, such as when an application stops processing requests. When this happens, users might tell you that they can't access a particular application, that their requests aren't being handled, or that they were kicked out of the application.
- Processes fail to release the CPU, such as when you have a runaway process that is using up CPU time. When this happens, the system might appear to be slow or nonresponsive because the runaway process is hogging processor time and is not allowing other processes to complete their tasks.

- Processes use more memory than they should, such as when an application has a memory leak. When this happens, processes aren't properly releasing memory that they're using. As a result, the system's available memory might gradually decrease over time and, as the available memory gets low, the system might be slow to respond to requests or it might become nonresponsive. Memory leaks can also make other programs running on the same system behave erratically.

In most cases, when you detect these or other problems with system processes, you'll want to stop the process and start it again. You'll also want to examine the event logs to see whether you can determine the cause of the problem. In the case of memory leaks, you'll want to report the memory leak to the developers and see whether an update that resolves the problem is available.

A periodic restart of an application with a known memory leak is often useful. Restarting the application should allow the operating system to recover any lost memory.

Examining Running Processes

To get a list of all processes running on a system, type **get-process** at the command prompt as shown in the following example and sample output:

```
get-process -computername fileserver86
```

```
Handles  NPM(K)    PM(K)      WS(K) VM(M)   CPU(s)     Id ProcessName
-------  ------    -----      ----- -----   ------     -- -----------
    127       4    13288      16708    59            1240 audiodg
    696       6     1872       5248    94             588 csrss
    495       7    21912      19672   155             644 csrss
     95       4     3160       6572    75     0.08   2752 CtHelper
    134       5     3808       7900    77     0.08   2708 Ctxfihlp
    189       5     9160       8764    72     0.22   3044 CTxfispi
     58       2     1236       4244    45     0.31   3260 ehmsas
```

Because the –ComputerName parameter accepts multiple name values, you can check the status of processes on multiple computers simply by typing the names of the computers to check in a comma-separate list as shown in the following example:

```
get-process -computername fileserver86, dcserver22, printserver31
```

Rather than type computer names each time, you can type computer names on separate lines in a text file and then get the list of computer names from the text file as shown in the following example:

```
get-process -computername (get-content c:\data\clist.txt)
```

Here, you get the list of remote computers to check from a file called Clist.txt in the C:\Data directory.

When you are looking for a specific process, you can reference the process by its process name or process ID. To match partial names, you can use wildcard characters as shown in the following example and sample output:

```
get-process win* -computername fileserver86
```

```
Handles  NPM(K)    PM(K)      WS(K) VM(M)   CPU(s)     Id ProcessName
-------  ------    -----      ----- -----   ------     -- -----------
    106       4     1560       4192    46             636 wininit
    143       4     2516       6692    56             804 winlogon
    485      26    45992      69220   441    83.34   5200 WINWORD
```

Here, you look for all processes where the process name begins with *win*.

Get-Process returns objects representing each process matching the criteria you specify. As you can see from previous examples and sample output, the standard output includes:

- **CPU** An alias for TotalProcessorTime.TotalSeconds. This item shows the number of seconds of CPU time the process has used.
- **Handles** An alias for the HandleCount property. This item shows the number of file handles maintained by the process.
- **NPM** An alias for the NonpagedSystemMemorySize property. This item shows the amount of virtual memory for a process that cannot be written to disk.
- **PM** An alias for the PagedMemorySize property. This item shows the amount of committed virtual memory for a process that can be written to disk.
- **VM** An alias for the VirtualMemorySize property. This item shows the amount of virtual memory allocated to and reserved for a process.
- **WS** An alias for the WorkingSet property. This item shows the amount of memory the process is currently using, including both the private working set and the nonprivate working set.
- **Id** The process identification number.
- **ProcessName** The name of the process or executable running the process.

As you examine processes, keep in mind that a single application might start multiple processes. Generally, these processes are dependent on the central application process, and from this main process a process tree containing dependent processes is formed. When you terminate processes, you'll usually want to target the main application process or the application itself rather than dependent processes. This approach ensures that the application is stopped cleanly.

To view all of the available properties, you need to format the output as a list, as shown in the following example and partial output:

```
get-process winword -computername server12 | format-list *
```

```
Name                        : WINWORD
Path              : C:\Program Files\Microsoft Office\OFFICE11\WINWORD.EXE
Company                     : Microsoft Corporation
CPU                         : 121.046875
FileVersion                 : 11.0.8237
ProductVersion              : 11.0.8237
Description                 : Microsoft Office Word
Product                     : Microsoft Office 2003
Id                          : 5200
PriorityClass               : Normal
HandleCount                 : 491
WorkingSet                  : 73142272
PagedMemorySize             : 47992832
PrivateMemorySize           : 47992832
VirtualMemorySize           : 463138816
TotalProcessorTime          : 00:02:01.0468750
BasePriority                : 8
Handle                      : 2752
MachineName                 : server12
MainWindowHandle            : 1573996
MainWindowTitle             : process.doc - Microsoft Word
MainModule               : System.Diagnostics.ProcessModule (WINWORD.EXE)
MaxWorkingSet               : 1413120
MinWorkingSet               : 204800
Modules                     : {System.Diagnostics.ProcessModule (WINWORD.
EXE), System.Diagnostics.ProcessModule (ntdll.dll),...}
NonpagedSystemMemorySize    : 27312
NonpagedSystemMemorySize64 : 27312
PagedMemorySize64           : 47992832
PagedSystemMemorySize       : 754224
PagedSystemMemorySize64     : 754224
PeakPagedMemorySize         : 48001024
PeakPagedMemorySize64       : 48001024
PeakWorkingSet              : 73150464
PeakWorkingSet64            : 73150464
PeakVirtualMemorySize       : 464146432
PeakVirtualMemorySize64     : 464146432
PriorityBoostEnabled        : True
PrivateMemorySize64         : 47992832
PrivilegedProcessorTime     : 00:00:36.2343750
ProcessName                 : WINWORD
ProcessorAffinity           : 15
Responding                  : True
SessionId                   : 1
```

```
StartInfo                  : System.Diagnostics.ProcessStartInfo
StartTime                  : 2/28/2009 10:22:34 AM
Threads                    : {5204, 5244, 5300, 5540...}
UserProcessorTime          : 00:01:24.8125000
VirtualMemorySize64        : 463138816
EnableRaisingEvents        : False
WorkingSet64               : 73142272
```

The output shows the exact configuration of the process. The properties you will work with the most are summarized in Table 14-1.

NOTE By default, many properties that measure memory usage are defined as 32-bit values. When working with Get-Process on 64-bit systems, you'll find that these properties have both a 32-bit and a 64-bit version. On 64-bit systems with more than 4 GB of RAM, you'll need to use the 64-bit versions to ensure you get accurate values.

TABLE 14-1 Properties of Get-Process and How They Are Used

PROPERTY NAME	PROPERTY DESCRIPTION
BasePriority	Shows the priority of the process. Priority determines how much of the system resources are allocated to a process. The standard priorities are Low (4), Below Normal (6), Normal (8), Above Normal (10), High (13), and Real-Time (24). Most processes have a Normal priority by default, and the highest priority is given to real-time processes.
CPU	Shows TotalProcessorTime in seconds.
Description	Shows a description of the process.
FileVersion	Shows the file version of the process's executable.
HandleCount	Shows the number of file handles maintained by the process. The number of handles used is an indicator of how dependent the process is on the file system. Some processes have thousands of open file handles. Each file handle requires system memory to maintain.
Id	Shows the run-time identification number of the process.
MinWorkingSet	Shows the minimum amount of working set memory used by the process.

TABLE 14-1 Properties of Get-Process and How They Are Used

PROPERTY NAME	PROPERTY DESCRIPTION
Modules	Shows the executables and dynamically linked libraries used by the process.
NonpagedSystemMemory-Size/NonpagedSystem-MemorySize64	Shows the amount of virtual memory for a process that cannot be written to disk. The nonpaged pool is an area of RAM for objects that can't be written to disk. You should note processes that require a high amount of nonpaged pool memory. If the server doesn't have enough free memory, these processes might be the reason for a high level of page faults.
PagedSystemMemorySize/ PagedSystemMemorySize64	Shows the amount of committed virtual memory for a process that can be written to disk. The paged pool is an area of RAM for objects that can be written to disk when they aren't used. As process activity increases, so does the amount of pool memory the process uses. Most processes have more paged pool than nonpaged pool requirements.
Path	Shows the full path to the executable for the process.
PeakPagedMemorySize/ PeakPagedMemorySize64	Shows the peak amount of paged memory used by the process.
PeakVirtualMemorySize/ PeakVirtualMemorySize64	Shows the peak amount of virtual memory used by the process.
PeakWorkingSet/ PeakWorkingSet64	Shows the maximum amount of memory the process used, including both the private working set and the nonprivate working set. If peak memory is exceptionally large, this can be an indicator of a memory leak.
PriorityBoostEnabled	Shows a Boolean value that indicates whether the process has the PriorityBoost feature enabled.
PriorityClass	Shows the priority class of the process.
PrivilegedProcessorTime	Shows the amount of kernel-mode usage time for the process.
ProcessName	Shows the name of the process.

TABLE 14-1 Properties of Get-Process and How They Are Used

PROPERTY NAME	PROPERTY DESCRIPTION
ProcessorAffinity	Shows the processor affinity setting for the process.
Responding	Shows a Boolean value that indicates whether the process responded when tested.
SessionId	Shows the identification number user (session) within which the process is running. This corresponds to the ID value listed on the Users tab in Task Manager.
StartTime	Shows the date and time the process was started.
Threads	Shows the number of threads that the process is using. Most server applications are multithreaded, which allows concurrent execution of process requests. Some applications can dynamically control the number of concurrently executing threads to improve application performance. Too many threads, however, can actually reduce performance, because the operating system has to switch thread contexts too frequently.
TotalProcessorTime	Shows the total amount of CPU time used by the process since it was started. If a process is using a lot of CPU time, the related application might have a configuration problem. This can also indicate a runaway or nonresponsive process that is unnecessarily tying up the CPU.
UserProcessorTime	Shows the amount of user-mode usage time for the process.
VirtualMemorySize/ VirtualMemorySize64	Shows the amount of virtual memory allocated to and reserved for a process. Virtual memory is memory on disk and is slower to access than pooled memory. By configuring an application to use more physical RAM, you might be able to increase performance. To do this, however, the system must have available RAM. If it doesn't, other processes running on the system might slow down.

TABLE 14-1 Properties of Get-Process and How They Are Used

PROPERTY NAME	PROPERTY DESCRIPTION
WorkingSet/WorkingSet64	Shows the amount of memory the process is currently using, including both the private working set and the nonprivate working set. The private working set is memory the process is using that cannot be shared with other processes. The nonprivate working set is memory the process is using that can be shared with other processes. If memory usage for a process slowly grows over time and doesn't go back to the baseline value, this can be an indicator of a memory leak.

Filtering Process Output

By redirecting the output to Where-Object, you can filter Get-Process using any of the properties available. This means you can specify that you want to see only processes that aren't responding or only processes that use a large amount of CPU time.

You designate how a filter should be applied using filter operators. The available filter operators include:

- **–Eq** Equals. If the property contains the specified value, the process is included in the output.
- **–Ne** Not equals. If the property contains the specified value, the process is excluded from the output.
- **–Gt** Greater than. If the property contains a numeric value and that value is greater than the value specified, the process is included in the output.
- **–Lt** Less than. If the property contains a numeric value and that value is less than the value specified, the process is included in the output.
- **–Ge** Greater than or equal to. If the property contains a numeric value and that value is greater than or equal to the value specified, the process is included in the output.
- **–Le** Less than or equal to. If the property contains a numeric value and that value is less than or equal to the value specified, the process is included in the output.
- **–Match** Pattern match. If the property contains a match for this string, the process is included in the output.

As Table 14-2 shows, the values that you can use with filter operators depend on the Get-Process property you use. Remember that all properties are available even if they aren't normally displayed with the parameters you've specified.

TABLE 14-2 Filter Operators and Valid Values for Get-Process

PROPERTY NAME	OPERATORS TO USE	VALID VALUES
BasePriority	–eq, –ne, –gt, –lt, –ge, –le	Any value from 0 to 24
HandleCount	–eq, –ne, –gt, –lt, –ge, –le	Any valid positive integer
MachineName	–eq, –ne	Any valid string of characters
Modules	–eq, –ne, –match	Dynamic-link library (DLL) name
PrivilegedProcessor-Time	–eq, –ne, –gt, –lt, –ge, –le	Any valid time in the format hh:mm:ss
ProcessID	–eq, –ne, –gt, –lt, –ge, –le	Any valid positive integer
ProcessName	–eq, –ne	Any valid string of characters
Responding	–eq, –ne	$True, $False
SessionID	–eq, –ne, –gt, –lt, –ge, –le	Any valid session number
Username	–eq, –ne	Any valid user name, with user name only or in domain\user format
UserProcessorTime	–eq, –ne, –gt, –lt, –ge, –le	Any valid time in the format hh:mm:ss
WorkingSet	–eq, –ne, –gt, –lt, –ge, –le	Any valid integer, expressed in kilobytes (KB)

By default, Get-Process looks at all processes regardless of their status. With the Responding property, you can find processes that either are or aren't responding. This property is set to a Boolean value. Consider the following examples:

```
get-process | where-object {$_.responding -eq $False}
get-process | where-object {$_.responding -eq $True}
```

In the first example, you list all processes that aren't responding. In the second example, you list all processes that are responding.

Because high-priority processes use more processor time than other processes, you might want to review the high-priority processes running on a computer when you are evaluating performance. Most processes have a normal priority and a priority value of 8. You can find processes with a priority higher than 8 as shown in the following example and sample output:

```
get-process | where-object {$_.basepriority -gt 8}
```

```
Handles  NPM(K)    PM(K)      WS(K) VM(M)   CPU(s)     Id ProcessName
-------  ------    -----      ----- -----   ------     -- -----------
    655       5     1872       5232    94             588 csrss
    493       7    22108      19876   155             644 csrss
    791      12     4820       2420    69             692 lsass
    280       8     3216       7732    51             680 services
     28       1      364        812     4             516 smss
    106       4     1560       4192    46             636 wininit
    143       4     2528       6700    56             804 winlogon
```

You also might want to find processes that are using a lot of CPU time. In the following example and sample output, you check for processes that are using more than 30 minutes of privileged processor time:

```
get-process | where-object {$_.privilegedprocessortime -gt "00:30:00"}
```

```
Handles  NPM(K)    PM(K)      WS(K) VM(M)   CPU(s)     Id ProcessName
-------  ------    -----      ----- -----   ------     -- -----------
    553      32    52924      80096   487  3026.42   5200 W3SVC
```

Viewing the Relationship Between Running Processes and Services

When you use Win32_Service with Get-Process, you can examine the relationship between services configured on a computer and running processes. The ID of the process under which a service is running is shown as part of the standard output when you work with Win32_Service. Here is an example and sample output for the Windows Search service:

```
get-wmiobject -class win32_service -filter "name='wsearch'"
```

```
ExitCode  : 0
Name      : WSearch
ProcessId : 2532
StartMode : Auto
State     : Running
Status    : OK
```

Using the ProcessId property of the Win32_Service object, you can view detailed information about the process under which a service is running, as shown in the following example:

```
$s = get-wmiobject -class win32_service -filter "name='wsearch'"
get-process -id $s.processid
```

```
Handles  NPM(K)    PM(K)      WS(K) VM(M)   CPU(s)     Id ProcessName
-------  ------    -----      ----- -----   ------     -- -----------
   1294      15    43768      40164   162            2532 SearchIndexer
```

Alternatively, you can get the same result using the following code:

```
get-wmiobject -class win32_service -filter "name='wsearch'" |
foreach ($a) {get-process -id $_.processid}
```

By default, the output of Get-Process is formatted as a table, but you can also format the output as a list. Beyond formatting, the important thing to note here is that Get-Process lists services by the base name of the executable that starts the service. Here, SearchIndexer.exe is the name of the executable that starts the Windows Search service.

You can use the correlation between processes and services to help you manage systems. For example, if you think you are having problems with the World Wide Web Publishing Service (W3svc), one step in your troubleshooting process is to begin monitoring the service's related process or processes. You would want to track the following:

- Process status, such as whether the process is responding or not responding
- Memory usage, including the working set, paged system memory, and virtual memory
- CPU time, including privileged processor time and user processor time

By tracking these statistics over time, you can watch for changes that can indicate the process has stopped responding, the process is a runaway process hogging CPU time, or there is a memory leak.

Viewing Lists of DLLs Being Used by Processes

When you use Get-Process, you can examine the relationship between running processes and DLLs configured on the system. In the output, the names of DLLs that the process uses are stored in the Modules property. However, the standard output might not show you the complete list. Consider the following example and sample output:

```
get-process dwm | format-list modules
```

```
Modules : {System.Diagnostics.ProcessModule (Dwm.exe),
System.Diagnostics.ProcessModule (ntdll.dll),
System.Diagnostics.ProcessModule (kernel32.dll),
System.Diagnostics.ProcessModule (ADVAPI32.dll)...}
```

> ***TIP*** **The preference variable $FormatEnumerationLimit controls how many enumerated items are included in a grouped display. The default value is 4, and this is why only four DLLs are shown here. If you increment this variable, you'll be able to see more values by default. In this example, you would have needed to set this variable to 30 or more to see all the DLLs.**

Here, per the default configuration of Windows PowerShell, you see only four values for the Modules property, and the rest of the values are truncated. To see all the DLLs, store the Process object in a variable and then list the value of the Modules property as shown in the following example and sample output:

```
$p = get-process dwm
$p.modules
```

```
   Size(K) ModuleName                  FileName
   ------- ----------                  --------
        96 Dwm.exe                     C:\Windows\system32\Dwm.exe
      1180 ntdll.dll                   C:\Windows\system32\ntdll.dll
       876 kernel32.dll                C:\Windows\system32\kernel32.dll
       792 ADVAPI32.dll                C:\Windows\system32\ADVAPI32.dll
       776 RPCRT4.dll                  C:\Windows\system32\RPCRT4.dll
       300 GDI32.dll                   C:\Windows\system32\GDI32.dll
       628 USER32.dll                  C:\Windows\system32\USER32.dll
       680 msvcrt.dll                  C:\Windows\system32\msvcrt.dll
      1296 ole32.dll                   C:\Windows\system32\ole32.dll
       564 OLEAUT32.dll                C:\Windows\system32\OLEAUT32.dll
       252 UxTheme.dll                 C:\Windows\system32\UxTheme.dll
       120 IMM32.dll                   C:\Windows\system32\IMM32.dll
       800 MSCTF.dll                   C:\Windows\system32\MSCTF.dll
        96 dwmredir.dll                C:\Windows\system32\dwmredir.dll
        28 SLWGA.dll                   C:\Windows\system32\SLWGA.dll
      1188 urlmon.dll                  C:\Windows\system32\urlmon.dll
       352 SHLWAPI.dll                 C:\Windows\system32\SHLWAPI.dll
       276 iertutil.dll                C:\Windows\system32\iertutil.dll
        40 WTSAPI32.dll                C:\Windows\system32\WTSAPI32.dll
       232 slc.dll                     C:\Windows\system32\slc.dll
        36 LPK.DLL                     C:\Windows\system32\LPK.DLL
       500 USP10.dll                   C:\Windows\system32\USP10.dll
      1656 comctl32.dll                C:\Windows\WinSxS\x86_microsoft....
      1984 milcore.dll                 C:\Windows\system32\milcore.dll
        28 PSAPI.DLL                   C:\Windows\system32\PSAPI.DLL
```

```
     132 NTMARTA.DLL                  C:\Windows\system32\NTMARTA.DLL
     296 WLDAP32.dll                  C:\Windows\system32\WLDAP32.dll
     180 WS2_32.dll                   C:\Windows\system32\WS2_32.dll
      24 NSI.dll                      C:\Windows\system32\NSI.dll
      68 SAMLIB.dll                   C:\Windows\system32\SAMLIB.dll
```

Alternatively, you can get the same result using the following code:

```
get-process dwm | foreach ($a) {$_.modules}
```

Knowing which DLL modules a process has loaded can further help you pinpoint what might be causing a process to become nonresponsive, to fail to release the CPU, or to use more memory than it should. In some cases, you might want to check DLL versions to ensure that they are the correct DLLs that the system should be running. To do this, you need to consult the Microsoft Knowledge Base or manufacturer documentation to verify DLL versions and other information.

If you are looking for processes using a specified DLL, you can also specify the name of the DLL you are looking for. For example, if you suspect that the printer spooler driver Winspool.drv is causing processes to hang up, you can search for processes that use Winspool.drv instead of Winspool32.drv and check their status and resource usage.

The syntax that you use to specify the DLL to find is

```
get-process | where-object {$_.modules -match "DLLName"}
```

where *DLLName* is the name of the DLL to search for. Get-Process matches the DLL name without regard to the letter case, and you can enter the DLL name in any letter case. In the following example, you are looking for processes using Winspool.drv, and the output shows the processes using the DLL, along with their basic process information:

```
get-process | where-object {$_.modules -match "winspool.drv"}
```

```
Handles  NPM(K)    PM(K)      WS(K) VM(M)   CPU(s)     Id ProcessName
-------  ------    -----      ----- -----   ------     -- -----------
    147       5     2696       8108    77     0.11   2956 DrgToDsc
    787      23    38444      49148   218    11.97   2132 explorer
    114       5     4708       7164    69     0.17    580 IAAnotif
    288      10    11516      18312   118     1.39    672 IntelHCTAgent
     71       4     2316       7068    69     2.13   5448 notepad
     68       3     2844       4544    57     0.03   2804 rundll32
    543      32    52304      79096   480   283.83   5200 WINWORD
```

Stopping Processes

When you want to stop processes that are running on a local or remote system, you can use Stop-Process. With Stop-Process, you can stop processes by process ID using the –Id parameter or by name using the –Name parameter. Although you cannot use wildcards with the –Id parameter, you can use wildcards with the –Name parameter.

By default, Stop-Process prompts for confirmation before stopping any process that is not owned by the current user. If you have appropriate permissions to stop a process and don't want to be prompted, use the –Force parameter to disable prompting.

If you want to stop multiple processes by process ID or name, you can enter multiple IDs or names as well. With process names, however, watch out, because Stop-Process stops all processes that have that process name. Thus, if three instances of Svchost are running, all three processes are stopped if you use Stop-Process with that image name.

> ***REAL WORLD*** **As you examine processes, keep in mind that a single application might start multiple processes. Generally, you will want to stop the parent process, which should stop the entire process tree, starting with the parent application process and including any dependent processes.**

Consider the following examples to see how you can use Stop-Process:

STOP PROCESS ID 1106:

```
stop-process 1106
```

STOP ALL PROCESSES WITH THE NAME W3SVC:

```
stop-process -name w3svc
```

STOP PROCESSES 1106, 1241, AND 1546:

```
stop-process 1106, 1241, 1546
```

FORCE PROCESS 891 TO STOP:

```
stop-process -force -id 891
```

To ensure that only processes matching specific criteria are stopped, you can use Get-Process and Stop-Process together. For example, you might want to use Get-Process to get only instances of Winword that are not responding and should be stopped, rather than all instances of Winword (which is the default when you use the –Name parameter). Or you might want to get and stop all processes using a specific DLL.

When you are stopping processes, you want to be careful not to accidentally stop critical system processes, such as Lsass, Wininit, or Winlogon. Typically, system processes have a process ID with a value less than 1000. One safeguard you can use when stopping processes is to ensure the process ID is greater than 999.

Consider the following examples to see how you can use Get-Process with Stop-Process:

STOP INSTANCES OF WINWORD THAT ARE NOT RESPONDING:

```
get-process -name winword | where-object {$_.responding -eq $False}
| stop-process
```

STOP ALL PROCESSES WITH A PROCESS ID GREATER THAN 999 IF THEY AREN'T RESPONDING:

```
get-process | where-object {$_.id -gt 999} | where-object
{$_.responding -eq $False} | stop-process
```

STOP ALL PROCESSES USING THE WINSPOOL.DRV DLL:

```
get-process | where-object {$_.modules -match "winspool.drv"} |
stop-process
```

Although Stop-Process doesn't support the –ComputerName parameter, you can use the following technique to manage the processes on remote computers:

```
get-process w3svc -computername engpc18 | stop-process

invoke-command -computername engpc18 -scriptblock { get-process w3svc |
stop-process }
```

Here, you use Get-Process to get a Process object on a remote computer, and then you stop the process by using Stop-Process. Note that this command reports only failure. It won't confirm that a process was stopped, but it will tell you that the process was not found or could not be stopped.

Digging Deeper into Processes

In addition to using Get-Process to get information about running processes, you can use Get-WmiObject and the Win32_Process class. If you type **get-wmiobject -class win32_process**, you'll see detailed information on every process running on the computer. To examine a specific process, you can filter by image name. As shown in the following example and sample output, the image name is the name of the executable for the process:

```
get-wmiobject -class win32_process -filter "name='searchindexer.exe'"
```

```
Caption                       : SearchIndexer.exe
CommandLine                   :
CreationClassName             : Win32_Process
CreationDate                  : 20090228102000.542640-480
CSCreationClassName           : Win32_ComputerSystem
CSName                        : TECHPC22
Description                   : SearchIndexer.exe
ExecutablePath                :
ExecutionState                :
Handle                        : 2532
HandleCount                   : 1323
InstallDate                   :
KernelModeTime                : 15156250
MaximumWorkingSetSize         :
MinimumWorkingSetSize         :
Name                          : SearchIndexer.exe
OSCreationClassName           : Win32_OperatingSystem
OtherOperationCount           : 34235
OtherTransferCount            : 2763510
PageFaults                    : 34156
PageFileUsage                 : 43696
ParentProcessId               : 680
PeakPageFileUsage             : 44760
PeakVirtualSize               : 174481408
PeakWorkingSetSize            : 41128
Priority                      : 8
PrivatePageCount              : 44744704
ProcessId                     : 2532
QuotaNonPagedPoolUsage        : 16
QuotaPagedPoolUsage           : 177
QuotaPeakNonPagedPoolUsage    : 29
QuotaPeakPagedPoolUsage       : 183
ReadOperationCount            : 9223
ReadTransferCount             : 45734098
SessionId                     : 0
Status                        :
ThreadCount                   : 16
UserModeTime                  : 55156250
VirtualSize                   : 169123840
WindowsVersion                : 6.0.6001
WorkingSetSize                : 41414656
WriteOperationCount           : 3845
WriteTransferCount            : 27617602
ProcessName                   : SearchIndexer.exe
```

Win32_Process objects provide some information that Process objects don't, including details on read and write operations. The rest of the information is the same as that provided by Get-Process, albeit in some cases the information is presented in a different way.

Process objects have a StartTime property, and Win32_Process objects have a CreationDate property. Whereas the StartTime property is presented in datetime format, the CreationDate property is presented as a datetime string. Using the StartTime property, you can search for all processes that have been running for longer than a specified period of time. In the following example, you look for processes that have been running longer than one day:

```
$yesterday = (get-date).adddays(-1)
get-process | where-object {$_.starttime -gt $yesterday}
```

Alternatively, you can get the same result using the following code:

```
get-process | where-object {$_.starttime -gt (get-date).adddays(-1)}
```

With the CreationDate property, you can perform the same search. Here is an example:

```
$yesterday = (get-date).adddays(-1)

get-wmiobject -class win32_process | where-object {$_.creationdate -gt
$yesterday}
```

Win32_Process objects have a property called *threadcount*, which is a count of threads associated with a process. You can list the thread count as shown in the following example:

```
get-wmiobject -class win32_process -filter "name='searchindexer.exe'" |
format-list name, threadcount
```

```
name        : SearchIndexer.exe
threadcount : 17
```

Process objects have a Threads property that contains all the threads associated with a process. You can count the threads as shown in the following example:

```
$p = get-process -name searchindexer
write-host "Number of threads: " ($p.threads).count
```

```
Number of threads: 17
```

You can view and work with each individual Thread object as well. As shown in the following example and sample output, you can list the information associated with each Thread object:

```
$p = get-process -name searchindexer
$p.threads
```

```
BasePriority             : 8
CurrentPriority          : 10
Id                       : 2536
IdealProcessor           :
PriorityBoostEnabled     :
PriorityLevel            :
PrivilegedProcessorTime  :
StartAddress             : 0
StartTime                :
ThreadState              : Wait
TotalProcessorTime       :
UserProcessorTime        :
WaitReason               : Executive
ProcessorAffinity        :

BasePriority             : 8
CurrentPriority          : 9
. . .
```

Or you can view details for a specific thread by referencing its index position in the Threads object array. For example, if you want to view the first Thread object, you can reference $p.threads[0].

Each thread has a base priority, a current priority, an ID, a start address, and a thread state. If the thread is waiting for another process or thread, the wait reason is also listed. Wait reasons include Executive (when the thread is waiting on the operating system kernel components) and UserRequest (when the thread is waiting on user-mode components).

When you are working with Win32_Process objects, you can use several methods to work with processes. These methods include the following:

- **GetOwner()** Gets the user account under which the process is running
- **GetOwnerSid()** Gets the security identifier of the user account under which the process is running
- **Terminate()** Stops a process that is running on a local or remote system

The basic syntaxes for getting the process owner and the owner's security identifier are

```
$processObject.GetOwner()
```

and

```
$processObject.GetOwnerSid()
```

where *$processObject* is a reference to a Win32_Process object. Here is an example and partial output:

```
$p = get-wmiobject -class win32_process -filter "name='notepad.exe'"
$p.getowner()
```

```
Domain          : CPANDL
ReturnValue     : 0
User            : WILLIAMS
```

Here, you examine a running instance of Notepad and get the owner of the Notepad process. In the return value, note the Domain and User properties, which show the domain and user account of the process owner, respectively. As shown in the following example and partial output, you can display the security identifier of the process owner by typing

```
$p.getownersid()
```

```
Sid             : S-1-5-21-4857584848-3848484848-8484884848-1111
```

In the return value, the Sid property contains the owner's security identifier.

As shown in the following example and partial output, you can stop the process by typing the following:

```
$p.terminate()
```

```
ReturnValue     : 0
```

The return value in the output is what you want to focus on. A return value of 0 indicates success. Any other return value indicates an error. Typically, errors occur because you aren't the process owner and don't have appropriate permissions to terminate the process. You can resolve this problem by providing credentials or by using an elevated administrator PowerShell prompt.

You can use the techniques discussed previously to work with processes when Get-WmiObject returns a single matching Win32_Process object. However, these techniques won't work as expected when Get-WmiObject returns multiple Win32_Process objects. The reason for this is that the objects are stored in an array and you must specify the instance within the array to work with. One technique for doing so is shown in the following example and partial output:

```
$procs = get-wmiobject -class win32_process -filter "name='notepad.exe'"
foreach ($p in $procs) { $p.getowner() }
```

```
Domain          : CPANDL
ReturnValue     : 0
User            : WILLIAMS

Domain          : CPANDL
ReturnValue     : 0
User            : WILLIAMS
```

Here, two instances of Notepad are running, and you list the owner of each process. This technique works when there is only one instance of Notepad running as well.

Performance Monitoring

Performance monitoring helps you watch for adverse conditions and take appropriate action to resolve them. Windows PowerShell has several commands for this purpose, and in this section, we'll look at the ones you'll use the most.

Understanding Performance Monitoring Commands

Commands you can use to monitor performance include:

- **Get-Counter** Gets objects representing real-time performance counter data directly from the performance monitoring instrumentation in Windows. You can list the performance counter sets and the counters that they contain, set the sample size and interval, and specify the credentials of users with permission to collect performance data.

```
Get-Counter [-MaxSamples NumSamples] [-Counter] CounterPaths
[-SampleInterval Interval] {AddtlParams}

Get-Counter -ListSet SetNames {AddtlParams}

{AddtlParams}
[-Credential CredentialObject] [-ComputerName ComputerNames]
```

- **Export-Counter** Exports performance counter data to log files in BLG (binary performance log, the default), CSV (comma-separated), or TSV (tab-separated) format. This cmdlet is designed to export data that is returned by the Get-Counter and Import-Counter cmdlets. Only Windows 7, Windows Server 2008 R2, and later versions of Windows support this command.

```
Export-Counter [-FileFormat Format] [-Path] SavePath
-InputObject PerformanceCounterSampleSets {AddtlParams}

{AddtlParams}
[-Force {$True | $False}] [-Circular {$True | $False}]
[-MaxSize MaxSizeInBytes]
```

- **Import-Counter** Imports performance counter data from performance counter log files and creates objects for each counter sample in the file. The objects created are identical to those that Get-Counter returns when it collects performance counter data. You can import data from BLG, CSV, and TSV formatted log files. When you are using BLG, you can import up to 32 files in each command. To get a subset of data from a file, use the parameters of Import-Counter to filter the data that you import.

```
Import-Counter [-Path] FilePaths {AddlParams}
Import-Counter -ListSet SetNames [-Path] FilePaths
Import-Counter [-Summary {$True | $False}]

{AddtlParams}
[-Counter CountersToInclude] [-MaxSamples NumSamples]
[-StartTime DateTime] [-EndTime DateTime]
```

Get-Counter is designed to track and display performance information in real time. It gathers information on any performance parameters you've configured for monitoring and presents it as output. Each performance item you want to monitor is defined by the following three components:

- **Performance object** Represents any system component that has a set of measurable properties. A performance object can be a physical part of the operating system, such as the memory, the processor, or the paging file; a logical component, such as a logical disk or print queue; or a software element, such as a process or a thread.
- **Performance object instance** Represents single occurrences of performance objects. If a particular object has multiple instances, such as when a computer has multiple processors or multiple disk drives, you can use an object instance to track a specific occurrence of that object. You can also elect to track all instances of an object, such as whether you want to monitor all processors on a system.
- **Performance counter** Represents measurable properties of performance objects. For example, with a paging file, you can measure the percentage utilization using the %Usage counter.

In a standard installation of Windows, many performance objects are available for monitoring. As you add services, applications, and components, additional performance objects can become available. For example, when you install the Domain Name System (DNS) on a server, the DNS object becomes available for monitoring on that computer.

Tracking Performance Data

Using Get-Counter, you can write performance data to the output or to a log file. The key to using Get-Counter is to identify the path names of the performance counters you want to track. The performance counter path has the following syntax:

```
\\ComputerName\ObjectName\ObjectCounter
```

where *ComputerName* is the computer name or IP address of the local or remote computer you want to work with, *ObjectName* is the name of a counter object, and *ObjectCounter* is the name of the object counter to use. For example, if you want to track the available memory on Dbserver79, you type the following, and the output would be similar to that shown:

```
get-counter "\\dbserver79\memory\available mbytes"
```

```
Timestamp              CounterSamples
---------              -------------
2/27/2010 4:26:54 PM   \\dbserver79\memory\available mbytes : 1675
2/27/2010 4:26:55 PM   \\dbserver79\memory\available mbytes : 1672
```

> ***NOTE*** **Enclosing the counter path in double quotation marks is required in this example because the counter path includes spaces. Although double quotation marks aren't always required, it is good form to always use them.**

Specifying the computer name as part of the counter path is optional. If you don't specify the computer name in the counter path, Get-Counter uses the values you specify in the –ComputerName parameter to set the full path for you. If you don't specify computer names, the local computer name is used. Although this allows you to easily work with multiple computers, you should familiarize yourself with the full path format because this is what is recorded in performance traces and performance logs. Without the computer name in the path, the abbreviated path becomes

```
\ObjectName\ObjectCounter
```

In the following example, you check the available memory on multiple computers by using the –ComputerName parameter:

```
get-counter -computername fileserver12, dbserver18, dcserver21
"\memory\available mbytes"
```

When you are working with a remote computer, you might need to provide alternative credentials. You can do this as shown in the following example:

```
$cred = get-credential
get-counter -computername fileserver12, dbserver18, dcserver21
"\memory\available mbytes" -credential $cred
```

When you use Get-Credential, Windows PowerShell prompts you for a user name and password and then stores the credentials provided in the $cred variable. These credentials are then passed to the remote computers for authentication.

You can easily track all counters for an object by using an asterisk (*) as the counter name, such as in the following example:

```
get-counter "\\dbserver79\Memory\*"
```

Here, you track all counters for the Memory object.

When objects have multiple instances, such as with the Processor or LogicalDisk object, you must specify the object instance you want to work with. The full syntax for this is as follows:

```
\\ComputerName\ObjectName(ObjectInstance)\ObjectCounter
```

Here, you follow the object name with the object instance in parentheses. When an object has multiple instances, you can work with all instances of that object using _Total as the instance name. You can work with a specific instance of an object by using its instance identifier. For example, if you want to examine the Processor\% Processor Time counter, you can use this command to work with all processor instances:

```
get-counter "\\dbserver79\Processor(_Total)\% Processor Time"
```

Or you use this command to work with a specific processor instance:

```
get-counter "\\dbserver79\Processor(0)\% Processor Time"
```

Here, Processor(0) identifies the first processor on the system.

Get-Counter has several parameters. –MaxSamples sets the number of samples to collect. –SampleInterval sets the time between samples where the default is 1 second. –ListSet lists installed counters for the specified objects.

Get-Counter writes its output to the prompt by default. You can redirect the output to a performance log by sending the output to Export-Counter. By default, Export-Counter exports performance counter data to log files in binary performance log format. Using the –FileFormat parameter, you can set the format as CSV for a comma-delimited text file, TSV for a tab-delimited text file, or BLG for a binary file. Consider the following example:

```
get-counter "\\dbserver79\Memory\*" | export-counter -fileformat tsv
-path .\dbserver79.txt
```

Here, you track all counters for the Memory object and write the output to a tab-delimited text file called Dbserver79.txt in the current working directory. When you want to work with this data later, you use Import-Counter. Type **import-counter -path** followed by the path to the performance log to view the performance data. Type **import-counter -summary -path** followed by the path to the performance log to get a summary view of the data. Type **import-counter -listset * -path** followed by the path to the performance log to see what counters were tracked. Optionally, use –StartTime and –EndTime to specify a datetime range to review. Consider the following example:

```
$startdate = (get-date).adddays(-1)
$enddate = (get-date)
import-counter -path .\data.txt -starttime $startdate -endtime $enddate
```

Here, you examine the performance data in a file in the current directory, called Data.txt. You review the performance details from yesterday at the current time to today at the current time.

If you need help determining how an object can be used and what its counters are, type **get-counter -listset** followed by the object name for which you want to view counters. The following example and sample output show how this can be used to get all the Memory-related counters:

```
get-counter -listset Memory
```

```
Counter: {\Memory\Page Faults/sec, \Memory\Available Bytes,
\Memory\Committed Bytes, \Memory\Commit Limit...}
CounterSetName     : Memory
MachineName        : EngPC85
CounterSetType     : SingleInstance
Description        : The Memory performance object  consists of counters
that describe the behavior of physical and virtual memory on the
computer.  Physical memory is the amount of random access memory on the
computer.  Virtual memory consists of the space in physical memory and on
disk.  Many of the memory counters monitor paging, which is the movement
of pages of code and data between disk and physical memory.  Excessive
paging, a symptom of a memory shortage, can cause delays which interfere
with all system processes.
Paths: {\Memory\Page Faults/sec, \Memory\Available Bytes,
\Memory\Committed Bytes, \Memory\Commit Limit...}
PathsWithInstances : {}
```

As with all results returned in PowerShell, the output is returned as an object that you can manipulate. To get a complete list of counter paths, you can reference the Paths property as shown in the following example and partial output:

```
$c = get-counter -listset Memory
$c.paths
```

```
\Memory\Page Faults/sec
\Memory\Available Bytes
\Memory\Committed Bytes
\Memory\Commit Limit
```

Alternatively, you can get the same result using the following code:

```
get-counter -listset memory | foreach ($a) {$_.paths}
```

If an object has multiple instances, you can list the installed counters with instances by using the PathsWithInstances property. An example and partial output follow:

```
$d = get-counter -listset PhysicalDisk
$d.pathswithinstances
```

```
\PhysicalDisk(0 E: C:)\Current Disk Queue Length
\PhysicalDisk(1 W:)\Current Disk Queue Length
\PhysicalDisk(2 D:)\Current Disk Queue Length
\PhysicalDisk(3 I:)\Current Disk Queue Length
\PhysicalDisk(4 J:)\Current Disk Queue Length
\PhysicalDisk(5 K:)\Current Disk Queue Length
\PhysicalDisk(6 L:)\Current Disk Queue Length
\PhysicalDisk(7 N:)\Current Disk Queue Length
\PhysicalDisk(8 O:)\Current Disk Queue Length
\PhysicalDisk(9 P:)\Current Disk Queue Length
\PhysicalDisk(10 Q:)\Current Disk Queue Length
\PhysicalDisk(_Total)\Current Disk Queue Length
```

Alternatively, you can get the same result using the following code:

```
get-counter -listset PhysicalDisk | foreach ($a) {$_.pathswithinstances}
```

Either way, the output is a long list of available counters arranged according to their object instances. You can write the output to a text file, such as in the following example:

```
get-counter -listset PhysicalDisk > disk-counters.txt
```

Then edit the text file so that only the counters you want to track are included. You can then use the file to determine which performance counters are tracked, as shown in the following example:

```
get-counter (get-content .\disk-counters.txt) | export-counter -path
c:\perflogs\disk-check.blg
```

Here, Get-Counter reads the list of counters to track from Disk-Counters.txt, and then it writes the performance data in binary format to the Disk-Check.blg file in the C:\Perflogs directory.

By default, Get-Counter samples data once every second until you tell it to stop by pressing Ctrl+C. This might be okay when you are working at the PowerShell prompt and actively monitoring the output. However, it doesn't work so well when you have other things to do and can't actively monitor the output—which is probably most of the time. Therefore, you'll usually want to control the sampling interval and duration.

To control the sampling interval and set how long to sample, you can use the –SampleInterval and –MaxSamples parameters, respectively. For example, if you want Get-Counter to sample every 120 seconds and stop logging after 100 samples, you can enter the following command:

```
get-counter (get-content .\disk-counters.txt) -sampleinterval 120
-maxsamples 100 | export-counter -path c:\perflogs\disk-check.blg
```

Detecting and Resolving Performance Issues Through Monitoring

Get-Process and Get-Counter provide everything you need for detecting and resolving most performance issues. However, you'll often need to dig deep to determine whether a problem exists and, if so, what is causing the problem.

Monitoring System Resource Usage and Processes

When you are working with processes, you'll often want to get a snapshot of system resource usage, which will show you exactly how memory is being used. One way to get a snapshot is to use the Get-Counter command to display current values for key counters of the memory object. As discussed previously, the Memory object is one of many performance objects available, and you can list its related performance counters by typing the following command at the PowerShell prompt:

```
get-counter -listset memory | foreach ($a) {$_.paths}
```

The Memory object has many counters you can work with. Most counters of the Memory object display the last observed value or the current percentage value rather than an average.

Sample 14-1 provides an example of how you can use Get-Counter to get a snapshot of memory usage. In this example, you use a counter file called Perf.txt to specify the counters you want to track. You collect five samples with an interval of 30 seconds between samples and save the output in a file called SaveMemData.txt. If you import the data into a spreadsheet or convert it to a table in a Word document, you can make better sense of the output and gain a better understanding of how the computer is using the page file and paging to disk.

I chose to track these counters because they give you a good overall snapshot of memory usage. If you save the command line as a script, you can run the script as a scheduled task to get a snapshot of memory usage at various times of the day.

SAMPLE 14-1 Getting a Snapshot of Memory Usage

Commands

```
get-counter (get-content .\perf.txt) -maxsamples 5 -sampleinterval 30 >
SaveMemData.txt
```

Source for Perf.txt

```
\memory\% Committed Bytes In Use
\memory\Available MBytes
\memory\Cache Bytes
\memory\Cache Bytes Peak
\memory\Committed Bytes
\memory\Commit Limit
\memory\Page Faults/sec
\memory\Pool Nonpaged Bytes
\memory\Pool Paged Bytes
```

Sample output

```
Timestamp                 CounterSamples
---------                 --------------
2/28/2009 5:04:37 PM      \\techpc22\memory\% committed bytes in use :
                          22.9519764760423
                          \\techpc22\memory\available mbytes :
                          1734
                          \\techpc22\memory\cache bytes :
                          390168576
                          \\techpc22\memory\cache bytes peak :
                          390688768
                          \\techpc22\memory\committed bytes :
                          1650675712
                          \\techpc22\memory\commit limit :
                          7191867392
                          \\techpc22\memory\page faults/sec :
                          3932.45999649944
                          \\techpc22\memory\pool nonpaged bytes :
                          70017024
                          \\techpc22\memory\pool paged bytes :
                          154710016

2/28/2009 5:05:07 PM      \\techpc22\memory\% committed bytes in use :
                          23.2283134955779
                          \\techpc22\memory\available mbytes :
                          1714
                          \\techpc22\memory\cache bytes :
                          389664768
                          \\techpc22\memory\cache bytes peak :
                          390701056
```

```
\\techpc22\memory\committed bytes :
1670549504
\\techpc22\memory\commit limit :
7191867392
\\techpc22\memory\page faults/sec :
617.601067565369
\\techpc22\memory\pool nonpaged bytes :
70008832
\\techpc22\memory\pool paged bytes :
154791936
```

If you suspect there is a problem with memory usage, you can obtain detailed information about running processes by using Get-Process. At a PowerShell prompt, you can view important statistics for all processes by typing the following command:

```
get-process | format-table -property ProcessName,
BasePriority, HandleCount, Id, NonpagedSystemMemorySize,
PagedSystemMemorySize, PeakPagedMemorySize, PeakVirtualMemorySize,
PeakWorkingSet, SessionId, Threads, TotalProcessorTime,
VirtualMemorySize, WorkingSet, CPU, Path
```

The order of the properties in the comma-separated list determines the display order. If you want to change the display order, simply move a property to a different position in the list. If desired, you can redirect the output to a file as shown in the following example:

```
get-process | format-table -property ProcessName,
BasePriority, HandleCount, Id, NonpagedSystemMemorySize,
PagedSystemMemorySize, PeakPagedMemorySize, PeakVirtualMemorySize,
PeakWorkingSet, SessionId, Threads, TotalProcessorTime,
VirtualMemorySize, WorkingSet, CPU, Path > savedata.txt
```

Whether you write output to the prompt or to a file, modify the properties of the PowerShell prompt and set the width to at least 180 characters. This ensures you can read the output.

Monitoring Memory Paging and Paging to Disk

Often, you'll want to get detailed information on hard and soft page faults that are occurring. A page fault occurs when a process requests a page in memory and the system can't find it at the requested location. If the requested page is elsewhere in memory, the fault is called a soft page fault. If the requested page must be retrieved from disk, the fault is called a hard page fault.

To see page faults that are occurring in real time, type the following at the command line:

```
get-counter "\memory\Page Faults/sec" -sampleinterval 5
```

```
Timestamp                  CounterSamples
---------                  --------------
2/28/2009 6:00:01 PM       \\techpc22\memory\page faults/sec :
                           172.023153991804
2/28/2009 6:00:06 PM       \\techpc22\memory\page faults/sec :
                           708.944308818821
2/28/2009 6:00:11 PM       \\techpc22\memory\page faults/sec :
                           14.5375722784541
```

Here, you check memory page faults every 5 seconds. To stop Get-Counter, press Ctrl+C. Page faults are shown according to the number of hard and soft faults occurring per second. Other counters of the Memory object that you can use for tracking page faults include the following:

- Cache Faults/sec
- Demand Zero Faults/sec
- Page Reads/sec
- Page Writes/sec
- Write Copies/sec
- Transition Faults/sec
- Transition Pages RePurposed/sec

Pay particular attention to the Page Reads/sec and Page Writes/sec, which provide information on hard faults. Although developers will be interested in the source of page faults, administrators are more interested in how many page faults are occurring. Most processors can handle large numbers of soft faults. A soft fault simply means the system had to look elsewhere in memory for the requested memory page. With a hard fault, on the other hand, the requested memory page must be retrieved from disk, which can cause significant delays. If you are seeing a lot of hard faults, you might need to increase the amount of memory or reduce the amount of memory being cached by the system and applications.

In addition to counters of the Memory object discussed previously, you can use other objects and counters to check for disk paging issues. If a particular object has multiple instances, such as when a computer has multiple physical disks or multiple paging files, you can use an object instance to track a specific occurrence of that object. You can also elect to track all instances of an object, such as whether you want to monitor all physical disks on a system. Specify _Total to work with all counter instances, or specify individual counter instances to monitor.

Sample 14-2 provides an example of how you can use Get-Counter to get a snapshot of disk paging. In this example, you use a counter file called PagePerf.txt to specify the counters you want to track. You collect five samples with an interval of

30 seconds between samples and save the output in a file called SavePageData.txt. If you import the data into a spreadsheet or convert it to a table in a Word document, you can make better sense of the output and gain a better understanding of how the computer is using the page file and paging to disk.

SAMPLE 14-2 Checking Disk Paging

Commands

```
get-counter (get-content .\pageperf.txt) -maxsamples 5 `
-sampleinterval 30 > SavePageData.txt
```

Source for PagePerf.txt

```
\memory\Pages/Sec
\Paging File(_Total)\% Usage
\Paging File(_Total)\% Usage Peak
\PhysicalDisk(_Total)\% Disk Time
\PhysicalDisk(_Total)\Avg. Disk Queue Length
```

Monitoring Memory Usage and the Working Memory Set for Individual Processes

You can use Get-Process to get basic memory usage for a process. The syntax you can use is

```
get-process -id ProcessID
```

where *ProcessID* is the ID number of the process you want to work with. The output from Get-Process shows you how much memory the process is currently using. For example, if you were tracking process ID 1072, your output might look like the following:

```
Handles  NPM(K)    PM(K)     WS(K) VM(M)   CPU(s)     Id ProcessName
-------  ------    -----     ----- -----   ------     -- -----------
    493      13    15520     13452    77             1072 svchost
```

In this example, the process is using 13,452 KB of memory. By watching the memory usage over time, you can determine whether the memory usage is increasing. If memory usage is increasing compared to a typical baseline, the process might have a memory-related problem.

Sample 14-3 provides the source for a PowerShell script that checks the memory usage of a process over a timed interval. The script expects the process ID you want to work with to be passed as the first parameter. If you do not supply a process ID, error text is written to the output.

SAMPLE 14-3 Viewing Memory Usage at the PowerShell Prompt

MemUsage.ps1

```
$p = read-host "Enter process id to track"
$n = read-host "Enter number of minutes to track"
for ($c=1; $c -le $n; $c++) {get-process -id $p; start-sleep -seconds 60}
```

Sample output

```
Enter process id to track: 1072
Enter number of minutes to track: 1

Handles  NPM(K)    PM(K)      WS(K) VM(M)   CPU(s)     Id ProcessName
-------  ------    -----      ----- -----   ------     -- -----------
    497      13    15548      13464    77             1072 svchost
    494      13    15520      13452    77             1072 svchost
    495      13    15520      13452    77             1072 svchost
    493      13    15520      13452    77             1072 svchost
    495      13    15548      13464    77             1072 svchost
    495      13    15520      13452    77             1072 svchost
```

In Sample 14-3, the process's memory usage shows small variances over time, but there isn't a trend of increasing memory usage over time. Because of this, it is unlikely the process has a memory leak, but to be sure you'd need to sample over a longer period.

You can use Get-Process to track detailed memory usage for individual processes as well. The syntax you can use is

```
get-process ProcessName | format-table -property `
NonpagedSystemMemorySize, PagedSystemMemorySize, VirtualMemorySize, `
PeakVirtualMemorySize, MinWorkingSet, WorkingSet, PeakWorkingSet
```

where *ProcessName* is the name of the process without the .exe or .dll. In a PowerShell script, such as the one shown as Sample 14-4, you can combine Get-Process and Start-Sleep to view the memory usage for a process at timed intervals.

SAMPLE 14-4 Viewing Detailed Memory Usage

DetMemUsage.ps1

```
$p = read-host "Enter process name to track"
$n = read-host "Enter number of minutes to track"
for ($c=1; $c -le $n; $c++) { get-process $p | format-table -property `
NonpagedSystemMemorySize, PagedSystemMemorySize, VirtualMemorySize, `
PeakVirtualMemorySize, MinWorkingSet, WorkingSet, PeakWorkingSet
start-sleep -seconds 60}
```

Sample output

```
 Nonpaged      Paged    Virtual        Peak        Min  Working       Peak
   System     System MemorySize     Virtual WorkingSet      Set WorkingSet
MemorySize MemorySize             MemorySize
---------- ---------- --------- ---------- --------- --------- ---------
      4776      96368  52891648  161480704              6946816    7282688
      8424     137056  61505536  161480704              8986624    9039872
     13768     121136 137351168  161480704             38670336   73658368
     13792     128904  82386944  161480704             13889536   73658368
     14320     167912 187904000  258859008             74432512  138919936
     44312     235704 221302784  429953024             65249280  278482944
     25288     156520  91754496  429953024             15536128  278482944
     30112     159376 123875328  429953024             23248896  278482944
     25296     118424  86568960  429953024             20758528  278482944
      2248      48088  24174592  429953024              2924544  278482944
      7112     105160  55832576  429953024              6393856  278482944
      5368     110960  63991808  429953024              7655424  278482944
      1472      30400  15618048  429953024              2330624  278482944
```

The Get-Counter properties examined in Sample 14-4 provide the following information:

- **NonPagedSystemMemorySize** Shows the amount of allocated memory that can't be written to disk
- **PagedSystemMemorySize** Shows the amount of allocated memory that is allowed to be paged to the hard disk
- **VirtualMemorySize** Shows the amount of virtual memory allocated to and reserved for a process
- **PeakVirtualMemorySize** Shows the peak amount of paged memory used by the process
- **WorkingSet** Shows the amount of memory allocated to the process by the operating system
- **PeakWorkingSet** Shows the peak amount of memory used by the process

When you focus on these properties, you are zeroing in on the memory usage of a specific process. The key aspect to monitor is the working memory set. The working set of memory shows how much memory is allocated to the process by the operating system. If the working set increases over time and doesn't eventually go back to baseline usage, the process might have a memory leak. With a memory leak, the process isn't properly releasing memory that it's using, which can lead to reduced performance of the entire system.

In Sample 14-4, the process's memory usage changes substantially over the sampled interval. Although it is most likely the process is simply actively being used by users or the computer itself, the process should eventually return to a baseline memory usage. If this doesn't happen, the process might have a memory-related problem.

Because memory is usually the primary performance bottleneck on both workstations and servers, I've discussed many techniques previously in this chapter that you can use to help identify problems with memory. Memory is the resource you should examine first to try to determine why a system isn't performing as expected. However, memory isn't the only bottleneck. Processors, hard disks, and networking components can also cause bottlenecks.

Index

Symbols and Numbers

A

D

E

F

H

I

J

K

L

M

O

P

Q

R

S

T

U

V

W

X

About the Author

William R. Stanek (*http://www.williamstanek.com*) has over 20 years of hands-on experience with advanced programming and development. He is a leading technology expert, an award-winning author, and a pretty-darn-good instructional trainer. Over the years, his practical advice has helped millions of programmers, developers, and network engineers all over the world. He has written more than 100 books. Current or forthcoming books include *Active Directory Administrator's Pocket Consultant, Windows Group Policy Administrator's Pocket Consultant, Windows 7 Administrator's Pocket Consultant*, and *Windows Server 2008 Inside Out*.

William has been involved in the commercial Internet community since 1991. His core business and technology experience comes from more than 11 years of military service. He has substantial experience in developing server technology, encryption, and Internet solutions. He has written many technical white papers and training courses on a wide variety of topics. He frequently serves as a subject matter expert and consultant.

William has an MS with distinction in information systems and a BS in computer science, magna cum laude. He is proud to have served in the Persian Gulf War as a combat crew member on an electronic warfare aircraft. He flew on numerous combat missions into Iraq and was awarded nine medals for his wartime service, including one of the United States of America's highest flying honors, the Air Force Distinguished Flying Cross. Currently, he resides in the Pacific Northwest with his wife and children.

William recently rediscovered his love of the great outdoors. When he's not writing, teaching, or making presentations, he can be found hiking, biking, backpacking, traveling, or trekking in search of adventure.

Follow William on Twitter at WilliamStanek.

What do you think of this book?

We want to hear from you!

Your feedback will help us continually improve our books and learning resources for you. To participate in a brief online survey, please visit:

microsoft.com/learning/booksurvey

...and enter this book's ISBN-10 or ISBN-13 number (appears above barcode on back cover). As a thank-you to survey participants in the U.S. and Canada, each month we'll randomly select five respondents to win one of five $100 gift certificates from a leading online merchant. At the conclusion of the survey, you can enter the drawing by providing your e-mail address, which will be used for prize notification only.*

Thank you in advance for your input!

Where to find the ISBN on back cover

Example only. Each book has unique ISBN.

* No purchase necessary. Void where prohibited. Open only to residents of the 50 United States (includes District of Columbia) and Canada (void in Quebec). For official rules and entry dates see: **microsoft.com/learning/booksurvey**

Stay in touch!

To subscribe to the *Microsoft Press® Book Connection Newsletter*—for news on upcoming books, events, and special offers—please visit:

microsoft.com/learning/books/newsletter